Religions Today

*Their Challenge to
the Ecumenical
Movement*

Edited by
Julio de Santa Ana

Religions Today

*Their Challenge to
the Ecumenical
Movement*

WCC Publications, Geneva

The following papers were translated by the Language Service of the World Council of Churches:

From Spanish: Introduction – Looking Ahead

From Portuguese: Nunes – Beozzo

Cover design: Rob Lucas

ISBN 2-8254-1459-X

© 2005 WCC Publications, World Council of Churches
150 route de Ferney, P.O. Box 2100
1211 Geneva 2, Switzerland
Web site: http://www.wcc-coe.org

Printed in France

Contents

Introduction

JULIO DE SANTA ANA

Context

During the last twenty years of the 20th century major changes took place. Some were of an obviously political nature, such as the fall of communist regimes in Eastern Europe. Others comprised developments in economics and finance, the most obvious of which was the increasingly rapid globalization and integration of various markets, which followed a similar process in financial transactions from the late 1970s onwards. The changes produced by these economic developments are very closely linked to advances in information technology. No one can now doubt that Marshall McLuhan was right when he described our planet as a "global village".

This technological evolution combined with high-level decisions by political leaders to create conditions favourable for a major expansion and integration of markets. Factors encouraging the widespread growth of consumer society were strengthened. Gradually, people began to call this complex phenomenon "economic globalization" and saw that it affected other areas of human activity, including the world's various cultures and the religious beliefs and practices within them.

In the realm of religion we have begun to question the universal validity of theories asserting that secularization (understood as the "disenchantment of the world" and the loss of influence of traditional religious institutions) is irresistible. Today, it is no longer possible to state that the secularization taking place in Western European society is a phenomenon that will affect other societies in the same way.[1] In various parts of the world, our oikoumene, the influence of religious beliefs and practices has demonstrated the vitality of religions today. In Poland, for example, Roman Catholicism (the religion of the majority) unhesitatingly supported the Solidarity union when it confronted and ultimately brought down the ruling communist regime. In Northern Ireland, religious influences existed in the conflict between Unionist Protestants and Republican Catholics. In Nicaragua, liberation theology was one of the ideological factors that motivated young people to join the Sandinistas, overthrow the Somoza dictatorship, and implement a programme of social, economic and political reform. More recently, people inspired by liberation theology contributed decisively to the victory of the workers party in Brazil. And in a different context, the revolution headed by Iman Khomeini put an end to the centuries-long rule of the monarchy in Iran, replacing it with an Islamic republic under the direction and control of the religious authorities. Indeed, it is in those countries where Islam is predominant that the influence of religious beliefs and practices on the population can be seen most clearly. Judaism is also experiencing a revival. And in south Asia, social and political confrontations in Sri Lanka and Indonesia are closely linked to religious beliefs.

The increasing flow of migrants in recent years, especially from the South to the North, and also from Eastern Europe to the USA, Canada and the European Union, is indicative of vast population movements. Such migrants include a considerable number of Muslims, which means that Islam is gradually gaining in strength and public influence in the nations that receive them. In South Africa, many campaigners against apartheid were motivated by the faith of various religious communities at home, while at the same time receiving support in solidarity from other religious communities abroad. The World Council of Churches' Programme to Combat Racism was one of many initiatives demonstrating the vitality of the ecumenical movement. In a different way, in the USA, the weight of the so-called Moral Majority, under the influence of the conservative religious media (particularly Protestant fundamentalists, evangelicals and conservative Catholics), was evident in the elections of 1980, 1984, 1988, 2000 and 2004, which brought Ronald Reagan, George Bush Senior and George W. Bush to the presidency. Some parts of church hierarchies (both Catholic and Protestant) in Latin America played a major role in defending and promoting human rights when various military dictatorships attempted to impose national security regimes by force between 1964 and 1988. Finally, in the Philippines, progressive religious sectors (both Christian and Muslim) took part in the movement that led to the fall of the tyrannical regime of Ferdinand Marcos and the introduction of new freedoms into public life when Corazon Aquino became president.

This is by no means an exhaustive list of examples demonstrating the vitality of religion in public life today. José Casanova has produced excellent research into this phenomenon by examining the different ways in which religion is present in the public sphere in a variety of countries that have set out to "modernize".[2] There is an indisputable convergence between Casanova's position and the research and thinking of S.N. Eisenstadt, a philosopher and social scientist who claims that the processes of modernization, while they share common elements, do not copy a universal pattern originating in Western Europe and the USA. According to Casanova, different religious traditions in different parts of the world demonstrate that it is not always possible to confine religious beliefs and practices to the private lives of believers, as happens – exceptionally – in Western Europe. Eisenstadt's view is that the processes of modernization are related to the growing influence of the new information media and their increasing penetration into community life, fostering greater participation by vast social sectors in activities and organizations created by groups occupying the centres of power in their respective societies.[3] Both Casanova and Eisenstadt agree that religious beliefs and practices continue to exert influence on society and have not ceased to be relevant.

The vitality of religion is not limited to public life. Over the last thirty years there has been noticeable growth in almost all religious communities (Western Europe is an exception). This trend is particularly evident within Islam. If population growth is maintained both in Muslim societies and in others (such as sub-Saharan Africa) where Islam is growing rapidly, it is possible that towards the end of the century Islam will have as many adherents as Christianity. Importantly, different interpretations of Islam influence not only those countries where it has been established for centuries, but also those parts of the world where Muslim communities are beginning to be established. In other words, debates within Islam are not limited to those countries where it has traditionally been the majority religion: they also take place in countries with an immigrant Muslim population.

As for Christian churches, in Europe there is a noticeable decline in church attendance. However, there remains a more or less stable number of those who declare themselves Christian, who present their children for baptism and confirmation, get married, and at the end of their lives request to be buried with the rites of the confession to which they have traditionally belonged. By contrast, in the churches of the South (Africa, Asia, the Caribbean, Latin America and the Pacific), there is a large increase in church attendance. Among the communities experiencing most rapid growth are the Pentecostals and the charismatics (especially in Africa and Latin America). This growth in countries where the churches have been established during the last four or five centuries leads Philip Jenkins to believe that, within a relatively short time (no more than thirty or forty years), most Roman Catholics will be Hispanics, and the highest percentage of Protestants will be in Africa, where Evangelicals are increasing very rapidly, both numerically and institutionally. In Africa, the number of African Instituted churches is multiplying. In Africa also we see a process of inculturation in various manifestations of the Christian faith that adopt features of local cultures at various levels – a thing practically unthinkable until a short time ago. These changes are so compelling that they now have an impact on the decisions taken by the large traditional churches. Jenkins observes that the attitudes of these "new churches" is weighing increasingly heavily on their "mother churches", which are attempting to introduce new perspectives, new values and new directions.[4] Some of these new churches (i.e. those that have come into being and developed out of the missionary efforts of the churches established in Europe and the USA) have a tendency to impose their traditional ideas, as happened at the last Lambeth conference of the Anglican communion, when there was a debate on whether or not to accept the ordination of clergy of homosexual or lesbian orientation. Jenkins believes this tendency will be strengthened and consolidated as the new churches continue to grow and the traditional Western churches continue to stagnate:

> The centre of gravity of the Christian world has shifted inexorably southward, to Africa, Asia and Latin America. Already today, the largest Christian communities on the planet are to be found in Africa and Latin America. If we wish to visualize a "typical" contemporary Christian, we should think of a woman living in a village in Nigeria or in a Brazilian favela.

Other new churches, mainly of a charismatic type, have also appeared and developed with an emphasis in their preaching on the importance of believers becoming prosperous, to achieve which they must be delivered from the devil in their personal lives. These churches practise exorcism and in some parts of Africa accept polygamy and other elements of traditional African culture. Such churches are growing numerically, and in the number of their preaching centres and ministers serving them.

According to the forecasts of Philip Jenkins, in the course of this century it is possible that the number of Christians in the world could reach somewhat more than 2500 million, of which some 640 million will be Latin Americans, around 235 million will be in Africa, 555 million in Europe and a little more than 450 million in Asia. Christianity has thus grown in recent decades and all the indications are that it will continue to do so, not only as a result of natural population growth within the Christian community, but also through evangelism and proselytism. This increase in Christian numbers is being matched by growth in other religious families. One result of this is the need for Christian communities to understand the importance of interfaith relationships, especially in those parts of the world where there is inter-religious conflict.

This same vitality can be seen in religions such as Judaism and in religious communities inspired by African traditions and practices, especially in groups that in South America and the Caribbean maintain their ancestral beliefs in "alien" lands. The slave trade uprooted those forcibly taken to the Americas, but despite their pain and suffering they held on to their beliefs and rites. The strength of religions in our time is also to be seen in societies where the predominant culture is Confucian, as is the case in Korea and Japan, where it has combined with Buddhist elements. In addition to all this, magical practices are flourishing more and more openly. [5]

The context of this renaissance in the vitality of religious practices is not traditional "primitive societies", which was where Emile Durkheim conducted his study of traditional religions. [6] Rather, it is where various processes of modernization are taking place. Consequently, it is occurring in situations where the modern ecumenical movement has taken shape since the end of the 19th century. We must thus acknowledge that the present state of religious life challenges and questions the ecumenical movement. An example here is the missionary practice of the churches. It also has to do with aspects of their confessions of faith and their internal discipline, their social ethics, their liturgical practices, their pastoral work and their forms of Christian education (catechesis). Thus, the issues we need to investigate revolve around the relation between modernization and religious life. However, not only do the processes of modernization affect religious practices and beliefs, but also those same practices and beliefs affect the processes of modernization. Thus, in addition, we also need to explore the relation in the opposite direction, between religions and modernization. The terrain within which religious life functions today is truly vast.

Study group

An awareness of these dynamic processes led the board of the Ecumenical Institute, Bossey, to set up a study group. Christian and ecumenical in nature, its aim was to reflect on the general theme "Religious Life in Today's World and Its Challenges to the Ecumenical Movement". The study group began its work at the end of May 1998. Priority was given to an interdisciplinary approach, which was reflected in the membership of the group, which included theologians, anthropologists, social scientists, political scientists and historians.

At the first meeting of the group, the members drew up a research programme, which was carried out in stages. The second meeting (January 1999) was devoted to the theme "Religions and Economy". The third meeting (August 1999) concentrated on "Religions and Politics". The fourth meeting (June 2000) studied the issue of "Religions and Identity", including the impact of migration on the religious beliefs and practices of migrants. At that meeting the group also considered Islam in different contexts where modernization was taking place. The fifth meeting (April 2001) was on various salient aspects of contemporary religious life: the significant increase in feminist movements within religions; the development of charismatic movements and Pentecostal churches in societies undergoing modernization; Protestant fundamentalism and similar movements in other religions; and Roman Catholicism at world level. The sixth meeting (April 2002) gave rise to a lively exchange of ideas on the theoretical tools that the group had gradually refined in the course of the programme. At that meeting the group members began to plan the present publication and to appoint those responsible for the tasks to bring it about. The seventh meeting (December 2002) received and discussed various contributions to the publication on the findings of the study. A small editorial team was appointed to decide on the final contents of the publication. Its members were Grace Davie, Wesley Ariarajah, André Droogers, Heinrich Schäfer and Julio de Santa Ana. They met in November 2003 and thereafter the various members and contributors to this study finalized their contributions.

Throughout its meetings the group was aware of its possibilities and limitations. Among the possibilities, the international and ecumenical composition of the participants should be noted. The information they were able to give was first hand, from direct sources, and formed a vast panorama enabling us to perceive the diversity of contemporary religious life. Among the limitations, it should be noted that, although the group was made up of people from five continents, its members were all Christians who were in one way or another associated with the ecumenical movement.

Our awareness of this self-imposed limitation increased as our thinking advanced. It became evident to all the group members that one of the major challenges facing the ecumenical movement is the need to take a further step towards what has come to be called "macro-ecumenism" or the "wider ecumenism". This needs to be conducted by means of more inclusive dialogues in the acknowledgment that the unity to which the ecumenical movement aspires should not be confined to that of Christians, but extends to all God's people in the service of all the peoples of the earth.

A further limitation, constantly present in the minds of members, was the fact that, despite the experience, abilities and knowledge of its participants, the group was not able to take into account the wide panorama of issues presented by the religious beliefs and practices of the world's peoples.

The methodology of the group gave priority to case studies and specific situations. Our more theoretical thinking was always rooted in references to facts and events in the daily lives of the followers and communities of the various religions. One of the major concerns of the group was to acknowledge the contribution made by women in each topic we studied and considered. We are aware that we have not always succeeded in doing this, which is a considerable deficiency in our work.

The aims of the group were to:
- contribute to a better understanding by the Christian churches of other religious families and the rich variety in the religious life of the various peoples of the world;
- confront real problems and challenges, attempting to respond to them within a broad perspective, taking into account the variety of situations in which these problems arise, and avoiding political and ecumenical jargon as much as possible, as it generally conceals rather than reveals;
- take into account that, in the face of problems common to the different religious families and their communities, there are many responses representing different traditions and contexts that are always specific and particular; one such issue is religious freedom, which merits in-depth consideration through multilateral and multicultural religious dialogue. An important example of this type of issue is the impact of the media on religious beliefs and practices in today's world.

The group was also aware of the crisis presently affecting the ecumenical movement. As the group sees it, this crisis could be seen as a judgment on the course taken by the ecumenical movement, but also as a promise of renewal: when something is losing momentum it can receive new strength when it follows a path that enables it to be more faithful to what God's mission requires of it.

The group also intended to contribute to the direction of some WCC programmes, especially the Programme on Inter-religious Relations and Dialogue and the Commission on World Mission and Evangelism, and above all to offer contributions of use to the large number of churches related to the WCC.

A further objective of the group – and always in a constructive spirit, working for reconciliation and peace between peoples – was to confront the tension between an ecumenical stance and the intolerant attitudes of Christians and followers of other religions. This led us to examine a variety of ways in which the exclusivism of various religious families could be approached. A typical example of such an attitude, which seems to characterize conflicts involving cultures and beliefs, is when people pay greater attention to hitherto latent confrontations and conflicts between different cultures (including the religions that form part of those cultures), thereby redrawing the geopolitical map following the cold war.[7] The group reflected on national and international conflicts in which various religious families are involved, or where divisions exist within each family, in order to see how a contribution could be made to overcome those conflicts.

We offer our work, the fruit of our thinking in the course of more than five years, to the body that commissioned it, the board of the Ecumenical Institute, Bossey, to the governing bodies of the World Council of Churches, to its member churches, and to all interested in the study of religions.

NOTES

[1] See Peter Berger, *The Desecularization of the World. Resurgent Religion and World Politics*, Grand Rapids MI, Eerdmans, 1999; Grace Davie, *Religion in Modern Europe: A Memory Mutates*, Oxford, Oxford UP, 2000.

[2] José Casanova, *Public Religions in the Modern World*, Chicago, Chicago UP, 1994.

[3] See S.N. Eisenstadt, *The Origins and Diversity of Axial Age Civilizations*, New York, SUNY Press, 1986; *Revolutions and Transformations of Society*, New York, Free Press, 1978; *Post-Traditional Societies*, New York, Norton, 1972; *Tradition, Change and Modernity*, New York, B Wiley, 1973; *Les antinomies de la modernité*, Paris, L'Arche, 1997.

[4] Philip Jenkins, *The Next Christendom: The Coming of Global Christianity*, Oxford, Oxford UP, 2002.

[5] The contemporary Brazilian author Paulo Coelho, whose books include *The Alchemist* and *The Pilgrimage*, is an example of those whose literature draws on magical traditions updated according to the various cultures undergoing modernization. His books, written in Portuguese, have been translated into many languages, and in many cases have gone through more than a hundred editions. The majority of those attracted to this type of literature belong to the fairly highly educated middle classes. The magical practices themselves are found much more frequently among more popular cultures.

[6] Emile Durkheim, *Les formes élémentaires de la vie religieuse. Le système totémique en Australie*, Paris, PUF Quadrige, 1960.

[7] See Samuel P. Huntington, *The Clash of Civilizations and the Remaking of World Order*, New York, Simon & Schuster, 1996; on a similar line, see Lawrence E. Harrison and Samuel P. Huntington, *Culture Matters: How Values Shape Human Progress*, New York, Basic Books, 2000.

Acknowledgments

The Ecumenical Institute received valuable financial support from the Council for World Mission, to whom it expresses its deep gratitude. Equally, the Ecumenical Institute places on record its appreciation to the executive secretaries of the World Council of Churches' Programme on Inter-religious Relations and Dialogue for their contribution to this process of research and reflection.

The study group received valuable advice from the director of the Netherlands Study and Action Group on Migration, Bas de Gaay Fortman (International Institute for Advanced International Studies, The Hague), Cees Hamelink (director, Institute for the Study of Media and Communications, University of Amsterdam and the Free University, Amsterdam), and José Oscar Beozzo (Theology Faculty, Nossa Senhora da Assunção, Archdiocese of São Paulo). To all the aforementioned the Ecumenical Institute, Bossey, expresses its thanks and appreciation. Their contribution to this research project has testified to their regard for the ecumenical movement and their commitment to it.

1

Theoretical Tools
Ways of Approaching the Question

GRACE DAVIE and HEINRICH SCHÄFER

Establishing frameworks in which to think has been an essential part of our task – looking, in other words, for theoretical tools that would help us to understand the myriad forms of religion that exist in the late modern world. Such tools must reflect not only the religions themselves, but also the very different ways that they relate both to the social and political context (in global terms) and to rapid economic change. Religion, for example, is part and parcel of the globalization process and of the social and political movements that bring this about, many of which are addressed in this book – they include large-scale migration, new social movements and transnational NGOs, and new understandings of gender and the struggle for economic justice in the aftermath of colonialism. Religion, however, can also act as a barrier to globalization, providing new understandings of identity for those who feel threatened by global change.

It is hardly surprising, therefore, that new forms of religion are emerging all the time, both inside and outside traditional structures. Some of these are transnational in character (evidenced in the global reach of Catholicism or in the mobilities of Pentecostalism), while others turn inwards rather than out (e.g. varieties of fundamentalism). Both tendencies find expression in political as well as religious life. Hence the complexities of the data, offering on the one hand evidence of secularization and on the other signs of religious resurgence. New forms of syncretism exist alongside ever greater exclusivity; growing individualization coexists with an increasing emphasis on group identity. The situation, moreover, is constantly changing: beliefs and practices mutate – as do their places in society.

The same point can be put in a different way. It is becoming increasingly clear that the relatively secular patterns of religious life that have emerged in Western Europe can no longer be considered a global prototype: indeed, Europe (from the point of view of its religious life) looks increasingly like an exceptional case. Think, for example, of what is happening elsewhere in the Christian world, starting with the vibrant religious market that exists in the United States, quite unlike the patterns that prevail in Europe. Even more significant, perhaps, is the changing nature of religion in both Latin America and sub-Saharan Africa, which together form the demographic centres of Christianity. Both have experienced exponential growth in recent decades, not least in Pentecostalism. Further east, the Philippines remain actively Catholic in terms of public (political) as well as private life and South Korea has Christianized at precisely the same time as it modernized, turning the European trajectory on its head. Add to this the indicators of religion that can be found in the Muslim world, in all its diversity, the surge in religious feelings (not to say ideologies) in the Indian subcontinent, and the dangerously polarizing situation in the Middle East, and Peter Berger's contention (1992) that the developing world is "as furiously religious as ever" becomes increasingly difficult to challenge.

A world "as furiously religious as ever" requires, however, new frames of reference and new forms of understanding if we are to grasp the significance of what is happening. This chapter offers a variety of starting points for that task. The explanatory frameworks that emerge help us to "order" the rich, diverse and frequently contradictory data that derive from empirical observations.

Theoretical tools 1: Secularization theory

One such framework has dominated both sociological and public thinking about religion in the modern world at least in the Western context: it is known as the secularization thesis. [1] More precisely this thesis assumes that the relatively strong connections between modernization and secularization that obtain in the European case will also occur elsewhere, other things being equal. The latter clause is important. Even the strongest advocates of secularization limit the application of their theory to relatively advanced and usually Christian democracies, a point that is frequently overlooked. [2]

The first point to grasp is that the paradigm fits relatively well with the European experience. The "fit" obtains moreover at a variety of levels, both empirical and theoretical. It is clear, for example, that the historic churches in Europe were seriously weakened by the onset of modernization in so far as this is associated with the twin pressures of industrialization and urbanization. European patterns of life extant for centuries, in which the church played a significant part, began to crumble – faster in some places than in others, but eventually across most of the continent.[3] Ecclesiastical structures, deeply embedded in a pre-industrial and a predominantly rural Europe, had difficulty adapting to the changes taking place. The territorial parish (the local manifestation of these arrangements) lost its resonance as the organizing feature of civil as well as church life.[4] And as the structures collapsed, so too did the disciplines (social, moral and religious) that went with them.

At the same time, new epistemologies (new ways of thinking) were challenging the old order. The European Enlightenment, particularly in its French forms, offered secular rather than religious narratives to the European citizen as he or she looked for explanations of life, both individual and collective. Such narratives, moreover, acquired institutions of their own. The (French) concept of *laïcité* offers an excellent example: in France, the state and the school system not only embodied the new philosophy, but also self-consciously replaced the Catholic church and the Catholic parish as the key institutions of modern living. Hence the particularly sharp conflict between church and state in this part of Europe, a theme that dominated much of French history from the time of the Revolution until the middle of the 20th century. Its legacies are still apparent – in, for example, the resistance to the Muslim *hijab* in the French school system.

In terms of the themes developed in this chapter, an important corollary follows from this discussion. It is from a European context that the discipline of sociology first emerged. A primary motivation for the new discipline lay in the attempt to apply Enlightenment thinking to the social as well as the physical order. With this in mind, the founding fathers of sociology set out to understand better the patterns of human living, powerfully stimulated by the economic and social upheavals of which they were part. Hence, there is in their work a constant preoccupation with the nature of modernization and what were thought to be its necessary adjuncts, including secularization – an assumption that worked well in the European context. The problem lies in extrapolating from the West European experience to other parts of the world: quite simply, the modern (or modernizing) world has not secularized in the way that was anticipated, and even the cursory look at the material set out in the first section of this chapter suggests that it will not in the foreseeable future.

The secularization paradigm is, however, resistant. It dominates popular as well as intellectual thinking about religion in the modern world. An exchange that took place in one of our meetings illustrates this point perfectly. Two of our number, neither of whom were Europeans, remembered "learning" the secularization thesis as part of their training in the 1960s and 1970s. It was already apparent (dramatically so, with hindsight) that the paradigm was misleading as far as their own experience was concerned, but learn it they had to – as part of a "proper" intellectual formation. Similar convictions have been true of public as well as academic discourse; hence, until very recently, the effective exclusion of religion from political negotiation or international relations. Religion, if it existed at all, was "really something else" – nationalism or ethnicity being prime candidates. Only relatively recently has religion become an accepted or "normal" category of public as well as private life, taken seriously by both analysts and policy-makers.

It is important that we do not discard the baby with the bath water. Many insights emerging from the secularization thesis are helpful, not least the emphasis on functional separation. It is equally clear, however, that many of the assumptions embodied in the secularization thesis (at least in its more intransigent forms) are no longer tenable. Nor, more profoundly, are they helpful to those, including the ecumenical movement, who are trying to grasp the realities of religion in the modern world and to work creatively within them. We have wrestled with this question in a variety of ways during the course of our work and looked carefully for possible alternatives.

Theoretical tools 2: Rational choice theory

One possibility is to replace one theoretical framework with another. If secularization has emerged from the European context and offers a plausible explanation for European patterns of religious life, the American equivalent can be found in rational choice theory (RCT) – a way of thinking which postulates that religious activity is stimulated by supply rather than demand. The theory, associated above all with the names of Rodney Stark and William Sims Bainbridge, rests on the assumption that the demand for religion is constant – it is part of being human.[5] Our demands, however, are diverse (different people and different communities want different things) and are better satisfied if the possibilities on offer are many and varied. In other words, religious pluralism stimulates demand; it does not, as the secularization theorists suggest, undermine plausibility. The growing pluralism of the modern world will, it follows, increase the likelihood of religious activity, rather than diminish it, this being one reason for the high levels of religious activity found in the United States, the quintessential religious market.

RCT is to America and Americans what secularization theory is to Europe and Europeans.[6] More precisely, RCT fits well with the specificities of American history in which no religious community was offered a privileged political position and which, in turn, stimulated forms of religion able to adapt to the conditions of modernizing America. Religious institutions in the new world had little time to embed themselves into a pre-industrial context; by the time that most of them arrived, the industrializing process was already underway. The churches responded positively – they simply became part of the process, moving easily into the expanding cities. American versions of the Enlightenment followed a similar, essentially creative path. In the United States both the positive nature of religion and the freedom to believe (or indeed not to) are defended; the assumed confrontations of European society, particularly in its French forms, are very largely left behind.

In short, the very different religious situations which obtain on different sides of the Atlantic have produced different forms of sociological theory: secularization theory in Europe and RCT in the United States. Both offer plausible explanations for the situation from which they emerge. Secularization theory accounts for low levels of religious activity in Europe alongside vestigial (sometimes rejected) state churches – the latter representing monopoly rather than choice; RCT explains high levels of activity in the United States in a society where church and state are kept rigorously separate and where an effective religious market has been able to emerge. Contrasting religious mentalities sustain these differences. Europeans think of their churches as public utilities: they are commendable institutions which will, indeed should, be available at the point of need. Americans (used to voluntarism in secular as well as religious life) are more market-oriented, seeing the need for *constant* religious activity if their institutions are to survive. Europeans assume that "someone else" (historically, the state) will keep the church going; Americans rely solely upon themselves.

Given these differences (in mentality as well as context), it is hardly surprising that neither theory travels well: secularization theory does not adapt well to the United States and rational choice theory is of little use in Europe. Attempts to insist otherwise are not helpful. Even more problematic, however, is the application of either theory to other parts of the world where both traditional and innovative forms of religion are increasingly present, but not necessarily along the lines that pertain in the United States.

Theoretical tools 3: Multiple modernities

How, then, can we make sense of these changes? Is it possible, in other words, to discover a theoretical framework within which to situate the chapters and material that follow in this book and which is able to take into account the very different religious situations that are emerging in different parts of the world? One such might be found in the notion of "multiple modernities", a concept elaborated by Shmuel Eisenstadt.[7] It is worth pausing for a moment to consider this somewhat innovative way of thinking; it proved very helpful to our deliberations.

Eisenstadt starts by describing what the idea of "multiple modernities" resists:

> The notion of "multiple modernities" denotes a certain view of the contemporary world – indeed of the history and characteristics of the modern era – that goes against the views long prevalent in scholarly and general discourse. It goes against the view of the "classical" theories of modernization and of the convergence of industrial societies prevalent in the 1950s, and indeed against the classical sociological analyses of Marx, Durkheim and (to a large extent) even of Weber, at least in one reading of his work. They all assumed, even only implicitly, that the cultural programme of modernity as it developed in modern Europe and the basic institutional constellations that emerged there would ultimately take over in all modernizing and modern societies; with the expansion of modernity, they would prevail throughout the world.[8]

Right from the outset, therefore, Eisenstadt challenges both the assumption that modernizing societies are convergent, and the notion of Europe (or indeed anywhere else) as the lead society in the modernizing process.

How then does the notion of multiple modernities develop from a *positive* point of view? In the introductory essay to a set of comparative cases, Eisenstadt[9] suggests that the best way to understand the modern world (in other words to grasp the history and nature of modernity) is to see this as a story of continual reconstitution of a huge variety of cultural programmes. A second point follows from this. These continuing reconstitutions do not drop from the sky; they emerge as the result of endless encounters on the part of both individuals and groups, all of whom engage in the creation and recreation of both cultural and institutional formations, but within *different* economic and cultural contexts. Once this way of thinking is firmly in place it becomes easier to appreciate one of the fundamental paradoxes of Eisenstadt's writing: namely, that to engage with the Western understanding of modernity, or even to oppose it, is as indisputably modern as to embrace it.

What then is the authentic core of modernity? The question becomes, in fact, very difficult to answer, in that modernity is more of an attitude (a distinctive epistemology) than a set of characteristics. In its early forms, it embodied above all a notion of the future which was realizable by means of human agency. As soon as the process was set in motion, however, even the core of modernity was beset by internal contradictions. Were such societies to be totalizing or pluralistic, for example? Or what degree of control/autonomy was considered desirable? Hence, to give an institutional illustration, the very different formulations of the nation-state, an essential feature of modernity, that emerged even in different parts of Europe – hegemonic in France and the Nordic countries, though differently so in each case, as opposed to the rather more pluralistic pattern adopted in Britain or the Netherlands. Should we be surprised therefore at the even greater transformations that took place, both culturally and institutionally, when the idea of modernity transferred itself to the new world (sometimes peacefully and sometimes less so), and then, bit by bit, out of the West altogether? Following Eisenstadt, diversity is simply assumed within the modernizing process; it becomes in fact part of modernity itself.

More specifically, it is part of *reflexive* modernity. Following Eisenstadt,[10] reflexivity in Western thinking not only means being aware of different interpretations of core values or ontological concepts, it also questions the givenness of transcendental visions altogether. Thus reflexive modernity relativizes both the religious and the political field. Positions must be discussed and bargains made; certainty comes from dialogue and negotiation, not simply from affirmation. Conversely, *instrumental* modernity or instrumental reason both affirms and asserts – and with conviction, given the power of modern technology and of the market. It is this side of Western modernity that assumes universal validity, leading at times to imperialist policies in both the economic and political sphere. In this sense, the notion of *multiple* modernities conveys at one and the same time both the essence of and reactions to Western versions of modernity.

The constantly shifting nature of modernity (or more accurately, modernities) is equally important – a point nicely illustrated in Eisenstadt's continuing analysis of the state, this time in late as opposed to early modern societies. Globalization, in all its diverse forms, has changed dramatically the "institutional, symbolic and ideological contours of the modern, national and revolutionary states".[11] No longer, for example, can these institutions adequately control much of modern living, whether in economic, political or cultural terms. Despite technologically developed means of restraint, the flows and counter-flows of modern living increasingly transcend political boundaries. The construction of multiple modernities continues nonetheless (that is its nature), but in constantly changing circumstances.

Central to this process in recent decades is the appearance of new actors and new entities, among them a whole range of social movements, who assume responsibility for the emergent problems of the modern world. Feminist or ecological organizations (often transnational in nature) provide excellent examples, but so too do religious movements – even those commonly known as fundamentalist. It is true that the latter are vehemently opposed to the West and to the ideologies embodied therein. Fundamentalist movements are, however, quintessentially modern in the manner in which they set their goals and in the means that they adopt to achieve them: their outlooks, for example, are truly global and their technologies highly developed. Just like their secular counterparts, they are redefining and reconstituting the concept of modernity, but in their own terms.

The crucial point to emerge from Eisenstadt's work is the continued space for religion and for religious movements within the unfolding interpretations of modernity. The forms of religion, moreover, may be as diverse as the forms of modernity. Indeed, the examples that follow in the same collection of essays offer Christian, Muslim, Hindu and Confucian illustrations. The author of one of these, Nilufer Göle, concludes that the essential core of modernity resides in its potential for self-correction, a capacity that by definition must be constant given that the problems that preoccupy us at the start of the 21st century could not even be imagined in the early stages of modernization. Thus, religion (in Göle's essay this is innovative forms of Islam) becomes one resource among many in the process of continual self-correction. More precisely, "modernity is not simply rejected or readopted but critically and creatively reappropriated" by a whole range of religious actors. [12]

Theoretical tools 4: Actor-centred theories

Eisenstadt's theory of multiple modernities presents an excellent macro-sociological framework within which to approach the role of religion in a global context. Other approaches can, however, be used alongside this, among which are a group of mid-range theories. The aim of these is to understand religious phenomena in a little more detail, paying particular attention to the point of view of the religious actor (both individual and collective) – an idea already introduced by Eisenstadt.

Linking each of the world religions with a different modernity is helpful up to a point: Christianity with the West, Confucianism and Buddhism with East Asian modernities, Hinduism with India, and so forth. This is not meant to imply, however, that religions are coterminous with civilizations. What happens, for example, with Indonesian Islam? Is it Asian or is it Muslim? If it is Muslim, in what sense is the Arabic component present? Or – to put the same point the other way around – to what extent does Islam have to be Arabic? Indonesian Islam seems simply to be both (i.e. Indonesian and Muslim) and as such it forms part of a specific, Indonesian modernity. In other words, recognizing the religious characteristics of different modernities should not imply that these are closed entities, the containers of states, groups and individuals, or, even more provocatively, civilizational blocs which exist only in opposition to one another. [13]

It is more helpful to focus on religious and cultural actors and their role in a great diversity of social processes – not least those which are taking place outside the conventional parameters. Excellent examples can be found in the religious activity of the last decades, much of which is located outside institutionalized religion and well beyond the traditional relationships between state and church. Institutional churches are, in fact, losing significance in exactly the same way as nation-states. Hence the anxieties provoked in both by the process of globalization, in a world where sociological and political perceptions have been deeply marked by the idea that the modern state is the natural point of reference – and not only for activities that are considered or labelled "political". Global communications, mobility and migration foster a huge variety of *non-state* actors: not only transnational corporations, but also transnational institutions, organizations and networks (the UN, Greenpeace, etc.), as well as a huge variety of social and religious movements. These actors do not limit themselves to the borders of nation-states, but create their own fields of action. Hence the increasing significance of "transnational social spaces". [14]

Religious communities are crucial players in these fields of action. The Jewish diaspora offers but one historical illustration – today, there are hundreds of such diasporas. The Jewish example shows, however, the way that religions function: they form and maintain identities over space and time, a crucial task in the conditions of late modernity.

Religion is a social practice that makes reference to a non-human entity in order that human beings may understand themselves better – offering, among many other things, both knowledge and emotional certainty. Such goals are achieved in different ways. Religion can encourage locally oriented practices or make claims to universal validity; it is able both to maintain tradition and to invent new stories; it can promote the group or encourage self-perfection. But whatever the means, religion forms identities: these are varied but distinctive. They can be thought of as "networks of dispositions", enabling both groups and individuals to perceive, judge and act in appropriate ways and thus to organize social life. The formation of religious identities becomes increasingly important as traditional authorities (the nation-state or tribal chiefs) give way to new and still very unclear forms of social organization.

As part of the same process, however, religious organizations – if this is in their interest – make claims to a greater share of power, the more so in circumstances where the dependence on democratic legitimation is relatively weak. Such a tendency revives an old characteristic of religion: its links with secular authorities. Religion has always been associated with worldly power or powers – so much so that many cultures institutionalized these links (Europe offers an obvious historical example). But as modernities redefine the social role of religion, so too do the relationships between "throne and altar" evolve. The crucial point to grasp in this connection is that religion appears to be gaining rather than losing influence in large parts of the modern world. Not only is this true with respect to "fundamentalisms", but the tendency also occurs as part of the democratic process – where even individualized forms of religion are able to exert pressure, through the electoral process, by participation in social movements and by the sheer weight of public opinion. And if the evidence for such pressure is limited in Western industrialized societies (though more so in some places than others), it is overwhelmingly present in Asia, Africa and Latin America.

Religious identities refer to non-human entities and to human (religious) traditions. In so doing they embody two opposing tendencies. On the one hand, they invite an open, indeed cosmopolitan appreciation of different forms of life and religion. But they are equally capable of reinforcing an inward-looking insistence on exclusive forms of religious and cultural practice. It is important to remember that these different possibilities do not depend on traditional or "modern" points of view. Traditional religion, for instance, is perfectly capable of respect for unfamiliar cultural and religious practices, seeing these as valid as well as significant – they are simply the practices of other people. Modern forms of religion, on the other hand, can be both excluding and exclusive, in the sense that they claim universal truth, but only for themselves – American civil religion and Islamic fundamentalism offer two very different examples.

If we classify religions (as Ariarajah does in chapter 14 of this volume) along a continuum, starting at one end with "natural" religions (with a strong sense of dependency on nature), through ethnic religions (which focus on specific ethnic groups), to universal religions (with claims to universal validity) at the other, it follows that the likelihood of exclusive claims will increase among the universalist religions. Such claims are part of their very nature. Further reflection suggests, however, that the most important determinant of such claims (or indeed of the lack of them) appears to lie in the degree to which the religion in question is rooted in everyday life. Religions that are engaged in the regulation of life (as opposed to the great stories with their universalistic aspirations) are less prone to exclusivist practices. An interesting suggestion follows from this. If women really are closer than men to the realities of life, it is possible that the increasing role of women in religious practice might encourage more rather than less open attitudes.

That may or may not be so. Whatever the case, religious identities offer an important means by which individual and collective actors cope with the challenges of the global environment. In multicultural societies, religion (traditional or modern) is able to offer stability as individuals and groups come to terms with religious and cultural differences. Alternatively, it can cultivate new religious identities as new syncretisms emerge out of older forms. More negatively, religion is also capable of fostering rather more aggressive or fundamentalist identities, by means of which religious actors mark themselves out as different from other groups. Such tendencies frequently become confused with ethnic and political claims. This distinction – between cosmopolitan openness and the affirmation of life on the one hand (frequently associated with global justice and an awareness of the natural environment), and a rather more fundamentalist or particularist politics on the other – offers a useful analytical frame.[15] It could also be used as the basis of ethical distinctions.

Conclusion

Three points bring this discussion to a close. The first is to underline once again that the European case with which we started this discussion is indeed distinct – it is an exceptional case rather than a global prototype. But secondly, it is not distinct from a single undifferentiated other. It is simply one modernity among many in the world of the 21st century, all of which are in a process of continual reconstruction. These multiple modernities are observed more closely in the pages that follow, which pay careful attention to the role of the religious actor (both collective and individual). The third point returns to the connections between Europe and the secularization thesis. If it can no longer be assumed that modernization and secularization necessarily go together, how can we explain the relatively secular nature of Europe? The answers must lie, surely, within the European case itself and not within the modernization process per se – there is no incompatibility as such between religion and modernity.

With this in mind, the following conclusion emerges: it is as modern to draw from the resources of religion in order to critique the secular, as it is to draw from the secular in order to critique the religious. Religion, for example, is a crucial feature of many modern identities. Only in Europe has the equation become seriously imbalanced. In terms of the work that we have undertaken together, a second question can no longer be avoided: has the ecumenical movement been too coloured by the European experience in its understandings of religion in the modern world and, therefore, in its aspirations for the 21st century? In so far as this volume offers a partial answer to this question, it rests in the desire not only to identify but also to affirm the opportunities that are developing for active ecumenism in the late modern world. In a world, that is, where religion remains an active and vital force, but in forms that were barely anticipated by the activists of the ecumenical movement in the early post-war decades.

NOTES

[1] The literature on the secularization thesis is immense. The following offer useful start-ing points: D. Martin, *A General Theory of Secularization*, Oxford, Blackwell, 1978; and "The Secularization Issue: Prospect and Retrospect", *British Journal of Sociol-ogy*, 42, 4, 1991. B. Wilson, *Religion in Sociological Perspective*, Oxford, Oxford UP, 1982. K. Dobbelaere, "Secularization: A Multi-dimensional Concept", *Current Soci-ology*, 29, 2, 1981; and *Secularization: An Analysis at Three Levels*, Brussels, PIE/Peter Lang, 2002. P. Berger, *A Far Glory: The Quest for Faith in an Age of Credulity*, New York, Doubleday, 1992; and ed., *The Desecularization of the World: Resurgent Religion and World Politics*, Grand Rapids MI, Eerdmans, 1999. J. Casanova, *Public Religions in the Modern World*, Chicago, Univ. of Chicago Press, 1994. S. Bruce, *From Cathedrals to Cult: Religion in the Modern World*, Oxford, Oxford UP, 1996; and *God Is Dead: Secularization in the West*, Oxford, Blackwell, 2002. G. Davie, *Europe: The Exceptional Case. Parameters of Faith in the Modern World*, London, Darton, Longman & Todd, 2002.

[2] Bruce, *God is Dead*.

[3] The exceptions to this "rule" (notably Poland and Ireland) are discussed in some detail in G. Davie, *Religion in Modern Europe: A Memory Mutates*, Oxford, Oxford UP, 2000.

[4] New forms of religion emerged to fill the gap, especially in the towns. The develop-ment of Methodism in Britain offers an excellent example of this process.

[5] Once again the literature is large and growing all the time. L. Young, *Rational Choice Theory and Religion: Summary and Assessment*, New York, Routledge, 1997, pro-vides a good summary. The *Journal for the Scientific Study of Religion* (from 1990 on) has become a central forum for this debate.

6 S. Warner, "Work in Progress towards a New Paradigm for the Sociological Study of Religion in the United States", *American Journal of Sociology*, 98, 5, 1993; and "A Paradigm Is Not a Theory: Reply to Lechner", *American Journal of Sociology*, 103, 1, 1997.

7 S. Eisenstadt, "Early Modernities", *Daedalus*, 127, 3, 1998; and "Multiple Modernities", *Daedalus*, 129, 1, 2000.

8 Eisenstadt, "Multiple Modernities", p. 1.

9 Eisenstadt, "Multiple Modernities".

10 *Ibid.*, p. 4.

11 *Ibid.* p. 16.

12 N. Göle, "Snapshots of Islamic Modernity", *Daedalus*, 129, 1, 2000.

13 The view taken by Samuel Huntington (1995) in his controversial "clash of civilizations" thesis. See *The Clash of Civilizations and the Remaking of the World Order*, New York, Simon & Schuster, 1995.

14 U. Beck, *Was ist Globalisierung?* Frankfurt, Suhrkamp, 1997, p. 55.

15 A point that resonates with the writing of Anthony Giddens, *Beyond Left and Right: The Future of Radical Politics*, Cambridge, Polity, 1994.

2

Religious Life Today

TODOR SABEV

Statistical data provide documentary support and comprehensibility of vast and complex subjects. Statistics regarding religious life are based on different sources and methods of reckoning religious adherents. Some use, as authoritative, the official figures of state institutions. Others depend on religious law. Most churches count baptised members. Others take into consideration practising believers and communicants. Still others number only the adults and/or constituents. Official state statistics approach in various ways the delicate questions of adhering or not to religion, personal belief, etc. For several decades, the censuses in the USA and in most communist and some other countries did not include questions on religion.

Often affected by ideological factors, political considerations and the exclusivity of dominant religious communities, statistics as historical sources require careful selection and study. Newly opened archives on closed societies and countries with anti-religious regimes have enlarged the documentary basis for a better assessment of religious life. Critical analyses of all sources and comparative studies in inter-related fields secure the credibility of modern statistical works.

Prevailing trends to 1980

The social, economic and political factors that characterized the 20th century had considerable implications for religious life in all its complexity and dynamic change. Any assessment of religion should take into consideration the fact that in many countries where persecution and curtailment of freedoms exist, a large number of religionists refused to register their communities or to publicize and manifest their religious beliefs. In other numerous cases the refusal to register came from hostile state authorities.

Tables 1–4 provide basic figures that show demographic increase at the world and regional levels. They provide comparative indications of population changes, and show a significant growth rate in regions and in several countries prominent on the international scene and in the life of religion. The centre of gravity is gradually oriented more and more towards the southern hemisphere. This is illustrated by the figures on macro regions and regions, the comparison between Europe and Latin America, the situations in the USA and China, and trends in Arab countries. Many other supportive arguments could be added.

Christianity has spread in all continents. By the end of the millennium it represented a third of the total population. Sizeable growth took place in several other religions as well. In 1980 Christians comprised 32.8 percent of the world population (34.4 percent of the adults). Practising believers comprised 23.3 percent. The annual rate augmented in net totals to over 23 million. About 524 million were children.

Christianity developed into seven confessional blocs representing 92 major distinct traditions, groups and communities in 220 countries. The proliferation of denominations attained a net increase of 270 each year. By 1970 their total number was 18,160. Within the next decade, 2620 new denominations were established. The largest ecclesiastical families had significant numbers of adherents in all continents. The greatest number (29 percent) of the world's Christians remained in Europe, followed by Latin America (24.3 percent), North America (15.3 percent) and Africa (14.2 percent). Christianity spread unevenly, with over 90 percent in 100 countries, less than 10 percent in 51 countries, less than 1 percent in 24 countries, and less than 0.1 percent in six Muslim countries in Asia.

The main contributory factor to the growth of Christian communities was demographic/natural/biological development. International migration and refugee issues were part of this demographic dimension. Civil strife and war, drought and hunger displaced people in masses.

Table 1: World population, 1900-2000

1900	1970	Mid-1990
1,619,625,741	3,696,148,141	5,266,442,000

Mid-1995	Mid-2000	Annual change, 1990–2000 rate	
5,666,360,200	6,055,049,000	78,860,791	1.41

Table 2: Macro regions and regions

	Mid-year estimates (millions)								Annual rate	Birth rate	Death rate
	1950	1960	1965	1970	1975	1980	1985	1990	1985–90	1985–90	1985–90
WORLD TOTAL	**2516**	**3020**	**3336**	**3698**	**4079**	**4448**	**4851**	**5292**	**1.7**	**27**	**10**
Africa	**222**	**279**	**317**	**362**	**413**	**477**	**553**	**642**	**3.0**	**45**	**15**
Eastern Africa	65	82	94	108	124	144	168	197	3.2	49	16
Middle Africa	26	32	35	40	45	52	60	70	3.0	45	16
Northern Africa	52	65	73	83	94	107	123	141	2.6	38	11
Southern Africa	16	20	23	26	29	32	36	41	2.4	34	10
Western Africa	63	81	92	105	122	141	165	194	3.2	48	17
Latin America	**166**	**218**	**251**	**286**	**323**	**363**	**404**	**448**	**2.1**	**29**	**7**
Caribbean	17	20	23	25	27	29	31	34	1.5	25	8
Central America	37	50	59	70	81	93	105	118	2.3	31	6
South America	112	147	169	191	215	241	268	297	2.0	28	8
Northern America*	**166**	**199**	**214**	**226**	**239**	**252**	**265**	**276**	**0.8**	**15**	**9**
Asia	**1377**	**1668**	**1861**	**2102**	**2354**	**2583**	**2835**	**3113**	**1.9**	**28**	**9**
Eastern Asia	671	792	874	987	1097	1176	1249	1336	1.3	20	7
Southern Asia	481	596	670	754	849	948	1070	1201	2.3	35	12
Southeastern Asia	182	225	253	287	324	360	401	445	2.0	30	9
Western Asia	42	56	64	74	85	99	115	132	2.8	36	9

	393	425	445	460	474	484	492	498	0.2	13	11
Europe**											
Oceania	12.6	15.8	17.5	19.3	21.2	22.8	24.6	26.5	1.5	19	8
Australia and New Zealand	10.1	12.7	14.0	15.4	16.7	17.8	19.0	20.3	1.3	15	8
Melanesia	2.1	2.6	2.9	3.3	3.7	4.2	4.7	5.3	2.3	34	11
Micronesia	0.2	0.2	0.2	0.3	0.3	0.3	0.3	0.4	1.6	27	7
Polynesia	0.2	0.3	0.4	0.4	0.4	0.5	0.5	0.5	1.5	34	5
USSR	180	214	231	243	254	266	278	289	0.8	18	11

* Hawaii, a state of the USA, is included in Northern America rather than Oceania.
** Excluding the USSR, shown separately. The European portion of Turkey is included in Western Asia rather than Europe.

Source: Based on Global Table 1, *World Christian Encyclopaedia* (WCE), ed. David B. Barrett, Oxford UP, 1982, p.3; Tables 1:1, 1–2, WCE, 2nd ed., 2001, pp.4–5; *Encyclopedia Britannica*, Book of the Year 1991, Report of 1990, p.29; 1990 *Demographic Yearbook*, New York, United Nations, 1992, p.2.

Table 3 : Comparative data on growth in Europe and Latin America

Region	Year	Estimated as of mid-year (in 000s)	Density (par km²)	Total reproductive value (in 000s)	Dependency ratio Youth <15 (×100)	Old age >65 (×100)	Departure from stability (%)	Crude rates (both sexes) Birth (×1000)	Death (×1000)	Standardized rates; Standard: USA 1980 Birth (×1000)	Death (×1000)
1	2	3	4	5	6	7	8	9	10	11	12
Europe	1950	392523	81		38.5	13.2		19.83	11.01		
	1960	425070	87		40.0	15.0		18.69	10.25		
	1970	460132	94		39.2	17.9		15.75	10.39		
	1980	484436	99		34.7	20.2		13.44	10.49		
	1985	492177	101		31.2	19.1		12.98	10.73		
Eastern Europe (Comecon)	1950	88500	89		40.3	10.6		23.62	11.28		
	1960	96713	98		43.8	12.9		17.52	9.37		
	1970	102998	104	23123	38.0	16.0	5.2	16.79	10.33	14.83	10.20
	1975	106180	107	22668	35.6	17.4	4.7	17.63	10.60	14.53	9.76
	1980	109400	110	22083	36.7	18.3	4.7	17.03	11.42	14.07	10.04
	1985	111681	113		35.8	16.3		14.61	11.25		
Northern Europe	1950	72477	46		35.5	15.6		16.73	11.09		
	1960	75647	48		37.4	17.5		17.89	11.21		
	1970	80457	51		38.2	20.1		14.76	11.22		

Year						
1980	82494	52	33.1	23.1	12.92	11.23
1985	83180	53	29.9	23.0	13.15	11.56

Southern Europe

Year						
1950	109014	83	42.9	11.4	21.21	10.35
1960	118197	90	41.9	12.9	20.68	9.42
1970	128339	98	41.7	15.6	17.81	9.15
1980	138806	106	38.0	17.9	13.16	8.87
1985	142342	108	33.1	17.7	12.63	9.51

Western Europe

Year						
1950	122532	123	35.2	15.2	17.65	11.35
1960	134513	135	37.1	17.1	18.24	11.05
1970	148209	149	38.4	20.3	13.75	11.11
1980	153740	155	31.1	22.1	12.07	11.06
1985	154974	156	27.1	20.2	12.04	11.01

Latin America

Year						
1950	165365	8	72.5	5.8	42.50	15.33
1960	217649	11	78.6	6.5	41.18	12.16
1970	285127	14	79.2	7.2	35.28	9.67
1980	361756	18	69.4	7.6	30.86	8.01
1985	403646	20	64.8	7.8	29.05	7.49

Caribbean

Year						
1950	16878	71	69.0	7.2	37.47	15.20
1960	20353	85	71.1	7.8	39.09	11.94
1970	24881	104	75.9	9.1	31.20	9.26
1980	29260	123	62.5	9.8	25.12	8.11
1985	31288	131	54.4	9.8	24.69	7.84

Table 3 : (Cont.)

Region	Year	Estimated as of mid-year (in 000s)	Density (par km²)	Total reproductive value (in 000s)	Dependency ratio Youth <15 (X100)	Old age >65 (X100)	Departure from stability (%)	Crude rates (both sexes) Birth (X1000)	Death (X1000)	Standardized rates; Standard: USA 1980 Birth (X1000)	Death (X1000)
1	2	3	4	5	6	7	8	9	10	11	12
Central America	1950	37241	15		82.1	6.0		47.30	17.07		
	1960	50456	20		88.6	6.2		46.04	12.34		
	1970	69665	28		93.7	6.5		42.69	9.55		
	1980	92677	37		84.8	6.6		33.49	7.01		
	1985	104746	42		76.3	6.4		31.07	6.29		
South America	1950	111245	6		69.9	5.6		41.64	14.76		
	1960	146840	8		76.5	6.5		39.77	12.13		
	1970	190580	11		74.9	7.2		33.04	9.77		
	1980	239820	13		64.8	7.8		30.53	8.39		
	1985	267611	15		61.8	8.0		28.76	7.92		

Source: N. Keyfit and W. Flieger, *World Population Growth and Aging. Demographic Trends in the Late Twentieth Century*, Chicago, Univ. of Chicago Press, 1987, pp.79ff.

**Table 4 : Some indications of significant changes
in a number of countries**

China
Demographic indicators, 2000 and 2025

	2000	2025
Births per 1000 population	14	11
Deaths per 1000 population	7	8
Rate of natural increase (%)	0.7	0.3
Annual rate of growth (%)	0.7	0.2
Life expectancy at birth (years)	71.4	77.4
Infant deaths per 1000 live births	29	11
Total fertility rate (per woman)	1.7	1.8

Mid-year population estimates and average annual period growth rates,
1950 to 2050 (population in thousands, rate in %)

Year	Population	Year	Population	Period	Growth rate
1950	562,580	1995	1,206,034	1950–1960	1.5
1960	650,661	1996	1,218,257	1960–1970	2.3
1970	820,403	1997	1,230,299	1970–1980	1.8
1980	984,736	1998	1,241,891	1980–1990	1.5
1990	1,138,895	1999	1,252,766	1990–2000	1.0
2000	1,262,474	2010	1,342,783	2000–2010	0.6
2001	1,271,085	2020	1,424,064	2010–2020	0.6
2002	1,279,161	2030	1,458,971	2020–2030	0.2
2003	1,286,975	2040	1,452,001	2030–2040	0.0
2004	1,294,630	2050	1,417,631	2040–2050	−0.2

Mid-year population, by age and sex, 2000 and 2025 (population in thousands)

Age	2000			2025		
	Total	Male	Female	Total	Male	Female
Total	1,262,474	649,774	612,700	1,448,447	734,939	713,508
0–4	95,883	50,111	45,772	82,707	42,516	40,191
5–9	103,615	54,199	49,416	90,309	46,501	43,808
10–14	119,965	62,817	57,148	93,180	48,150	45,030
15–19	99,059	51,386	47,673	85,465	44,291	41,174
20–24	95,889	49,357	46,532	80,674	41,889	38,785
25–29	118,814	61,095	57,719	93,556	48,611	44,945
30–34	125,139	64,435	60,704	100,920	52,416	48,504
35–39	102,806	52,752	50,054	116,432	60,500	55,932
40–44	82,271	42,780	39,492	95,432	49,046	46,386
45–49	84,031	43,199	40,832	91,856	46,811	45,045
50–54	61,054	31,731	29,323	112,578	57,227	55,352
55–59	45,823	23,851	21,973	115,737	58,617	57,120
60–64	40,726	21,071	19,655	91,212	45,574	45,637
65–69	34,634	17,488	17,146	67,238	33,407	33,830
70–74	25,085	12,131	12,954	61,101	29,147	31,954
75–79	15,899	7,055	8,845	36,159	16,664	19,495
80–84	7,908	3,114	4,793	19,202	8,240	10,963
85 +	3,871	1,203	2,668	14,688	5,331	9,357

Source: US Census Bureau, International Data Base, October 2002 version; cf. Marlita A. Reddy, ed., *Statistical Abstract of the World*, Detroit, Gale Research, 1994, p. 194.

USA

	2000	2025
Births per 1000 population	14	14
Deaths per 1000 population	9	9
Rate of natural increase (%)	0.6	0.5
Annual rate of growth (%)	1.0	0.8
Life expectancy at birth (years)	76.6	80.5
Infant deaths per 1000 live births	7	5
Total fertility rate (per woman)	2.1	2.2

Mid-year population estimates and average annual period growth rates, 1950 to 2050 (population in thousands, rate in %)

Year	Population	Year	Population	Period	Growth rate
1950	152,271	1995	266,557	1950–1960	1.7
1960	180,671	1996	269,667	1960–1970	1.3
1970	205,052	1997	272,912	1970–1980	1.0
1980	227,726	1998	276,115	1980–1990	0.9
1990	250,132	1999	279,295	1990–2000	1.2
2000	282,339	2010	309,163	2000–2010	0.9
2001	285,024	2020	336,032	2010–2020	0.8
2002	287,676	2030	363,811	2020–2030	0.8
2003	290,343	2040	392,173	2030–2040	0.8
2004	293,028	2050	420,081	2040–2050	0.7

Mid-year population, by age and sex, 2000 and 2025 (population in thousands)

Age	2000			2025		
	Total	Male	Female	Total	Male	Female
Total	282,339	138,596	143,743	349,666	171,918	177,748
0–4	19,218	9,831	9,387	23,518	12,015	11,503
5–9	20,483	10,489	9,994	23,163	11,831	11,332
10–14	20,608	10,561	10,048	22,888	11,692	11,195
15–19	20,250	10,413	9,837	22,469	11,496	10,972
20–24	19,185	9,822	9,363	22,125	11,296	10,829
25–29	19,317	9,785	9,531	21,441	10,882	10,559
30–34	20,587	10,373	10,214	22,993	11,647	11,347
35–39	22,648	11,305	11,343	23,080	11,654	11,425
40–44	22,535	11,180	11,355	22,319	11,232	11,087
45–49	20,231	9,959	10,271	20,682	10,327	10,355
50–54	17,791	8,707	9,084	20,044	9,914	10,130
55–59	13,559	6,553	7,006	20,292	9,945	10,346
60–64	10,865	5,166	5,699	21,128	10,185	10,944
65–69	9,534	4,403	5,131	19,647	9,284	10,363
70–74	8,850	3,904	4,946	16,041	7,346	8,695
75–79	7,425	3,051	4,374	12,268	5,377	6,891
80–84	4,985	1,854	3,131	7,557	3,079	4,478
85–89	2,803	884	1,919	4,353	1,609	2,745
90–94	1,124	286	837	2,312	750	1,562
95–99	290	59	231	1,018	282	737
100 +	51	10	41	327	74	253

Source: US Census Bureau, International Data Base, October 2002 version, p. 974 (3rd ed., p. 993).

Arab countries (with large population and/or high growth rate per annum)

Year Country	1900	1970	Mid-1990	Mid-2000	Mid-2025	Growth rate, 2000 (%)
Egypt	10,500,000	35,285,000	56,333,000	68,470,000	95,615,000	1.70
Algeria	4,600,000	13,746,184	24,936,000	31,471,000	46,611,000	2.11
Morocco	5,200,000	15,180,676	23,804,000	28,221,000	38,530,000	1.57
Iraq	2,250,000	9,356,000	18,078,000	23,115,000	41,014,000	2.85
Saudi Arabia	2,730,000	5,744,758	16,045,000	21,607,000	39,965,000	2.57
Yemen	2,530,000	6,331,600	11,590,000	18,112,000	38,985,000	3.47
Syria	1,750,000	6,258,000	12,386,000	16,125,000	26,292,000	2.46
Palestine/ Palest. Authority	260,000	809,664	1,535,000	2,215,000	4,133,000	4.01

Source: WCE, 2nd ed., Part 4: Countries.

Table 5: Adherents of religions, mid-1980

Religions	Adherents (%)		Annual change, 1970–1985, natural conversion rate	
Christians	1,432,686,519	32.8	21,414,259	196,449	1.64
Jews	16,938,230	0.4	185,873	– 10644	1.09
Muslims	722,956,504	16.5	17,063,381	140,371	2.74
Hindus	582,749,920	13.3	12,144,744	– 248,235	2.30
Buddhists	273,715,590	6.3	5,112,463	– 908,123	1.67
Sikhs	14,244,360	0.3	333,367	29,849	2.94
Shamanists	13,502,770	0.4	308,883	– 551,336	0.41
Baha'is	3,822,630	0.1	78,906	37,413	3.63
New religionists	96,021,800	2.2	1,830,567	127,301	2.28
Non-religious	715,901,416	16.4	9,314,352	7,969,260	2.76
Atheists	195,119,360	4.5	2,446,459	536,627	1.66

Source: Based on Global Tables 4, 23, WCE, 1st ed., pp. 6,782.

Table 6: Adherents of religions in the world, mid-1990 and mid-2000

Major religions	1990 adherents (%)		2000 adherents (%)	
Christians	1,747,461,964	33.2	1,999,563,838	33.0
Jews	13,188,955	0.3	14,434,039	0.2
Muslims	962,357,235	18.3	1,188,242,789	19.6
Hindus	685,998,940	13.0	811,336,265	13.4
Buddhists	323,106,550	6.1	359,981,757	5.9
New religionists	92,396,355	1.8	102,356,297	1.7
Non-religious	707,117,959	13.4	768,158,954	12.7
Atheists	145,718,604	2.8	150,089,508	2.5

Source: Based on Table 1–1, WCE, 2nd ed., p. 4; *Encyclopedia Britannica*, Book of the Year 1991, p. 299; 1999 Britannica of the Year, p. 315.

Table 7: Major religions in the world, annual change of adherents, 1990–2000

Religions	Annual change, natural conversion rate		
Christians	22,708,799	2,501,396	1.3
Jews	194,962	−70,444	0.5
Muslims	21,723,118	865,558	2.1
Hindus	13,194,111	−660,337	1.6
Buddhists	3,530,918	156,609	1.0
New religionists	1,032,400	−36,405	1.0
Non-religious	6,639,206	−535,100	0.8
Atheists	1,315,322	−878,227	0.3

Source: Table 1–1, WCE, 2nd ed., pp. 4,5.

Table 8: Global Christianity; Christians in various continents and regions, 1980

Continents/regions	Mid-1980* adherents (%)		Annual change, 1970–1985, natural conversion rate	
Africa	203,490,710	14.2	4.7	4,586,648	1,466,149	3.55
East Asia	19,026,270	1.3	1.4	276,181	359,622	4.04
South Asia	109,051,740	7.6	2.5	2,645,668	447,043	3.35
Europe	415,600,780	29.0	9.5	2,197,458	−1,150,645	0.26
Latin America	348,658,275	24.3	8.0	8,419,292	−291,821	2.66
Northern America	219,833,450	15.3	5.0	2,008,880	−669,881	0.63
Oceania	20,298,794	1.4	0.5	372,894	−128,200	1.28
USSR	96,726,500	6.7	2.2	907,238	164,182	1.17

* The first column indicates the percentage of all Christians, and the second one is the percentage of the world population.

Source: Global Tables 2 and 23, WCE, 1982 ed., pp. 4,782–5.

Table 9: Population and Christians on continents, 1990, 2000

Continents	Population (1) Christians (2)	Mid-1990 (%)	Population (1) Christians (2)	Mid-2000 (%)
Africa	614,846,200		784,537,686	
	276,497,939	45.0	360,232,182	45.9
Asia	3,192,397,000		3,696,988,087	
	248,728,290	7.8	312,849,430	8.5
Europe	722,206,100		728,886,949	
	550,418,843	76.2	559,642,545	76.8
Latin America	440,469,700		519,137,936	
	409,345,790	92.2	481,102,373	92.7
North America	281,988,200		309,631,092	
	240,458,450	85.3	260,624,388	84.2
Oceania	26,411,875		30,393,392	
	22,010,352	83.3	25,109,520	82.6

Source: Based on Table 1–4, WCE, 2nd ed., pp.13–15.

Table 10: Muslims in the late twentieth century

Continents	Mid-1970 adherents	(%)	Mid-1990 adherents	(%)	Mid-1995 adherents	(%)	Mid-2000 adherents	(%)
Africa	143,095,965	40.1	251,066,766	40.8	282,641,990	40.6	317.374.423	40.5
Asia	391,407,279	18.2	676,677,775	21.2	751,779,485	21.8	832,878,936	22.5
Europe	17,622,610	2.7	29,206,045	4.0	29,866,635	4.1	31,566,311	4.3
Latin America	488,630	0.2	1,373,320	0.3	1,546,300	0.3	1,672,011	0.3
Northern America	842,000	0.4	3,810,010	1.4	4,105,010	1.4	4,449,696	1.4
Oceania	71,309	0.4	223,279	0.9	259,295	0.9	301,292	1.0

Annual change 1990–2000

Continents	Natural	Conversion	Total	Rate
Africa	6,500,296	130,471	6,630,767	2.37
Asia	15,156,928	463,200	15,620,118	2.10
Europe	6,035	229,994	236,029	0.78
Latin America	20,296	9,572	29,868	1.99
Northern America	37,040	26,929	63,969	1.56
Oceania	2,790	5,012	7,802	3.04

Table 11: Population and Muslims on continents, 1900, 1990, 2000, 2025

Continents	1900 population Muslims (%)		Mid-1990 (%)		Mid-2000 (%)		2025 (%)
Africa	107,808,100		614,846,200		784,537,686		
	34,485,292	32.0	251,066,766	40.8	317,374,423	40.5	40.0
Asia	956,196,200		3,192,397,000		3,696,988,087		
	156,139,610	16.3	676,677,775	21.2	832,878,936	22.5	25.7
Europe	402,607,550		722,206,100		728,886,949		
	9,234,890	2.3	25,206,045	4.0	31,566,311	4.3	5.1
Latin America	65,142,300		440,469,700		519,137,936		
	57,710	0.1	1,373,320	0.3	1,672,011	0.3	0.4
North America	81,625,500		281,988,200		309,631,092		
	10,050 0.0		3,810,010	1.4	4,449,696	1.4	1.8
Oceania	6,246,350		26,411,875		30,393,392		
	13,372	0.2	223,279	0.9	301,292	<1.0	1.3

Source: WCE, 2nd ed., pp.13–15.

Table 12: Organized Christianity: global membership ranked by seven Christian/ecclesiastical blocs, 1980

Name	Membership 1980 Affiliated (total membership)	In number of countries 2000
Roman Catholic	802,659,904	220
Catholic (non-Roman)	3,439,375	59
Protestant	262,155,904	212
Marginal Protestant*	14,077,333	176
Orthodox	160,737,744	107
Anglican	49,803,974	165
'Indigenous' Christians	82,180,415	145

* Mormons, Jehovah's Witnesses, Christian Science and others.
Source: Based on Global Table 9, WCE, 1st ed., p.14.

Table 13: Global Christian membership, 1990 and 2000

Name	1990	%	2000	%
Roman Catholic	929,701,934	17.7	1,057,328,093	17.5
Protestant	296,349,246	5.6	342,001,605	5.6
Orthodox	203,765,600	3.9	215,128,717	3.6
Anglicans	68,195,625	1.3	79,649,642	1.3
Independents*	301,536,352	5.7	385,745,407	6.4
Marginal Christians	21,832,515	0.4	26,060,230	0.4
Evangelicals	173,272,155	3.3	210,602,983	3.5
Pentecostals/ Charismatics	425,486,472	8.1	523,777,994	8.7
Great Commission Christians**	560,665,961	10.6	647,820,987	10.7

* Mainly African Indigenous Protestant churches.
** Wedded to Witness/martyrdom.
Source: Based on table 1–1 (cf. also tables 1–3, 1–4), WCE, 2nd ed., pp. 4,5,12–15; *Encyclopedia Britannica*, Book of the Year 1991, Report of 1990, p. 299; 1999 Britannica Book of the Year, Events of 1998, p. 315.

The most dramatic of such occurrences were in Africa (with some 5 million refugees), Latin America and Southern Asia.

The combination of Christian mission and inculturation with economic and political relations with third-world countries was also very important. By 1980, in Africa alone, over 6 million Christians were baptised each year. In Latin America there was an annual net increase of nearly 9 million. A driving force in the process of Christianization was the "social gospel".

Also noteworthy is the rapid growth of "indigenous" Christians (particularly in Africa) and "marginal Protestants" (Jehovah's Witnesses, Mormons, Christian Scientists, Unitarians). The movement of non-Roman Catholics is also surprising.

Undoubtedly, by the year 1980 world evangelization had made significant progress. Despite the success of mission endeavours, however, there remained nearly 1400 million unevangelized people. In 77 countries there was moderate church growth (from 1 percent to 3 percent yearly). In another 48 countries the increase was under 1 percent. A net decline (less than zero growth) occurred in 26 countries.

The number of evangelizers from Europe and North America declined, while missionaries from the third world became more active. Waves of secularization, the cold war and other divisive factors affected religious life. Mainline Western European and North American churches experienced a tide of demographic increase and declining membership. The number of countries traditionally considered as religious decreased from 114 in 1970 to 101 in 1980. Some 50 countries in various parts of the world became closed to foreign missions.

A good number of churches witnessed in 38 Marxist countries. This included the majority of Orthodox churches, most of which were limited in their missionary work and their natural growth, instead bearing the cross of martyrdom and searching for new ways and means to survive. "Secular" countries increased to 92 and were not eager to provide all the necessary conditions for religions to flourish.

Other problems that Christianity faced by 1980 were poverty, illiteracy, social injustice, racial tension, divisive political and ethical issues, and missionary rivalry. Around 780 million people in 172 less developed countries lived in poverty and suffered malnutrition, illiteracy and disease. A significant proportion of citizens of these less developed countries (26 of which were defined as the poorest in the world) lived in Christian communities.

Christian conciliarism progressed. Some 550 national, 55 regional, 27 continental, and 3 international councils were involved Christians in ecumenical work. However, a trend of non-conciliarism continued.

Around 66 million Christians remained unaffiliated to confessional councils. Another 144 million did not join world ecumenical bodies. Some 315 million were outside continental structures and another 315 million were non-associated to regional councils. By 1980 some 115 million church members were not participating in ecumenical structures. The main reasons for this non-conciliarism were the geographic, cultural, social and political isolation of Christian communities, and ignorance about modern ecumenism or disagreement with programmes, positions or the working style of organizations. In other cases isolated and persecuted churches (e.g. Orthodox and Protestant churches in Central and Eastern Europe) tried to find in conciliar membership a new identity, fellowship, witness and life.

Studies and reports mention a variety of dialogues and other vital ecumenical work by churches and communities. However, conservatism, fundamentalism, divergent opinions, strained relations between adherents of different religions, competing interests of communities, and clashes and violence persisted.

Along with Christian churches, other religions asserted their presence and increased their membership across many regions. Islam continued to spread in 162 countries, as did Hinduism (84 countries), Buddhists and others. The general increase in non-believers and atheists (together forming over 911 million people) was also impressive.

This gradual extension of other religions and non-believers was again due to demographic change, migration, missionary zeal and tenacity. Muslims, Buddhists and some others found ways of surviving even in countries hostile to religion (e.g. in Asia and Eastern Europe). Orthodoxy and the conservative and reformed streams of Judaism did not reverse these trends of modernity.

Religious pluralism became a living reality, expressed through over 20 world religions, religious systems or quasi-religions, for whom shared living space remained an important issue and a common challenge (e.g. crises in the Middle East, conflict between Hindus and Muslims, religious fundamentalism and intolerance in many countries). Although some revivals of religion occurred in secularized areas of the modern world, the erosion of Christianity is noticeable. A gradual decline occurred within most world religions. The percentage of religionists declined from 80.4 percent in 1970 to 79.2 percent in 1980.

The last two decades of the 20th century

The end of the 1980s was marked by transformations in Central and Eastern Europe that had implications for the whole world and led to optimistic predictions about religion. Events in Europe and the Middle East aggravated the problems of migration, national minorities, asylum-seekers, resettlement and unemployment, and had consequences for the global refugee population (about 15 million), especially in Africa and Asia.

According to the statistics, in 1990 the world population was almost 5300 million, with a growth of 93 million from the previous year. This growth is explained by increases in life expectancy and other demographic factors. Over the last two decades population levels increased rapidly in the South. For example, in 2000 the growth rate per annum in some large countries was as follows: Argentina: 1.19 percent, Brazil: 1.20 percent, India: 1.41 percent, Indonesia: 1.22 percent, Pakistan: 2.50 percent. By way of comparison, the UK rate was 0.11 percent.

The historically large churches and other world religions gained strength in terms of membership and practising adherents, yet many of them experienced difficulties with disaffected members, dissidents and continual exodus to other denominations (often "missionary centred" Christian communities and proselytizing movements). Apart from these traditional Christian blocs and ancient religions, the statistics for 1990 include the following categories: *Other Christians* (non-Roman Catholic, marginal Protestants and crypto-Christians – secret believers – and indigenous Christians from the South); *Other religionists* (which represent about fifty minor religions, the New Age and para-religions); *New religionists* (various religions and movements, "new crisis religions" and Christian syncretistic mass religions). Most of them increased numerically and geographically. Pentecostals, Baptists, other evangelicals, Adventists, Jehovah's Witnesses, Mormons and "sects" were highly visible and very active in the missionary field.

The total Christian increase (as a result of factors mentioned above) for the 1980s was around 326 million.

Let us now look at statistical data illustrating a stable religious situation in the USA. In February and March 2002 the Pew Research Council conducted a survey of 2002 adults. Questions about religious preference were included. The results are shown in tables 14 and 15.

In the "communist world", despite restrictions and persecution of religions, most of the churches and other faiths witnessed vitality and gradual improvement during the 1980s. At the beginning of the 1990s they started a new period of reconstruction. John Meyendorff observed a "continuous and spectacular revival of religious practice in formally communist countries". Some signs of freer expression of religion appeared also in China. The number of Christians there increased from 5 million in 1949 to over 50 million in 1990.

Table 14

Religious preference %	June 1996	March 2001	March 2002
Christian	84	82	82
Jewish	1	1	1
Muslim	*	1	*
Other non-Christian	3	2	1
Atheist	*	1	1
Agnostic	*	2	2
Something else *(specify)*	*	1	2
No preference	11	8	10
Don't know/refused	1	2	1

Table 15: Self-identification, American Religious Identity Survey

Religion	1990 est. adult pop.	2001 est. adult pop.	% of US: Pop. 2000	% Change 1990–2000
Christianity	151,225,000	159,030,000	76.5%	+5%
Non-religious/ secular	13,116,000	27,539,000	13.2%	+110%
Judaism	3,137,000	2,831,000	1.3%	−10%
Islam	527,000	1,104,000	0.5%	+109%
Buddhism	401,000	1,082,000	0.5%	+170%
Agnostic	1,186,000	991,000	0.5%	−16%
Atheist		902,000	0.4%	
Hinduism	227,000	766,000	0.4%	+237%
Unitarian Universalist	502,000	629,000	0.3%	+25%
Wiccan/ Pagan/Druid		307,000	0.1%	
Spiritualist		116,000		
Native American Religion	47,000	103,000		+119%
Baha'is	28,000	84,000		+200%
New Age	20,000	68,000		+240%
Sikhism	13,000	57,000		+338%
Scientology	45,000	55,000		+22%
Humanist	29,000	49,000		+69%
Deity (Deist)	6,000	49,000		+717%
Taoist	23,000	40,000		+74%
Eckankar	18,000	26,000		+44%

Foreign missionary work and proselytism within the dioceses of the traditional Orthodox churches in the former USSR and other Eastern European countries jeopardized ecumenical relations, particularly after the collapse of the communist system. Roman Catholic policy concerning Eastern rite Catholics (uniates) was regarded as a major obstacle to dialogue.

Religions in most socialist countries had already been involved in dissident events and the move towards freedom. For some churches and communities this also meant religious and political independence. This process furthered ethnic/national rivalries and conflicts with far-reaching implications for the autonomy of church structures and religious life in general.

Elsewhere, clergy and lay people, as well as ecumenical councils, contributed to socio-political changes in Namibia and South Africa, and to major events in Latin America. Religion remained a conservative force in spiritual and cultural traditions. A great number of churches were concerned with identity and followed the way of integrism. In most religions conservative fundamentalists manifested their views and claimed orthodoxy. "Liberalism" and extreme and moderate conservatism often alternated or paralleled each other as streams of religious life. They influenced interchurch relations and dialogue with other faith partners. Christian divergence and polemics focused often on personal morality and social ethics. Particularly important subjects were homosexuality, family, contraception, abortion, women's ordination, antisemitism, xenophobia and violence.

Numerous churches, denominations and organizations resisted the reappearance of the fascist spirit in antisemitic and far-right politics, racial discrimination, nationalism, and ethnic and religious conflicts. Churches in the South (particularly Latin America) saw renewal, new dynamism in spirituality and mission, and commitment to development, justice and ecumenism. Women in various countries moved into high-ranking church leadership. Others were ordained pastors. In the Roman Catholic Church and Orthodox churches the issue of the role of women and the ministry of deaconesses was voiced with theological argument and inspiration to renewal.

There was unrest among Muslims in the Islamic republics of the former USSR. Muslims were also active in Eastern Europe. Buddhists, Baha'is and others acquired more adherents and also became better equipped to work in those regions. Local churches lacking adequate resources and personnel for mission reacted nervously without discernible effect. Ecumenism entered a period of transition.

By mid-1998, world population numbered 5,926,000 billion and soon went beyond 6 billion. (The churches were reaching an estimated level of one-third of the total population.) The annual rate of growth, however, declined (from 1.47 percent in 1997 to 1.41 percent in 1998) as a result of a falling birth rate due to socio-economic problems in less developed countries. Over 90 percent of the total births in 1998 occurred just in those regions. The population in the less developed countries constituted 80 percent of the people in the world.

In comparison to the figures for 1990, the percentage of Christian presence in the rest of the world changed from 33.2 percent to 32.8 percent in 1998, and 33 percent in 2000. This occurred in the main Christian blocs, with Roman Catholics declining by 0.5 percent, Protestants declining by 1.6 percent, the Orthodox increasing (in the post-communist period) by 0.4 percent, and the Anglicans declining by 0.3 percent. The figure for "Other Christians" (unaffiliated with traditional Christian communions) augmented by 3.3 percent due to missionary work and aggressive proselytism. "Marginal Protestants" and post-denominationalists have become prominent for Christian witness and claimed a major role in the renewal of Christianity.

Numerically and in terms of evangelical zeal Christianity has further grown in the southern hemisphere. By 2000 it reached over 360 million in Africa (almost half the continental population), with a net increase of 8.4 million a year. In Asia the net increase was 2.4 million a year. At the end of the second millennium, Christians formed the majority of the population (over 50 percent) in two-thirds of the world's 238 countries. They numbered over 90 percent of the population in 84 countries, less than 10 percent in 51 countries, and less than 1 percent in 22 countries.

Other world religions also strengthened their influence in several regions in the South. The statistical data in the last two decades gives reason to speak not only of significant Christian gains but also of massive losses. There is a continual erosion of Christianity's numerical strength. Every year a large number of the 2,700,000 church members in Europe and North America cease to be active Christians. Stagnation is occurring in the life of other religions as well.

Muslims have grown by 1.6 percent in an additional 36 countries; Buddhists have grown by 0.3 percent in an additional 42 countries; Hindus declined by 0.5 percent but reached 26 new countries; Baha'is declined by 5.6 percent but spread to another 16 countries.

Today, there are large Muslim communities in 204 countries of the world, Jews in 134 countries, Buddhists in 126 countries, Hindus in 114 countries, and Baha'is in 218 countries. The annual increase of major world religions is as follows: Christians 1.4 percent; Muslims 2.1 percent; Hindus 1.7 percent; Buddhists 1.1 percent; Baha'is 2.3 percent; Sikhs 1.9 percent; Jews 0.2 percent. The figures for Christian popular religionists (500 million), non-religionists (918 million) and non-religious (768 million) are very sizeable.

The great majority of adherents of world religions face basic social problems. Over 110 million Christians live in the poorest countries. About 24 percent of the 1.1 billion absolutely poor people are members of Christian churches. Ethnic conflicts, divisions, war and insecurity have further increased the number of refugees (over 23 million) and reinforced continual international migration. Comparatively small numbers of displaced people have been enabled to return home. These events have influenced human relations and cultural and religious life in a number of regions. Precious help was provided by international organizations and religious bodies. Churches and other faiths have gradually learned how to respond to common challenges in a pluralistic society. New impetus and impediments were intertwining with concern, care and hope for a better future.

Millions of Muslim immigrants live in former colonial countries (e.g. France and the UK) and in other regions as citizens, political refugees, temporary residents and workers. The attacks of 11 September 2001, associated with Islamic violence, inhibited the pluralistic spirit in modern society and also affected Christian–Muslim relations, which are easily influenced by reference to history and local and regional events. Destabilization of society, together with further security measures, can endanger lives, jobs, housing, education, transnational networks, etc.

The internal life of churches has often been dominated by ethical issues. There are important concerns over the breakdown of essential Christian values, mission and evangelism, religious freedom and ways towards unity. Differing interpretations of the gospel and the church's attitude to contemporary society still persist. Peace, justice and reconciliation often sparked discussions with unspectacular outcomes or recommitment to common Christian witness.

A large number of Western churches, evangelicals, new religionists and other faiths adherents continued to focus missionary attention on former socialist countries. The local churches, however, had expected to receive missionary know-how and financial resources in a spirit of ecumenical fellowship. Polemical discussion about religions in central and Eastern Europe during the communist era and after continued to trouble internal church life and interchurch relations. Newly verified statistical data provide the basis for a reassessment of Christian life in the former European socialist countries. Here are some examples of nominal membership and practising adherents:

Christians (except those in Russia, Armenia, Georgia, GDR)
Orthodox: over 60 million baptised Christians
Reformed and Lutheran: about 4 million
Roman Catholic: 62,153,216
Eastern rite Catholic : 6,243,740

Christians and others in Russia (population over 146 million)
Orthodox: 16.3 percent
Protestants: 0.9 percent
Muslims: 10 percent
Jewish: 0.4 percent
Other (mostly non-religious): 72.4 percent

Ukraine (population over 50 million)
Orthodox: 30.8 percent
Protestants: 3.6 percent
Roman Catholic: 1.2 percent
Uniates: 7.0 percent

Romania (population over 22 million)
Orthodox: 86.8 percent
Roman Catholic: 5.1 percent
Uniates: 1.0 percent

The percentage of Christian attendance at mass or a religious cere-mony at least once a month was as follows: Poland: 83 percent; Slova-kia: 42 percent; Slovenia: 36 percent; Lithuania: 28 percent; Hungary: 24 percent; Czech Republic: 13 percent; Latvia: 12 percent.

Statistics and studies in recent years indicate signs of decreasing ecumenical commitment. There is some hesitancy regarding traditional global programmes, disappointment with classical dialogues, and con-fusion about the continuing multiplicity and divisions of Christian denominations. Churches and religious communities are called to new visions for life together in democratic and pluralistic societies. All this strengthens the hope for renewal of the ecumenical movement.

3
Aspects of Religious Life
in the Context of Globalization

JULIO de SANTA ANA

Over the past thirty years a series of situations predicted by analysts of world affairs has come to pass. Events and processes that started in the second half of the 1970s surprised many people tracking developments in various aspects of the world. In the wake of the upheavals and disturbances caused by the student uprisings in the late 1960s, a marked increase was noted in the growth rate of trade and financial operations, greatly helped by the development of new information technologies and by decisions taken in the centres of power that opened the way for market deregulation, especially in financial markets. Economic liberalism had gained a new lease of life. The new conditions helped to create a growing divide between financial transactions on the one hand, and the trade in goods and services on the other. These changes came as a surprise to many, as they began to take note of the very rapid progress of financial and business integration.

Another important factor was the high rate of population growth in almost every continent with the exception of Western Europe, which forced ever-growing numbers of people from the poorest countries to migrate to places where it might be easier to earn a living. Around the turn of the 20th century, population movements were mainly from Europe to different parts of the American hemisphere, whereas in the past thirty years or so waves of migration have increased from the South to Western Europe and North America. These movements are happening all over the world as millions of people try to escape from poverty or oppression, or simply leave their places of origin in search of a better future. Analyzing the demographic evolution in the late 1980s, Paul Kennedy noted in 1993 that "the world economy is becoming increasingly integrated as the production of wealth increases, but the creation and use of this wealth is very disparate".[1] It is a well-known fact that an increase in trade and financial transactions is based on strong economic growth. This in turn benefits people living in the highly industrialized countries more than those in the so-called developing countries.

The process observed by Kennedy and other students of the international scene became more obvious from the beginning of the 1990s onwards. The term "globalization" came into fashion to describe the complex world situation in which these and other processes affecting the social, political, cultural and religious life of the world's peoples were taking place. Globalization has become an important aspect of our times. As we try to fathom it, analyze its complexity and take appropriate action, we realize that this "novelty" has its roots in the last four or five centuries of human history. Of course, there were great powers and empires in the past that tried to impose their political might and economic interests on the peoples they subjugated. Yet none of these processes of domination became worldwide. It was not until the political and commercial expansion of the West towards the end of the 16th century that there began the economic system that would eventually stretch around the globe.

There are various reasons for this. One was the emergence and development of modern Western culture, which pursued its instrumentalist outlook to its logical conclusions, conquering not only countries and cultures, but also nature and the environment. Religious institutions were involved in this project of conquest and helped shape it. It was given practical support and theological legitimacy by the Christian missionaries who accompanied the Spanish conquistadores and colonists, ambitious Dutch traders, and people seeking to free themselves from religious persecution by setting sail for North America to found "free" colonies. Sadly, their leaders did no better than other conquerors and imposed their yoke on the native peoples of the east coast of what is now the USA. This Western domination also thrived on the slave trade. These facts highlight a paradox that has been implicit in modern Western culture from the start: its ambivalence. On the one hand, it aims to create conditions that will enable human beings (or at least some human beings) to live in greater freedom, while on the other its instrumental approach causes it to reduce human beings and the natural environment to the status of objects.

Today's globalization is clearly modern in character. It takes place in very diverse contexts, with different processes of modernization. Its history can be traced to the period when Western Europe underwent the cultural revolution that took it from the Middle Ages into the modern world. This transition was closely bound up with the influence of the new bourgeoisie that subsequently emerged in Europe, and went on to extend its power and influence to the rest of the world, imposing a cap-

italist economic system which has governed the international production, circulation and distribution of goods since the early 17th century.

Process and project

Globalization is the subject of passionate ideological, political and
economic debate. There are those who support and welcome it as the
culmination of history, while others are strongly critical and condemn
it for creating unacceptable and ever-growing social differences in
every part of the world. This poses important challenges for the ecumenical movement. One such challenge is voiced by many Christian
churches and congregations and other religious families, for the most
part in the less industrialized, developing countries. These religious
communities and institutions warn in tones of moral outrage that globalization is heightening differences, injustices and imbalances, and
increasing social tensions both in international relations and within
individual countries. The World Economic Forum that meets in Davos,
Switzerland, in January every year is an occasion for the partisans of
globalization to celebrate their successes. At the World Social Forum,
on the other hand, participants call for resistance to the ideologies and
practices that guide the activities of those who make profits and acquire
economic, social, political and cultural advantages through globalization.

Critics of globalization are not entirely unanimous among themselves. Some reject it totally, while others say we need to look for ways
to develop a different kind of globalization (e.g. by globalizing solidarity). However, everyone in the amalgam of critical groups attending
the World Social Forum is agreed that "a different world is possible".

What makes the people in Davos sing the praises of globalization is
the fantastic growth of international trade and financial transactions
over the past thirty years. What then makes the participants at the Porto
Alegre meetings reject globalization? First, prevailing trends during
these years of market integration have made it almost impossible for the
poor to find ways of improving their living conditions and overcoming
unacceptable social exclusion. Second, their rejection is prompted by
the tendency of those ideologues who defend globalization to state cat-
egorically that it is the only viable way forward for humanity. If this is
so, it seems that globalization does not lead to the development of
"open societies" – indeed, quite the opposite.

Those in favour of globalization are well aware that the economic
growth of the past quarter of a century is due to the fact that the governments of a majority of countries have agreed to apply policies that
give priority to the laws of the market. In the view of those in the cen-

tres of power where decisions affecting people's lives are taken, this is what has allowed the expansion of trade and commerce and financial transactions, and they want it to continue. They maintain that this approach creates more favourable conditions for generating wealth than when the state exercises greater control over economic life. Arguing against this apology for market reasoning and the wish to see commercial transactions continue their unlimited expansion, opponents of the present course of globalization point out that, starting in late 1994, a succession of serious financial crises occurred that inevitably required state intervention to enable markets (most notably financial markets) to regain a measure of stability (Mexico 1994; Russia 1995 and 1998; southeast Asia 1996; east Asia and Brazil 1997; Argentina 2000, etc.).

The supporters of globalization adhere to an economic ideology that prescribes economic deregulation as an essential condition to give those operating in the market greater room for manoeuvre. This is what is known as economic neo-liberalism. Its origins can be traced to the classical economic liberalism propounded by Adam Smith, David Ricardo and John Stuart Mill in the 18th and 19th centuries. It was taken up again by economists in the 20th century (e.g. von Hayek, von Misses, Friedman), who modernized and redefined it. When the United States decided in 1971 to abandon the fixed exchange rate system that had been in operation since the end of the second world war, this deregulation had an unexpected effect: it gave a huge impetus to growth, boosting the rate of wealth creation and, above all, making it easier for private capital to assert its interests. The government of Margaret Thatcher in the United Kingdom opted to pursue this neo-liberal line of "more market, less state". It is important to note that this affirmation of the supremacy of the market over the state assumes the continued unrestricted expansion of the mercantile world as an essential condition.

This situation owes much to the development of new information technologies, which have made it possible for agents operating in markets (particularly financial and stock markets) to act very rapidly. Little by little, the financial market gained in importance and tacitly imposed itself as the paradigm for the market integration that characterizes globalization. In globalization there are thus very close links between financial capital interests and the impact of new technologies. The integration of the global financial market could not have taken place without this technological base, which allows a money flow of more than US$1,500,000,000 every day. Modern biology tells us that information is essential for life to evolve and increase its viability. The new information technologies help to build networks that make it possible to share knowledge and take decisions at a speed that was unimaginable only a short time ago.

However, it is clear that not all the world's population can enjoy the use of these technical innovations. Although a certain percentage of people on earth can join in what Manuel Castells has called the network society, [2] a much greater number of individuals and groups are not yet part of any such network. Paradoxically, although some of these networks are purely concerned with individual interests, others enable people and institutions to combine their efforts to achieve objectives with a genuinely global or (in Kantian terms) universal dimension. In other words, there is a contrast and a tension between those who use information technologies to set themselves apart and to impose their own interests and exclude others, and those who use the same means to try to promote causes which aim to bring about a world of greater justice for all, giving priority to the least advantaged. To those trying to promote social progress and defend the cultural identity and rights of the people who have been left by the wayside in the advance of globalization, the ones who assert their own interests and exclude others are viewed as a threat.

The history of globalization goes back a long way, to the long journey over several centuries that led to the building of a world economy based on the interests of the Western European merchant classes. Originally, this system was the product of modern Western culture. It has spread to all the corners of the world by means of a process which gave pride of place to capitalism. Today, bourgeois interests are no longer exclusively Western. The process which has enabled the middle classes successfully to extend their vision of the world, based on private appropriation of wealth and goods, has encompassed the whole world. It is a process that will help us understand the development of capitalism as the global economic system.

In 1995 one of the seminars on social progress organized to follow up decisions taken at the UN Development Summit (Copenhagen, March 1995) drew a distinction between globalization as a phase in the process of building and propagating modernization and capitalism, and globalization as a project guiding the activities of groups that hold economic, social, political and cultural power within the capitalist system. [3]

The Bossey Ecumenical Institute and the Visser 't Hooft Endowment Fund organized a consultation as one of a series of events commemorating the first general secretary of the World Council of Churches. The theme of the seminar, held in June 1997, was "Sustainability and Globalization". [4] The final report of this consultation notes that globalization has three main elements. First of all, from an economic point of view, it reflects the process of market integration that has been going on for the past three centuries. From about the middle of the 19th century, economists were already observing that the market had assumed a global dimension. Local markets were being subordinated and integrated into the dynamic of international trade. From the second half of the 19th century, this led to the emergence and gradual expansion of transnational companies which, both industrially and financially, went on to become the main actors in the world economy. For some analysts, the transition from the phase of transnationalization of large companies to that of globalization marked a step forward in the evolution of capitalism. The rapid integration of markets was driven by financial capital and it should come as no surprise that it follows the model of the financial market, which has become a solid reality over the past two decades. This development has allowed financial capital to assume an increasingly influential role in contemporary economic life.

However, it is important to note that there is one market which, so far at least, is not integrated with the others, nor is it like the others. It is the labour market, which is highly disparate at the global level. The value of labour is very unequal in the world today. There are enormous differences between workers performing relatively similar tasks depending on where they are doing their work. This encourages investment fund managers to place the capital at their disposal in countries where labour is cheapest. Not only does this practice endorse unjust situations, it also helps to accentuate the diversity that exists in this market, which continues to be fragmented.

Second, the process of combining different markets and reducing their diversity has been accelerated by the development of new information technologies. Some argue that this technological evolution took place before the integration of markets and actually provided the basis for it. Others maintain that it was the inherent dynamic of capitalism itself that set the direction and gave the impetus, encouragement and support to the research and technological application that led to the development and spread of the new information tools. For us, the most interesting thing to note in this connection is that the rapid integration of trade and commerce over the past few decades cannot be separated from this scientific and technological evolution and its crucial influence on the development of our societies.

Third, these financial, economic, scientific and technological achievements have generally been accompanied by two strong assertions. One of these is that this is the only path open to the world's peoples if they are to create the conditions for a better future. Margaret Thatcher, while prime minister of the UK, put it very clearly: "There is no other alternative." According to this point of view, the peoples of the oikoumene are bound to follow the path taken by the capitalist process at a global level. Globalization is the global project that the capitalist modernization process is going through today. The other assertion follows from the first: it insists that cultural diversity has to adjust to the demands of this dominant culture, which is presented as the only viable one in our day and age. The French call this *la pensée unique* (the single frame of thought). Many of the world's poor and excluded people feel that they have to conform to the cultural uniformity sought by those who hold the reins of financial, economic, scientific and technological power. Yet there are also many others who resist the direction set by the dominant culture that gives top priority to the market and its reasoning, and pursues its expansion at all costs.

These positions have strong ideological support. Neo-liberal economic ideology has supplied all the necessary arguments and instruments to drive globalization forward. Heated ideological debates take place between those who support neo-liberalism and those who believe that its positions do nothing to help solve the world's principal economic problems (distribution of wealth to reduce poverty; social security; basic needs such as health care, education and a decent living; guaranteeing the reproduction of life on a sustainable basis). The religions do not escape these tensions. Members of all the religions are implicated in the process, and accept or oppose the trends built into the dominant project that sets the direction of globalization. Opinions are divided. It is quite understandable that there are many voices, both within the different religious families and outside them, calling on the religions to assume their share of responsibility with regard to globalization. However, there is no consensus among the faithful about how to take responsible action.

The report of the Independent Commission of the International Labour Organization (ILO) emerged from discussions among some twenty people from different parts of the world. They examined the social dimension of globalization. The report is entitled *A Fair Globalization: Creating Opportunities for All*,[5] a title which in itself shows that the group did not believe that globalization contributes to the creation of justice, since it accentuates social differences. Most of the members of this international group believed globalization is an irreversible phase of the global economic process. Consequently, globalization needs to be guided in a different direction. The report notes that globalization has the potential to become a force for freedom and well-being, as well as helping to consolidate democracy and community development. However, the enforcement of the demand for a general adjustment to the needs of globalization generates conflicts, which unfortunately lead in many cases to the use of violence, whether by those trying to force through the integration of markets and impose the *pensée unique*, or by those resisting such domination. This point in particular clearly shows up the political dimension inherent in the project of globalization: it would seem that a "global world" would require the existence of a "global power" to administer it. The reaction of many peoples to this imperialist line is to struggle and resist. Members of the different religious families are inevitably involved in these conflicts, which in turn influences the positions taken by religious groups, and their beliefs, practices and doctrines.

Some important aspects of modernization and globalization

Scholars studying the cultural history of the world's peoples say that the Western bourgeoisie supported a number of cultural trends which led eventually to the process of modernization: the desacralization of reason, with the consequent development of Western science; the application of the new scientific knowledge to the invention of new technologies; the imperial dominance of certain Western powers which imposed their rule on the rest of the world, this being necessary if the economic interests of the bourgeoisie were to prosper worldwide. Little by little, and by different paths, the system that governs the world economy today took shape. It is the only system that has ever achieved a worldwide, global dimension. Like any system, it is a hierarchical regime which has gradually evolved its own laws, norms and conventions and has also created its own institutions to manage global economic activity, safeguarding the advantages enjoyed by the centres of power, imposing conditions and demanding adjustments from those who have no share in these positions of power. [6]

In keeping with the avowed intentions of those who supported and encouraged processes of modernization in Western countries, the culture they expressed was one that also inspired democratic regimes and the defence of human rights. A series of revolutions in a number of countries in Western Europe triggered by the treaty of Westphalia (1648) provided the opportunity for the bourgeoisie to acquire political power. Subsequently, with the industrial revolution, the proletariat – a social class which had its origins in the economic activities led by the bourgeoisie – embarked on its own struggle for the recognition of its rights. The revolutions in Britain in the 17th century, and in the USA and France in the late 18th century, gave impetus to a political process which also achieved a worldwide dimension. This period of history from the late 17th to the mid-19th century has been described by Eric Hobsbawm as the age of revolutions.[7]

It is important to remember that this political process was taking place concomitantly with the intellectual movement known in the West as the Enlightenment, *die Aufklärung*, which Kant described as being the stage when human beings were finally able to affirm their autonomy and assume their responsibility as adult beings, following the paths of reason and deploying practical wisdom based on rational principles.[8] The vision of history produced by the Age of Enlightenment is optimistic: it affirms the supremacy of reason as the ideal instrument for solving the problems facing humanity. Originating and taking shape in the West, it went on to assert the superiority of Western science over the beliefs and traditions of other peoples and to proclaim the constant progress of human history. In emphasizing these tendencies, modern culture confirmed its instrumental bias, which drew strong criticism from Nietzsche at the end of the 19th century and from members of the Frankfurt School (Theodor Adorno, Max Horkheimer) in the last century.[9] These criticisms stress the positivist trend prevailing in the sciences, the fragmentation of knowledge, the utilitarian treatment of human life and its natural environment, and the illusion of constant human progress that so fascinated the thinkers who lauded the virtues of the Enlightenment. The remarks of Adorno and Horkheimer concerning the ambiguous nature of modernization processes highlighted the fact that the very intellectuals who were proclaiming the necessity of democracy as a political system had no scruples (when it suited them) about using force to prevent people from freely expressing opinions that differed from those that the holders of power wished to see enforced. This brings to light a paradox inherent in these processes of modernization: human rights have on many occasions been promulgated and violated at one and the same time.

As for religious life, the process of modernization has led to radical secularization in the majority of Western European societies. In recent decades this has been accompanied by a strong tendency to assign religious beliefs and practices to the private sphere, while traditional religious institutions have steadily lost much of the social legitimacy and authority they enjoyed until about the middle of the 20th century. Nevertheless, traditional religion still has its intransigent defenders, like those who in the USA adhere to what is known as "the old-time religion" and who use modern means to combat modernization (Protestant fundamentalism is one of the clearest instances of this).

Various case studies show that this process is not advancing in the same way in other parts of the world, at least up until now. On the basis of various studies, S.N. Eisenstadt has noted that in different places the process of modernization is occurring in ways that do not exactly reproduce what has happened in the West: in Japan, Mexico, Brazil and many other places in the world, for example. Yet, for all this diversity, the relation between globalization and modernity is undeniable.

For Eisenstadt, however, the most important thing is not this paradox inherent in the processes of modernization. In his view (which I share), we have to accept that there is no one single, universally valid path for premodern societies to follow in their transition to modernity. Thus the secularization in Western Europe is not necessarily a phenomenon that all modernizing societies have to undergo. It might even be said that, in the evolution of peoples that accept the transition to modernity, traditional religious beliefs may play a role that is both positive and negative – as one might expect, given the inherent ambiguity of religious beliefs and practices. In Brazil, for example, traditional popular Catholicism, with its amalgam of different ethnic and cultural elements, has proved to be both a help and a hindrance in Brazilian society's transition to modernity.

Most analysts of the process of globalization highlight the relation between religion and globalization. We shall now examine three aspects of this relation that seem to me to be of particular importance.

Population growth and population movements

Demographic development is one factor that has a clear impact on processes of social change. It has repercussions on the transformations taking place in societies around the world and on other aspects of the present situation (e.g. deterioration of the environment, technological innovation, the volume and quality of international trade, etc). Demographic experts have calculated that the earth had some 6 billion inhabitants at the start of this century and are forecasting a steeply rising growth rate that will bring the figure to almost 9 billion by the year 2050. They also predict that by the start of the 22nd century, following a trend towards stability that may intervene in the second half of this century, there will be more than 10 billion people on earth.[10]

As with all such predictions, it has to be remembered that population growth is very unequal in different regions of the world. Africa is the continent with the fastest growing population, despite the devastating effects of the HIV/AIDS pandemic, which is obviously having a negative effect on population numbers. Nonetheless, Africa's demographic development is still very strong: in 1950 its inhabitants represented only half of those living in Europe, but the figures had levelled out by 1985 and it is estimated that within twenty years Africans will outnumber Europeans by three to one. The Middle East is another region where sustained population growth is taking place. In Latin America, which had an annual population growth index of 3 percent until the mid-1960s, this index has been declining in almost all countries. China is estimated to have a total of around 1.4 billion inhabitants, while something over 1 billion people live in India. In contrast with these trends, the natural growth rate in Europe struggles to reach 1 percent. In North America demographic development is very uneven: the growth rate is very high in Mexico and very low in Canada, while in the United States – which saw a steep increase in the birth rate following the second world war – the trend is now also downwards. It is migrants from other countries who are helping to keep the US figures rising, and the same phenomenon can be noted in some countries of the European Union.

These figures show that, unless there is a corresponding increase in wealth indicators and, above all, unless appropriate mechanisms are introduced to ensure the equitable distribution of wealth, the numbers of poor people in the world are inevitably going to increase. This situation has already led to massive migration, first of all from the countryside to the cities, and on an even larger scale, from the less developed countries to the more highly industrialized ones. These two trends mean that, on the one hand, the waves of migration from the countries of the South (the least developed countries, but also those which are developing but where the population still cannot make a decent living and satisfy its basic needs) towards the more modern countries is bound to continue, and indeed will probably increase. One such migration movement is in Europe, as people from Eastern Europe move to countries in the West of the continent. In the late 19th and early 20th centuries the great flow of migration went from Europe to the American hemisphere, and even from Asia to north America. In recent decades waves of migrants have fled from poverty in their places of origin and sought to travel by whatever means possible – even at the risk of their lives – to places where they can hope for a better life. Large groups of such people venture across oceans and deserts, mostly without any proper resources, to reach a world they have heard about, but of which they know nothing. Very few of them have papers that would allow them to live there legally and they are obliged to lead a clandestine existence simply in order to survive. Thus, after a long and difficult path, they become cheap labour that is easy to exploit. It is very difficult (indeed, almost impossible) in situations of this kind to avoid social clashes, as many citizens in the countries where these migrants arrive are hostile, which leads to a corresponding increase in xenophobia and racism. Of course, there are some people who are prepared to welcome migrants; nevertheless, confrontation with the citizens of the countries they come to in search of a better future is almost inevitable.

These population movements have caused a huge and rapid expansion of urban centres. The number of large cities where many millions of people are concentrated is increasing all the time: this is the case in places such as Mexico City, São Paulo, Lagos, Cairo, Calcutta, Bombay, Shanghai, Djakarta, Manila and Johannesburg, not to mention New York, London, Paris or Moscow, which have had very large populations ever since the 19th century. Historically speaking, these large urban agglomerations create a favourable climate for major social changes to take place, and sooner or later they begin to influence religious beliefs and practices.

As a result of these migrations, there has been a drastic reduction in the number of people living in the countryside and working in agriculture. The rural exodus is one of the principal factors in the proliferation of urban centres in the world today, but at present it does not help to satisfy the demand for work, as the industrial sector no longer offers the jobs it did only a short while ago. Increasing robotization and the impressive growth of the tertiary sector (white collar jobs) as a result of the immense power accruing to financial capital and the activities connected with it have led to an increase in the number of unemployed in the cities. Consequently, many of those who leave the countryside under the illusion that they will find better living conditions in the city discover that they cannot fulfil their ambitions. In order to survive, they turn to illegal, marginal activities, which often involve violence. The increase in urban violence is a worldwide phenomenon which reflects the anomie prevailing among many of those who have left rural areas for the cities, and among the migrants who have come from the developing to the industrialized countries. This is a global phenomenon.

The use of violence is often linked to the resentment generated among immigrants by the antagonism they encounter in the receiving country. It is most often seen among members of the second generation in migrant families. The children of the people who migrated often have difficulty in finding their way in life, whether in the formal education system or in the traditional forms of vocational training. Manifestations of racism and a lack of consideration and respect for their beliefs and their traditional culture cause bitterness, which sometimes finds an outlet in violence. Situations like this help to explain why a significant number of Muslim youths have been pressed into joining militant movements engaging in violent action, which they justify with radical interpretations of the religious books of Islam. In varying degrees, something similar also occurs among members of other religions.

The communities belonging to different religious confessions are directly involved in these processes. On arriving at the place where they wish to settle, the people who migrate try to reproduce, at least in part, some of the spaces that will help them to cope with the situation of anomie and social and cultural maladjustment which often causes anxiety and depression. One way of doing this is to try to recreate in their new home religious communities like those in the places they come from, so that they can practise their beliefs, speak their own language and rediscover the familiar environment they were forced to leave. This being so, the proliferation of non-Christian religious communities is hardly surprising, nor is the growing number of temples, mosques and Islamic centres found, for example, in Europe. The development of the religious beliefs of the peoples of the South, the Middle East and the East in Western countries is linked to the waves of migration that include people who belong to the Muslim and Buddhist faiths, as well as other religious groupings. What is more, in Western European countries and in the United States, the established churches are setting up services to help and support immigrants, which very often include pastoral care for the new arrivals. Some foreign congregations show tremendous vitality, in stark contrast to the general apathy of the parish services in the traditional churches. More important still is the establishment of communities of other faiths, with their corresponding institutions. This is happening, for example, in Birmingham in the UK, where Muslim communities now outnumber Christian congregations, displaying a vitality lacking in the latter, which are strongly affected by the secularization that has accompanied the process of modernization in the West.

All these factors have led to the emergence of multicultural, multifaith societies – one of the most important phenomena influencing religious beliefs and practices in the context of globalization. The cultural homogeneity which reflected the predominant cultural traditions of each people is gradually crumbling and, in some places, is doing so very rapidly. To give some examples, there are many citizens of the Philippines who are mostly Roman Catholic working in the Emirates of the Persian Gulf, which are predominantly Islamic. Large numbers of Latin Americans, most of them Mestizo, are migrating to the USA and the countries of Europe. Many Kurds are settling in Central Europe; Chinese, Koreans and Japanese are moving to the United States, Canada and Western Europe; thousands of men and women from north Africa are travelling to the countries of southern Europe and summoning their families from their countries of origin to join them. As a result of these population movements all these societies are gradually being transformed. The changes do not only affect the people who migrate, they also affect the customs and habits of the societies where they are trying to establish themselves.

Of course, population movements are not the only factor promoting social mutations. These flows of migration influence both the culture of those involved in the exodus and the culture of the countries where they end up. These processes unleash a series of changes that show the strength of the processes of modernization. They contribute, for example, to changing the forms of interaction in particular places where communities of different traditions live together, when the more modern and democratic forms of community and institutional organization of some groups call in question and challenge others which are less adapted to the demands of modern life. At the same time, the resolution of those who insist on maintaining more traditional positions represents a threat to those who are aware that the strength of their beliefs has been somehow eroded in the process of modernization, and more specifically in its present phase of globalization. These questions not only have repercussions on the formulation of religious thought and the celebration of the rites of the different faiths, they also raise questions about the organization of the institutions that administer religious life. Suffice it to say that one of the issues that is disturbing the different families of believers today is the complex question of gender relations. The fact that traditional beliefs are being exposed to others that are more evolved because of the influence of modern factors is generating tensions and mutations that cannot yet be predicted. On the other hand, the vitality of certain traditions enables them to hold in check attitudes that claim to be modern and innovative. (The chapters that follow will attempt to clarify some of these topics.)

Repercussions of intercultural communication

Societies that give priority to traditions, customs and habits whose origins are often lost in the mists of time, and values that express ancient beliefs handed down over the centuries, try to preserve a life wisdom that is called into question by factors which, sometimes gradually and sometimes abruptly, introduce outside elements that clash with traditional ways of life. This can occur when some cataclysm challenges the men and women of the traditional world to re-examine the usual paths of their existence. When this happens, it is a historical exception. Generally, the influence of such agents of change can be seen when time-hallowed ways of life are confronted by others that cause people to begin to doubt the beliefs and values expressed in their life-style.

This confrontation may be sudden and violent, as in Mexico, with the arrival of the Spanish conquistadores. Indigenous ethnic groups were taken by surprise by a group of adventurers clad in metal breast-plates, wielding lethal weapons of war that spat fire, killing and ready for anything as they set about conquering the Aztecs, Toltecas, Zapote-cas and other native peoples. This clash of cultures made the original Mexican peoples aware of the technological superiority of the Spanish. Some of them submitted voluntarily, finding justification for the new situation in their traditional religious myths and symbols. Others resisted this superior power with admirable courage, though not without a degree of resignation. Thanks to their technological dominance, the invaders were able not only to impose their rule on the vanquished peoples, but also a new conception of life, a rationality that differed from ways of thinking that had until then governed the life of these peoples who, for many centuries, had lived in a culture that was accustomed to the use of violence and sacrifice. When the established societies in the region realized the supremacy of the implements used by the Spanish and recognized their own inability to withstand such violence and efficiency, they accepted that they had to make sacrifice to the conquerors. The sad end of the Aztec chief Moctezuma is symbolic in many ways. Among other things it denotes the total submission of a once-powerful state that had to bow to others unexpectedly using greater force and violence.

Technological development is an extremely important element in intercultural relations. Even when cultures meet in a spirit of peace, a certain degree of violence is still involved when the technological development of one of the parties calls the other in question. This type of confrontation produces cultural asymmetry that reflects the greater power of one in comparison with the other. Unconsciously, more often than not, those whose fate it is to give way to others who display greater strength and ability in handling existence will then conceive a desire to imitate them. Those who have been subordinated aspire to be like those who hold the power of command; the oppressed want to be like the oppressors.[11] In order to do that, they need to acquire the technological capacity of their conquerors.

Nevertheless, in most cases, there are pockets of resistance that show that the culture of the subjected is still alive. Very often, this last resistance of the dominated culture lives on in the minds of those who have had to submit to others (and can often be translated as plain bad faith) and can only be expressed symbolically. An example of this is what happened among the millions of Africans who were forced to submit to the power of the coalition engaged in the slave trade. Displaced and uprooted, they recast some of the symbols of their ancestral culture and religion so that, although they might seem to have adapted to the culture of their oppressors, they still preserved their African cultural identities, albeit in a concealed way. Voodoo in Haiti, Candomblé in northeast Brazil, with the various transformations it has undergone since the end of the 19th century, both express a degree of submission and symbolic resistance at one and the same time. This took more concrete form in the Haitian revolution at the end of the 18th century and the beginning of the 19th, and in the organization of *quilombos* or independent republics of African Brazilians, where slaves trying to escape from the despotism of their Portuguese overlords could find refuge and freedom.

For those who have been obliged to submit to a dominant power, religious practices (sometimes involving the recasting of traditional myths) provide an ideal terrain for subtly implanting their resistance. Somehow, the preservation and refocused use of traditional symbols in religious practices helps many people to hold on to their culture and traditions. This is what happened in Eastern Europe under communist rule, when the spirit of resistance showed itself above all in liturgical celebrations and the (often secret) continuation of religious observance in family life. Whether at the subjective level or the more rational level of dogmatic formulation, religious life, with its beliefs and practices, is a sphere of existence that helps many people hold on to the sense of belonging to a tradition which is still very much alive and valid, even though it has been downtrodden. This is one of the reasons why less developed peoples – and also the less privileged sections of populations in industrialized societies – attach so much importance to keeping their traditions alive.

There is a very strong and indissoluble link between cultural identity and religion. This is obvious when we see local identities standing firm before the advance of the *pensée unique* that accompanies neoliberal globalization, with its claim to domination. In doing so, they resist the totalitarianism of market reasoning, which sees itself as universal and sets out to impose a uniform way of thinking and uniform patterns of social behaviour. However, the distinction between globalization and traditional identities is not clear-cut. The agents of globalization often draw on elements of traditional cultures to help them achieve their objectives more effectively. In this way, cross-fertilization takes place between local cultures and the modernity that seeks to be global or universal. At the same time, case studies show that social groups that strive to survive and hold on to their traditions do adapt these in various ways to the logic of globalization, which helps to ensure that their resistance to the dominant culture does not disappear.

In Mexico, for example, there is evidence for the above in the image of Our Lady of Guadalupe, revered by Christians and imposed on the indigenous peoples of the region, which actually bears the face of the Aztec goddess Tonantzin. And the ruins of the great temples in the area of Mexico City have some surprising features: the chapels for the celebration of the eucharist are not inside these vast edifices, but outside, and they have no roof. This is because the Catholic priests responsible for evangelizing and converting the indigenous people understood that, for them, God could not be contained or worshipped in a closed space. God is infinite, and a relationship with the divinity is only possible under the open sky. The vast spaces inside these buildings were used to gather thousands of local people together for the teaching of the catechesis. It is easy to understand that symbols, rites, myths, values and even life-styles came to permeate one another. This hybridization is continuing right up to the present time, as various anthropological investigation have found. [12]

Consequently, in a world marked by globalization, there can be no question of claiming or asserting that cultures have remained absolutely pure and immaculate, uncontaminated by outside factors. The phenomenon of cultural hybridization shows that the processes of modernization do not result in the disappearance of traditional cultures. There is constant cross-fertilization between the traditional and the modern as cultures come into contact and influence one another. This inevitably has an impact on religious life, beliefs and practices. We only need look at what happens when the pope visits countries that are not traditionally Christian. The presence of the supreme authority of an institution which is visibly concerned to maintain its traditions, some of which are clearly premodern, draws huge crowds who are organized and prepared by specialists using the most modern information techniques, for the purpose of leaving the biggest possible impression on the minds and collective memory of the peoples visited. In the specific case of these papal visits, one of the results is a better understanding of the dimensions of the pontifical ministry and its institutional charisma.

Development of multifaith societies

Processes of cultural hybridization are only one of the manifestations of the interaction taking place between cultures and religions.

Some people, like Samuel Huntington, have tried to construct a new geopolitical world map based on the "clash of civilizations".[13] As they see it, relations between cultures lead to tensions which can erupt into violent conflicts, as happened in Kosovo between the population of Albanian origin, the great majority of whom are Muslim, and the Serbs, who are traditionally Orthodox Christians. The war which took place in this region of the Balkans at the end of the 1990s is often quoted as an example by those who adopt Huntington's line, aiming to establish a new conception of world order following the end of the cold war and the collapse of the communist regimes in Eastern Europe. Another example is the situation in Northern Ireland, where Protestant Unionists and Catholic republicans have been engaged in a violent confrontation for many years. Among those who insist that the "war on terrorism" must necessarily have a global dimension, there are some political scientists who use Huntington's propositions to support their view that confrontation between the modern West and Islam is inevitable. There are others, however, who see the respectful development of intercultural relations as full of promise for a new style of international coexistence, geared to creating peace. They point to the way in which believers of different religious families now live together in social contexts which, until about thirty or forty years ago, were culturally and religiously homogeneous. However, for a variety of reasons, these have gradually been transformed into societies where individuals belonging to different traditions and different religions can all participate.

Very often, of course, relations between communities with differing beliefs and customs can be extremely tense. In most cases, people who come from elsewhere are viewed with suspicion, even repulsion, by local inhabitants. In such situations xenophobia is often rife; foreigners are treated with hostility, and the resentment and contempt they encounter calls forth an intransigence on their part that reflects the habits of their traditional societies, where social life is strictly regulated according to long-established norms. But we also find other situations where people who have been hostile gradually come to realize that they are in fact citizens of a country governed by the rule of law, where all the inhabitants, and not only those belonging by birth to the national community, have formal powers, rights, prerogatives and freedoms, as well as duties and obligations. Foreigners who have managed to find the means of a decent livelihood have to be respected under the terms of the law, which in many countries penalizes racist attitudes and discrimination. This means that, to a greater or lesser degree, tolerance is gradually coming to be recognized as essential. To put it another way, the "Other" has to be recognized and respected. All the world's religions – even those with strong exclusive and dogmatic tendencies – preach the need for tolerance and the importance of reconciliation. If intolerance prevails it can generate bitterness and resentment. The arrogance typically displayed by families and groups that have lived in the same place from generation to generation can be painful and humiliating for those who arrive as migrants, especially if they are rejected or treated aggressively. Such situations do not contribute to peaceful coexistence, but are more likely to unleash a spiral of violence.

Attitudes to foreigners cover a vast range, from outright rejection to welcoming respect. This is not the place to examine the countless cases that exist. What is important for us to note is that, first, the appearance, development and proliferation of multicultural, multifaith societies in which minorities are tolerated, recognized and respected is a relatively recent process in modern societies. Historically, however, there have been situations where communities with different beliefs and different specific cultural features were able to coexist satisfactorily. One example was in Andalusia, where Jews, Christians and Muslims lived together for centuries, respecting and even esteeming one another, until the faithful of the synagogues and the mosques were expelled from Spain following an arbitrary decree by the Catholic kings in 1492.

As we have seen, some people see these new attitudes and arrangements as being full of promise. They believe that this coexistence, and some cases of harmonious intercultural relations, point to an effort to build societies that affirm peace, justice and social rights, both at the level of values and convictions and in systems of jurisprudence that testify to more inclusive social pacts, reflecting the awareness that "Others" too have a place that has traditionally been denied them in societies fiercely opposed to processes of modernization.

All the same, in a context dominated by the neo-liberal project of globalization, we have witnessed the proliferation of situations characterized by rigidity and rampant intolerance and animosity within communities of different cultures. This is even to be found in positions (also involving expressions of faith and religious practice) which condemn the growing pluralism as a danger to societies governed on the understanding that their security depends above all on their ideological cohesion. In many cases, this element forms part of a central nucleus in the conception a society has of itself, its beliefs and its integrity. The frequent use of religious symbols, ostentatiously or otherwise (e.g. the *chador* by Muslim women, the *kipa* by Jewish men, the cross by Christian men and women), can be interpreted in a variety of ways. It can be seen as affirming a particular identity or testifying to certain beliefs, or it can be perceived as an act of provocation towards those who are different. When the latter happens, the social fabric of a country can be torn apart, at least on the ideological level. (Incidentally, when state authorities lay down rules stating that such symbols may or may not be used, they create a situation that affects the exercise of religious freedom. When that happens, it is generally social minorities who are most affected. This has occurred not only in Islamic countries, but also in countries with a Christian majority.)

Both locally and internationally, the situations in which different cultures and religious families coexist in the context of globalization vary greatly. Against this historical background, one group of Christian theologians has argued for the need for a different approach to this new reality.[14] Besides emphasizing the need for interfaith dialogue, they have also begun to formulate a "theology of religions" (from a Christian point of view, obviously). All of them echo the call that Pedro Casaldáliga, the bishop of São Felix de Araguaia, in Matto Grosso, Brazil, has been tirelessly repeating for the past twenty years, urging that ecumenism should step beyond the boundaries of the Christian confessions and become much broader and more inclusive, opening itself up to all the beliefs and spiritual families of the peoples who inhabit our oikoumene.

Anxious to bar the way to these proposals, some people summon the spectre of syncretism. Would it not be more appropriate if they directed their criticism against the various forms of fundamentalism and extremism that are at work among the different religions in the world today?

Militants of the ecumenical movement: between Babel and Pentecost

Using biblical images, we may say that we are in a post-tower-of-Babel situation, or living within the perspective of what the first Christians experienced on the day of Pentecost. According to the story recounted in Genesis, God decided to thwart the wishes of the tower builders. They wanted to impose one language, one culture on all the peoples of the world. Therefore:

> The Lord came down to see the city and the tower which mortals had built. And the Lord said, "Look, they are one people, and they have all one language, and this is only the beginning of what they will do; nothing that they propose to do will be impossible for them. Come, let us go down, and confuse their language there, so that they will not understand one another's speech." So the Lord scattered them abroad from there over the face of all the earth. (Gen. 11:5–8)

Interpreting this text for our own times, we could say that God does not want cultural uniformity for the peoples of the earth. The diversity that exists among the nations is a rich treasure that should be cherished.

On the other hand, for Christians, one dimension among others in the historical perspective is Luke's rendering of what happened at Pentecost, when the disciples were all "filled with the Holy Spirit and began to speak in other languages, as the Spirit gave them the ability" (Acts 2:4). Everyone who was in Jerusalem for that feast day, many of them pilgrims who had come to the holy city from different parts of the diaspora to celebrate the Jewish harvest festival, was bewildered, because each one heard them speaking in the native language of each. Amazed and astonished, they asked, "Are not all these who are speaking Galileans? And how is it that we hear, each of us, in our own native language? Parthians, Medes, Elamites, and residents of Mesopotamia, Judaea and Cappadocia, Pontus and Asia, Phrygia and Pamphylia, Egypt and the parts of Libya belonging to Cyrene, and visitors from Rome, both Jews and proselytes, Cretans and Arabs – in our own languages we hear them speaking about God's deeds of power."

One dimension of God's mission is to go out to all the peoples of the oikoumene and tell them the message of God's wonderful deeds, each in his or her own language and culture, and in terms that speak to their own specific existence. This does not mean opposing globalization. Rather, it means bringing about a change of direction and rejecting the prevailing neo-liberal version of globalization, so that each and every one of us with our own distinctive characters can be part of it.

It is obvious that these Bible narratives pose for us the challenge of recognizing, respecting and loving the "Other". Participating in a globalization that involves everyone, respecting our cultures and beliefs, requires us to do whatever we can to steer the global process towards creating situations in which it is possible for people to live together in respect and freedom, and in which religious practices, including love of our neighbour, and especially those in greatest need, can be expressed in concrete form.

NOTES

[1]   Paul Kennedy, *Preparing for the Twenty-first Century*, New York, Vintage, 1993, p. 47.
[2]   Manuel Castells, *The Information Age: Economy, Society and Culture. Vol. 1: The Rise of the Network Society*, Oxford, Blackwell, 1996.
[3]   Jacques Baudet ed., *Building a World Community: Globalization and the Common Good*, Copenhagen, 2000. On p. 44 we read: "[Globalization] is a process in the

historical evolution of humanity, [and also] a political project steering the world economy in a particular direction. Calling the first a 'trend' is to state that the narrowing of physical distances between peoples and the growing interdependence of countries represents both an unstoppable course of history, moved essentially by the application of human reason to the development of science and technology, and a general direction of change that can be navigated by human decision. The project is 'global capitalism', or the application of the ideas and institutions of the market economy to the world as a whole... Globalization is not moved by an invisible and benevolent hand. It is shaped by powerful actors and influenced by a multitude of forces, not all operating in the economic realm."

4   See Julio de Santa Ana ed., *Sustainability and Globalization*, WCC Publications, 1998. The book presents the report of the consultation and its main presentations.

5   World Commission on the Social Dimension of Globalization, *A Fair Globalization: Creating Opportunities for All*, Geneva, ILO, 2004.

6   Fernand Braudel, *Civilisation matérielle, économie et capitalisme. XV–XVIII siecle*, 3 vols, Paris, Librairie Armand Colin, 1979.

7   Eric Hobsbawm, *The Age of Revolution 1789–1848*, Ontario, Penguin, 1962; *The Age of Capital 1848–1875*, London, Weidenfeld & Nicolson, 1975.

8   Immanuel Kant, *Was its die Aufklärung?*, 1784.

9   Max Horkheimer and Theodor W. Adorno, *Dialectic of Enlightenment*, New York, Seabury. See also N. Eisenstadt, *Les antinomies de la modernité. Les composantes jacobines de la modernité et du fondamentalisme*, Paris, L'Arche, 1997.

10   Data taken from *The Economist*, 20 Jan. 1990, p. 19.

11   On the desire to emulate, see René Girard, *La violence et le sacré*, Paris, Grasset, 1972; *Le bouc émissaire*, Paris, Grasset et Fasquelle, 1982.

12   See Néstor García Canclini, *Culturas en Globalización*, Caracas, Nueva Sociedad, 1996; "Hybrid cultures and communicative strategies", in *Media Development*, London, vol. 44, 1997, pp. 22–29; *Consumidores y Ciudadanos. Conflictos multiculturales de la globalización*, Mexico, Grijalbo, 1995.

13   Samuel P. Huntington, *The Clash of Civilizations and the Remaking of World Order*, New York, Simon & Schuster, 1996.

14   See, among others, Wesley Ariarajah, *The Bible and Peoples of Other Faiths*, WCC Publications, 1985; J.B. Cobb, *Christ in a Pluralistic Age*, Philadelphia, Westminster; Jacques Dupuis, *Towards a Christian Theology of Religious Pluralism*, Maryknoll NY, Orbis, 1997; J. Hick. *The Rainbow of Faiths: Critical Dialogues on Religious Pluralism*, London, SCM Press, 1995; P.F. Knitter, *Towards a Protestant Theology of Religions*, Marburg, Elwert, 1974. See also "Interreligious Dialogue: What? Why? How?", in L. Swidler et al. eds, *Death or Dialogue? From the Age of Monologue to the Age of Dialogue*, London, SCM Press, 1990, pp. 19–44; R. Panikkar, *Religión y Religiones*, Madrid, Gredos, 1965; Stanley Samartha, *One Christ – Many Religions: Towards a Revised Christology*, Maryknoll NY, Orbis, 1991.

4

Media Globalization and Its Challenge to the Ecumenical Movement

CEES HAMELINK

Globalization has many different manifestations. In a very general sense it encompasses processes of expansion, integration and interdependence in the domains of trade, finance and communication. These processes are driven by economic incentives, technological innovations, and regulatory preferences for privatization and commercialization. Among the institutions affected by globalization are the media. In recent years a global media market has matured in which the fifty largest companies received in 2001 over 400 billion euros in revenues. Compared to such revenues in 1997, this represents growth of more than 150 percent. [1]

Although the process of media globalization is complex and broad it can be reduced to three essential dimensions: conglomerates, commercial messages and ownership of content.

Conglomerates

Media globalization refers in the first place to the worldwide expansion of media production and distribution companies that trade in the emerging global media market. This expansion is facilitated by technological developments. However, it is largely supported by pressure on countries to open their domestic markets to foreign suppliers, with the concomitant neo-liberal claim that cultural products should not be exempt from trade rules.

Effective operations in the global market are possible only for large-scale, integrated companies: conglomerates that combine several sectors of the media industry, such as hardware, software and distribution networks. These conglomerates are presently involved in a process of global consolidation that results in a high degree of concentration. Media globalization is therefore primarily the global proliferation of a small number of media conglomerates.

Over recent years the trading of media products on the world market has grown exponentially. A key feature of the global media market is consolidation. Increasingly, control of the world communication market is consolidated in the hands of a few mega-conglomerates. The emerging mega-industries combine message production (ranging from digital libraries to TV entertainment), the manufacturing and operating of distribution systems (ranging from satellites to digital switches), and building the equipment for reception and processing of information (ranging from HDTV sets to telephones). Illustrative of this is the Japanese company Sony, which was already active in the equipment sector before it acquired access to the message component via Columbia Pictures and CBS.

This process is a continuation of earlier waves of media concentration, but is increasingly international in scope. Several of the key players have in recent years consolidated their market position through merger. The most sensational merger in 2000 was the first Television/Internet marriage: the combination of Time Warner with AOL. Internet service provider America On Line (with 1998-99 revenues of US$4.7 billion and 12,100 employees) purchased multimedia conglomerate Time Warner (1998-99 revenues of US$14.6 billion and 67,500 employees). This deal between the new and the old economy cost around US$183 billion. The merger brought content producers such as print media *(Time, People, Sports Illustrated, Money and Fortune)*, audiovisual media (Warner Brothers and Turner Classic Movies), broadcasters (CNN, HBO and TNT) and the music publisher Warner Music together with distributors like Time Warner Cable and internet service provider AOL. In January 2000 the *Financial Times* wrote that this merger was an important move towards a global society in which all media platforms will be integrated.

In early 2000 Warner Music (part of Time Warner) and British recording company EMI also announced a proposed merger. This deal would create the largest music publisher in the world, with revenues exceeding US$8 billion. The European Commission objected to the merger and the companies subsequently announced that they would not fully merge, but instead explore other forms of cooperation.

In several of its sub-sectors the media market demonstrates a strong degree of concentration. In 2001 the world market for entertainment was almost totally dominated by six firms (see p. 64).

On the world market for music in 2000, Seagram Universal Music (which bought Polygram from Philips in 1998 and has itself been acquired by the French conglomerate Vivendi) was the leader, with a share of 21 percent. Behind it were Sony Music (17 percent), EMI

Company	Revenues (billions of euros)
AOL/Time Warner (USA)	42,691
Walt Disney (USA)	28,200
Vivendi Universal (France)	28,115
Viacom (USA)	25,930
Bertelsmann (Germany)	14,811
News Corporation (Australia)	14,769

Source: *Fortune, Business Week,* company annual reports

(14 percent), Warner Music (12 percent) and multimedia firm Bertelsmann (11 percent).

Equally, the international news market demonstrates a strong trend towards consolidation. For printed news, the world market is largely controlled by the US agency Associated Press, the British Reuters, and Agence France Presse. (World visual news is largely an Anglo-Saxon duopoly with a marginal role for the French agency Agence France Presse.) Production and distribution of worldwide audiovisual news is largely the domain of the US companies APTV (the film branch of press agency Associated Press), CNN (part of AOL/Time Warner), NBC (owned by General Electric), ABC (owned by Walt Disney), CBS (owned by Viacom, the company that controls MTV) and the British firm Reuters TV (the film branch of press agency Reuters). [2]

A crucial feature of the companies that emerge from mergers and acquisitions is their integration of diverse commercial activities. As a result the largest actors on this world market are conglomerates. Conglomerates are made possible through the application of digital technologies that facilitate the convergence of formerly separate fields such as computer, telecom and audiovisual technologies. The technical convergence of all signals makes it both possible and attractive to operate in the three different domains of the market simultaneously: hardware, software and network distribution.

Examples of such conglomerates include the German firm Bertelsmann (which sells books, CDs, TV programmes and magazines) and the company owned by Italian media tycoon Sylvio Berlusconi (which trades in TV programmes, spaghetti, insurance and supermarkets). In June 2000 the French conglomerate Vivendi expanded its media investments (among others, pay-TV station Canal Plus, publisher Haves and 24.5 percent participation in Rupert Murdoch's B Sky B station) with the acquisition of the Canadian firm Seagram (owner of Universal Studios and Polygram).

An important issue in the operation of conglomerates is that of independence of information provision. Industrial concentration inevitably implies the establishment of power. The mega-media companies are centres of power that are at the same time linked into other circuits of power, such as financial institutions, the military establishment and the political elite. A problem arises when the mass media that provide news and commentary are part of an industrial conglomerate. The conglomerate may engage in activities that call for critical scrutiny by the media, but which those in control may prefer to conceal from the public gaze.

Ideally, media consumers should have access to a large variety of autonomous media managed by a diversity of individuals and groups. Consolidation may effectively diminish the number of (independent) channels that people have at their disposal to express or receive opinions. In consolidated markets it thus becomes easier for controlling interests to refuse to distribute certain opinions.

Commercial messages

The primary messages of the global media conglomerates are of a commercial nature; they are the key vehicles in creating a "billboard society" in which people worldwide are better informed about consumer goods and where to fun-shop than about the environmental consequences of the global rate of consumption. As a result, media globalization is to a large degree the worldwide proliferation of messages that propagate global consumerism

As the 1998 UNDP report claims, "Globalization – the integration of trade, investment and financial markets – has also integrated the consumer market."[3] The opening of markets for consumer goods, mass production, mass consumption and mass advertising has both economic and social dimensions. The latter imply that "people all over the world are becoming part of an integrated global consumer market – with the same products and advertisements". As a result they begin to share the same standards of the "good life". However, the increasing *visibility* of consumer goods is not the same as their *availability*. "While the global elite are consumers in an integrated market, many others are marginalized out of the global consumption network." On the global consumer market most people are merely gawking. As markets open worldwide and more advertising for consumer products arrives to promote the expansion of a global fun-shopping culture, there develops an explosive disparity between visibility and availability around the world. In the global shopping mall in 1998 the world spent some US$24 trillion. Over 80 percent of this was spent by 20 percent of the world's population. Propagating the standards of the good life worldwide happens against the backdrop of globalizing poverty. In 1989, as poverty increased around the world (e.g. in Eastern Europe it has risen sevenfold since 1989), the richest 20 percent of people had 86 percent of the global gross domestic product.

The ratio of the richest 20 percent to the poorest 20 percent in the world reduced from 1 in 30 in 1960 to 1 in 74 in 1997. As the 1999 UNDP reports warns, "Global inequalities in income and living standards have reached grotesque proportions."[4] The potentially explosive conflict between the rich and the poor is reinforced by today's global media.

More than anything else, media audiences get commercial messages. This is the heart of the global media market and it is expanding. Per capita advertising expenditures around the world are rising steeply: at an average of 7 percent per annum it is more than the GDP growth rates of many countries. The worldwide advertising market represents a US$300 billion business. And the general expectation is that spending for advertising will continue to rise. McCann-Erickson predicts an increase from US$335 billion in 1995 to US$2 trillion in 2020. Growth is projected especially for Asia (in particular, China) and Eastern Europe. Even the African continent reports that in 1995 the six largest advertising agencies sold over US$360 million of commercial messages.

Global advertisers and marketeers are in hot pursuit of new targets. Children especially are becoming top audiences for commercials. The average 7-year-old child in an affluent country sees over 20,000 commercials a year. At the age of 12, most children have complete consumer profiles in the databases of major marketeers.

The central significance of advertising is manifested in the number of deals that advertisers make with media companies, such as the recent cooperative arrangements between the Disney Studios (owner of ABC News) and McDonald's, or between the NBC TV network and IBM. The result is unprecedented influence of advertisers upon editorial policies. There is a good deal of empirical evidence to demonstrate this worrisome development.

An increasingly common format for advertising is also the blurring of the difference between selling and informing by means of "advertorials", "infomercials" or sponsored messages. The launching of new forms of advertising is important, since many markets are saturated and the overproduction characteristic of advanced capitalism needs to be sold. In an average year an American supermarket will offer over 15,000 new products on its shelves.

In 1998 the trend emerged to offer more advertising in the open air. Large advertisers began spending more of their budgets on billboards.

The American Outdoor Advertising Association estimated that in 1998 over US$2 billion were spent on open-air commercials. Using digital and holographic technologies, billboards are rapidly becoming more spectacular and their production less expensive and faster. Per 1000 people that can be reached with a commercial message, digital billboards require half the expense of advertising in newspapers. Thus today in many countries there is an increase in the numbers of billboards along motorways, but also in sports stadiums and in schools.

Among these new developments is the expansion of product placement in feature films and TV programmes. Whereas in films there was usually a brief exposure of products, now they can be seen throughout most of the movie. In this way cinema films help to advertise products and the advertiser promotes the film worldwide. The audience is not only entertained but also sold a product. Fashion designer Tommy Hilfiger's products represented 90 percent of the wardrobe of the new teen science-fiction horror production *The Faculty*. Hilfiger funded half of the US$30 million expense for the promotion of the film. The general expectation in the advertising industry is that product placement and entertainment will blur as part of the merger between advertising and the entertainment industry.

Advertising proclaims a single cultural standard for its audiences: consumption fulfils people's basic aspirations and fun-shopping is an essential cultural activity. It subjects all a region's cultural differences to the dominance of a consumption-oriented life-style. People's fundamental cultural identity is that of a consumer. Advertising teaches the values of materialism and the practices of consumerism.

The neo-liberal commercial agenda has a strong interest in the expansion of global advertising. Among other things this implies more commercial space in the media (mass media and internet), new target groups (especially children), more sponsorship (films, orchestras, exhibitions) and more places to advertise (the ubiquitous billboards).

Ownership of content

The core business of the media conglomerates is content; and several of the recent mergers are motivated by the desire to gain control over rights to contents such as are, for example, invested in film libraries or in collections of musical recordings. German media tycoon Leo Kirch made much of his enormous fortune through the acquisition of rights to content. Kirch bought from United Artists/Warner Brothers the rights to some hundred successful American TV programmes: he holds rights to over 50,000 hours of such TV series as Baywatch and owns copyrights to 16,000 film titles which he bought from Columbia Pictures, Paramount and Universal. He also acquired the Pay-TV rights to Disney films. British music company EMI owns the copyrights to over a million of the world's most popular songs.

Recent developments in digital technology that open up unprecedented possibilities for free and easy access to and utilization of knowledge have also rendered the professional production, reproduction and distribution of content vulnerable to large-scale piracy. It has made content owners very concerned about their property rights and interested in the creation of a globally enforceable legal regime for their protection.

Media globalization involves the worldwide protection of proprietary content through the imposition of a global system of intellectual property rights (IPRs) protection. The emerging global regime for the protection of IPRs administered by the World Trade Organization (WTO) has crucial effects on the accessibility, distribution and innovation of knowledge. The relations between this regime and the development of "knowledge societies" require analysis and debate.

The WTO plays an increasingly important role, since it oversees the execution of the legal provisions of the agreement on Trade-Related Intellectual Property Rights (TRIPS). This global agreement emerged in the GATT negotiations (as Annex 1C to the General Agreement on Tariffs and Trade in the Uruguay Round of Multilateral Trade Negotiations, 1993). TRIPS contains the most important current rules on the protection of IPRs. It is implemented within the WTO regulatory framework. In this agreement the economic dimension of IPR protection is reinforced. As Venturelli correctly summarizes, "The balance has tipped entirely toward favouring the economic incentive interests of third-party exploiters and away from both the public access interests of citizens and the constitutional and human rights of creative labour."[5] As IPRs have achieved a prominent place among the world's most important tradable commodities, the current trade-oriented IPR regime favours the corporate producers (publishers, broadcasting companies, music recording companies, advertising firms) against individual creators. The provisions of the TRIPS agreement protect the economic rights of investors better than the moral rights of creative individuals or the cultural interests of the public at large. There is growing evidence that the legal provisions of the 1993 TRIPS agreement hamper the independent development of knowledge in developing societies and facilitate the plunder of knowledge resources (e.g. bio-genetic materials) from those societies.

It is ironic that whereas international law has not codified a basic human right to knowledge, the right to the protection of (private) knowledge is enforced by a robust and expanding set of rules and remedies. The kind of neo-liberal global governance that is currently emerging is neither in the interests of the consumer, nor to the benefit of producers of artistic works. In order to disseminate their work, performing artists, writers and composers increasingly transfer their rights to the big conglomerates with which they sign contracts. Ultimately, these companies will determine how creative products will be processed, packaged and sold. One of the serious problems with the current trend in IPR protection is that the emerging regulatory framework stifles the independence and diversity of creative production around the world. The regime is particularly unhelpful in the protection of "small" independent originators of creative work. It establishes formidable obstacles to the use of creative products, since it restricts the notion of "fair use" under which these products traditionally could be freely used for a variety of purposes (e.g. education). Its narrow economic view focuses more on the misappropriation of corporate property than on the innovation of artistic and literary creativity.

With the increasing economic significance of intellectual property, the global system of governance in this domain has moved away from moral and public interest dimensions and emphasizes in its actual practice mainly the economic interests of the owners of intellectual property. Today, such owners are by and large no longer individual authors and composers who create cultural products, but transnational corporate cultural producers. The individual authors, composers and performers are low on the list of trade figures and as a result there is a trend towards IPR arrangements that favour institutional investment interests over individual producers. The recent tendency to include IPRs in global trade negotiations demonstrates the commercial thrust of the major actors. Copyright problems have become trade issues and the protection of the author has taken second place to the interests of traders and investors. This emphasis on corporate ownership interests implies a threat to the common utilization of intellectual property and seriously upsets the balance between the private ownership claims of the producer and the claims to public benefits of the users. The balance between the interests of producers and users has always been under threat in the development of the IPR governance system, but it would seem that emerging arrangements provide benefits neither to the individual creators nor to the public at large.

It seems sensible that holders of copyrights would want to protect their interests against theft. Even the most active defenders of neo-liberalism (who argue for the withdrawal of the state) will encourage states to act decisively against the piracy of their properties. Protecting intel lectual property is, however, not without risks. The protection of intellectual property also restricts access to knowledge, since it defines knowledge as private property and tends to facilitate monopolistic practices. The granting of monopoly control over inventions may restrict their social utilization and reduce the potential public benefits. The principle of exclusive control over the exploitation of works someone has created can constitute an effective right to monopoly that restricts the free flow of ideas and knowledge.

Challenges

The ecumenical movement is challenged by the process of media globalization in terms of global governance, media professionals and media literacy.

Global governance: The media have become crucial institutions in modern societies and the social responsibility for their future course should be shared among private media proprietors, media professionals, governments and citizens. Media are crucial elements of our cultural environment and the quality of this environment should be a public concern. Policy discussions in relation to media concentration, global advertising and intellectual property rights cannot be the exclusive mandate of states and markets. Multi-level forms of governance should be designed and implemented in which civil society has a legitimate place. In today's international politics of information and communication, the concerns of citizens receive no priority. This requires the active participation of civil groups (such as are present in the ecumenical movement) to promote fundamental humanitarian standards in media policy frameworks and policy-making processes.

Professionals: In the media professions around the world one finds committed and capable people who are willing to reflect on their social responsibility and public accountability. The ecumenical movement should open up the dialogue with these professionals about such issues as the desirability of public control over mega-conglomerates and limits to the influence of large advertisers on editorial policies.

Media literacy: In the early 21st century the media have become in many societies the most important story-tellers. They tell their audiences through entertainment, news and advertising who they are, where they come from, what their destinies are, and which values are important. They condone certain forms of conduct and reject what they label "deviant" behaviour. But story-tellers need a critical audience. They need a media-literate public that monitors their trustworthiness and calls them to account in cases of deception, misinformation and unprofessionalism. The urgent need for critical media awareness implies a challenge for the ecumenical movement: actively to support efforts to make training for media literacy a standard provision in a wide range of formal and informal educational curricula.

Conclusion

Today's global media market is at the core of an expanding cultural environment that can best be described with the metaphor of *Disneyland*. It is important for the ecumenical movement to reflect on what religion in Disneyland means.

In Disneyland the citizen has become more than anything else a consumer. People do not relate to Disneyland through the category of citizenship, but through their enjoyment of sensational thrills. They do not participate as active agents, but constitute audiences to be sold (through entertainment) to advertisers. Politics in Disneyland is theatrical and trivial. Debates are based upon sound-bites and focus primarily on personal images and avoid structural concerns. All images and logos can be commercially used and exploited. Anything – including religion – can be merchandized. Brand names become new idols, and the new places of worship are the shopping malls. In Disneyland shopping equates with worshipping. In Disneyland there are no conflicts between social classes. Advanced technology represents human moral progress and the key motivation for individual conduct is not communal solidarity but the individual "I Deserve It" syndrome.

This "Disneyzation" of the world through the three essential dimensions of media globalization poses a key challenge to the ecumenical movement. In past decades the issues discussed in this chapter have not been a major concern to the movement. Today, the luxury of this negligence can no longer be afforded.

NOTES

[1] See L. Hachmeister and C. Rager eds, *Wer beherrscht die Medien?*, C.H. Beck, 2002.
[2] In 2001 the Reuters Group had revenues of 6247 billion euros.
[3] UNDP, *Human Development Report 1998*, Oxford, Oxford UP, 1998.
[4] UNDP, *Human Development Report 1999*, Oxford, Oxford UP, 1999.
[5] S. Venturelli, "Cultural Rights and World Trade Agreements in the Information Society", *Gazette*, 60, 1, 1998, p. 63.

5

The Dynamics of Political Migrations as a Challenge to Religious Life

FELICIANO V. CARINO

Political drama on the high seas

For several days in August 2001, not long before the explosions in New York and Washington, DC, on 11 September, and in the lead-up to the Australian national elections, a political and humanitarian crisis erupted in the Pacific that threatened to explode into a major diplomatic row and fuel continuing worldwide controversy on issues surrounding policies and practices relating to migrants, political refugees and asylum-seekers. Responding to the distress signals of the sinking Indonesian boat *Aceng*, and following accepted humanitarian practice on the high seas, the Norwegian vessel *MV Tampa* rescued some 430 passengers, who were in fact Afghan asylum-seekers, and proceeded to transport them to their declared destination on the Australian outpost of Christmas Island. Rather than allow the *Tampa* to proceed to and unload its passengers on Australian territory, and asserting that those rescued were not legitimate refugees and asylum-seekers but simply sought illegal immigration to Australia, the Australian government ordered Australian SAS troops to board the *Tampa* and forcibly stop it. [1]

There ensued a diplomatic and political stand-off on the high seas that directly involved the Indonesian, Norwegian and Australian governments and the UNHCR, and indirectly several countries in the Pacific, notably Nauru, Papua New Guinea and Aotearoa New Zealand. The reported discussions and the commentaries that accompanied them criss-crossed old animosities but also raised some new issues. The Australian government denied claims that it had fuelled fears about asylum-seekers and dramatized its strong response against the Tampa passengers to assuage increasing domestic feelings against uncontrolled "foreign arrivals" on Australian soil in order to help win the November 2001 national elections. Indonesia was accused of refusing to receive asylum-seekers and was in fact tacitly aiding and abetting illegal migration of people into Australia. Norway was mildly rebuked for unwittingly becoming party to the illicit movement of people into Australia. Indonesia responded by pointing out that Australia was negating long-accepted humanitarian obligations on the high seas and rejecting asylum-seekers by invoking facile technicalities. Norway, in particular, strongly asserted that its vessel had simply made a customary response to disaster and the need for humanitarian assistance and objected to the forcible boarding of its vessel. Meanwhile, the UNHCR kept reminding everyone of the international conventions on refugees and of the obligations of the signatories to respect them. When the drama finally ended and the smoke of the diplomatic stand-off cleared, the Afghan asylum-seekers were transferred from the *Tampa* to an Australian navy warship and taken instead to Nauru, Papua New Guinea and Aotearoa New Zealand.

The immediate result of the incident was the unveiling and perhaps first practice of what has become known as the Pacific Solution to the refugee and migration problem by the Australian government. Presumably, as the crisis began to unfold, the Australian government asked a number of neighbouring countries in the Pacific region to receive the asylum-seekers and to set up offshore detention centres where they would be based temporarily while their applications for refugee status would be processed. The cost of establishing and maintaining these centres would be met by Australia. Nauru and Papua New Guinea (PNG) responded positively to the Australian proposal. Since late 2001 they have set up detention centres – Nauru almost immediately after the crisis in September, and PNG shortly thereafter in October. In part to help diffuse a possible international incident, Aotearoa New Zealand received some of the *Tampa* passengers, but did not accept any Australian assistance. Since then, several other Pacific countries have been approached (e.g. Timor Laroa'ese, Fiji, Kiribati, Palau and Tuvalu). [2]

The appeal of the proposal to those who have so far accepted it seems to lie primarily in the access it provides for much-needed financial assistance. Australia in a sense was temporarily buying or renting residence for possible refugees instead of allowing them to enter its territorial household. Initial estimates of the cost of setting up and maintaining the centres are some $72 million in Nauru and $24 million in PNG. In addition, substantial supplementary funds have been pledged that are coupled with development aid. [3] Australia, in short, seems willing to spend large amounts to protect itself – its "boundless plains" as the Australian national anthem puts it – from refugees, asylum-seekers and so-called unwelcome arrivals.

The Australian refusal to allow the *Tampa* to unload its passengers embodied patent distinctions between refugees and migrants and equally patent references to national boundaries, and reiterated the responsibility of government to protect political sovereignty, territorial integrity and to uphold the best interests and well-being of its people. Official Australian government statements on the crisis firmly stressed it "is firmly committed to ensuring the integrity of Australia's borders and to the effective control of the movement of people to and from Australia... Underlying these commitments is the fact that Australia is a sovereign country, which decides who can and who cannot enter and stay on its territory."[4] Asserting that the crisis was not precipitated for national election purposes, the immigration minister, Philip Ruddock, added that the people on the *Tampa* had already been "safe and secure in Indonesia and wanted to leave Indonesia and come to Australia to have a better outcome". Ruddock also suggested that some of the refugees were coming to Australia, not for reasons of racial or political persecution, but because they had made a "life-style choice". He told parliament that new legislation was needed to change perceptions that Australia is a "soft touch" for refugees and "unwelcome arrivals". Even more direct and blunt (and consonant with the subsequent actions of Australia after the events of 11 September) was the warning from the defence minister, Peter Reith, that unauthorized arrivals of boats in Australian territory "can be a pipeline for terrorists to come in and use your country as a staging post for terrorist activities".[5]

Forgettable incident or precursor of war?

For a while, the crisis attracted significant international attention because of the obvious importance and sensitivity of the issues it raised, the circumstances that precipitated it, and the international actors involved. However, it was soon swept aside and diverted from public attention by the overwhelming take-over of media coverage by the events of 11 September and the ensuing bombing of Afghanistan and the "war on terrorism".

The incident is recalled here for one critical reason. The asylum-seekers who were on the *Tampa* were Afghans. In other words, they were people fleeing a country whose government has been described as comprehensively and incorrigibly oppressive, evil and satanic and whose political leadership needed to be bombed out of existence and brought to justice "dead or alive". Who are "migrants" and who are "refugees" from such an economic, social and political context? Who are leaving in terror or fear for their lives and their future, and who are moving elsewhere simply for reasons of "life-style choice"? The incident, in short, should have been an occasion for a frank, honest and critical discussion of the legal, economic, political and other issues that could provide a more pertinent, creative and human framework for understanding the movement of people across national boundaries in the increasingly global, "borderless" and still very unjust and cruel world in which we live. Obviously, this did not happen. Instead of it providing an occasion for hope, the events of 11 September diverted attention to a new rhetoric of war.

Where are the passengers of the *Tampa* now? What has happened to them and the thousands of other asylum-seekers who have sought entry to Australia and other countries in the Pacific? How is the Pacific Solution working? Is this the promise for a better future for asylum-seekers or retrogression to some of the worst elements of past practice and policy? Was the *Tampa* crisis a mere passing and forgettable incident, or a precursor of the war into which the world has been drawn?

Nearly a year after the incident, the *Tampa* passengers, along with thousands more who are seeking refuge in Australia, remained "adrift in the Pacific", still temporarily held in detention centres in various Pacific countries, and still uncertain of their final destinations. Independent visitors to some of the detention centres noted the squalid and harsh physical conditions in which they lived, and the trauma and severe psychological pressures they suffered – conditions that have caused protests, riots and acts of self-harm. The fact that some of the countries in which the asylum-seekers have been detained are not signatories to the 1951 Convention on the Status of Refugees has worried many that they would engage in practices that would be contrary to accepted refugee rights, including the use of asylum-seekers as unpaid labour for public works projects.[6]

In June 2002 another political explosion was detonated from the *Tampa* incident, this time from Nauru, one of the countries that received the *Tampa* passengers. Leading up to his own national elections, the president of Nauru, Rene Harris, condemned Canberra for its Pacific Solution. Claiming that Australia had barely provided half of the financial commitments it had made and that the date for the processing of the asylum-seekers was now well passed, he noted acerbically that the "Pacific Solution, as it has been named, has somehow become a Pacific nightmare for us". Noting the linkage between the *Tampa* crisis and the Australian national elections, he continued, "*Tampa* won it for them at the last election. I have an election coming up in ten months' time and I am not riding too well."[7]

Shortly thereafter, word spread that the processing of the Tampa asylum-seekers had been completed, and that most of them were not refugees and would therefore have to be repatriated.[8]

Does the story end there, or is it the beginning of another nightmare? It was not clear even after the processing where the so-called "legitimate refugees" would end up. It was reported that those who were rejected would present an appeal for a reconsideration of the decision. Meanwhile, Australia made a cash offer to those who would return to Afghanistan. Acknowledging that there were dangers in returning to Afghanistan, the immigration minister, Philip Ruddock, said he was still hoping that many would accept the cash offer and go home. "It is a very generous offer," he said. "It's of the order of A$2000 per person and up to A$10,000 per family. When you understand that the yearly income for an Afghan is A$200, you can see that this is ten times what a person expects to earn during the course of the year."[9] After leaving Afghanistan under probably the most unimaginably difficult circumstances, being shunted to Indonesia, boarding a makeshift boat and being shipwrecked on the high seas, and after months in a detention centre, that indeed is a very generous offer.

Across boundaries, beyond borders

Dramatic and depressing as the *Tampa* incident might be, it is in fact only a tiny part of the very large picture of the vast movement of people across all sorts of boundaries and for all sorts of reasons. It is also only partially illustrative of the depth of human tragedy and suffering, cruelty and horror, and complex economic, social, political and legal issues and realities that accompany the massive scale of human displacement in our contemporary world.

Throughout human history, there have always been movements of people beyond native borders, and there have always been migrants, refugees and exiles. It was in the last century, in the wake of the human tragedies brought about by two world wars and the political upheavals in various parts of the world that marked the beginning of our global era, that issues related to the movement and displacement of people began to draw public attention and elicit a response from non-governmental and governmental institutions.[10] Today, as the world lurches further into globalization in all fields of human endeavour, the movement and displacement of peoples have reached unprecedented proportions and constitute one of the central issues for the future of humanity. They are in this sense a major expression of the "human component" in the question of globalization.

Elizabeth Ferris provides as a historical note a sense of amazement over the fact that in 1915, at the time of the Armenian genocide, the Armenian Committee for Relief in the Middle East raised "$20 million, sent relief teams to affected areas, fed an average of some 300,000 people a day, established and administered all hospital services in Armenia and took charge of over 75,000 orphans". [11] She goes on, however, to cite figures for migrants, refugees, asylum-seekers and displaced people nearly a century later that make the Armenian example look puny.

Recent estimates place the number of refugees and asylum-seekers at over 17 million, internally displaced people at over 20 million, "regular" migrants at over 30 million and another 30 million who are in another country on an "irregular" basis. This puts the total at over 100 million people. This surpasses the total population of nearly all the countries of central Europe. It also surpasses by far the total population of Australia and Aotearoa New Zealand. It does not even include the displacement of people brought about by more recent political events in various parts of the world (e.g. wars in the Middle East and on the Indo-Pakistan border, and the attack on Afghanistan after September 2001). It has been estimated that at the height of the military action in Afghanistan, there were some 2 million refugees strewn across the Afghan-Pakistan border alone, a figure that has been noted as constituting potentially the greatest humanitarian disaster of all times. When one adds to this the continuing and exponentially growing number of people who are travelling temporarily and crossing national boundaries for reasons of pleasure or educational and professional advancement and commitments, it is no wonder that population movement and political migration in our times are described in terms of vast waves or massive movements of people rather than in terms of exceptional or emergency cases, or in the language of "migratory elites". [12] It seems clear that in the years ahead these vast waves and massive movements will be even greater than they are now.

Migrants, refugees and displaced people

The more than 100 million migrants, refugees and displaced people are defined in categories provided by current legal and international systems and conventions. There are varying conditions and ways in which these categories have been determined; principally, however, they are based on "the reasons the person has left his or her country, on the degree of coercion, and on the extent to which protection of the host government is available". [13] Migrants are generally those who leave their country for *economic or personal work* reasons and who *choose* or who have a large degree of choice to do so. Refugees are generally those who leave their country for *political* reasons and who are *forced* to do so or who face some form of danger to their lives if they do not do so. The distinction may also be stated in terms of access to the protection of the person's government. Refugees are considered to be those who no longer enjoy the protection of their government, while migrants may have economic difficulties if they return to their home countries, but still enjoy the protection of their government.

To date, the principal legal definition of a refugee (and the most widely developed and respected) is the one provided by the UN Convention Relating to the Status of Refugees (adopted in 1951) and its 1967 Protocol, which extended the Convention's provisions to current refugees. The Convention defines a refugee in the following terms:

> Any person who, owing to a well-founded fear of being persecuted for reasons of race, religion, nationality, membership of a particular group or opinion, is outside the country of his nationality and is unable or, owing to such fear, unwilling to avail himself of the protection of that country, or who, not having a nationality and being outside the country of his former habitual residence, is unable or, owing to such fear, unwilling to return to it. [14]

The Convention also provides a set of rights for refugees, including the right not to be repatriated to the country of origin. Over a hundred countries have ratified either the 1951 Convention or its 1967 Protocol. Indeed, the laws of many nations have adopted or incorporated this definition of a refugee. The Convention and the Protocol are in this sense critically important for understanding the issue.

There are however very clear and grave shortcomings to the Convention and the definitions it provides. These allow nations and other actors in the international arena to disclaim responsibility for responding to the massive human needs that migrants, refugees and displaced people have, and even callously to use such people in economic and political games.

Both the language and the substance of the definition are very clearly time-bound. It uses the term "persecution", for example, and pins the protection and obligations it seeks entirely on the fear of it. Political life and international relations have changed drastically since 1951. They have made more varied and more complicated the conditions that create fear among people and cause them to move beyond the boundaries of their countries "of nationality" or "habitual residence".

Consequently, there are glaring exclusions in who might be considered a refugee. People who are fleeing from violence or warfare and who have not been *specifically singled out for individual persecution* are not included. Neither are the millions of people who are fleeing violence, warfare or persecution, but who for one reason or another cannot leave their country. What many now call internal refugees are, in short, excluded. Meanwhile, the emphasis on individual persecution – what others call "targeting" of individuals – provides a very wide latitude of discretion for governments to reject asylum-seekers. Some, like the Australian government in the *Tampa* case, refer to them as people who have merely made a "life-style choice".[15] There are also conspicuous ambiguities in the distinctions the definition makes. Where really is the divide between economic and political reasons, and why are economic conditions left out of the causes of fear or oppression of people? When a Filipina who is a teacher at home moves to Hong Kong to become a domestic helper because a teacher's salary is not sufficient to support her family and put her children in school, is it a matter of changing to a better job or is it a matter of survival? Is the decision to move a matter of choice, or a matter of necessity and therefore "by force"? When a group of Afghans cross dangerous terrain because of war and oppressive economic and political conditions in their country, is this a matter of life-style choice or fear of persecution? What is the difference between fleeing for fear of your life in an oppressive economic and political situation and fear of persecution?

All these things take no account of today's "global" world and its possible consequences for redefining political life and international relations, particularly policies and perspectives on migration and the movement of people. The defence that the Australian government provided for its actions against a few hundred Afghan asylum-seekers stressed principles of sovereignty and national boundaries provided by the political framework of the nation-state and its supremacy. If the same language and principles had been used with regard to economic life (e.g. in the movement of capital, goods and services, and in the determination of investment policy) they would immediately have been attacked and rejected as embodying the abhorrent practice of protectionism. What does it mean that in economics we speak approvingly of a borderless world and of breaking down barriers, but in politics we speak in terms of national borders and territories? More specifically, what does it mean that the migration of goods and resources must be free, but the migration of people is and should be bordered?

Religion, globalization and migration

If we needed reminders of how important religions are for understanding and dealing with the affairs of economic and political life in a
global world, the attacks on the World Trade Center and the Pentagon
and their aftermath provide stark and sombre lessons. This is not to say
that such events may not have happened or will not happen again if
there is or had been greater understanding and cooperation between
religions, and between Islam and Christianity in particular. Neither is it
to say that our political and military enemies should be defined or
named in terms of their religious identities, or that international conflicts should be traced to their religious or cultural roots, or be understood as a clash of civilizations. [16] What the assault on the United States
and the response to it tell us is how human community is made so much
more difficult when God or Allah or religious traditions are invoked as
reasons for violence, or to undergird patently economic or political
interests with the semblance of universal righteousness. It is clear now
that a world split along religious lines or between peoples of different
religious traditions is fraught with trouble and danger. A new global
community cannot emerge when people of different traditions and
faiths are not given space to live together as creative components of a
more inclusive political community.

The issue of migration (political migration in particular) is an urgent
focus of religious concern in this context. We live in a world where
more and more people are increasingly on the move and crossing formerly
forbidden and prohibited borders. It is not, as Bert Hoedemaker has
rightly noted, that modern technology has created a "new world". What
is new is the fact that, as a consequence of technological innovation and
a combination of historical forces, we now live in a world confronted
by the "permeability of all sorts of boundaries", and overwhelmed by
the "growing consciousness that all segments of the world are
inescapably bound together in a traffic of network and communication
that is there to stay". The result is specific experiences and manifestations
of the "proximity of humankind" affecting wider and wider areas of
human life that have not been seen before, and which take precedence
over older ways of dividing the globe into "worlds" or "cultural regions".
As such, it has become increasingly difficult – if not obsolescent – to
think of the world in terms of absolute "contexts" or "entities" that can
be understood independently of each other. On the contrary, more and
more "contexts" are fast becoming deterritorialized and hybridized. [17]

The growing movement of people across and beyond previously
defined borders is one of the major transnational forces that is pushing

the world, for better or for worse, towards a global community. It constitutes the human component of the task of incorporating this incipient global world into new and equitable structures and systems of economic, social and political life and international relations. This is one of the supreme tasks of social and political imagination and construction in the 21st century. It is also one of the supreme challenges to the religions of the world: to incorporate it into new expressions and structures of religious life and inter-religious understanding and cooperation.

The movement of people across boundaries takes place for various reasons. People move as goods and products are planned and marketed transnationally. People move as capital, resources and information now move so fast across national boundaries that structures and borders of nation-states become irrelevant. People move as their perceptions of and opportunities for a better life and for professional advancement go beyond the locus of national boundaries. People move as transnational economic corporations and organizations of intellectual, social and political life grow in number and require more transnational personnel to operate and serve them. People move as transport facilities improve and become more accessible to more people. People move as new affluence causes them to seek entertainment and enjoyment, rest and relaxation.

People also move because the fields are dry, the crops have failed, and there is famine in the land. People move because there are no jobs at home, or the jobs pay so little that they do not have enough to survive or to send their children to school. People move because there is war and conflict in their land and it is not safe to remain in their homes. People move because they could not speak freely or participate freely and fully in the economic, social and political life of their land.

People move because they could not worship their God freely and fully in their country, or because they could not profess and practise their religion in a country that is dominated by another religion.

For these reasons and many more, people now move in such enormous numbers that the phenomenon of migration can no longer be ignored in determining what it means for us to live in a global community. Political migrants such as refugees and displaced people have traditionally been given little attention, as having little real social, political or religious significance. They are viewed as exceptional or aberrational cases that require emergency relief, but are marginal to the central processes of national or international life. Social and political institutions – even churches and other religious bodies – look at them mostly as tragic but largely irrelevant victims of political or military conflict. Consequently, politicians in both democratic and authoritarian regimes play political games with them, either seeking to contain political fall-out or gain politically from the way in which they are treated.

The constancy and enormity of political migration in our time changes this situation substantially. Political migrants, refugees and displaced peoples have become a symbol of the political violence and intolerance that pervades our world and the changes that are taking place and must take place in various aspects of economic, social, political and religious life.[18]

Political migrations, political order and inter-religious community

For the religious life in particular, migrants raise an immense issue of humanitarian concern and therefore of human service. Beyond this, however, they also raise issues of justice, and of war and peace in a global but unjust and conflict-ridden world. Most importantly, they raise issues related to the reconstruction of political order and religious community in a world whose old borders now begin to look tenuous and antiquated.

Service and justice

The humanitarian dimensions of this issue are obviously immense. Refugees are uprooted people. Having been forcibly lifted out of home, community and country, they are completely denuded of the most basic support systems and resources for survival. When they come in the hundreds of thousands and even millions as they did during the attack on Afghanistan after September 2001, or as a result of seemingly interminable and intermittent political conflict in African countries (e.g. Liberia, Ethiopia, Sudan, Côte d'Ivoire, Algeria, Burundi), they tax humanitarian and relief agencies beyond their capabilities. As a result, there has been talk of "humanitarian fatigue".

As the World Council of Churches noted not too long ago, the agony and anguish of uprooted people in our time constitute a "moment of choice" for the churches and the expression of Christian concern. Such a moment of choice might be the starting-point for common religious concern and a common response.

Refugees and displaced and uprooted people are not just the visible face of human need in our time. More importantly, they reveal the tragic dimensions and broken character of current economic, political and international arrangements. Refugees and other political migrants exist because things are tragically wrong and oppressive in our world: in the way in which economic resources are exploited and distributed and political power is exercised. In addition to military and other authoritarian regimes there are more subtle forms of this tragic brokenness. There is something terribly wrong and unjust when a Filipino teacher earns less than a domestic helper in Hong Kong or the Middle East. There is something terribly wrong and unjust when Afghan oil helps supply the energy needs of the richest nations, but Afghans wallow in abject poverty and are unwelcome in those same countries that benefit from their national resource. Migrants, in short, show in a vivid way something of the injustice of our time and our heavy responsibilities in this globalizing world.

War and peace

Thus, political migration and displaced people are indissolubly linked to the issue of war and peace. We cannot simply say that if only the fruits of globalization were more abundant and more widely shared then wars would end and peace would be achieved. It is clear that a world split between those who benefit from increasing wealth and openness and those who do not will be a world of greater trouble and conflict, including environmental degradation, political instability, military conflict and terrorism.[19] It is clearer than ever before that where this split is combined with religious identities the conflicts it engenders are more violent and unpredictable.

The character of war and the problems of peace have changed over the last ten years. Not too long ago, war was conducted among nations and empires that subjugated other nations, expanding and amassing wealth and resources, and competing for control and areas of influence. Then war became a matter of ideological alliances, accompanied by arsenals of weaponry so destructive and so powerful that they required the maintenance of a "balance of terror" – an arms race equilibrium. Wars of ethnic or religious character seemed slight in comparison. National and civil strife in non-aligned territories was dwarfed in magnitude and importance.[20]

It would be a mistake to regard these kinds of political and military conflict as mutually exclusive. There remain some terrifying remnants of all these wars in many places around the world. Today, however, two new dimensions have emerged.

On the one hand, in addition to the fact that the religious components of war have become more prominent, wars of ethnicity and religion have arisen in places and in ways that were unexpected. These are wars that are rooted in ethnic or religious identities and loyalties, and are mainly directed not at material goals (e.g. conquest of territory or natural resources), nor ideological or class-specific goals, but to promote the power of an ethnically or religiously defined population.

Waged mostly by non-state actors, they use irregular armies and avowedly ethnic and religious movements in the pursuit of their goals. Their methods are unorthodox and involve deep expressions of loyalty and persistence. Most importantly, they engage natural populations in war activities. In Indonesia, Sri Lanka, India and Pakistan, Bosnia, various parts of the Middle East, and in various African countries, such wars have predominated in recent times.

On the other hand, there is now a bureaucratization of war that has not been seen before. Using highly sophisticated technological instruments and deadly weapons, war is waged at a distance while executives, commanders and generals meet in well-furnished conference rooms to devise strategies and designate targets, before unleashing mass destruction from afar. Undertaken either by air or by sea, the direct deployment of troops is kept to a minimum so that the "messiness" of war is avoided at close range by the attacking armies. The result is a reduction of the moral or social damage "at home", while the damage "abroad" is immense. Whole cities and large populations are involved, but the operations are described as "clinical" and the suffering and damage inflicted on non-combatants and innocent victims are known as "collateral damage". Symbols of religious fervour and devotion are invoked to provide justification for the war effort.

The political migrations and displacement of people that such wars create have a more pronounced religious identity. How can the common response to such human need be the starting point for inter-religious understanding and cooperation –a new inter-religious fellowship? Beyond the need for a common humanitarian response, how can people of various faiths assist in seeking peace and help bring about a structured agreement among nations that will allow cultures, languages, religions and ways of life to flourish and prosper together peacefully?

Political order and inter-religious community

It is in this sense that the issue of migration requires the remaking of political order and religious community. Several areas could serve as the starting points for such an effort.

Seeking reforms: The magnitude of the issues involved in the displacement and movement of people requires at the very least the reform of various practices, policies and components of national and international systems. Elizabeth Ferris suggests alternative criteria for dealing with the issues that would entail reforms in the international system, more particularly the United Nations and its operational humanitarian work. She also makes proposals for the reform of international law, particularly the 1951 United Nations Convention on the Status of

Refugees, the setting up and strengthening of regional initiatives, and changes in national policies and practices.[21] Her proposals are worth serious examination by governmental and non-governmental organizations and humanitarian agencies, and deserve wider ecumenical concern across confessional and religious boundaries.

Towards methodologies of complementarity: Samuel P. Huntington has linked the quest for the "remaking of world order" with the "clash of civilizations", in which religious components will constitute and define the primary character and expression of international conflict.[22] Noting the provocative and dangerous nature of this suggestion, some Asian intellectuals and social analysts have pointedly asked why, in a globalizing world with proliferating global partnerships necessary for success and survival in various human undertakings, we should be bound by methodological paradigms of conflict rather than complementarity. Methodological paradigms that presuppose views of society and human relations as essentially in conflict have formed a basis of much of Western sociological and political analysis. Is Huntington's assertion not in fact a self-fulfilling prophecy of war and a self-serving justification for programmes and policies of political and military aggression by the established powers of Western Christian cultures?

The world should not be drawn into another cold war based on the presumed polarities of civilizations. It is imperative for religious bodies and people of religious faith not to become involved in prognostications of an inevitable clash of civilizations or religions. Julius Lipner's appeal for Christians and people of other faiths to exercise and explore "methodologies of complementarity" rather than exclusion in their relationships is urgent in this context.[23] What does it mean to affirm religious integrity, to respect and live with the religious and cultural traditions of others who not only profess, but also live these traditions as part of the basis of the common life of all? What is the form of political community that best expresses such a methodology of complementarity?

A look at political borders: A fresh and constructive look at the idea of political borders is obviously one area of exploration. The issue of borders is essentially a problem resulting from the emergence of the nation-state as the primary structure of political community and international relations. Nation-states insist on territorial integrity and impermeability. Insisting on exact definitions of borders and justifying territorial claims in terms of historical continuity, racial homogeneity, customary law and (if possible) treaties and agreements, nation-states regard the defence of territorial integrity and borders as a supreme ingredient of national interest. It is for this reason that so many of the flashpoints of international conflict are related to borders and territorial claims.

The problem of borders in many non-Western areas (e.g. in Central and Eastern Europe) is that they were drawn up or distorted on the basis of conquest, diplomatic convenience and bargaining by imperialist powers. The territorial borders of the major countries in southeast Asia were established from the remains of colonial territories; they exhibited the extent of territorial holdings of Western powers. As for Africa, "the Congress of Berlin... carved out large portions of Africa and distributed them like so many portions of beef". Indeed, in world history, "there is hardly a single boundary which was not a product of conquest and violence at one time or another". [24] Obviously, these are not in themselves sufficient reasons to denigrate or gloss over the issue of borders. It is striking, however, that after setting up the artificial, forced borders of the new African states, forced migrations and refugees in Africa also increased. More than a third of refugees and displaced people in the world are now in Africa. [25] What does it mean to maintain political borders in such a situation? Amid the increasingly massive flow of people across borders, what kinds of borders to political community should we have?

A look at religious composition: The religious composition of political order is a critical area for exploration. Religious history and tradition in regard to this issue are ambivalent. On the one hand, the experience of exile and displacement has very important religious significance. It should provide a hospitable environment for the discussion and exploration among the religions of the world. It was while he was in exile in Medina that the Prophet Mohammed led the decisive battle and was finally vindicated in his calling as Prophet. It was the experience of exile and wandering in the desert in search of a homeland that proved to be the vehicle for the people of God in the Judeo-Christian tradition to receive the promise and fulfilment of God's care and protection and his love and grace for all peoples. Christ was an outcast in his own country, yet in him there is no "Jew nor Greek, slave nor free, male nor female". Exile and wandering in the desert became the paradigmatic experiences out of which the religious fellowship of Christ understands itself as transcending political and other borders. Embedded in such religious traditions are the values of love, compassion and hospitality, and care for orphans and widows, strangers and exiles.

On the other hand, in the current definition of a refugee provided by the 1951 UN Convention, religion is recognized as one of the sources of persecution for which a person may seek asylum or refugee status. In other words, religious factors have been among those that have caused the persecution of people, and have been among the prominent reasons why people have been displaced or have decided to move. The waves of migration from the old world to the new, across various borders in Asia and Africa, and in the Middle East, carry the marks of violence in the name of religion and show the ambivalent role that religions play in political life

This "ambivalence of the sacred" means it is critical that the building of inter-religious community become part of the project of remaking political community and world order in this global era.[26] What might be the structure of such an inter-religious community and the larger political order of which it should be a part and which it should nurture? Ecumenical thought on inter-religious dialogue has underscored the fact that dialogue is not primarily between belief systems or ideas, but between and among people. It is in this sense a dialogue of life. The permeability of borders and the movement of people that globalization and the new world of technologies have brought about make it clear that the religious composition of political order will become increasingly plural. They also make it clear that the dialogue of life will now begin to take place "up close" and not "from afar". It will be a dialogue among neighbours,[27] in the common avenues of human intercourse, seeking common ground, where a better life can be shared by all. A new and creative definition of inter-religious community is a necessary and critical component of the remaking of political order.

NOTES

1   This account of the *Tampa* crisis is based on daily news items reported in the *Philippine Daily Enquirer* and the *Philippine Star* in Manila, and the *South China Morning Post* in Hong Kong.

2   *Adrift in the Pacific: The Implications of Australia's Pacific Refugee Solution*, Fitzroy, Victoria, Oxfam Community Aid Abroad, 2002, p. 5. See also pp. 8ff.

3   *Ibid.*, p. 5. See also pp. 12ff.

4   As quoted in *ibid.*, p. 8.

5   As quoted in *ibid.*, p. 8.

6   *Ibid.*, pp. 6, 14–15.

7   "Refugees a Nightmare, says Nauru President", *South China Morning Post*, 11 June 2002, p. 13.

8   "UN Deals Blow to Afghans' Hopes for Asylum", *South China Morning Post*, 14 June 2002.

9   Quoted in *ibid.*

10 See Elizabeth G. Ferris, *Beyond Borders: Refugees, Migrants and Human Rights in the Post Cold War Era*, WCC Publications, 1993, pp. 4–10.

11 *Ibid.*, p. 4.

12 See *ibid.*, pp. 129–272.

13 *Ibid.*, p. 10.

14 Quoted in *ibid.*, p. 12.

15 *Ibid.*, pp. 12–13.

16 See Samuel P. Huntington, *The Clash of Civilizations and the Remaking of World Order*, New York, Simon & Schuster, 1996.

17 Bert Hoedemaker, "Mission and the Challenge of the New World of Technology", in *The People of God among All of God's Peoples: Frontiers in Christian Mission*, Philip L. Wickeri ed., Hong Kong, Christian Conference of Asia, 2000, p. 125.

18 See Ferris, *Beyond Borders*, p. xvii.

19 On this point, see Supachai Panitchpakdi and Mark L. Clifford, *China and the WTO: Changing China, Changing World Trade*, Singapore, John Wiley, 2002, p. 1.

20 See Charles C. West, "The Changing Ideological Climate in Church and Society", in *Faith and Life in Contemporary Asian Realities*, Feliciano V. Carino and Marina True eds, Hong Kong, Christian Conference of Asia, 2000, p. 72.

21 Ferris, *Beyond Borders*, pp. 273–304.

22 Huntington, *The Clash of Civilizations*.

23 Julius Lipner, "Religion and Religious Thinking in the New Millennium", in *Plurality, Power and Mission: Intercontextual Theological Explorations on the Role of Religion in the New Millennium*, Philip L. Wickeri et al. eds, London, Council for World Mission, 2000, pp. 83–97.

24 Ishwer C. Ohja, *Chinese Foreign Policy in an Age of Transition: The Diplomacy of Cultural Despair*, Boston, Beacon, 1969, p. 146.

25 Ferris, *Beyond Borders*, pp. 129ff.

26 See R. Scott Appleby, *The Ambivalence of the Sacred: Religion, Violence and Reconciliation*, New York, Rowman & Littlefield, 2000.

27 S. Wesley Ariarajah, *Not without My Neighbour: Issues in Interfaith Relations*, WCC Publications, 1999.

6
New Wars
and Religious Identity Politics

HEINRICH SCHÄFER

Within a framework of globalization and the development of different modernities, religion has become an important element in a new type of conflict: regional war between mobilized cultural (mostly ethnic) identities. Conflicts in Sri Lanka, Kashmir, Rwanda, the former Yugoslavia, Sudan, Nigeria, East Timor and elsewhere mix ethnic, religious, political, social and economic factors. Many scholars have called this new type of war post-modern, privatized, unofficial, post-national or simply new. Concepts are still in flux, as the phenomenon is recent. Nevertheless, one thing is obvious: broadly speaking, such conflicts are distinct from classical modern warfare between nations.

Globalization and the reculturing of politics

These "new wars" stem from the different consequences of the transformation of modern political and economic structures under accelerated globalization.

In terms of economic structures, Dieter Senghaas[1] points to the failure of post-colonial development-nationalism in third-world countries as an important factor in the rise of a militant reculturalization of politics. Often, those elites who are largely responsible for economic failure seek to elude the opposition of frustrated middle classes and the marginalized by inciting ethnic conflict. In addition, strategies of reculturalization of politics focus on the reaffirmation of rights and identity over against strong influences from outside. The goal of such reformulations is a new and feasible political project for the actors involved.

Another context for militant ethnic and religious reorientation is the decline of the modern nation-state. It has given way to "new visions of collective identity",[2] such as multicultural or fundamentalist movements and communal religious or ethnic movements. And it paves the way for new forms of conflict, since the power and legitimacy of the nation-state are severely damaged. From above, transnational economic and political organizations reduce the state's ability and competence for effective action; while from below, the increasing lack of financial resources (e.g. tax revenues), the increase and privatization of violence, and the very social movements themselves scatter the state's authority. Inside, ineffectiveness and corruption dissipate state legitimacy.

Finally, growing social differences between the winners and losers in globalization are becoming increasingly apparent. Declining social classes all over the world have a clear sense of reduced opportunities. In the absence of a clearly articulated political consciousness of this situation,[3] the field of cultural relations – ethnic or religious – becomes attractive for the mobilization of people in order to achieve political goals. Religion and ethnicity can become a resource for political and military power.

Old and new wars

Modern war has its origins in the nation-state. Pacification inside the state (e.g. the end of feuds) brought about the creation of conscripted and (later) professional armies and potentially hostile relations with other states. Between the 15th and 19th centuries war developed into a highly governed and controlled activity. The kind of war described by Clausewitz is (at least in theory) a rational instrument of political power, and the various Geneva conventions aimed to regulate and minimize the impact of military activity on civilians. Modern war was organized according to three basic distinctions: public vs private, domestic vs external and civilian vs military.

Religion in classic modernity belonged only in the private sphere, and thus lost its importance as a rationale for war. The state's interests dictated and legitimized military activity. Along with nationalism, religion only served as a means to instil loyalty in troops and populations.

A first step in the dissolution of the three basic distinctions of modern war was the "total war" of the 20th century. Whole societies were subdued under the logic of war: an all-encompassing war economy turned everything important towards war and so everything had to be bombed. A second step was guerrilla and counter-insurgency warfare: in both (in very different ways) the civilian population and the use of propaganda came to be a central factor for military activities.

New wars go a step further. Mary Kaldor analyzed the conflict in Bosnia (1992–95) as an example of a new kind of war. Yugoslavia was transformed from communism to capitalist modernity with less precipitation than the Soviet Union, but with considerable friction. From above, the break-up of the state delegitimized ruling political elites. From below, economic decline and separatist politics fuelled insecurity. Over against this increasing scarcity of political resources, the discourse of elites changed from communism to nationalism, mediating nationalism through ethnic and religious identities.

Ante bellum society in Bosnia, on the other hand, did not in itself embody centuries-old hatred, as some politicians put it. It was ethnically and religiously heterogeneous and thus provided the raw material for political polarization. The distinctive element in the groups to be polarized was not language but religion. Bosnian Muslims are ethnic Serbs who converted during Ottoman rule and went on to become the economically strongest members of Bosnian society. Orthodox Serbs and a Catholic Croatian minority generally had weaker social positions. The Ottoman empire's millet system (different religions in one administrative unit) created the space for the coexistence of these groups in Bosnia. This "good neighbourhood" *(komsiluk)* was even called an institutionalized communitarianism by Xavier Bougarel. Intercultural ties, via intermarriage and an encompassing city-based secular culture, were fostered by the communist secularism of Tito. On the other hand, social differences persisted between the more urban Muslims and the more rural Serbs and Croats.

It is very striking that six months before the elections of 1990, 74 percent of voters welcomed the possible proscription of nationalist parties in order to preserve good neighbourhood. Afterwards, however, political mobilization occurred along ethnic-nationalist lines. People had little choice other than to gather around their own ethnic tradition. But this tradition was mobilized into a dynamic of political polarization and heated up by religious institutions. It would not be long before snipers fired on the peace movement in Sarajevo, paramilitary groups organized and a new war broke out, the main goal of which was the elimination of a "secular, multicultural, pluralistic society".[4]

According to Kaldor, the most important characteristic of the war in Bosnia is that it was a war of different power groups (not *the* state) *against* civilians. This turns the concept of modern warfare (according to which regular troops fight against each other) upside down. It also changes the concept of guerrilla and counter-insurgency warfare, for the state is no longer the most important military actor. Instead, private actors have become increasingly important: paramilitary groups under criminal leaders cooperate with the state and conduct their own business by means of warfare and collateral damage. Foreign mercenaries (e.g. mujahedin or US military firms) engage with different parties for the sake of money, recognition by political elites, or simply adventure.

Local militias seek to protect villages from these groups. The regular troops of interested states or state-like structures also engage in the fighting, as well as international regular military units (e.g. UN, NATO or US troops). In Bosnia as in many other places (e.g. Rwanda and Somalia), regular troops were in no position to protect civilians, even if they wanted to. The most important military actors were irregular forces that acted flexibly and were widely dispersed, but remained in close contact by means of communication technology. Their target was the civilian population.

In order to gain political control of the population, terror against civilians was systematically employed to achieve religious/ethnic "cleansing" and the division of territories. Amid economic circumstances that did not allow for much more than living on humanitarian aid, fleeing or becoming criminals, members of paramilitary groups decided on the latter. Meanwhile, regular troops and mercenaries are mostly paid from outside by governments or diasporas, and irregular troops are financed to a great extent by illegal "war taxes", extortion, robbery, pillage, smuggling (weapons, drugs, diamonds, etc.) and black-market activities. Thus, the economic logic of war also gets turned around. Members of paramilitary forces – especially higher ranks – find in war and common insecurity a source of income. Consequently, their goal is not to re-establish civil institutions and public security, but to maintain for as long as possible a state of common insecurity and the rule of the strongest. As war is business and civilians are the main target, it is no wonder that irregular forces neither establish clear fronts nor seek to battle enemy forces. On the contrary, they may even deal with the enemy for economic benefits.

One thing is always very probable: any group of irregular forces will repress, terrorize or exterminate moderate civilians. According to Kaldor,[5] while members of other ethnic groups are targeted, another very important target group are those who seek to moderate conflicts and help their neighbours: Serbs who hide or defend their Muslim neighbours, Jews who help Muslims flee, and many other courageous people.

This new war is not premodern. It is not really a regression to "medieval" conditions. Its actors rely on transnational contacts and allegedly promote national interests. According to Kaldor,[6] such alleged national interests moulded the way in which the Bosnian war was perceived by international observers. International diplomacy dealt with the war as a conflict between competing nationalisms instead of a war waged by power groups against civilians and civilized life. Its discourse constructed ethnic-national units and their representatives, while

1990 pre-election conditions showed completely different (more social and economic) fault lines among the population. Such an essentialist view corresponds perfectly to the ways in which modern nation-states regulate external affairs. Precisely for this reason it fails to recognize the power relationships in informal warfare between paramilitary (and proto-national) troops and civilians. On the contrary, diplomacy recognized "warlords" (e.g. Karadzic) as representatives of a potentially national population. Thus, "ethnic cleansing" created facts and the policy of territorial division acknowledged them. If the genocidal character of what happened had been perceived and reckoned with, priorities might have been different. The foremost priority should have been the protection of civilians, the inclusion of local civil-society organizations in policy planning and negotiations, and the creation of safe territories for the reconstruction of democratic institutions (e.g. an international protectorate), all under a more powerful UN military presence. "The real challenge was not to preserve peace, but to enforce humanitarian law."[7]

Identity politics

Many of the new conflicts follow the logic of an ethnicization of social relationships.[8] According to this approach, it is erroneous to think that ethnic belonging itself is the reason for conflict. Such an opinion corresponds to the nationalist theory (going back to Herder) that nations themselves are rooted in ethnicity. Instead, in a process of ethnicization, actors overstate ethnic traditions for the sake of political power. Much like religious fundamentalism, this process is anchored in traditions of everyday life, selects certain symbols and stresses them as emblematic for certain "ethnic identities", and combines them with political programmes over against others. Such ethnic identities are at the same time traditional and constructed; they correspond to feelings of belonging and emphasize artificial contradictions. They are traditional in terms of central contents of their discourse: they use old and well-known symbols, refer to collective memory and operate according to habitual practices of certain populations. They are constructed in terms of the boundaries that they draw by overstating certain contents over against alleged enemies: they use symbols to mark differences and contradictions and to produce self-recognition through the exclusion of others. Emblematic labels serve for both aspects of this process.

In such a way, traditional ethnic belonging can be transformed into a resource for political power. In situations in which economic or political resources are too scarce to achieve political goals or control over economic goods, elites can construct conflictive scenarios and mobilize people in terms of ethnicity and/or religion. Such a situation can involve the breakdown of a nation-state, developmental crises and collective confrontation with an extremely strong external pressure. As the once overarching distinction between left and right becomes more and more meaningless, and as political opposition to globalization becomes more and more global itself, a political articulation of the social contradictions between the winners and losers in globalization is not clearly developed. The void of political self-definition is ready to be filled with ethnic and religious identity discourse, and socio-economic problems transform into symbolic violence.

Collective identity is a resource for those with and those without economic and/or political power.[9] But identity politics bring with them the danger of an uncontrollable development, for they bargain with a good that cannot be bargained with: identity. It is neither true nor false that new wars lack rationality. For ethnic-nationalist, religious and (para) military elites, a new war is primarily a purposive rational enterprise to further political and economic benefits – even if at the same time they identify with their ethnic or religious backgrounds. For the mobilized marginal population, however, ethnic and religious identity is much more than a political calculus. Their religious and/or ethnic identity represents for them truth, life and dignity.

Goldstein and Rayner[10] describe the differences between identity and interest-related conflict. Conflicts about material interests have a clear focus and can be addressed quite easily because they involve "third things" like material goods and political positions. Strategies point towards material betterment, which people value less than life itself. Negotiation is possible. Interest-related conflicts correspond to the highly developed rational choice framework of modern politics. Identity conflicts, on the other hand, are very hard to address politically. Negotiation is much more difficult, especially under the presuppositions of a rational choice framework. This is because identity conflicts resist the clarification of goals and reasons, and tend towards mystification. Moreover, they involve the intricate logics of self-esteem, dignity and recognition, the sense of belonging and the habitus of actors. Actors orient their strategies (e.g. from negotiation to suicide bombing) with dispositions anchored beyond the limits of the individual in religion and community, which means that individual life is not of primary importance. But it is precisely this trait of collective identity affirmation that answers the demands of individuals when they are uprooted and lack the cognitive and emotional dispositions to get along in a new situation.

In such circumstances (former) governmental, political or intellectual elites, traditional leaders, religious personalities and skilful criminals can serve their material interests by mobilizing people through ethnic and religious discourse. The higher the insecurity that they themselves produce, the more attractive is their offer and the fewer possibilities are left for alternatives on the basis of everyday cooperation or religious syncretism. And the more people can be engaged in collective violence, the more cohesion is produced by the bonds of guilt and hatred. Such an environment fosters a typical combination of factors for identity politics in the context of new wars. The main actors are more and more non-governmental groups, movements and organizations; the main resource for mobilization is discourse and the main resource for implementation is symbolic and physical violence; and the main contents of discourse are ethnic and/or religious. The conducing logic is Janus-faced: purposive, materially oriented rationality among the elites, and ethnic or religious identity affirmation among their followers.

Religion

Religion is an important part of ethnic identity, especially in non-European modernities and traditional societies.

On the macro level, the development of ethnic units and the boundaries between them followed religious differences, for in traditional societies religion was of pivotal importance. Even the missionary activities of Christianity and Islam did not change this pattern, but followed pre-existing social boundaries, including ethnic ones. Thus, material religion might have changed in certain social units, but it still goes together with boundaries between neighbours. Only in rapid migrational movements and multicultural societies like Canada or Malaysia does this picture seem to change. There have been multicultural and multireligious formations before (e.g. under the Ottomans, or Muslim rule in Spain); and even in a multicultural setting, religion often plays an important role as a cultural identity marker of ethnic groups. As the example of the USA shows, civil religion can overwhelm different religious identities as an ideology of national unity and implicitly confirm the dominion of one ethnic group over the whole multicultural setting.

On the micro level of collective identities, religion can be understood as a specific condensation of culture. We can think about a collective cultural identity as a broad network of dispositions to perceive, to judge and to act, common to all actors of a certain culture and, at the same time, comprising some specific differences according to individuals, groups, etc. Religion traditionally is a region of this network, where the fabric of signification is very densely woven. Even in European secularized societies, religion serves as a common reference, be it positive or negative. In the event of an ethnic revival, religion mostly acquires the role of an important, if not pivotal, operator for mobilization.

Symbolic violence

In a context of decaying nation-states and the growing significance of non-governmental actors, public discourse becomes increasingly important in general and, more specifically, for the exercise of power.[11] Especially in new wars, social movements and organizations (like paramilitary groups) act against one another. Ethnic and religious identity mobilization operates with symbolic boundaries.[12] As an identity is being constructed, some people are included and others excluded. This is normal and does not lead to problems in everyday life as long as communication is flowing and expectations are basically positive. But when there are very scarce resources and increasing polarization of interests, identities reaffirm themselves and the gaps between them widen. Actors perceive any competing identity as a threat, not to some delimited interests, but to their own identity – to everything they are.

In these clashes of mobilized identities, symbolic violence gains an important role. First of all, it means not recognizing the identity of others as legitimate. Thus, it implies negative ascription (labelling). Strong actors opt for racism, the weak for the "strategy of exclusive self-recognition",[13] which means fundamentalism.

Religion plays an important role in these processes, especially in combination with ethnic identity. Religious socialization – in life-cycle rites, schools, family traditions, etc. – closely combines with the formation of cultural habitus. In ethnic mobilization, therefore, religion for many people represents an anchor point for ethnic self-recognition. Habitual dispositions to combine religious and cultural practices (learned since primary socialization) can become salient and most significant in situations of conflict and construction of (counter) identities. Deep-rooted experiences of belonging can thus be used as widely recognized emblematic markers for political identification. It helps even more that religion provides many ancient and long-standing means for dramatizing and representing identities, like processions, shrines, life-cycle rites, everyday rites, meaningful buildings, etc. Often, these practices and objects are combined with places or territories, but with modern mobility and growing diaspora, religious symbols become transnational as well – even though they still might be linked to significant places like Mecca or Rome. In times of crisis, these anchor points provide a source of emotional security for individuals and, at the same time, they link these people to strategies of politically interested identity mobilization. In this context, religion offers a double usage to those who manipulate it. It is generally open to combining with arguments from reason and common sense; thus, it is possible to link to secular political discourse and even to further secularist goals. On the other hand, religion does not have to be reasonable in a "worldly" sense. Consequently, religion is a strong means to overcome instrumental rationality, such as presupposed in rational choice scenarios about human action. The example of Palestinian suicide bombers shows that the sense of belonging to a community and concrete expectations of paradise introduce another kind of rationality, the criteria for which reside far beyond individual benefits.[14] Finally, religion also comprises a certain tendency to make actors believe that their positions are absolute (not relative to others), which leads to fundamentalist mobilization.

New wars

In new wars religion serves as a resource to mobilize people behind (ethnically framed) political interests. As an example, we take a closer look at the Bosnian experience.

As a result of the Ottoman *millet* system and Tito's Yugoslavia, urban culture in Bosnia was quite secular in pre-war society. Spoken language was not an identity marker, since Serbocroatian was common to all. Religious differences were the only important markers of difference between ethnic groups, even though much of the Muslim population is ethnically Serbian as well. Under Ottoman rule the Serbian Orthodox Church became an important agent of self-affirmation for the regional non-Muslim population. Nonetheless, religious differences in urban life lost their importance amid increasing secularization and religious intermarriage. And all over the place "good neighbourhood" *(komsiluk)* in everyday life had its counterpart in syncretic religious practices. Nevertheless religion was still a strong *possible* resource for differences. The conflictual history of the region had contributed to the development and spread of ethnic-religious myths like that of the Christ-like Serbian King Lazar, which anchor deeply in the collective memory and can link to remembrances of particular events like second world war atrocities. And they can serve as a rationale for counter-action later on, as was the case with the alleged destruction of Serbian monasteries and genocide against Serbs by Kosovar Albanians in 1986.

Again, because they are rooted in everyday socialization – mothers' tales and family chats at lunch – these socio-religious myths have a strong potential for mobilization.

Such myths are of direct use to political interest groups, church leaders and elites in their strategies of ethnic identity mobilization by discourse. A good example of the political construction of an ethnic-religious myth can be found in the activities surrounding the 600th anniversary of the battle at Kosovo Polje in 1989. According to Sells, [15] this celebration served as the culmination of many activities with the same focus: to construct a belligerent ethnic-religious Serbian identity. The alleged destruction of monasteries was one element. Another was that the bones of Nazi-killed Serbs were ritually exhumed and nationalist propaganda depicted Muslim Serbs, Croats and Albanians as genocidal. At the commemoration of the battle these symbols were put together by Slobodan Milosevic and leaders of the Serbian Orthodox Church. The medieval Prince Lazar, killed by the Turks in the 1389 battle, was depicted as a Christ-like figure so that the defeat could be called the Serbian Golgotha. The historical Serbian heartland of Kosovo thus appears as the Serbian Jerusalem. Against this background, the Nazi killings of the second world war and alleged attacks against Orthodox religious symbols (the symbolically most important monasteries) became religiously *and* militarily charged symbols.

This symbolic operation reaches still deeper when seen in the context of "Christoslavism". The belief that Slavs are Christian by the very fact of their being Slavs uses religion to absolutize ethnic identity and substitutes ethnic belonging for religious orientation. In consequence, all those Serbs who (historically) converted to Islam are not Serbs any more, but "Turks". And as such they are to be made fully responsible for the death of King Lazar on the Serbian Golgotha.

This combined political, ethnic and religious discourse produced (or invented) a new combined religious-ethnic identity: the strictly Orthodox Serbian identity. The most important boundary was drawn over against Serbs with a Muslim credo. This means that these people were most dangerous for this new identity, precisely because of similarities and not differences. As a partly invented identity, the Orthodox Serbian identity had to focus on preserving itself from "alien contamination". [16] This could be done very effectively by means of ethnic-religious "cleansing" by military force. It is precisely to this that the combination of symbols in the Kosovo Polje commemoration points. The effect of this symbolic conglomerate on (potentially mobilized) Serbian people is quite obvious: "All Muslims have the blood of King Lazar and the Serbian people since 1389 on their hands."

Finally, religion is not just a legitimation of political violence. It is a driving force that gives it direction. According to Kaldor,[17] in new ethnic warfare it is important to make certain religions uninhabitable for certain people. Genocidal action is incomplete if it leaves the symbols for religious identification intact. People of a region can be driven out, but they wish to return as long as their memory links them to it with pleasant bonds. Therefore, systematic rape and physical atrocities are possible weapons to destroy the willingness of people to reclaim their homes. Another is the systematic destruction of sites of religious identification. No wonder (para) military forces composed of Bosnian Serbs systematically destroyed non-Serbian sacral sites, removed the rubble and turned them into something else, such as car parks. Religious symbolic violence is an important element in extinguishing a sense of belonging, uprooting people and making a region psychologically uninhabitable.

Religious polarization does not tear everything apart. Traditional syncretism in the context of good neighbourhood provides strong roots of faith and solidarity in everyday life. Even under the extreme stress of ethnic-religious "cleansing" there are religious people willing to risk their lives to help those from other religions. These attitudes – though strongly traditional – are closely related to the cosmopolitan worldview of the peace movement, NGOs, etc., that search to mediate and reconstruct civil society under the conditions of new wars.

Perspectives

New wars involve ethnic and/or religious identity politics. Against the background of decaying nation-states and scattered post-colonial economies, political forces reorganize along ethnic and/or religious boundaries. Thus, religious actors come to be significant for politics and warfare. Respective conflicts are waged largely by a mixture of regular and irregular forces, most of which make a living out of the disorder that they themselves produce. One of the most important characteristics of new wars is that the civilian population is the main target. A very specific target is that part of the population which resists being mobilized for one of the fighting parties, but instead searches to reconstruct legitimate and legal institutions, defend human rights, maintain or reconstruct inter-religious tolerance, and foster multicultural, pluralistic and democratic societies. Thus, new wars can be seen as a specific means by which particularists (fundamentalists) try to eliminate cosmopolitan orientations from the political landscape.

Religion plays an important role in increasing polarization and hatred. In this sense, it is a significant resource for particularists. Yet religion has capacities to foster cosmopolitan attitudes even at the grass-roots. These reside partly in its ability to relativize any human action over against the sacred and partly in the close connection of traditional folk religion with the unorthodox practical logic of everyday life.

Enforcement of cosmopolitan law

According to Kaldor,[18] habitual international strategies of intervention treat elites as the representatives of the people and the fighting parties as if they were fighting each other: Orthodox Serbs against Muslims, Hutu against Tutsi, etc. If we follow Kaldor's analysis of the Bosnian war (and her references to Rwanda and other places), we can perceive another practical logic of new wars: politically interested particularist elites against civilian populations (especially those of cosmopolitan orientation). This might not be wholly the case in any particular conflict, but it is most important that this viewpoint allows for a completely different approach to new conflicts: it makes cosmopolitan local actors the key figures for the re-establishment of law and justice.

Kaldor[19] proposes a "cosmopolitan alternative" for intervention in new wars. Fundamental to this is a focus on international law instead of geopolitics. Consequently, the major goal should be the restitution of democratically legitimate government. The rule of law can then be the basis for the execution of a legitimate monopoly of force by the state. Key partners in such a process are local cosmopolitan activists like NGOs, civil and human-rights groups, non-particularist intellectuals, etc. Such a political strategy relies on a strong and combined military and police presence of international ground forces to protect civilians active in the process of political reconstruction. This military presence should be recognized as legitimate by the civilians concerned. Finally, humanitarian aid that asphyxiates local economic activity should be transformed as fast as possible into support for the construction of a feasible local economy and political institutions. The goal of the whole process is not to go back to the pre-war situation, but to establish political institutions and civil actors that promote a society based on democratic and pluralistic standards. This is not to be taken as a universalist formula, but the intention that local political structures are shaped according to the will of the majority of the people who live in that place.

Of course, such a strategy confronts local and international antagonism. Local particularist elites do not want to negotiate power on this basis, and the dynamics of religious mobilization can be turned against international intervention as well. International powers tend to emphasize geopolitical criteria for interventions, rather than international "cosmopolitan" law. This is especially the case with US unilateralism, which looks at ethnic-religious conflict through the lens of Huntington's "clash of civilizations" theory,[20] and undermines the enforcement of international law by constantly breaking it and refusing to take part in a human community of legal standards. This ends up as particularist as the main protagonists in the new ethic-religious wars and tends to produce more problems than solutions.

Religion and cosmopolitanism

There is no doubt that cosmopolitan and long-standing ecumenical strategies fit well together. Obvious ecumenical counterparts are those pragmatic humanists who look for good neighbourhood and mutual understanding in terms of practical humanitarian legality and legitimacy. But without addressing the dynamics of religion in an ethnic-religious conflict it is not possible to decide on opportunities for action and the possible hazards that this action might face.

In the context of new wars we have seen a marked tendency of religion to polarize actors and to escalate cultural conflicts. Religion is drawn into the logic of identity politics, which is characterized by a complex mixture of interest-oriented and identity-oriented elements. The Janus face of the conflicts consists in the fact that the interests of political protagonists are channelled through the mobilized religious and ethnic identities of ordinary people. Purely political negotiations with protagonists do not address the religious and ethnic mobilization motifs of the people; thus, negotiations give in to the logic of particularist elites: territorial division. Mobilized religious identities, on the other hand, do not fall from heaven. They are rooted in everyday experiences and at least partly legitimate social grievances as well. There is not much sense in talking dogmatics or political opinions with particularists or fundamentalists. The problem is to understand the social and political overtones in their specific religious language and to make the long hermeneutical way back from religious enunciations to social practices by sound socio-religious analysis.

More specifically, traditional religion can play an important role in rescuing opportunities for linkage. Where particularists claim universal validity, traditional religion focuses on everyday experience; where purity is proclaimed, traditional practices are syncretic; where particularists promote long-term pretension, folk religion looks for short- and mid-term solutions to practical problems; and where political power is at stake, it will not be much more than a slight influence on decision-making. Traditional and practical everyday religion is a tool for problem solving and establishing a basic feeling of dignity. But as particularist or fundamentalist constructions are based on traditional religion, both have quite a lot of vocabulary in common – and traditional religion has the advantage of being closer to everyday life. This gives a certain plausibility to the semantic relinkage of mobilized religion to everyday problem-solving in the context of the pluralistic reconstruction of civil societies. Under the conditions of international intervention by UN forces and the reconstruction of legitimate political institutions, the pressure on people for ethnic-religious mobilization eases and new opportunities for a regular life arise. Relinkage to traditional religion might help in this context to demobilize exclusivistic and belligerent religious dispositions in order to assist people on their way back into ordinary life – a task that again has to be worked on together with local religious cosmopolitans.

Recommendations

What challenges do new wars pose to ecumenical policy? In general, the Colombo consultation (1994) made much headway. As for general recommendations, we can follow the advice of its authors.

Political action

The main target and victim in new wars is the civilian population, especially those who promote cosmopolitan perspectives for social and political life. It is the policy of the ecumenical movement to support and promote church and non-church groups that fight for the well-being of disadvantaged people in conflicts. It might be of use not to view the victims from one's own perspective and project one's own ideas of problem-solving onto them, but to develop a capacity for perceiving their needs from their own standpoint. More specifically, it might be of interest to link up with local strategies of specific groups to reconstruct legitimate political and social institutions in affected regions.

Military terror against proactive pluralist civilians is the most serious obstacle to the restitution of basic conditions for political and economic stability. It therefore seems to be justified within Christian social ethics to promote a stronger and more offensive military presence for UN forces in conflict zones, in order to defend civilians and stop the terror. Local partner churches might also be encouraged to cooperate with UN intervention forces.

The goal for peace-making in conflict areas is to promote the creation of legitimate institutions and local economic production. This requires the enforcement of cosmopolitan humanist law, including human-rights standards, etc. An indirect contribution to these strategies might be the public promotion of international institutions of law such as the International Criminal Court and the United Nations, in order to foster support for them among member churches and the broader public.

Religious action

Very important recommendations (e.g. to foster inter-religious dialogue) have already been made by the Colombo consultation. Here is one more specific idea. Particularist religious strategies mobilize people by polarizing religious symbolism. They choose elements of traditional religious practice to amplify them in one direction only. Thus, they take extreme forms, exalt "purity" and separate from traditional religious practice. It might be useful to help theologians and pastors of ecumenical churches to recognize the importance of traditional religions and syncretic practices for good neighbourhood and religious peace and to acknowledge the relativity of their own religious practices over against others. In this way they can be an example of recognizing the "other" where recognition does not seem to be possible.

The "essentialist" ideologies of ethnic particularists follow the logic of "we are right, because we are us". Some confessionalists have the same tendency and are easily caught up in alliances with the former. It might be of use for churches to take a close look at those tendencies within confessionalism that might overstate their specific identity at the expense of the capacity to perceive opportunities for cooperation with other churches and religions. The search for institutional unity tends towards essentialist views, too. It might be more useful and realistic to search for good opportunities for mid-range cooperation.

Religious mobilization plays an important role in particularist strategies of polarization and conflict provocation. In such a situation, any missionary activities can be caught in the dynamics of provocation and conflict escalation. Thus, it might be useful to refrain from any attempt at missionary activity and instead give a simple and human testimony of one's own faith as a basis for common life. This should of course include the firm assertion of the fundamental values of life. This does not mean an affirmation of the ecumenical movement as such, but the intention to provide criteria for mediation.

Civilians in new wars are not "collaterally damaged". Military actors target them intentionally. A theology of the cross might take this into account. Identification with the victims, then, is more than humanitarian aid. It is proactive defence.

104   Part II: Modernization and Religions

NOTES

1   Dieter Senghaas, *Zivilisierung wider Willen. Der Konflikt der Kulturen mit sich selbst*, Frankfurt, Suhrkamp, 1998, pp. 161ff.
2   Shmuel Eisenstadt, "Multiple Modernities", *Daedalus*, vol. 129, 2000, p. 16.
3   Mary Kaldor, *Neue und alte Kriege. Organisierte Gewalt im Zeitalter der Globalisierung*, Frankfurt, Suhrkamp, 2000, p. 117.
4   *Ibid.*, p. 72.
5   *Ibid.*, pp. 91ff.
6   *Ibid.*, pp. 92ff.
7   *Ibid.*, p. 106.
8   Klaus Eder, Bernd Giesen, Oliver Schmidtke and Damian Tambini, *Collective Identities in Action: A Sociological Approach*, manuscript, in preparation, 2003. Klaus Eder, "Protest und symbolische Gewalt. Zur Logik der Mobilisierung kollektiver Identitäten", *Forschungsjournal Neue Soziale Bewegungen*, 11, 1998, H. 4, pp. 29–40.
9   "Protest und symbolische Gewalt", p. 30.
10   Jonah Goldstein and Jeremy Rayner, "The Politics of Identity in Late Modern Society", *Theory and Society*, 23, 1994, pp. 367–84.
11   Klaus Eder, *Kulturelle Identität zwischen Tradition und Utopie. Soziale Bewegungen als Ort gesellschaftlicher Lernprozesse*, Frankfurt, Campus, 2000, p. 29.
12   *Ibid.*, pp. 201ff.
13   *Ibid.*, p. 203.
14   See Nasra Hassan, "An Arsenal of Believers", *New Yorker*, 19 Nov. 2001, pp. 36–41.
15   Michael Sells, *The Bridge Betrayed: Religion and Genocide in Bosnia*, Berkeley, Univ. of California Press, 1998; and "How Serbs Used Monasteries to Entice Ethnic Hatred", www.alb-net.com/kkc/061499e.htm#15 (15 June 1999).
16   Goldstein and Rayner, "The Politics of Identity", p. 372.
17   Kaldor, *Neue und alte Kriege*, p. 159.
18   *Ibid.*, pp. 92ff.
19   *Ibid.*, pp. 177ff.
20   Samuel Huntington, *Kampf der Kulturen. Die Neugestaltung der Weltpolitik im 21. Jahrhundert*, Munich, Europaverlag, 1996 (*The Clash of Civilizations and the Remaking of World Order*, New York, Simon & Schuster, 1996); and "The Clash of Civilizations?", *Foreign Affairs*, vol. 72, 1993, no. 3, pp. 22–49.

ADDITIONAL BIBLIOGRAPHY

Ettrich, Frank, "'Neue Kriege' und die Soziologie des Krieges", *Berliner Journal für Soziologie*, vol. 11, 2001, no. 3, pp. 391–404.

Giddens, Anthony, *Jenseits von Links und Rechts. Die Zukunft radikaler Demokratie*, Frankfurt, Suhrkamp, 1997.

Tiryakian, Edward, "Der Kosovo-Krieg und die Rolle der Vereinigten Staaten", *Berliner Journal für Soziologie*, vol. 11, 2001, no. 2, pp. 201–16.

Tschuy, Theo, *Ethnic Conflict and Religion*, WCC Publications, 1997.

7
Religions, Politics and the State
Some Revisions and Discordant Notes

FELICIANO V. CARINO

> Those who say that religion has nothing to do with politics do not know
> what religion is all about. *(Mahatma Gandhi)*

An old question revisited

Recent events in various parts of the world seem to have put an end to prognostications (made mostly by Western social and religious analysts) about the secularization of politics and the anachronism of religious symbols and movements in political life. They seem at last to have driven home the point that we need to give new attention to and make alterations in our understanding of the relationship between religion and politics. More specifically, they have raised the urgent need for us to revisit, if not revise, our conceptions of and attitudes towards the relationship between the nation-state and people and communities defined by their religious affiliations and identities.

In all parts of the world religious bodies and organizations of various kinds have become politically active and openly critical of the secular processes that have dominated national and international life. In keeping faith with what they consider to be the divine will, they have increasingly refused to provide either material or moral tribute to secular powers or to recognize them as having final social or political authority. They have also projected themselves as bearers of alternative religious and confessional options.

People of all faiths continue to insist that their religion is not only a private matter but also a public faith. They will become more actively social and political in character and will enter the public sphere with definitions and proposals not only for the good life but also for the good society. As a result they will be increasingly and directly concerned with political issues. The religious challenge to the legitimacy of primary secular spheres – political organization, the nature and form of governance, the character and structure of the economy, and the state itself – will intensify. More and more will refuse to limit their activities to the spiritual care of individuals and will instead raise questions about the interconnection between private and public behaviour, and the claims of states and other economic and political institutions to be above normative religious considerations and scrutiny. They will also question the extent of temporal authority and usurp political functions and powers. In short, what is emerging as new and "news" in the contemporary social and political scene is the "widespread and simultaneous refusal of the so-called 'world religions' to be restricted to the private sphere". [1] The epigraph from Mahatma Gandhi that began this chapter could well be rephrased thus: "Those who say that religion has nothing to with politics do not know what politics is all about."

Religion, religions and the state

In various parts of the world, at various critical points of national and international life, religion and the state (and state religious policy in particular) have become subjects of intense and contentious political and policy discussion. Even in China, for example, which is a declared secular socialist state, it is a lively subject of policy discussion. As this huge country of nearly 1.4 billion people moves forward with modernization, discussions of religious policy go beyond general debates about the place of religion in a socialist society. They include relatively detailed discussions about where in social and political life religious bodies and organizations may operate, the foreign control of religious bodies and movements, the intellectual and cultural contributions of world religions to Chinese life, and the distinctions that need to be made between "good" and "evil" religions. Such discussions are fought out in the streets, in judicial courts in Hong Kong and other cities in China, and in foreign policy meetings about the smuggling of Bibles into the country. These are just a few specific examples of how the issue of religion and politics – in particular, religion and the state – must be raised in a new and critical manner.

The enduring problem

At the heart of the question of religion and the state is the fact that both of them represent and constitute centres and claims to authority, obligation and power over the lives of people. They are poles around which groups and movements are organized for the promotion of and adherence to certain goals, principles, values and demands on individual and corporate life.

Many definitions of religion or of the religious life incorporate the notion that they have something to do with what is perceived as ultimate or sacred and around which beliefs and practices encompassing the whole of human existence are affirmed to be inviolate. Paul Tillich summed this up with his description of religion as "the state of being grasped by an ultimate concern which qualifies all other concerns as preliminary and which itself contains the answer to the question of the meaning of our life".[2] This character of religion as the bearer and interpreter of what is ultimate and sacred in the light of which all other aspects of life are to be considered as preliminary has in its theistic form been proclaimed in the notion of "none other gods", used by Christians in the struggle against fascism and authoritarian expressions of the state.

Definitions of the state may not seem so sublime. However, even in their non-authoritarian forms they embody equally encompassing – if not transcendent – notions of authority and allegiance. The state in modern political life is the embodiment of supreme political organization and power. Few, if any, are exempted from its encroaching hand. We do not choose the state to which we belong. On the contrary, it is the condition into which we are born. We might at a later time have the opportunity to change its form, or to leave it in favour of another, but life in a state is something we cannot escape. There are varying degrees of freedom, opportunity and obligation that different states accord to their members. The state by its very nature, however, is empowered to use instruments of violence and force to compel obedience to its laws and regulations. This is a power that is given to nobody else. It can restrict and limit personal freedoms, desires and activities in the preservation of its security. It collects economic contributions from its constituents for the support of its programmes. It can call on and compel the obedience and service unto death of its people in the defence of its existence and interests.

There is in short an inherent clash in the existence and practice of one in relation to the other. Given their reach, how can they coexist? This in fact has been one of the primary issues of modern political construction. In the light of the increasingly self-conscious political involvement of religions around the world, and the equally intense relations of religions with each other, the issue remains fresh and urgent. Is there really such a thing as a secular, non-religious sphere in which the life of the state is defined and within which the life of religion or religions is regulated? How do we look at all of these things in the global world into which we have been drawn?

Secular salvation or heavenly mandates?

Ideas of a secular society have emerged in the modern period as part of a supposedly larger historical process of secularization described by an earlier ecumenical study as "the withdrawal of areas of life and thought from religious – and finally also from metaphysical – control and the attempt to understand and to live in these areas in the terms which they alone offer".[3] The term secularization in short refers to a change in the relation between religion and culture and between religion and the various institutions of social life. It projects the perception and the experience that the dominant institutions of modern culture and society have been freed or removed from the ambit of religious control, and that conversely traditional religious institutions and religious perceptions and motivations of human activity have become marginal, if not obsolescent.[4]

Within this wider process of secularization, ideas of a secular state or of the separation of church, religion and the state emerged in part because of the perceived failings and inadequacies of the religious or church control of society and political life. At the heart of the idea of a secular state is the notion that the state as a whole is not grounded in or based upon a particular religious view of the nature of the universe and the place and destiny of humanity. It explicitly refuses in this sense to commit itself to a particular doctrine of the ultimate purpose of human society and of individual human beings within it, and does not require subscription to any particular religious doctrine or overt forms of religious behaviour as conditions for claiming the full rights and benefits of being a citizen. It is in this sense not necessarily anti-religious but religiously neutral and tolerant of a multiplicity of religions and religious groups.[5]

Much more can be said of the ideals. The reality is that secularization as a description of the relationship between religion and culture or between religion and politics and of the patterns of religious activity in the world is now beginning to be recognized as mostly an exceptional rather than a general phenomenon. Far from being universal, it seems to be mostly a European case and embodies assumptions about the place of European experience in relation to those of the rest of the world.[6] The social and cultural life of most of the rest of the world meanwhile surges with "furious" religious activity and "breathtaking" religious expansion.[7] In politics, this has meant that religious prescriptions are directly being brought into the affairs of the state and the definition of the character and goals of political community. In short, if in Europe the failings and inadequacies of the religious and ecclesiastical control of political life have been an impetus for the emergence of the ideas of a secular state, in Asia and in many other parts of the world the failings and inadequacies of the secular definitions of the state and the rapaciousness and oppressions of secular powers nationally and internationally have given rise to longings for "heavenly mandates" and religious contributions to social and political construction.

Some questions for revision and reconstruction

This leads to some very critical questions for revision and reconstruction of political life and orientations. Does democracy presuppose or require a secular state? Are secular powers any more hospitable to human freedoms and plurality than religious ones? Conversely, are religious powers necessarily more authoritarian and dogmatic than those who espouse secular perspectives?

Given the fact that in many parts of the world the nature and form, the populations and boundaries of the state are a legacy and creation of colonialism, in other words a product of conquest, what revisions and rearrangements need to be made to make them more viable and more a product of collective will in a globalizing world? What would be the religious components of such revisions?

Does economic development also presuppose the secularization of economic life or is it not in fact rooted in and does it not need a religious base from which to take off? On the one hand, there have been recent discussions of Confucian ethics and economic development in relation to economic modernization and the new economic spirit in China. On the other, discussions of economic progress in "secular circles" have underscored the importance of "courage", motivation, honesty and purpose as primary ingredients of economic development – ingredients that are not in the realm of the science of economics but in its religious base. Are we being brought back here to a new discussion of the relationship between religion and the formation of economic life?

Recent ecumenical social and political thought has tilted strongly towards an affirmation of the secular state and "the renewal of society in the direction of a truly secular and man-made order of life".[8] Is this still a viable position or are there now critical revisions that need to be made? Is there really such a thing as an independent and neutral secular sphere or secular power that stands above the religions and regulates their life together? On the contrary, as more and more people from the other religions are asking, is not secularization or the secular society really a "hidden" Christian project and a kind of Trojan horse for Christian mission?

What is religious liberty in a world in which we have become much more conscious of the depth and plurality of religious faith? In what sense and in what form is it really a universal human right? When are claims of religious liberty really a matter of exercising and projecting a "religious free market"? If, in economic life, there is need for protectionism from inordinate economic invasion and artificial products, when is there a need for a form of religious protectionism against inordinate religious invasion and artificial religious products? When is religious liberty religious imperialism?

Are religions because of their passion inevitable sources of conflict and division, or do their avowed values make them inherent partners in the search for peace and harmony?

Towards pluralistic human communities

These kinds of questions could very well be on the agendas of much-needed inter-religious dialogues at various levels and locations. They could also be an agenda for the revision and reconstruction of ecumenical social and political thought. They all point to the need to draw attention to the challenge of incorporating (not negating or avoiding) the issue of the plurality of religions in the construction of human community.

The project of a religiously plural human community as a principle for nation-building has in fact been a part of the political experience of countries in Southeast Asia. What may be the methodology and expression of such a project? Some notes on this experience might be instructive in this context, not so much as a matter of historical recollection but as a way of drawing attention to the issues that have made this project difficult but also promising.

As in other parts of the world, the people and territorial boundaries of many of the countries of Southeast Asia were literally constituted and carved out of the remains of colonial territories. At their beginnings, they exhibited more than anything else the territorial holdings that various Western powers controlled in this part of the world. The Philippines, for example, were defined as those territories that were ceded by Spain to the United States at the treaty of Paris that ended the Spanish-American war. This meant some 7000 islands, 86 linguistic groups and hundreds of ethnic identities. For Indonesia, which was constituted by the territories and peoples that were controlled by and which collectively declared independence from the Dutch, the numbers possibly triple and the territories widen considerably. It did not matter what previous boundaries were erased. It did not matter what ethnic, cultural or religious lines of loyalty were ignored. It did not matter what international relations and activities were previously established. The sheer force of Western colonial power put certain territories and their peoples together under one political control. When that political control was removed, what was left over were not the natural ingredients of nation-states but fragments of economic, social, political, cultural and religious life that had to be held and put together to form a viable political community. So many of the dimensions of conflict in Southeast Asia to this day issue from this colonial past.

The cultural, linguistic, ethnic, geographic and political ingredients and infrastructure that provided foundations for the nation-state in the West were not present. What were and still are present were multifarious conglomerates of sometimes hostile and antagonistic ethnic, religious, cultural and political forces that do not easily hold together. What can hold or bring people together in such a context? What can hold together Aceh in Sumatra and Ambon in the Moluccas under one national entity? What can hold together Muslims, Hindus and Christians in Java? What can hold together Christians and Muslims in Southern Philippines? It is indeed a wonder that these Asian nation-states have held together this long. It is also no wonder that the emergence and experience of modern Asian nation-states contain the explosive ingredients of conflict and division.

The task of nation-building in this context is, as Aristotle once said of politics, an architectonic task. In Southeast Asia, however, the building blocks include a plurality of ethnic, religious and cultural groups and traditions that are passionately self-conscious and jealous of their identities. It means literally building, designing and forging a new political community and structure amid religious plurality rather than simply assuming a national inheritance. Even the principles on which this new building is to be founded have had to be rethought. Pantjasila in Indonesia is an example of such design and the principles on which it is founded.

Pantjasila is a set of five principles enunciated by President Sukarno, the first president of Indonesia and one of the architects of the Indonesian republic, by which the preparatory committee for Indonesian independence defined the foundations of free Indonesia. In their original form, the five principles were nationalism, internationalism or the principle of humanity, political and economic democracy, social justice or social welfare, and belief in God. It is noteworthy that the five principles were rearranged when they were finally incorporated into the Indonesian constitution so that they now appear in the following sequence: belief in God, just and civilized humanity, Indonesian unity, democracy and social justice.[9]

This transfer of the principle of religion or belief in God as the first principle is important. In the words of M. Hatta, the first vice president, this provided the moral and religious base for both state and government. It also established "belief in God" as the guiding principle for the other four. It was also a principle that was meant to establish not only tolerance and mutual respect but also truth, justice, well-being and fraternity among all of the people. Article 29 of the constitution subsequently and expressly declares "the state is based upon belief in God". In this sense, instead of being a 'secular state' that is regulating religious activity, the Indonesian state is avowedly a "religious state" that recognizes religious plurality and encourages the practice of religious tolerance as the basis for justice, freedom and democracy and for a common human community. Sukarno and Hatta, in other words, recognized the deeply religious character of the Indonesian people and affirmed this as a positive rather than as a negative political value. They realized rightly that not to do this would have been fatal to the birth of the Indonesian republic.

There were many who scoffed at Pantjasila when it was first enunciated and viewed it as an artificial political concoction that was unrealistic and unworkable. M.M. Thomas, the eminent ecumenical leader from India, thought otherwise. He declared at a consultation of Muslims and Christians held in Manila in February 1996 that he considered Pantjasila as one of the most imaginative political constructs to have emerged anywhere in the world, without which the Indonesian republic would not have been born, much less survived. Thomas went on to say that without Pantjasila internecine strife would have broken out immediately after independence and the new Indonesian state would have been dismembered. [10] Pantjasila has been tested severely through the period of military government after Sukarno. It is being tested again, as religious conflict has broken out in several places in Indonesia. So far it is holding. Hopefully, it will continue to hold. The alternative to its idealism is more open and widespread religious conflict, the "clash of civilizations" in Indonesia.

Is religiously plural human community possible? Those who crafted Pantjasila thought so and believed that religion, "belief in God", is and should be the basis of a modern state or a modern world, and the guiding principle of justice, freedom and democracy, rather than the burden they should grudgingly carry or skilfully avoid. Pantjasila, in short, is not an old story that must now be laid to rest. It is a vibrant past that must be revisited and re-envisioned, revised perhaps but certainly not forgotten. Jeff Haynes has warned that the varieties of religious situations require us to identify common issues but also to recognize specific cases.[11] Indonesia in this sense is unique, but in many ways it is also typical. Despite continuing reports of religious conflict in the country, there are also dramatic reports of emerging manifestations of religiously plural human communities. They happen where people of various faiths and religious affiliations begin to be part of and cooperate in natural collective activities and organizations of the common life; for example, in civic organizations, health clubs, sports bodies, service agencies, and corporate associations and joint ventures of the economic life, so that as a result the key ingredients of their daily lives are the products of their joint endeavours. It is one of the supreme challenges of our time to imagine and build the political structures where more of these joint endeavours can take place, and make these the foundations for the remaking of world order.

NOTES

[1] J. Casanova, *Public Religions in the Modern World*, Chicago, Univ. of Chicago Press, 1994, p. 6.

[2] Paul Tillich, *Christianity and the Encounter of World Religions*, Minneapolis, Fortress, 1994, p. 3.

[3] Charles C. West, *The Meaning of the Secular. Report on a Consultation for University Teachers, 15–20 September 1959, Geneva*, Ecumenical Institute, Bossey, 1959, p. 14.

[4] Bert Hoedemaker, *Secularization and Mission: A Theological Essay*, Christian Mission and Modern Culture Series, Harrisburg PA, Trinity, 1998, pp. 1–11.

[5] D.L. Munby, *The Idea of a Secular Society and Its Significance for Christians*, Riddel Memorial Lectures, Oxford, Oxford UP, 1963, pp. 9–35.

[6] Grace Davie, *Europe: The Exceptional Case. Parameters of Faith in the Modern World*, Sarum Theological Lectures, London, Darton, Longman & Todd, 2002.

[7] Peter L Berger, "The De-Secularization of the World" (unpublished paper).

[8] Arend T. Van Leeuwen, *Christianity in World History: The Meeting of the Faiths of East and West*, London, Edinburgh House, 1964, p. 420. On this point, see also Charles C. West, "Community – Christian and Secular", in *Man in Community: Christian Concern for the Human in Changing Society*, Egbert de Vries ed., New York, Association Press, 1966, pp. 330–58.

[9] Peter D. Latuihamallo, "The Search for Consensus Democracy in the New Nations", in *Responsible Government in a Revolutionary Age*, Z.K. Matthews ed., New York, Association Press, 1966, pp. 217–18.

[10] M.M. Thomas, "Faith and Community: Muslim–Christian Cooperation and Understanding in a Changing Asia" (unpublished paper).

[11] Jeff Haynes, *Religion in Global Politics*, London, Longman, 1998.

8
Religious Liberty

TODOR SABEV

The specific nature of religious sentiments, the intimacy and depth of convictions, as well as the strength of community spirit within religious confessions, have generated and sustained their sensitivity to freedom. This particularly concerns witness and life in community. The aspiration to religious liberty has found new dimensions and a new dynamic in the process of shaping a pluralistic world, in a surprising resurgence of religions and their role in societies. The issue of liberty of religion has come to the fore as a major challenge and urgent task.

The history of religions is a long series of sufferings for believers and faith communities, a struggle for survival, and boldness to acquire space for witness in a hostile environment. Most religions have endured persecutions from neighbouring religionists, political powers and state institutions. No less embittered – and at times violent – were the fights within religious communions: orthodoxy versus heresy, sects and schismatics; divisions between Eastern and Oriental (post-Chalcedonian) Orthodox; fatal schisms between Eastern and Western Christians, then between Catholics and Protestants during the 16th and 17th centuries. Above all there were the events related to the crusades in the East, the inquisition and religious wars in the West. Intolerance and discord also occurred within the Protestant family. Nevertheless, the proliferation of confessions and congregations and confrontation with Catholics opened the way towards consideration of the value of religious freedom.

In more recent history, trends towards "majority" and "minority" religions, of "national churches" and "traditional" and "predominant" confessions, have sometimes led to the inappropriate interdependence of religion, nation and state, and tension between denominations at a national level.

However, history also provides examples of positive inter-religious attitudes and contacts. There have been periods of peaceful coexistence between Orthodox, Jews and Muslims, often sustained for centuries.

Mutual understanding and conversations between adherents of different religions also took place. Such dialogue is illustrated by the great missionaries Cyril and Methodius in the 9th century. It was inspired by theological ideas (e.g. *Logos spermatikos*) and the humanism of early church writers, especially Justin Martyr, Tertullian, Clement and Athanasius of Alexandria, and Lactantius. They thought, in summary, that "nothing is more contrary to religion than restraint". Religious conviction and practice "is a fundamental human right (and) a privilege of nature". Religion "must be adopted freely and not by force". According to Lactantius, religion is an issue of personal will and conviction. "Nothing is so much a matter of free will as religion, and no one can be required to worship what he [or she] does not will to worship."

Similar considerations were taken into account and articulated by enlightened people during the middle ages, the Renaissance and the Reformation. The peace of Westphalia in 1648 contributed to putting an end to extreme religious divisions. A number of great personalities defended freedom of thought, conviction and religion. From the 19th century onwards, systematic persecution motivated by anti-religious philosophy was gradually diminishing. In post-war situations, due attention was given to the problems of minorities, including religious groups. At its conference in Jerusalem in 1928, the International Missionary Council spoke loudly in favour of freedom and defence of minorities, as well as of dangerous "symptoms of a religious imperialism". The Life and Work conference in Oxford in 1937 established the framework of ecumenical tasks for religious liberty.

The tragedy of the second world war and subsequent years affected human rights and the life of religions. Atheistic ideologies and totalitarian regimes in many countries, fanaticism, tribal and ethnic problems, and the cold war all troubled the international community. The establishment of the United Nations and other means for strengthening solidarity, peace and renewal gradually led to new hope and new challenges for religion.

The United Nations and other organizations as promoters of religious liberty

The issue of human rights was at the heart of the UN from its foundation in 1945. Article 1 of the UN charter proclaimed respect for the fundamental liberties of all people, without distinction of race, sex, language and religion.

In 1948 the UN general assembly adopted the Universal Declaration of Human Rights, recognizing the "inherent dignity" and equal rights "of all members of the human family". They "should act towards one another in a spirit of brotherhood" (art. 1). "Everyone has the right to freedom of thought, conscience and religion." This includes "freedom to change his/her religion or belief, and freedom, either alone or in community with others, in public or private, to manifest his/her religion or belief in teaching, practice, worship and observance" (art. 18).

Two international covenants of 1966 affirmed civil, political, economic, social and cultural rights. Three conventions – European (1950), American (1969) and African (charter, 1981) – contributed to regional human rights. Some of them supported the liberty "to have or to adopt a religion" (art. 18 of the Covenant on Civil and Political Rights) as well as to choose and guarantee religious and moral education of children (art. 13 of the Covenant on Economic, Social and Cultural Rights). The principles of the Final Act of Helsinki (1975) were very important for countries, churches and other faiths in Central and Eastern Europe.

Subsequent to these, the Declaration on the Elimination of all Forms of Intolerance and of Discrimination based on Religion or Belief (1981) was of particular value. Referring to positions already expressed in previous statements, the Declaration emphasized that religion and belief are among the fundamental elements in people's conception of life. Therefore, "freedom of religion... should be respected and guaranteed" (preamble and art. 1:1, 2). It "may be subject only to such limitations as are prescribed by law and are necessary to protect public safety, order, health and morals or the fundamental rights and freedoms of others" (art. 1:3). Any discrimination and intolerance based on religion or other beliefs should be prohibited (arts 2–4). Children "shall be brought up in a spirit of understanding, tolerance, friendship among peoples, peace and universal brotherhood". An important means for achieving this ideal is the "respect for freedom of religion or belief of others" (art. 5:3). Article 6 articulates more comprehensively the nature, frame and function of religious liberty:

– worship, appropriate places of worship, and right to assemble;
– charitable and humanitarian institutions;
– necessary articles and materials for religious life;
– relevant publications;
– teaching of religion in suitable places;
– right to receive voluntary financial and other help;
– training, appointment, election or designation by succession of appropriate religious leaders;
– observance of religious holidays, ceremonies, days of rest;
– communications at national and international levels.

At its 43rd session in 1987, the UN Commission on Human Rights urged all states to contribute to the implementation of the declaration of 1981. They were asked to encourage understanding, tolerance and respect in matters relating to freedom of religion, working at all levels and by effective means: supervision, training, education, etc. This would strengthen people's awareness about respect of "different religions and beliefs" (para. 7). Universities and other academic and research institutions were invited "to undertake programmes and studies" towards that aim (para. 8).

The authority of these various documents (reached through an arduous process of preparation) became a driving force for international law and national legislation. The declaration of 1981 is still a point of reference for universal standards, inspiration and correction in dealing with liberty of religion.

Since 1982, praiseworthy efforts have been made towards the implementation of UN decisions and recommendations about religious liberty. The working process has involved all the structures of the UN concerned with human rights and related problems. There was close interaction with UNESCO, NGOs, ecumenical bodies and specialized associations on religious liberty. A long series of conferences and studies was dedicated to vital subjects. Several reports were presented to the Commission on Human Rights by the UN special rapporteur assessing incidents, intolerance and discrimination in the area of religious liberty.

Contribution of the ecumenical movement

As already indicated, some early ecumenism of the 20th century expressed concern about freedom of religion. The Life and Work conference in Oxford in 1937 formulated the essential requirements for religious freedom; soon after, these provided a basis for the Commission of the Churches on International Affairs (CCIA)/WCC work in that field, an inspiration for UN documents on human rights, and even a kind of pillar for article 6 of the declaration of 1981.

Historically, and in terms of humanitarian presuppositions, the WCC and the UN have run a parallel course. The inaugural assembly of the WCC in 1948 shaped the ecumenical understanding of religious liberty. The assembly stressed freedom of religion as "an essential element in a good international order". In pleading for this freedom, Christians are not asking for any privilege "denied to others". "All men should have freedom in religious life"; namely, to determine their own faith and creed, their policies and practices; to express religious liberty in worship, teaching and practice; "to associate with others and to organize with them for religious purposes". WCC governing bodies were critical of totalitarianism and atheistic ideology, restrictions on religious liberty by state authorities, "dominant religious majorities" and "religious groups seeking dominance".

In its report entitled "Christian Witness, Proselytism and Religious Liberty", the WCC's third assembly in 1961 reiterated earlier pronouncements. It stressed that "freedom to manifest one's religion or belief, in public or in private and alone or in community with others, is essential to the expression of inner freedom" (art. 8). "It includes... preaching with a view to propagating one's faith and persuading others to accept it" and "performance of action of mercy or expression... of the implication of belief in social, economic and political matters". Christians have "responsibility for the rights of others" (arts 8, 9, 11) because "religious liberty as a consequence of God's creative work, of his redemption of man in Christ ... is not coercive" (art. 3). Churches should promote "the realization of religious liberty for all men" (art. 11). The assembly expressed its support for the UN Universal Declaration of 1948 (arts 5, 10). In 1963 the newly established WCC Secretariat for Religious Liberty published a scholarly study on the theological basis for Christian commitment to religious freedom.

The next assembly (Uppsala 1968), mindful of the inter-relatedness of all human rights, appealed for "a common understanding" and application of "the instruments of the UN and other organizations" concerning the "protection of human rights and fundamental liberties". The assembly asked "for the recognition and protection of the inherent dignity of men... full human equality... and respect for the adherents of all religions and ideologies".

The CCIA consultation in St Pölten in 1974 marked another important stage in Christian pilgrimage, responsibility and comprehensive understanding of human rights.

The statement of the WCC Nairobi assembly in 1975 paid due attention to basic guarantees for life, personal dignity and self-determination, participation in decision-making, cultural identity, minorities, sexism, racism, right to dissent, and religious freedom. The statement expressed "solidarity with people who suffer because of their religious faith and practice and... who stand in favour of political and social justice". "Religious liberty should never be used to claim privileges." "No religious community should plead for its own religious liberty without active respect and reverence for the faith and basic human rights of others." Churches are called to provide witness, intercessions, remedial assistance and effective support for all wronged believers. Religious bodies have "the right and duty to criticize the ruling powers when necessary, on the basis of their religious convictions". The statement reminded us that "many Christians in different parts of the world are in prison for reasons of conscience or for political reasons as a result of their seeking to respond to the total demands of the gospel" – a reverberation from a stormy discussion of religious liberty in Eastern Europe, especially the USSR. Some of these points were further elaborated in the WCC Study Paper on Religious Liberty (1980–81).

Ecumenical work on human rights, including the protection of religious liberty, brought together WCC structures (with the CCIA as the main instrument), the offices of Christian world communions (CWCs), regional and national ecumenical bodies, churches, available means of dialogue with other faiths, and secular organizations. Several of these partners worked together during the International Colloquium on the Contribution of World Religions to Human Rights (Paris 1989). The International Association for Religious Liberty and similar study centres in European countries shared in particular tasks.

Response: churches and other faiths

A significant number of churches involved in ecumenical councils and CWCs contributed to programmes, documents and actions relating to major issues of human rights. Good will was manifested in endeavours for an international standard of religious liberty. Yet, most often, priority was given to local problems, confessional concerns, and aspects of social life enabling Christian witness – the latter particularly in Eastern Europe and less developed countries.

The coordinating role of the Human Rights Advisory Group within the CCIA, the Human Rights Resource Office for Latin America, and the working committee of the Churches' Human Rights Programme for the Implementation of the Helsinki Final Act facilitated inter-regional exchange, ecumenical cooperation, growing awareness and solidarity about religious liberty.

Apart from collective contributions to the ecumenical process of theological interpretation of religious freedom, many individual churches – Protestant, Catholic, Orthodox, and CWCs – have elaborated their particular views on human rights and liberty of religion. Their common ground is the Bible, especially God's creative work, redemption in Christ, all-embracing love and peace, compassion and solidarity, reconciliation and forgiveness. The variety of views is due to different theological approaches, historical traditions and experience.

The renewal of the Roman Catholic Church that began with Pope John XXIII's encyclical *Pacem in Terris*, consolidated through the

Second Vatican Council, encompassed a constructive attitude to the international standard on human rights and religious liberty. The Catholic theological foundation and commitment to various dimensions of these matters are given in the Vatican II pastoral constitution *Gaudium et Spes*, and especially in *Dignitatis Humanae*. The Council declared its attachment to "the permanent binding force of universal natural law and its all-embracing principles". "Religious freedom has its foundations in the dignity of the person... created in the likeness of God." Therefore, "every type of discrimination, whether social or cultural... based on sex, race, colour... religion, is to be overcome and eradicated". The protection and the promotion of human "inviolable rights" is part of the "essential duties of government". A responsible society has the right "to defend itself against... abuses committed on pretext of freedom of religion".

In 1966 the WCC central committee expressed satisfaction with the Vatican Declaration on Religious Liberty, which proclaimed "full civil religious freedom, both individual and collective, for everybody everywhere". The WCC was "encouraged by the fact that there is now a large measure of agreement among all the churches in these matters". It opened up new perspectives "through brotherly consultation to overcome the practical difficulties which still exist".

The Roman Catholic Church participated in a series of human rights-religious liberty conferences and publications. Catholic representatives elaborated principles on religious freedom that were presented to the Madrid conference in 1980 as a contribution to the Helsinki follow-up. In his message to the heads of states and international organizations in January 1988, Pope John Paul II emphasized "religious freedom, inasmuch as it touches the most intimate sphere of the spirit, is a point of reference of the other fundamental rights and in some way becomes a measure of them". It is "a cornerstone of the structure of human rights, and... an irreplaceable factor in the good of individuals and of the whole of society". As far as state churches and other confessions are concerned, if in "peculiar circumstances... special recognition is given to one religious community... it is... imperative that the right of all... communities to religious freedom should be recognized and made effective in practice".

The Vatican remained consistent with former statements and practice. Nevertheless, a number of obstacles had appeared in connection with new religious movements (NRMs), conservative minorities and dissident voices within the Catholic church, as well as some restrictive attitudes of the holy see towards champions of liberation theology. NRMs and "sects" – with their peculiar structures, ways of proselytizing new adherents, scope of activity, methods of imposing "religious renaissance", and negative attitudes towards mainline religions – gradually provoked resistance and hostility. This jeopardized inter-religious relations and led to certain infringements of religious liberty. An anti-cults opposition took shape in several churches. Compared with similar situations in church history, the ecumenical movement was slow in its reactions and definitive stands. It suggested studies, discernment and an individual approach to multiform movements.

Inter-religious dialogues, international meetings and dramatic examples of intolerance in several regions exposed the attitudes of world religions to issues of human rights. Like Christian churches, representatives of other faiths based their theological reflections mostly on sacred scripture and tradition. Specialists in Judaism expressed a positive attitude to freedom and fundamental liberties in the light of the Old Testament, particularly the Law, the prophets, the psalmists and the experience of God's chosen people. Islamic visions were grounded in the Quran's texts about creation, fraternity, love and respect for the religions and peoples of the Book (e.g. prophets, patriarchs, Jesus Christ). They refer also to Surahs dealing with tolerance in relationships, wisdom and exhortation in missionary work, and discussion with others. Buddhists were ready to apply international standards of religious liberty in harmony with their own understanding of life and ethics, especially the Buddhist concept of liberation from suffering as accessible to all people. Buddhism values life in common. Altruism, friendship and love are considered the best virtues. Instead of fundamentalism there should be liberty of conscience, and a friendly disposition towards different religions and ideologies. The disciples of Confucius were proud of his humanistic doctrine of the dignity and equality of people, harmony in difference, love for neighbours as brothers and sisters, and care for those in need.

However, such generous religious/ethical dispositions were not easy to put into practice. For instance, some Muslim representatives had already stated that a clause about changing religious adherence in article 18 of the Universal Declaration of Human Rights was unacceptable. Others thought that, as the Quran claims the right to persuade people to change their faith, non-Islamic religions should have the same right of mission. Since 1981, and on several occasions, Islamic states have asserted they could not guarantee an individual's right within the Muslim community to change religion. Publicly or in private, many confessions experienced similar problems.

Problems implementing international agreements

Until the mid-1970s, churches and other religions in Marxist/communist countries sought only to survive. This was especially true in the USSR and Central and Eastern Europe in the Stalin and Khrushchev eras, with their aggressive anti-religious campaigns and cruel persecution. Similar conditions prevailed in Albania and in China during the cultural revolution. In 1967 China proclaimed itself as the first atheistic state in the world.

Many leaders and members of religious communities in such countries accepted a modus vivendi of collaboration with civil authorities on issues related to peace and justice – in the spirit and the intention of Christian witness, but also in compliance with state policy. This had some positive effects on religious freedom, as well as implications of compromise with those who were trying to mould an atheistic society. A large number of believers opted for non-conformity and martyrdom. The constitutions and resulting laws officially guaranteed basic human rights, including some aspects of the functioning of religions, but other aspects of religious life were restricted or bluntly ignored, especially religious education, work with youth, charity associations and political activity. Brutal atheistic propaganda, protected by state legislation, operated as an ideological tool for decades, while Christians and other believers were prevented from disseminating religious propaganda. Trials, persecution, imprisonment, heavy loss of clergy and lay people, and martyrdom were all experienced during this tragic time for religions. The slow process of change in government policy and attitudes towards religion started in the 1960s and continued for two decades. Even then, suppression of dissent and other movements continued throughout *perestroika* and *glasnost* until 1990–91.

Religious revivalism in many countries around the world led also to increased fundamentalism, proselytism, intolerance and discrimination towards other religions. In Islamic countries these trends found expression in religious-based laws. In other parts of the world, legislation enforced inequality between "traditional", "national" and "patriotic" religions and other confessions. Minority religions almost everywhere experienced a high degree of intolerance and disadvantage, particularly "sects" and NRMs. In 1977 Philip Potter, general secretary of the WCC, identified the following problems: harassment, torture, deprivation of rights, and assassination of Christians because of their faith and solidarity with those who struggle for rights.

In 1986 the UN Commission on Human Rights expressed its concern about "frequent... reports from all parts of the world" revealing that "because of governmental actions, universal implementation of the Declaration [on Human Rights] has not yet been achieved". Its statement spoke of "incidents and... actions inconsistent with the provisions of the Declaration". In 1987 the special rapporteur of the Commission on Human Rights referred to legislative discrimination, forced assimilation of religious minorities, and the intransigent attitudes of one religion to another.

Voluminous reports presented to the UN Commission on Human Rights over the years revealed a variety of problems for the implementation of religious liberty. The report for 1990 spoke of extremist and fanatical governmental actions as "the principle cause of discriminations or of explosions of violence of a religious character". This became a destabilizing factor in the international system, a source of tension and conflict between states.

In the final decade of the 20th century, dramatic changes in Central and Eastern Europe, some improvement in other countries, and the options for globalization promised a better climate for international relations. This also nourished hope for more freedom of religion.

Role of secular international bodies

The UN special rapporteur's 1991 assessment expressed gratification over the changes "in the enjoyment of the rights and freedoms" (including religion) "that have taken place in Eastern Europe". The tenth anniversary of the Declaration on the Elimination of All Forms of Intolerance and of Discrimination Based on Religion or Belief in 1991 was a propitious occasion for the UN and other organizations to call upon states and all parties concerned to fulfil their commitment to religious freedom. In the same year, the UN general assembly adopted resolution 46/131 on the elimination of all forms of religious intolerance. Having reaffirmed the declaration of 1981, the document exhorted states to provide constitutional and legal guarantees for liberty of religion. This implies work for elimination of intolerance, promotion of comprehension and mutual respect, and protection of worship places and sanctuaries, as well as setting up the necessary observation, information, publicity and communication (arts 2–6, 11, 13–16). Specific attention was given also to universities and institutes – their research work, programmes and studies related to religious liberty (arts 7–9).

By 1992 the international pact on civil and political rights had been ratified by 111 countries. It endorsed earlier statements on religious liberty and made the commitment to respect parents' and legal tutors' liberty concerning the religious education and morality of their children.

Parallel with meetings of specialized UN bodies, several international conferences took place in the course of the 1990s, attended by representatives of states, cultural institutions and religions. Among the most significant were the World Conference on Human Rights (Vienna 1993), the International Congress on Education for Human Rights and Democracy (Montreal 1993), the UNESCO meeting on "the contribution of religions to the culture of peace" (Barcelona 1994), another UNESCO seminar on the same subject (Grenada 1995), and still another (Sienna 1995) with more specific focus on "tolerance and the law". There followed the International Congress on Religious Liberty (Rio de Janeiro 1997), the Oslo conference on liberty of religion and of conviction (1998), the International Conference (under the auspices of UNESCO) on Interreligious Dialogue (Tashkent 2000), the Millennium World Peace Summit (New York 2000), and the UNESCO International Colloquium on Human Rights and Liberty of Religion (Paris 2001). Some of the documents of these fora draw attention to the following points:

- Religions have contributed to peace and mutual comprehension in the world, but they have also been responsible for divisions and hostilities.
- There is need for repentance and mutual pardon, for cultivation of spirituality and its manifestation in acts of compassion, charity and love.
- We are called to respect freedom of religion and the rights of minorities.
- Preventive measures against violence and terrorism are significant.
- Religions are expected to be a constructive force in society.
- Dialogue should be encouraged as part of the culture of peace-making.
- Religious education is important, with a need to plan for education favouring human rights and democracy in a pluralistic society.
- Religions are expected to share their theological bases, attitudes and commitment to tolerance and peace.
- International organizations and state authorities reinforced their attempts to adapt legislation to new requirements.

Throughout the programmes of all these conferences, the UN and other partners helped clarify topical issues such as the confessional state, church–state relations, the constitution and religion in Islamic countries, minorities and new political entities in international law, human rights and religious liberty in various continents and states (particularly in Europe), and "sects" and democracy. Specialized associations such as the International Association for Defence of Religious Liberty were instrumental in sponsoring several conferences on religious liberty and helped publish relevant studies and documents.

Reactions of ecumenical organizations, churches and other religions

The WCC, regional and national ecumenical bodies, CWCs, a number of churches and other faiths increased their participation in the work for human rights and religious liberty. Many of them were partners in the events listed above. For example, representatives of more than a dozen religious traditions attended the Barcelona conference. The meeting of the Parliament of Religions (Chicago 1993) provided impetus to dialogue and tolerance. The Atlanta (1994) and Oslo (1998) conferences endorsed the ideas of an international coalition and a strategy for progress in the defence of religious liberty. Both were echoed in churches and religious organizations. Attention concentrated on dialogue, education, studies, mediation and prevention of violence.

Ecumenical organizations approached the issue of religious liberty within the spectrum of human rights, regional perspectives and proposals made by churches. Statements were issued on the death penalty, indigenous people and land rights, foreign debt, cultural minorities, national ethnic religions, ethno-religious nationalism, and new developments in former socialist countries.

Church leaders, theologians, sociologists and others elaborated on the theological grounds for defending religious freedom; for example, human rights according to the Bible (D. Tutu) and religious dimensions of human rights (M.E. Marty).

Persisting difficulties, signs of hope

New constitutions and laws on religion in the Russian Federation and Central and Eastern Europe protect religious liberty, but the privileged position of majority and national confessions remains. In most cases these are the Orthodox churches, but in Croatia it is the Catholics and in Baltic countries it is Protestant churches. Some "non-traditional" and "foreign-origin" communities have been suspected of undermining the national ethos, unity and security. Nationalism, xenophobia and antisemitism have harmed Christian witness and inter-religious collaboration. Ethnic and religious conflicts and war in former Soviet republics and Yugoslavia have had harmful consequences. Internal divisions in the Orthodox churches and state registration of "schismatics" also raised questions of religious discrimination, intolerance and disagreement between secular and canon law.

Signs of positive change in state policy towards religion also appeared in other countries influenced by Marxist ideology. Old problems and the usual government justifications for the restriction of religion also persisted. "Patriotic religious organizations" in China enjoy traditional favour.

Legislation in some regions with prevailing Christian populations took new steps towards overcoming discrimination, but still faced serious challenges. Even more democratic countries have been addressed by the UN rapporteur on particular cases, alleging restriction of religion (e.g. problems in practising traditional religion in the USA; wearing head-scarves in French state schools; conscientious objection to military service in Switzerland; new procedures for the selection of muftis and limitation of religious minorities in Greece). Western Europe has achieved a "relatively unified attitude to the issues of religious liberty", yet experience has demonstrated that countries are far from unanimity. The local implementation of internationally agreed principles met with a "variability of limits". Specialists revealed five persisting polarizations: geo-cultural (West-East), Occidental-Oriental; theory and practice; public and private; majority and minority; pluralism and proselytism.

Developments in a number of Muslim countries were characterized as growing religious fundamentalism and fanaticism, engendering extremism and violence. The religious life of minority Christian communities was restricted, whereas hundred of mosques and Islamic cultural institutions were established in Europe, the Americas and Australia. In a few regions with traditional Christian populations (e.g. Armenia and Ethiopia), representatives of the majority church were tempted to revenge themselves on Muslim neighbours.

On the positive side, some Muslim governments (e.g. in Tunisia, Libya and Egypt) restrained intolerance. Unfortunately, Islamic laws disregarded some UN agreements of the international community. Comparative studies of religions identified both convergence and divergences between international agreements and recent Islamic documents on human rights. Muslims and Hindus were becoming more intransigent regarding people leaving their communities. Proselytism gradually reached a critical stage in interconfessional relations (Christian and others), not only in Europe, but also worldwide.

Tragic events and illicit activities within sects and NRMs increased inter-religious tension. A new round of discussions considered the delicate space and inter-relations between democracy, law, liberty of religion and restriction of practices which endanger good order, the stability of state institutions, and tranquillity in society.

Many countries refuse to register communities such as Jehovah's Witnesses, Christian Scientists, the Unification Church and the Hare Krishna Movement. In many countries today there are various structures in place to defend religious groups, alongside anti-cult associations and NGOs that aim to protect pluralistic society from abuse and manipulation by pseudo-religions.

Summarizing the problems reflected in UN reports on religious liberty, one can identify the following permanent factors: complexity, variety, hesitancy, inconsistency and controversial assessment. Tension, intolerance, conflict, persecution, punishment and continuous suffering of religious minorities throughout the world are reported by official documents. In 1999 the UN again emphasized and named "persistent violations" of religious liberty, such as restrictive state policy, pending problems of restitution of property of religions, inter- and intra-communitarian struggles, politico-religious movements, and schismatics. A UN report in 2000 again reported the basic tendencies and violations of human rights.

Ecumenical service for religious liberty

Embracing a large number of organizations and churches, the ecumenical movement provided a valuable service to the common ideal and aspiration of religious liberty. Its contribution included propitious initiatives, sharing in the UN programmes, and active participation in conferences, studies, statements and discussions on vital topics. The WCC, in particular, facilitated churches' access to UN structures. It monitored, advocated and made public statements. Especially appreciated were interfaith dialogues, the development of inter-regional exchange programmes, the elaboration of the notion of religious liberty (its substance, components and significance) and theological considerations for the protection of freedom.

Through the Joint Working Group, the WCC and the Roman Catholic Church came to a better understanding of the nature and the harm of proselytism. The WCC and the Conference of European Churches mediated to overcome Catholic-Orthodox tensions over uniatism relating to Eastern rite Catholic churches. Orthodox, Catholic, Protestant and Muslim leaders, accompanied by the WCC, CEC and the Vatican, have maintained dialogue and rendered conciliatory witness in times of trouble in Yugoslavia and the ex-Soviet republics.

The WCC and sister ecumenical organizations worked on the delicate matter of religious liberty in hostile atheistic or totalitarian environments through discernment, taking into consideration the results of previous experience, and following the advice of local churches. Thus, the ecumenical movement took the risk of passing through some "silent years", honestly recognized in 1990 as a weakness. Both the ecumenical organizations and the churches (East and West) "could have done much more" to defend the "majesty of truth".

Besides letters, statements and conversations with state representatives and leaders of churches in Eastern Europe (e.g. on the problems of dissidents, the Turkish minority in Bulgaria, and recent legislation in the Russian Federation), the WCC, Western churches and ecumenical partners joined in sustaining local efforts for protection of religion. Meetings of ecumenical governing bodies, conferences and consultations on peace and justice, ecumenical team visits and staff travel in communist countries enabled private and public contacts, listening to people, raising questions and expressing disappointment concerning religious life. The participation of Eastern churches in the Human Rights Programme for the Implementation of the Helsinki Final Act was another incentive to liberty. The "East–West human contacts group" and bilateral dialogues between churches in Eastern and Western Europe also had an effect on relaxation of restrictions and openings to freedom.

Conclusion

Much has been achieved in the struggle for religious liberty. However, there is still a long way to go. We live in a fragile, divided world. Healing and uniting comprise a great task. Religion is a fundamental factor for peace and democracy. Freedom of religion is the "foundation of all other civil liberties".

The protection of religious liberty has become more demanding. Many religions, "sects", NRMs and schismatics consider any restriction in their activity and expression of liberty as repression. Regional, cultural, social and political differences intertwine with religious integrism. The decline of state anti-religious ideology and policy is a promising sign, but other disturbing phenomena persist all over the world. In most countries the state authority continues to be "the main actor on the scene of religious liberty". There are ambiguities in the wording of legislation and even more so in its performance. The principle "neither privileges nor disadvantages" remains inapplicable in many countries. Often, religion is considered as a synthesis of social, cultural and national values. The social and political manifestations of religion are frequent. As in previous decades, issues of religious liberty are politicized by governments with different social and political orientations. Human rights and religious freedom have been subordinated to economic pragmatism and political interests.

Christians and other faith adherents complain about the growing scale of anti-religious liberalism and the erosion of traditional moral values. This may generate hatred, hostility and new forms of persecution. All these matters reinforce the continuing challenges and urgent tasks of the ecumenical movement.

9
Religion and Feminist Thought

MARIA JOSÉ ROSADO NUNES and JANE I. SMITH

The great advance achieved by feminist study of religion has been to introduce the experience of women into a body of knowledge believed to be neutral. *(Monica Tarducci)*

It is possible to claim that religion is one of the areas which has been most exposed to the impact of feminism, both by the changes brought about in women's religious practices and by its influence on the development of a new discourse – feminist theology – and on the study of religion in general.

It is not easy, and perhaps not even appropriate, to distinguish between the feminist study of religion and feminist theology, given the close connections between these two approaches to religion. However, the following two essays pursue these two lines of feminist thought – the feminist study of religion and feminist theology – and suggest some of the ways in which they overlap and the careful distinctions that must be maintained between them.

Feminism and the Study of Religion

MARIA JOSÉ ROSADO NUNES

Just as has happened consistently in the field of theology with the establishment of a new field of study (feminist theology), so, in the humanities, innovations have come about by applying theories and methods drawn from feminism to the analysis of religion. Despite men's historic predominance in the study of religion, feminist thinkers have been very successful in their efforts to become a respected and influential presence in all areas of the discipline.

Initially, criticism of religion was political and militant. Religion was seen as an effective instrument for controlling women and keeping them socially and religiously subordinate. More recently, the development of more analytical research with an empirical foundation has applied feminist research concepts and methods to the domain of religion. It has thus become possible to evaluate the complexity of relations existing within the religious field. The ambiguous and contradictory links of women with religion and of religion with women within religious organizations have been laid bare.

Feminist theoretical and methodological concepts have enabled us to call religion into question from the point of view of social relations between the sexes, or of gender, and examine the ways in which religious beliefs, practices and images contribute not only to reproducing inequality between women and men but also to overcoming it. Empirical observation has shown that religions are complex social phenomena, full of contradictions, which do not function always and in all societies as conservative forces. Given certain circumstances, they can function as mobilizing forces, inspiring women to resist their power to exercise discipline over them. In a significant number of research projects, religion has appeared as a motivating force for political action and social change.

In all fields of the study of religion it has become one of the fundamental issues to understand the way in which symbolic activities – beliefs, rituals and religious discourse – which seem to be immune from sexual differentiation, are in fact shaped by it. It has thus become a concern of feminist researchers to demonstrate how religion is presented in its social and historical reality as permeated and shaped by gender relationships, as well as by relationships of class and race. This assertion is based on evidence from sociology: "Men and women interpret religious symbols differently... Many hypotheses suggest that gender is a mediator of religious experience, which lends weight to existing studies that suggest the importance of 'developing an understanding of ways in which gender shapes one's experience of being and becoming a religious person'."[1]

However, doubts have persisted in many feminist approaches to religion as to whether a movement initiated in a male-dominated church is capable of emancipating women and being open to their demands. In Canada in 1995 a multidisciplinary symposium, "Femmes et Religions", directed by the sociologist Denise Veillette, sought to discover the reason why men had appropriated the sacred to themselves. How has the male gender been able to control the rites and practices, discourse and belief, and images of the divine?

Feminist analyses of religion have led to criticism of institutional power and of the social and political effects of the involvement of women in religion. Feminist criticism of the sociology of social organizations has provided the tools necessary to criticize existing analyses of religious institutions. Women studying religion have shown that it is inadequate to employ categories that are supposedly gender neutral. Employing such categories actually prevents us from seeing factors that are essential for analyzing religion as it really is. In Catholicism, for example, the generic use of categories such as clergy and hierarchy, without reference to the fact that they are referring to an exclusively male group, hampers analysis of the power relationships that dominate the organization of that particular religious institution.

Apart from empirical study, feminist researchers have further devoted themselves to theoretical criticism by analyzing classical authors in the sociology of religion. Bologh[2] and Erickson[3] have pointed out the inherently sexist nature of their thought, which distorts their analysis of religion. The rigid division between sacred and profane in Durkheim's work, which he presents as a constitutive element in religion and society, results in women being relegated to the profane/private domain. Only men are the bearers of the sacred, protagonists of beliefs and rites by which new relations are forged and society itself is created. Max Weber, too, associates men with religions that are based on rational asceticism, which enables the figure of the leader, or hero, to emerge. What remains for women is magical religion, embodying eroticism and removing them from "action in the world". The result is men who are active and women who are passive, both in religion and in society as a whole.

A further area in which feminists have made significant contributions is that of the history of religion. In assessing the present state of feminist religious science, Lacelle[4] places women historians among "the first to become aware of the selective and sexist memory underlying historical constructs". By questioning existing historical writing and its silence surrounding female leaders and by confronting the problem of sources, women historians of religion have sought to write an alternative history in which facts, personalities and processes are shaped by relationships between the sexes. "Including the category of gender and linking it with those of social class and race is useful not only for writing the history of religion, but is also an essential key to understanding the invisible history of women in religion and their relations with all forms of power structures."

Finally, among the main critical concerns of feminist studies of religion is the issue of real opportunities for change favourable to women in the historically mainstream religions. For some women researchers and for a certain number of women theologians, androcentrism (male-centredness) is an inherent element in religion: the involvement of women in religion is then seen as an expression of their conservatism. These researchers and theologians are proposing the creation of alternative religious spaces in which women can enable new and innovative ways of relating to the sacred to emerge. For others, the problem of the historical religions is that men have appropriated them to themselves. One of the objectives of future research must be to recover the traditions and foundations of the historical religions, so that women can find their own place within them.

Present challenges and future perspectives

One of the major problems confronting women in contemporary religion is the resurgence of conservative forces, their power and their organization. They are not limited to religious groups, but are also political. This connection is important because religious fundamentalism cannot be understood without reference to the growing political conservatism in international relations. It began in the 1980s, became particularly strong in the 1990s, and is the basis on which religious conservatism is sustained and expanded. European elections, the policies of the Bush government (especially after 9/11), the war by Israel against the Palestinian people, the way in which the crisis in Argentina has been dealt with – all these are trends in international policy which are expressions of this kind of politico-religious fundamentalism. Such actions are extremely damaging to the world's poor, among whom women and blacks are present in significant numbers.

The presence of conservative religious groups and their activities has been somewhat surprising, as one of the debates current in the analysis of religion in the 1970s was on so-called "secularization", understood either as the decline in the ability of religion to guide people's daily behaviour or as the decline in its political influence on nation-states. Today, however, countless studies identify religious fundamentalism as a powerful and active political force. It is a force that resists ratification of international agreements concluded by various meetings and assemblies arranged under the auspices of the United Nations and other international bodies. These meetings have made proposals for implementing government measures in favour of human rights, specifically (in the context of this chapter) the rights of women.

In the case of Latin America, for example, despite the acknowledged tendency towards fragmentation and diversification in the field of religion, with a decline in Catholic dominance, it can be said that, on the one hand, Christian cultural patterns persist and pervade society. They guide people's (particularly women's) behaviour, especially in terms of sexuality and human reproduction. On the other hand, there is a constant attempt by religious groups to influence public policy and to guide national legislation in the direction of the values and standards they defend. These are exactly the characteristics of what has been called "religious fundamentalism", fundamentalism as distinguished from its original meaning, which was limited to Protestantism. Courtney Howland states,

> One of the key aspects of religious fundamentalism … is its tendency to direct its political action towards making the laws of a state, of a country, conform to religious teachings, particularly in areas affecting the rights of women... Fundamentalists concentrate especially on the sexuality of women – which they consider a danger and threat to society – and they thus mobilize to regulate and control women's sexuality and reproduction by means of various measures... Thus a number of standards are established to ensure that women's sexuality is controlled, not by women themselves, but by men.[5]

In this regard it is relevant also to speak of a "catholic fundamentalism". But the most extreme cases of this type occur in Islamic countries, where restrictive andocentric understandings of women's rights prevail.

Rosemary Radford Ruether recalls that all fundamentalist movements have in common "rejection of modernity and attempts to re-establish the public role of religion, if not religious nation-states, so as to contain what has been seen as the demon of secularism, with its lack of established public values". But she adds,

> Perhaps the strongest likeness between the various fundamentalisms is their attempt to re-establish rigid patriarchal control over women and their hostility to the principle of equality, freedom of action, and one's right to control one's own sexuality and fertility... It would be difficult to say that the Vatican is less obsessed (than other religious groups) with equality and women's reproductive rights, considered to be the synthesis of the evil of modern secularism and the cause of the death of civilization.[6]

Promotion of a patriarchal family model, emphasis on the role of women as wives and mothers, and restriction of their activity in the public sphere – all of them values common to the various religious fundamentalisms – combine with local elements of culture shaped by a religious ethos.

One of the strategies for action by conservative religious groups opposed to the agenda of women's rights is to make a contrast between proposals concerning women's rights and values presented as typical of the cultures and traditions of the South. Thus,

> It is ironic for women that those who support and promote world globalization – with contradictory consequences for women and in large part harmful to the countries of the South – are frequently the same people who support the break with the traditional patriarchal order. On the other hand, among those who oppose globalization, there are those who do so for the sake of values and control systems that openly oppress women.[7]

The Vatican, particularly, strives to appear on the international scene as a defender of economic justice for the countries of the South, while at the same time attempting to replace talk of "human rights for women" with more abstract talk about "human dignity" based on the Christian religious tradition.

In this regard, feminism is viewed as part of "Western domination by the first world", an expression describing cultural domination by the North over the South. "This demonization of feminism as Western", says Ruether,

> totally ignores the fact that for more than two decades women in Asia, Africa, Latin America and the Middle East have been creating their own contextualized forms of feminism and with their own voices speaking of their rights and demands. Such a globalization of feminism was evident at the world conference of women in Beijing, where representatives of women's movements from all nations met and networked, forming relationships with one another.[8]

At this historic moment, when women's movements are attempting to articulate social justice and affirm the rights of individuals, these contradictions make it more difficult to engage in the political negotiations necessary for the advance of women's rights. In the case of Latin America these tensions are yet more acute, since for a large number of women from poor social strata, the churches often appear as places where they can find protection and help. This is a contradiction that in practice hampers recognition of the negative elements in religion for women regarding their freedom in the field of reproductive health and sexuality.

Another particularly relevant issue, when discussing the human rights of women, is the argument based on cultural relativism. How is it possible to defend women's rights in face of the huge differences to be found among women – economic, social, religious, racial and ethnic? Criticism is directed at the use of terms such as woman, motherhood, family and sexuality in specific situations as basic categories.[9] Exaggeration of these culture-bound, anti-universalist positions ultimately makes it difficult to present women's rights as universal human rights. In a review of these debates in recent years, Susan Moller Okin, similarly to Ruether, states that, at the very moment when those debates were taking place among feminist theorists, "feminists in the third world active at local level, as well as some Western feminists who were ready to overcome difficulties, were working together to achieve recognition of women's rights as human rights by the international human rights community".[10] She continues by recalling that these women from widely differing cultures – Africa, Asia, Latin America, and the rich countries of the North – after hearing women from their own countries, organizing encounters and creating regional and sub-regional networks, and sharing their knowledge in international encounters, came to the conclusion that all women have much in common. Discrimination, certain patterns of gender violence and economic and sexual exploitation appear as virtually universal phenomena.

It is not a question of denying differences arising from the different forms taken by the nation-state because of local cultures and different class situations. "What was happening was that, through the channels of NGOs and other similar groups operating at different levels, many of the silent (silenced) voices of women were at last heard... Once they had spoken, they recognized that women are greatly affected by laws and customs concerning sexuality, marriage, divorce, childcare and family life as a whole."[11]

Even considering this immense diversity, it is possible to recognize a common experience of subordination and resistance. In the most recent international conferences appeal to the universality of human rights has had a positive effect. "Many of the violations of basic human rights suffered by women occur within the family, and are justified by appeal to culture, religion or tradition."[12] Thus, one of the great gains of the Beijing action platform was "a powerful rejection, as never before, of cultural justification for the violation of women's rights". Current perceptions of the family, of religion and of tradition were challenged in international documents. "The family" is now spoken of in the plural, which is what it really is, and tradition and religion have been relativized and stripped of their aura of timeless untouchable sacredness. On the basis of the principle of universality, all states should ensure that the physical integrity of the person's body is respected as a fundamental human right and commit themselves, for example, to abolishing practices of mutilation. This debate demonstrates how issues of women's rights and of sexuality are intrinsically related to the cultural and religious problems of their respective peoples and need to have universally accepted paradigms as a point of reference in order to confront them.

Note should be taken of the practice – sometimes legitimate, but often inappropriate – of appealing to respect for local cultures in order to discredit struggles against gender inequality, branding such struggles as divisive, secondary, illegitimate and attributable to "Western culture". Magdalena de Leon[13] quotes the case of indigenous Andean women who experience pronounced disadvantage and discrimination. The prevailing mindset among them causes them to affirm themselves as "Indigenous peoples", thus overshadowing any specific demands for them as women. The author's assessment is that this results in women's rights losing out. Even those Christian religious sectors considered to be progressive use this logic to deprive women's demands of legitimacy.

Conclusion

The issues discussed here provide an extensive agenda for religious leaders who are committed to proposals for social change leading to a situation of justice and peace. The demands of organized women's movements in the most widely differing countries, in different settings – political, social, cultural and religious – and in highly differing ways, are inextricably linked to struggles for social justice.

NOTES

[1] In Carol Drogus, *Women, Religion, and Social Change in Brazil's Popular Church*, Notre Dame IN, Univ. of Notre Dame Press, 1997, p. 11.

[2] Roslyn W. Bologh, *Love or Greatness: Max Weber and Masculine Thinking – A Feminist Inquiry*, London, Unwin Hyman, 1990.

[3] Victoria Lee Erickson, *Where Silence Speaks: Feminism, Social Theory and Religion*, Minneapolis, Fortress, 1993.

[4] Elisabeth J. Lacelle, "Les sciences religieuses féministes: Un état de la question", in Denise Veillette dir., *Femmes et Religions*, Québec, Corporation canadienne des sciences religieuses/Les Presses de l'Université de Laval, 1995, p. 61.

[5] Courtney Howland ed., *Religious Fundamentalisms and the Human Rights of Women*, New York, St Martin's, 1999, pp. xii,xx.

[6] Rosemary Radford Ruether, "The War on Women", in *Conscience: A New Journal of Prochoice Catholic Opinion*, vol. XXII, no. 4, Washington, USA, 2001-2002, p. 26.

[7] Gita Sen and Sonia Onufer Corrêa, "Justiça de Gênero e Justiça Econômica: reflexões sobre as revisões de cinco anos das conferências da ONU da década de 1990", docu-

ment prepared by UNIFEM, in preparation for revision of five years of the platform of action, Beijing, 1990.

[8] Ruether, "The War on Women", p.28.

[9] Susan Moller Okin, "Feminism, Women's Human Rights, and Cultural Differences", in *Hypatia: A Journal of Feminist Philosophy*, vol. 13, no. 2, Bloomington IN, Indiana UP, 1998, p.42.

[10] *Ibid.*, p.44.

[11] *Ibid.*

[12] *Ibid.*, p.39.

[13] Magdalena de León T., "Direitos Reprodutivos na Constituição Equatorial", in Maria C. Oliveira and Maria I. Baltazar Rocha orgs, *Saúde Reprodutiva na Esfera Pública e Política Na América Latina*, São Paulo, Editora Unicamp, 2001, p. 138.

Further Reading

Bidegain, Ana Maria, "Gênero como Categoria de Análise na História das Religiões", in Ana Maria Bidegain org., *Mulheres: Autonomia e Controle Religioso na América latina*, São Paulo/Petrópolis, Vozes/CEHILA, 1996.

Curran, Charles E., *Catholic Social Teaching: A Historical, Theological and Ethical Analysis*, Washington, Georgetown UP, 2002.

Gross, Rita M., *Feminism and Religion*, Boston, Beacon, 1996.

Howland, Courtney W., *The Challenge of Religious Fundamentalism to the Liberty and Equality Rights of Women: An Analysis Under the United Nations Charter*, Collum. J. Trasnat'l, 1997.

Mernissi, Fatima, *Sexe, idéologie, Islam*, Paris, Tierce, 1983.

Orozco, Yury Puello, *Mulheres, AIDS e religião. Uma análise da experiência religiosa de mulheres portadoras do vírus HIV e AIDS*, São Paulo, 2001, dissertação de mestrado, Pontifícia Universidade Católica de São Paulo.

Poulat, Emile. *Les discours sur les droits de l'homme. Ses paradoxes et ses contraintes*, Tunis, Centre d'études et recherches économiques et sociales, 1986.

Rosado Nunes, Maria José, "Religion and Women's Rights: The Fundamentalist Face of Catholicism in Brazil", in Courtney Howland ed., *Religious Fundamentalisms and the Human Rights of Women*, New York, St Martin's, 1999.

Shepard, Bonnie. El "Doble Discurso" sobre los Derechos Sexuales y Reproductivos em América Latina: el Abismo entre las Políticas Públicas y los Actos Privados", in *Consciencia Latinoamericana*, vol. XII, no. 3, 2000.

• This text has been published in Portuguese as "O Impacto do Feminismo sobre o estudo das religioes", in *Cadernos Pagu*, Campinas, UNICAMP, no. 16, 2001.

Varieties of Post-1970s Feminist Thought

JANE I. SMITH

The 1960s and 1970s saw a new phenomenon arise in the West, sweeping the imaginations of women in new and exiting ways. That phenomenon was loosely referred to as feminism. Many of those calling themselves feminists in the early days of the movement were not thinking about its applications to religion. In fact, much feminist thought was and is either post-religious or specifically non-religious, on the assumption that religions are inherently disadvantageous to women and should be abandoned forthwith. Rosemary Radford Ruether, in the Christian case, refers to this as "post-Christian rejectionism". So-called secular feminists do not allow the possibility that women can find any empowerment in religion. In Western Europe feminism and secularism tend to be more closely bound together than in America, where the relatively greater interest in the church has supported the development of specifically religious feminism. [1]

In any case, the influences and interpretations of these feminist pioneers have been deeply influential on many women trying to find ways in which to affirm full communal participation with men. At first these efforts were confined in the West to Christianity and Judaism, with Christian and Jewish women, ranging from ultra-liberal to very conservative, struggling to see how feminist insights might be applied to their respective traditions, sects and denominations. [2] Conversations were located almost exclusively among white, class-privileged and economically advantaged women. Gradually, other voices began to be heard, especially from within the Christian community, as women of colour and others outside of the "elite" group claimed their own kinds of interpretations. Sometimes they continued to use the term feminist, but with broader definitions, and other times they specifically chose new designations to reflect their own particularities, such as womanist for black theologies [3] and *muherista* for Hispanic theologies. [4]

Meanwhile, of course, women in cultures around the world have themselves been engaged in movements of nationalism and liberation and for some time have been thinking about issues of parity with men within their own cultural or religious traditions. Some have ventured to consider what it means to say that one is a Hindu feminist, or a Buddhist feminist, or a Muslim feminist.[5] Always their definitions of that meaning have been clearly differentiated from those that they see as characterizing the positions and attitudes of Western (especially Anglo) women. Feminist gatherings in the West over the past several decades have often included the participation of non-Western women, whose insights and critique are invited (though in reality not always welcomed) by their Western counterparts.

This essay will deal with the concerns and issues of women who are working from within their respective religious traditions, whether they are advocating revolution, reform or (in some definition) reaffirmation of the ways in which the tradition works for women. As the Christian church takes stock of the many different ways in which its constituent members must address the concerns of the 21st century, many are arguing it is crucial to think seriously about (a) how Christian women are addressing "feminist" concerns, (b) how women in non-Western (including Christian) traditions are learning from and also reacting against feminist movements as they have developed in the West, and (c) what can be learned from the mutually enhancing exchanges that are starting to take place both in the West and in other parts of the world as women representing different cultures and perspectives come into contact with each other. It is also important to note that while women have been at the forefront of conversations vitally important to their own identity and well-being, many men have seen themselves as partners in the endeavour and are working with and supporting women as they move forward with these efforts.

Feminist theology, now a recognized if not always appreciated Christian theological alternative, arose as a critique of the patriarchal bias of traditional theology. Its goal is the development of an inclusive understanding of God that affirms the full humanity of both genders and of all races.[6] Christian feminist theology now includes biblical studies, history, theology, ethics and other disciplines within the study of religion. For theologians such as pioneer Rosemary Ruether, the task of feminist theology is not merely a tinkering with reinterpretation but a basic restating of the norms and methods of theology.[7] A feminist hermeneutics critiques the androcentrism and misogyny of patriarchal theology. For many feminist theologians, the issue has been how to speak "properly" about God in light of the fact that so much of the divine imagery in the Christian tradition has been male. Some insist that it presupposes the openness to the possibility of the divine as feminine.[8] New non-hierarchical models of relationship between men and women and between humans and God, say feminist thinkers, need to be developed that celebrate difference rather than fear it.[9]

Much of the work of Christian and other religious feminists has been a kind of internal response to the faith traditions of which they are a part. A key ingredient in the conversations of Christian women, struggling to affirm their full participation and recognition in the practice of the faith, is the way in which scripture continues to function as authoritative in their lives. This conversation, of course, is being engaged in similar ways by women in a range of religious traditions today. A few women over the past several decades have determined that scripture can no longer be considered holy or sacred because it appears to be too patriarchal at its core. Most, however, are unwilling to make such an assertion, and turn their attention to determining how what have been considered "patriarchal" interpretations of texts can be discarded in favour of new ways of viewing scripture. For some, this means simply ignoring certain verses, eliminated by virtue of their supposed lack of authenticity or because they do not support the general message of the text. Many prefer to engage the hermeneutic task of reinterpreting passages of scripture so that they can be understood in the light of what they believe to be God's intention of equality between the sexes. For conservative Christians and Jews (and the same is true for virtually all Muslims), such reinterpretation is the only viable alternative. One of the first tasks to be engaged in the hermeneutic process, of course, is reclaiming the right of women themselves to serve as interpreters of scripture, a function that in virtually all religious traditions has long been considered to be the exclusive province of men. In some cases women are being recognized by their respective communities as having the right, and the training, to fulfil this function; in other cases they are simply claiming it for themselves and proceeding with the task. The study and analysis of the language of scripture itself has occupied the attention of many feminist thinkers as they struggle to free scripture from patriarchal readings based on gender-exclusive renderings.

Women (and men) who are working from positions of self-conscious identification with the Christian tradition, as is again true of many women of other faiths, in addition to reflection on scripture are also looking again at the writing and reading of their own religious histories. They are turning back to the documents that have formed the corpus of the history of their branch of Christianity, as well as Judaism, Hinduism, Buddhism, Sikhism and other traditions, and are examining them for alternative interpretations to those that have favoured the exclusion of women from decision-making processes. "His-story" has been reclaimed by some as "her-story", bringing to light new narratives and traditions that highlight the lives and contributions of women whose stories have been forgotten in the official telling of the history of the tradition. Some feminists claim that everything beyond the initial experiences and records of those who serve as the "founders" of the tradition, however that might be understood, is suspect and to be seriously questioned and often discarded. Others refuse to reject everything "post-scriptural" as simply male invention and interpretation, and are struggling to invest the entire history with new dimensions of meaning in which women's contributions are honoured. In traditions where "sacred law" has served as a regulative force in the lives of adherents, feminists have examined the strictures of that law in the effort to find what new vehicles might be possible for a fresh understanding of those elements that have served as repressive for women. Sometimes they champion completely cancelling those elements. In some cases those elements have simply been deleted.

One of the first Christian reinterpreters of early Christian history was Elisabeth Schüssler Fiorenza, a critical historian looking to understand the real role of women in the early church. Working on the assumption that scripture was written from a male perspective, she determined that the task is to try to recover what she calls repressed memories of the role of women in the early church.[10] Now scholars in many different fields are working to uncover the "real" lives and contributions of women throughout the history of the church, sometimes learning to extrapolate from the paucity of known records to fill in the gaps in information that male historians have neglected to attend to.

One of the challenges of the contemporary period posed by some Christian women as well as by women from other faiths is that of seeing the tradition as dynamic rather than static. Often, women are among those who are arguing that Christianity, Judaism, Islam or some other faith is not to be seen as rigid, fixed for all time and immune to new interpretations. Rather, they insist, religious traditions must be understood as both changing and capable of adapting to that change, thus serving as appropriate vehicles for faith in new and rapidly evolving circumstances. Dynamism and flexibility are watchwords for many religious feminists, who have found themselves almost inevitably excluded from the confines of a faith that is "set in stone" for all time. Vested interests are high, of course, and often feminists have had to pay a price for what has been perceived as a challenge to the understanding that a religion represents a kind of changeless eternality.

For religious feminists, as important as looking internally into their own religious traditions for new interpretations and understandings has been the task of responding to the external realities of the cultural situations within which they live and operate and of which their religious traditions are a part. Some women refer to this task as trying to meet the challenges of contextualization. Clearly, religion and culture cannot be fully distinguished, and one of the key issues in many traditions today is the attempt to extract the "essence" of the faith from the cultural accretions that have determined its manifestations in different cultures around the globe. Feminists are contributing to that effort by trying to identify those elements of cultural world-views that are clearly not supportive of the full role and participation of women. They are attempting to determine when and if the apparent "lower" status accorded to women in many cultures is a factor of religion or culture, in the attempt to exonerate the faith and to reappropriate for themselves what they understand as the proper roles accorded by their religious tradition. Many factors impinge on these considerations, of course, including the potentially different understandings of what "lower" status might mean for Western and for two-thirds world women. Non-Western feminists are struggling to come up with their own definitions that do not buy into the stereotypes of their Western sisters,[11] about which more will be said below.

Basic to all feminist discussions is the matter of authority. Women are challenging, in many different ways, hierarchical notions of authority that generally serve the advantage of men. How, many are asking, can male hierarchies be identified as culturally determined and supported rather than part of the inherent structure of their religious tradition? Some Asian Christian women, for example, struggle with the double oppression of cultural patriarchy and what are clearly patriarchal tendencies in their adopted Christian tradition. In some cases, however, the effort to separate religion and culture does not serve them well. Women who are working to reconcile elements of their traditional cultures with the new religions of which they are now a part (efforts sometimes referred to disparagingly as syncretism) may actually find themselves in more empowering positions. Christian attempts to blend part of native American or Korean spirituality with Christian faith and practice, for example, may well serve to provide new possibilities for participation and leadership for women.

One of the most important concerns facing religious communities today is that of appropriate roles and responsibilities for women within the structures of the faith. In some cases women are demanding that they be allowed to perform all of the leadership roles that have traditionally been available to men. Within the Roman Catholic Church, for example, the issue of women serving as priests is hotly debated in some quarters and a matter of "no discussion" in others so long as the magisterium continues the long-held policy of the church that women cannot be ordained. Muslim women and men are virtually unanimous in affirming that women cannot serve as Imams to men (they can to women), although a few isolated voices are being raised to challenge that interpretation. In Hinduism, Buddhism, Judaism (the 20th century saw the ordination of numbers of women rabbis from all but the Orthodox branches) and other traditions, women are in the process of assuming roles that traditionally have not been open to them, and are finding justification in scripture and other religious sources for doing so.

With religious leadership, of course, comes access to all of the physical space and paraphernalia that have been available to men. Many women and men question the appropriateness of that access, while feminists in general wonder how the lack of it can reasonably be challenged. One of the difficult issues both within and across religious faiths is how women and men who have different understandings of appropriate women's roles can talk with each other and understand each other's perspectives. Western feminists tend to equate power with authority, while non-Western women (as well as those from more conservative Western Christian branches) often work from the assumption that "non-authoritarian" positions can still afford power. Is there a basis for conversation between these perspectives?

Also part of the equal access question is whether the structures of a given faith tradition support women's participation in the range of ritual activities associated with that tradition, as well as the appropriate role of women in the religious education of children, women and men. Congregations of various faiths that work on a model of elected leadership are facing the question of whether women can/should be elected to serve as presidents of congregations and communities in churches, mosques and synagogues. In many cases women are assuming responsibility as interpreters of scripture, law, doctrine and religious opinion, while opposition to those functions for women continues to be raised. The critique of feminists is often seen to be very helpful in the efforts to claim "appropriate" access, although some women who prefer to move more slowly and who may be reluctant to easily cede full parity with men to women sometimes find themselves feeling pressure from their more liberal sisters that they do not appreciate.

While it was initially the endeavour of more liberal Protestant, Roman Catholic and Jewish Western women, feminism in its many forms and varieties is now being engaged by women (and men) from a great range of ideological and theological perspectives. Orthodox Christian women are working to determine what is essential to their full participation within their tradition. Evangelical feminism, once a contradiction in terms, is now an accepted activity in many branches of the conservative Christian church. Evangelical feminists try to combine women's rights and biblical Christianity without abandoning scripture or history, at the same time that they recognize what they believe to be inequities in the church's treatment of women.

As Western feminism has increasingly come under attack for being too monolithic, too white and too upper middle-class in orientation, a number of new attempts have arisen to formulate different kinds of responses to understanding the relationship of women to religious traditions. In some cases these have a particular focus in given communities, while in other cases they are attempts to be more global in outlook. In addition to womanist (the name given initially to African American Christian feminist interpretations) and *muherista* (developed initially by Latin American feminist theologians) feminism, other "branches" of the movement have arisen, including ecofeminism (which may provide a creative way of finding cross-cultural commonalities in its concern for ecology, social transformation and a reform of the means of production and reproduction),[12] gay/lesbian feminism (which by very definition will have limited appeal in cultures and traditions in which homosexual life-style is not acceptable), spiritual feminism, feminism for peace, and the like. Some of these new forms find resonance in the responses of two-thirds world women, both Christian and non-Christian. More radical forms of feminism, however, and certainly those seen to promote gay and lesbian life-styles, are generally not appreciated outside of certain circles in the West.

Women from religious traditions other than Christianity and Judaism, whether they are resident in the West or living in two-thirds world countries, share many of the same issues as have been raised by Western women when it comes to interpretation and reinterpretation of the foundations of their faith. Their response to what they understand to be Western feminism, however, is complex and closely related to the history of Western imperialism in much of the developing world. Non-Western women often reject even the use of the term patriarchy on the grounds of its association with Western feminism, even though they are well aware of, and are struggling against, various forms of male oppression and domination in their own cultures.

Western incursion into non-Western lands has taken many different forms: religious, political, economic, educational, etc. Often, it has been accompanied by narrow attitudes of paternalism and bias about the condition of women in the religious traditions and cultures to which Westerners have come (some would say intruded themselves). Quick to judge and to render Western culture and religion superior, they have identified Muslim, Hindu, Buddhist and other women as oppressed, suffering and downtrodden, but often have done so through Western rather than indigenous lenses. Such critique has served both to prod the thinking of non-Western women about their own circumstances and to confuse and impede their efforts to work within their own religions and cultures. Two-thirds world women who are interested in looking seriously at the roles and opportunities possible for women in their own religious traditions often need to ask themselves how they can critique those traditions and cultures without necessarily buying into Western argumentation.

Liberation, long a watchword for Western feminists, has always had strong political overtones in lands that have been colonized or dominated by the West. Freedom for the last century for many two-thirds world women has connoted not so much liberation from men as from the West. Part of that movement for freedom has entailed a rethinking of the roles of women and the importance of engaging women as full and functioning members of their respective societies. Often that has meant that women in these countries are left with the perplexing task of engaging in a kind of feminist discourse and investigation that is culturally relevant without buying into the very structures that their societies have struggled to get rid of. Western feminists are often seen by their counterparts in other cultures to be interested in consciousness-raising in order to identify ways in which women are exploited by males. Non-Western women are therefore struggling to figure out how to affirm that goal at the same time that they are working to see that members of their societies are not exploited by outsiders (such as Western feminists). Two-thirds world women often question the universality of some of the rights declared by Westerners to be applicable to all people. At the same time, however, they express a range of opinions as to the degree to which definitions of rights and values should be determined by specific cultural realities.

Aside from imperialist intrusion – whether 19th and 20th century incursions or new forms of 21st century economically exploitative "neo-imperialism" – a number of basic assumptions sometimes make it difficult for women in non-Western cultures to understand, agree with or adopt the principles that have seemed to drive Western feminism. Many two-thirds world women prefer the term activism, working for women's rights, to feminism, on the grounds that feminism is too Western, too elitist, and does not properly attend to the larger issues of class struggle and community welfare. They see their Western sisters as being too focused on liberation as freedom of opportunity for the individual, a critique they sometimes apply even to women claiming rights to religious leadership and interpretation. Non-Westerners often want to mould individual goals and interests to accord with the welfare of the larger group. Freedom in this interpretation is not for the sake of the individual but for the progress and development of the nation. This can lead to tensions between cultural identity and sexual identity. Some Arab Christian women, for example, have argued that the "sisters unite" that seems to be the watchword of Western Christian women must take second place to the importance in the context of the Middle East or Arabs uniting against the forces that may be working to challenge their society and culture. Two-thirds world women are thus often in the position of needing to define their feminism in such a way that they do not end up attacking the very societies and religious traditions that have been and are being critiqued by the West.

NOTES

[1]   In many two-thirds world areas the designation secular feminism refers specifically to the attitude of those who favour the separation of religion and politics (especially those who actively oppose religious "fundamentalism") and is not necessarily anti-religious.

[2]   One of the earliest of these efforts was the work of Mary Daly. See *The Church and the Second Sex*, New York, Harper & Row, 1968.

[3]   See, for example, Jacqueline Grant, *White Women's Christ and Black Women's Jesus*, Atlanta GA, Scholars, 1989.

[4]   See Ada Maria Isasi-Diaz, *Mujerista Theology: A Theology for the Twenty-First Century*, Maryknoll NY, Orbis, 1996.

[5]   See Arvind Sharma and Katherine Young eds, *Feminism and World Religions*, Albany NY, State Univ. of New York Press, 1999.

[6]   Rosemary Ruether, "Feminist Theology in the Academy", *Christianity and Crisis*, 4 March 1985, pp.67–61.

[7]   See, for example, Ruether's *Sexism and God-Talk: Toward a Feminist Theology*, Boston, Beacon, 1983.

[8]   See Carol P. Christ, "Why Women Need a Goddess", in *Womanspirit Rising*, Carol Christ and Judith Plaskow eds, New York, Harper, 1979.

[9]   See Elizabeth Johnson, *She Who Is: The Mystery of God in Feminist Theological Discourse*, New York, Crossroad, 1993.

[10]   Elisabeth Schüssler Fiorenza, *In Memory of Her: A Feminist Theological Reconstruction of Christian Origins*, New York, Crossroads, 1984.

[11]   See Katie G. Canon, Ada Maria Isasi-Diaz and Kwok Pui-Lan eds, *Inheriting Our Mother's Gardens: Feminist Theology in Third World Perspective*, Philadelphia, Westminster, 1988.

[12]   See Rosemary Ruether, *Gaia and God: An Ecofeminist Theology of Earth Healing*, San Francisco, Harper, 1992.

10
African Women and Globalization
A View from Ghana

MERCY A. ODUYOYE

The UN decade of women provided an unparalleled opportunity to unveil women's lives worldwide. In the process there were attempts to create a hierarchy of suffering that often placed African women at the bottom of the pile. This kind of approach has been more or less discredited by perceptive researchers who continue to point out the commonalities in women's experience and the common roots of their status, wherever they may be.

The biological definition of woman as female – childbearer and nurturer of infants – seems to be at the heart of all definitions of womanhood. It is this that stimulates the urge to own her, to protect her, to direct her life and to adore her. Concentrating on femaleness has determined the upbringing, education and training of women and defines their economic status and power. Hedged in by all things domestic, women have limited public participation in policy-making and politics. This further defines their social status. Confined to the periphery of religious structures, women serve as clients to religious ministration.

While globalization of the world economy tends to disadvantage Africa, its impact on African women and children also tends to be negative. Globalization assumes equal opportunities for all, but in terms of wealth creation this is not at all the case. Land is still to a large degree managed by men; it is controlled and sold by men, in the process denying women the land they need for subsistence farming in favour of large-scale farming for agricultural products for the global market. It has led to the cordoning-off of water sources for the use of bottling companies, so that people who used to walk miles to fetch water from a spring now have to find money to buy "pure water". The income from these sales has not been used to provide clean water for rural populations, and cities like Accra go for months without tap water. When this happens young people (mostly girls) have to roam the town with containers, seeking water.

The social consequences of economic structural adjustment have fallen heavily on women, who are ground down by the wheels of an economy in a hurry to reduce welfare and sacrifice women and children. Education and training are too expensive and take too long, so children have to learn to grow up faster. Globalization also means the globalization of terrorism and militarism, which affect entire civilian populations, but particularly women and children. None of this can be offset by technological miracles like the information super-highway. Indeed, communications technology makes the vulnerable feel more threatened and deprived by increasing their awareness of global events and those things that are missing in their lives. They may not know what hit them, but they know how hard they are being hit.

Globalization and judgment

All of us who exist within this unjust system cry out from the depths of our common humanity, just as Amos does in the Old Testament:

You have threshed the earth with sledges of iron.
You have delivered entire communities into slavery and refugee camps.
You have not remembered the covenant of kinship.
You have pursued other people with a sword.
You have cast off pity and maintained our anger and wrath in perpetuity.
You have ripped open pregnant women in order to enlarge your territory.
You have set villages on fire to rout your siblings, those you now call enemies.
You have sold the righteous for silver and the needy for a pair of sandals.
You have trampled the head of the poor into the dust of the earth and pushed the afflicted out of the way.   (adapted from verses in Amos 1–2)

Then we shall look at one another and cry out, "When did we participate in all these atrocities?" And our common humanity will respond, "In as much as you have passed the struggling women and children without seeing them, you have displayed callousness towards our common humanity."
(adapted from Matt. 25:31–45)

The statistics are overwhelming, but actual day-to-day experiences are even more overpowering and depressing. For example, human communities have distanced themselves from contemporary child sacrifice by calling homeless city children "street-children", as if it is the streets and not people who beget them. Now that market forces operate everywhere and profit is the new idol, it is the blood of women and children that feeds its all-consuming desire. Women are obliged by their cultures to bear more children to throw on the rubbish heaps of globalized economies or give them over as fodder for armed conflicts that enrich the few and traumatize the many.

In Ghana, the "innocent" days of colonial elitism and Nkrumaist socialism at least ensured that those who found themselves within the Western educational system could make something of themselves, and people close to a hospital or clinic could obtain adequate, free health care. Life was never perfect or blissful, but the safety net of traditional communalism prevented anybody from becoming a child of the streets. Women worked for nothing, but they never broke stones for a living until contemporary globalization arrived.

In one sense, globalization has affected Africa for the past five hundred years. Political, economic and cultural developments, structures and policies pulled Africa into the Euro-American world for the benefit of people of European descent. As for religion, Christianity has had a globalizing aim and the founding of churches has been its instrument. One could almost say that globalization means the exploitation of the weak with impunity beneath a veneer of free and equal participation. Africans – especially black Africans – have had a raw deal in this new culture that does not allow for the possibility of alternatives.

Those who benefited from the trade in human beings, from colonial dictatorship and expropriation of the land and wealth of Africa, the Americas, Australia, Aotearoa New Zealand and the Caribbean, remain the major forces in globalization. Those who reap abundantly from the unjust trade practices surrounding so called "raw materials" continue to direct the affairs of the globalized world economy. Naturally, they remain the key beneficiaries. They are also wise enough to know that other people must be kept at subsistence level in order to play the role of workers in this colony of ants.

What's new?

The globalization of market forces means that human beings have to pass the test of viability before they are accorded the right to food, clothing and shelter. Those who fail the test are clothed from the discarded wardrobes of the wealthy. They are fed from the left-overs of harvests and the manufacturing of beef and fish steaks; they build their dwellings from the cartons that protected the precious goods of the rich. And for most of Africa, being poor is also equated with deeply pigmented skin. The under-privileged exist side by side with the privileged.

Women have been deemed to be "helpers" only; they and their children are described as unproductive people who contribute nothing to the national economy because they are not on the labour market. The trouble is, they too have to live and move and have their being. And their being as humans does not depend on their economic viability. Whether or not they generate wealth, their health should be the concern of the whole community. The discards of the economic system – especially those of the labour market – land by the hearths of their mothers, wives and sisters, who do not have the heart to leave them hungry. The sick and the aged, who cannot afford the health care that has to pay for itself, crawl home to seek refuge under the roofs of women who nurse them even when they themselves are hungry, naked and exhausted. The HIV/AIDS pandemic has left thousands of orphans in the care of grand-mothers who also continue to nurse their dying offspring.

Structural adjustment programmes

Economic structural adjustment programmes (SAPs) – foisted on debtor countries by the financial instruments of the owners of the world's wealth – forced many governments to abandon the ideas and practices of the welfare state. To keep consciences at peace, people were praised for their resilience in constituting themselves into "civil societies" in order to assume the responsibilities shed by governments. Most of their structures belong to women's organizations, some of which now find themselves overloaded and underfunded. Thus, women and children do not share in the wealth they helped to create.

What role have women played in the sacrificing of children to market forces? When Abraham was marching his young son to the sacrificial altar, did he consult the mother? Did she know? We are not told. When our governments sell our countries and manufacture conflicts to immolate our sons and rape our daughters they do not consult us. Few women have the necessary skills and knowledge of what their governments are planning to be able to cry enough is enough. Governments themselves (at any rate, those in Africa) have little control when market forces are the bosses. Knowingly or unknowingly, they discontinue the life-support machinery that are expected to provide. Women are milked dry and blood is drained from young bodies with bloated bellies. And so the sacrificing of the most vulnerable of the human community continues.

SAPs are out to sap the blood of weaker economies, especially that of women and children in Africa. Globalization wears the cloak of liberalization and openness; however, its doors have laser beams sensitive to wealth and different kinds of people. Visa requirements are structured to keep out the poor and those in need of help from the very regions where they might have a chance to transform themselves. On the other hand, nations and people with economic and financial clout can march into regions with more primary resources, land, forests, fresh water and human labour and invest. Nobody invests where they are not going to reap a hundred-fold. Most people from countries labelled poor cannot do the same in rich countries; globalization is one-way liberalization that expands the opportunities of the rich. The flip side of this is that children and women of "poor" countries are forced to sell on our road-sides those articles that they themselves cannot afford to own, including bottled water – water sources that were free for all have now been globalized for the benefit of the rich.

The few people from the South who squeeze through the visa net and obtain economically viable positions in the North often have to leave family behind because what they earn cannot support all of them. These are the economic widows and orphans created by the poverty-enhancing mechanisms of globalization. Africa has known many traumatic displacements of its population – men, women and children – but globalization's contribution has increased the scale of the sacrifice. Women and children are run over by Africa's armies and pushed onto trucks and boats destined for refugee camps in neighbouring countries and beyond.

When Southern African men left women and children to serve in the mines of Egoli there began a trend of the dissipation of family life that continues to this day and that has become an Africa-wide phenomenon. Women and children who expected fathers and sons to return or send money have not always had their hopes fulfilled. These women and children have had to work the land and try to survive. Such resilience should be recognized and praised, but the fact remains that they have been led by hunger and privation onto the altar of globalization. Globalization has become a poverty-maker for the women of Africa, especially in rural areas.

African women are not given to mourning. We need to seek a way out of the negativity of globalization and appropriate its benefits and challenges for the enhancement of our lives together and to stimulate our creativity. A victim mentality will not empower women and children. Globalization must not be allowed to continue to feed on the blood and sweat of women and children. This sacrifice of human potential must stop. There are no easy solutions. We all need to bring our suggestions to the table. And where profit is enthroned and welfare trampled underfoot, the weak turn to religion for solace.

Healing the hurt

Religion attracts women striving to hold on to the one treasure they have: their own lives and the lives of those around them. Indeed, with women, it is always others first. This ecumenical study recognizes the power of religion. Yet we cannot ignore the fact that religion is a two-edged sword. How will religion act as a life-giving force in the lives of women and children battling to live with globalization? What practical acts of solidarity will religious bodies undertake to support women and children living under globalization? Can religious ideals and personalities from faith communities become active advocates for women and children?

Globalization has shaken the centrality and preciousness of human life. Today, it is profit and wealth that count in people's lives. It seems that all many people care for are the profits that will enable them to have all that money can buy. Religion has to help people rediscover their dignity and sense of worthiness. Society has to be called back to the principle of being the other's keeper and of building a caring community. Religion should call people's attention to the God who constantly reminds us "I made you better than you are living". Faith communities have to live out the image of the Transcendent they claim to know. They have to point to the Sacred as undergirding the sacredness of human life.

Faith communities can express diakonia in a spirit of service with the understanding that "to whom much is given, much is expected". Those who have benefited from globalization must be made to realize the need to create safety nets for those who have become its victims, while at the same time seeking alternatives to it. Globalization must become a partnership in which all can contribute and all can reap what is necessary for a life that deserves to be called human.

The divine economy according to Christianity does not expect human sacrifice, only that people should make themselves a living sacrifice. This means living lives for the well-being of all and for the ecology that God has put in place. It means that those who plan the globalization of the world's structures and systems must put women and children at the centre.

We are challenged by Luke 4:18–19 and the prophecies of Amos. We need to hear Isaiah cry, "The whole body is sick." Healing can come when faith communities can discuss globalization with economic planners and with governments. Only then can we say with Isaiah 65:23–25 that they shall not labour in vain or bear children for calamity.

11
Catholicism, Modernity
and the Second Vatican Council

JOSÉ OSCAR BEOZZO

The Second Vatican Council, a rich and complex event, and probably the most important in the religious history of the 20th century, can be approached in many different ways.[1]

This chapter will look at it from two viewpoints: (1) the changes that have taken place in the understanding of Catholicism and (2) its relation to modernity. Modernity is an equally complex phenomenon, a vast movement comprising cultural, political, economic and social elements with far-reaching repercussions in the field of religion, providing many entry points to examine and understand it.

Contemporary Catholicism

It is a risky task to make an assessment of contemporary Catholicism, its major trends, tensions and issues, locating it within the network of its complex relations with other Christian churches and the great world religions, and also amid the problems of today's globalized world. It is risky because this branch of Christianity alone represents 52.8 percent of all Christians, and is to be found in 240 different countries, located in an even greater number of cultures, with more than a billion (at least nominal) followers. This will therefore be only a tentative assessment, inevitably incomplete and partial.

What we call the Catholic world is not limited to its best-known, Latin, branch, but also comprises some twenty Eastern Catholic churches. It thus needs to be examined in all its diversity, even though that diversity has been overlaid by many centuries of increasing centralization and uniformity.

Liturgically, Catholicism finds expression in six different rites: the Latin rite and five Eastern Catholic rites. The Latin rite, numerically the greatest, predominates in the West, but is also present in some parts of the East. It is the dominant Catholic rite, but it is undergoing an increasing process of inculturation in the new churches of Africa, Asia, Central and South America and Australasia.

Among the Eastern rites there are the Byzantine rite, its principal ethnic and cultural base being the Ukrainian and Russian Catholics, located in Ukraine and the diaspora;[2] the Chaldean rite, its most important group being the Chaldean-Malabars of India;[3] the Antiochene rite, whose major strength is in the Maronites of Lebanon, the Melkites of Syria, Lebanon, Palestine and the diaspora;[4] the Alexandrine rite, made up mainly of the Catholic Copts of Egypt and the Catholics of Ethiopia; and, finally, the Armenian Catholic rite, in Armenia and among Armenian immigrants in other continents.

Without wishing to go into complex details, it is essential to consider the current concept of the Catholic Church and the habitual use of the term in its historical context.

Catholicism: a concept in mutation

Up to at least the council of Trent the name by which the Western branch of Catholicism was known was the Latin Church, to distinguish it from the Christian East.[5] After the great schism of 1054, the churches of the East, grouped in the ancient Eastern patriarchates, took to calling themselves Orthodox, to distinguish themselves from the Latin Church, which was reckoned to have departed from correct doctrine (i.e. orthodoxy).

In Rome, the Orthodox were regularly called Greeks. That was the term used at the councils of reconciliation: the council of Lyon (1274) and the council of Florence (Ferrara, Florence and Rome, 1438–45); and also at the council of Trent (1545–63).

With the Lutheran Reformation, we witness a dramatic change in the vocabulary used up to that time. In the tradition of the Lutheran Reformation, the Latin Church at first came to be known as the Roman Church and now today as the Roman Catholic Church (RCC), which is also the name given to it in World Council of Churches publications.

The Latin Church, for its part, was compelled to redefine its identity at the time of the council of Trent, when the main religious division ceased to be between Latins and Greeks with the capture of Constantinople by the Turks (29 May 1453), to be replaced by the tension between Catholics and Protestants.

Historically, the term "Catholicism" in its modern sense stems from that period. The Dutch reformer Philipp van Marnix (1540–98) gave the name "Catholic" to the traditional believers who had remained loyal to the pope. On their part, however, the new term to describe themselves was accepted only slowly and with some hesitation. Only at the time of the Enlightenment, when all the churches and doctrines arising from the Reformation were grouped under the general term Protestantism, did the notion of Catholicism become a term meaning the opposite of Protestantism and thus become more widespread.

Thus, the former Latin Church came to be called, and to call itself, the Apostolic Roman Catholic Church, or simply the Catholic Church or the Roman Church.

The Second Vatican Council (1962–65), particularly with its reformulation of the doctrine of the church and the entry of the Catholic Church into the mainstream of the modern ecumenical movement, marked to an extent an end to the post-Tridentine period and the so-called Catholic Counter-Reformation, thereby producing an identity crisis as they left behind the earlier Catholic identity arising out of its conflicts with Protestantism.[6]

From another perspective, there arose questions concerning the current use of the term Catholicism to describe the Roman Church.

Catholics, but not Roman

During the Second Vatican Council the Eastern Catholics reacted strongly against this identification of being not only Catholic but Roman. The Melkites, for example, rejected on one hand being branded as a "uniate church",[7] which is not applicable to them because of their history of unbroken communion with the see of Rome since the 5th century, and on the other hand claimed to be fully Catholic. They did not feel Latin or Roman, but Eastern.

In this regard the speech by the Antiochene Patriarch of the Melkites, Maximus IV Saigh, on this issue during the first session of the Second Vatican Council (1962) is both striking and illuminating. Declining to speak in Latin, the official Council language, he caused a sensation by deliberately breaking the rule and addressing the gathering in French:

> It should, in fact, not be forgotten that we are speaking here of the Eastern church. It is a church that is fully apostolic in its constituent elements, and it is clearly distinct from the Latin churches. It is a first-born church of Christ and the apostles. Its historical development and organization are exclusively the work of the fathers, of our Greek and Eastern fathers. It owes what it is to the college of the apostles, which lives on in its college of bishops, with Peter at its centre and with its distinctive rights and responsibilities.

This church historically does not owe its origin, its rites, its organization nor anything that is part of its life to the see of Rome. In short, it has no fathers in the faith other than the apostles; no one, apart from the fathers, has created its whole heritage of prayer, organization and activities. Is it possible to hold that St Basil, St Gregory, St Cyril, St Chrysostom and others, when you consider what they received and passed on, are second-class Catholics because they were not Roman?[8]

It can thus be seen that the Catholic Melkites feel themselves to be in full communion with Rome, but in no way accept being described as Roman or being identified with the "Roman" Catholic Church, or (in their language) with the "Latin" Church. On the other hand, culturally and spiritually, they feel themselves to be an integral part of the Christian East and of the "orthodox" heritage and feel called to be a bridge to re-establish the former communion *(sobornost)* between East and West.

This fluctuating vocabulary, within the present context of ecumenical relationships and the internal changes in the Catholic Church, largely springing from the Second Vatican Council, results in it being possible to speak of the Catholic Church or the Latin Church in connection with its relations with Eastern Catholics or the Orthodox; of the Roman Catholic Church (RCC) when we consider the terminology used by Protestants, and particularly Lutherans, to describe it; and of simply the Catholic Church, which is the current Brazilian usage. All this, however, does not deny the nature of catholicity to other churches that claim it.

If the way one is seen by others is always revelatory of one's own identity, at least from the viewpoint of those receiving the signals one sends out, I leave the final assessment to one of the pioneers of ecumenism, the Greek Orthodox Prof. Alivisatos of Athens, at the end of the Council after Rome and Constantinople had simultaneously on 7 December 1965 lifted the mutual condemnations of 1054. He declared, "By holding this Council, the Roman Catholic Church, from being Catholic, has incontestably become ecumenical."[9] It is obvious that that statement by Alivisatos must be taken with all the necessary nuances. It is correct in that John XXIII and the Council decided to set out on the road of ecumenism, which the Catholic Church had not trod up to that time. It has, however, to be qualified when we consider the difficulties and setbacks in many of its positions, taken without due consideration of the tradition of other Christian churches and without the essential consultation marking the quest for a common way forward.

Catholicism between old and new identities

Even within what is commonly called the Roman Catholic Church we should take note of particular identities, inherited from the past and not totally abandoned. Thus, the church of Milan maintains its ancient liturgy going back to the 5th century, the Ambrosian rite. In the church of Toledo in Spain, in some of its parishes and in one of its cathedral chapels, the Mozarabic rite has been preserved to this day. During the Second Vatican Council the Spanish bishops had printed and presented to Paul VI and the other Council fathers the *Ordo Missae Ritu Mozarabico Peragendae*. [10] Braga in Portugal and Lyon in France kept their own distinctive liturgical features until the liturgical reforms of Vatican II. Religious orders such as the Dominicans also still continue to observe their own rite. [11]

On the other hand, after Vatican II we should note the diversity emerging in the churches of Asia, Africa, Latin America and Australasia, as they each forge their own identity. These churches are in communion with Rome, but are following the path of increasing linguistic, liturgical, pastoral and theological inculturation. We see in them a progressive diversity which, sociologically and historically, means that they cannot be described simply as Latin or Roman churches, but rather as Zairian or Brazilian, or even Zapotecan, Mixtec, Maya-Quiche, Aymara and so on.

Granted all that, it cannot be denied that the numerical weight is with the Latin branch of Catholicism by comparison with the small Eastern Catholic churches, which are surviving in difficult circumstances among populations with a majority of Muslims, Hindus or Orthodox, and with a large proportion of their faithful dispersed in countries outside the East because of continual emigration.

It should equally be noted that the cultural diversity that is giving the churches of Asia, Africa, Latin America and Australasia a more distinctive profile has led to tension with Rome. Rome, at one and the same time, is both conniving at their local cultural expressions of the faith, liturgy and theology, and also contradictorily urging them to continue to observe the Roman rite in its entirety in their worship, and views Latin American, Asian and African contextualized theology with suspicion. In other words, the healthy principle of the autonomy of the particular churches, collegially organized in local churches, which was recovered by Vatican II, and the principle of the apostolic college presiding over the church with Peter at its head, but without reducing the proper authority of the bishops, is being eroded by a renewed centralizing tendency. That is to the detriment of the particular churches and their collegial organization in their national or regional bishops conferences. [12]

Traditionally, the pope has always been regarded as *primus inter pares* (first among equals) and not as *primus solus* (sole head). The direction taken by the pontificate of John Paul II once again isolated the Roman centre, moving it away from a more collegial practice and communion with two-way, rather than one-way, communication.

We normally define post-Tridentine Catholicism by taking as our point of reference the division of the 16th century, but also its numerical and qualitative development in the course of the 20th century. The outstanding features of that last century were the changes that led to the Second Vatican Council or arose from it. Many observers and historians saw in Vatican II the end of the post-Tridentine era and thus the end of a particular type of Catholicism, a term directly derived, in its classic sense, from the so-called Counter-Reformation of the 16th century.

Later developments in Catholicism can be followed in some recent collegial assemblies, such as the synod on evangelization in 1974, which produced the apostolic exhortation *Evangelii Nuntiandi* by Paul VI, the extraordinary synod to mark the twentieth anniversary of the closing of Vatican II in 1985, and the regional synods leading up to the Jubilee Year 2000.

The many faces of contemporary Catholicism

I take as an example of this development the third general assembly of the synod of bishops in Rome, 27 September–3 November 1974, on the theme "Evangelization in the Modern World", just ten years after the closing of Vatican II. Central to the lead-up to the synod was the awareness that the church does not exist for its own sake, but for mission, and that its prime task is to "proclaim" and at the same time "be" God's good news in the life of humankind. Philip Potter, the general secretary of the World Council of Churches, in his speech to the synod, struck the same note.

The synod, on the other hand, reflected the rediscovered central role of the individual church, rooted in one part of the people of God, with its own distinctive culture and profile, in its inter-relationship with other local churches, through bishops conferences and in its wider links by regions in the various continents, and marked by distinctive cultural and linguistic features after the discontinuance of the exclusive use of Latin.

The differing views and perspectives on the main challenges to evangelization coming out of the different language groups brought the synod to an impasse. The final statement voted on by the bishops was rejected for not having adequately included the rich and sometimes conflicting variety of views. The *Relatio Finalis* rejected by the synod was the responsibility of the then Archbishop of Cracow, Karol Wojtyla. The solution arrived at was to pass to Paul VI the different reports from the language groups with the request that he undertake to write an apostolic exhortation reflecting the variety of views arising from the debates and proposals.

A good summary by specialists among the Brazilian bishops attending the synod gives the major themes arising from the debates:

- The theme of *indigenization*, referring to the mutual relationship between the gospel and the life or culture of a people or continent. This theme was particularly stressed by the fathers from Africa, who strongly emphasized the self-awareness and importance of the individual churches.

- The theme of the great *non-Christian religions*, highlighted particularly by the fathers from Asia, the Near East and the Far East, who live alongside the great religious traditions of their peoples outside Christianity.

- The theme of *liberation*, in the theological, ethical and social sense, which was introduced above all by the fathers from Latin America, where the vast marginalized masses are awakening Christians to act as a church to free the oppressed by defending human rights as an urgent necessity, and by establishing justice, solidarity and peace, as proclaimed throughout the Jewish-Christian revelation.

- The theme of *secularization*, with its tendency towards secularism, both in theory and practice, and consumerism. This theme was raised particularly by the fathers from Western Europe and North America. They even spoke of a post-Christian civilization, and of a religious indifference which makes people deaf to the newness of the gospel.

- And, finally, the theme of a *programme of atheism*, and the total denial of a place for the gospel and religion in general, both in the life of the individual and in the life of any society. This theme was experienced most sharply by the synod fathers from communist countries, where militant atheism is a constant challenge.

- The church in various parts of the world was becoming increasingly aware of the *presence and activity of the Holy Spirit* in the world and the church through the present-day "charismatic renewal", a feature that was also quite profoundly evident in the synod meeting itself.
13

The challenge of liberation as an integral part of the gospel message and of credible evangelization was equally felt to be a common challenge by the other third-world countries. On this issue Paul VI wrote in *Evangelii Nuntiandi*:

> But evangelization would not be complete if it did not take account of the unceasing interplay of the gospel and of man's concrete life, both personal and social. That is why evangelization involves an explicit message, adapted to the different situations constantly being realized, about the rights and duties of every human being, about family life without which personal growth and development is hardly possible, about life in society, about international life, peace, justice and development – a message especially energetic today about liberation.
>
> It is well known in what terms numerous bishops from all the continents spoke of this at the last synod, especially the bishops from the third world, with a pastoral accent resonant with the voice of the millions of sons and daughters of the church who make up those peoples. Peoples, as we know, engaged with all their energy in the effort and struggle to overcome everything which condemns them to remain on the margin of life: famine, chronic disease, illiteracy, poverty, injustices in international relations and especially in commercial exchanges, situations of economic and cultural neo-colonialism sometimes as cruel as the old political colonialism. The church, as the bishops repeated, has the duty to proclaim the liberation of millions of human beings, many of whom are her own children – the duty of assisting the birth of this liberation, of giving witness to it, of ensuring that it is complete. This is not foreign to evangelization.
>
> Between evangelization and human advancement – development and liberation – there are in fact profound links. These include links of an anthropological order, because the man who is to be evangelized is not an abstract being but is subject to social and economic questions. They also include links in the theological order, since one cannot dissociate the plan of creation from the plan of Redemption. The latter plan touches the very concrete situations of injustice to be combated and of justice to be restored. They include links of the eminently evangelical order, which is that of charity: how in fact can one proclaim the new commandment without promoting in justice and in peace the true, authentic advancement of man?[14]

Before moving on to the second theme of our study, modernity, I shall give a brief overview of some statistics showing developments in Catholicism in the course of the 20th century.

Development and demographic distribution of Catholicism in the 20th century

Extraordinary changes have taken place in the cultural and geographic distribution of present-day Catholicism. In 1900 around 90 percent of Catholics were to be found in only two regions: Europe (67.8 percent) and Latin America (21.98 percent), with Europe clearly predominant. A comparison of the two regions shows that there were three times more Catholics in Europe than in Latin America. However, in the course of the 20th century, Europe and Latin America changed positions. In the year 2000, Europe's share had gone down to 27.04 percent and Latin America's share had gone up to 45.5 percent.

The second significant movement is the growth of Catholicism in Africa (from 0.71 percent to 11.37 percent of its adherents) and in Asia (from 4.16 percent to 10.44 percent). These two continents have taken the place occupied at the beginning of the century by North America (from 4.87 percent to 6.71 percent), coming third and fourth after Latin America and Europe, and pushing North America down from third to fifth place, numerically considered.

In the course of the 20th century and increasingly so after 1970, Catholicism became a church with two-thirds of its faithful (67.31 percent) based in areas outside the main centres of modern capitalism: Europe and North America. It is now a church more and more involved in the everyday problems of the peoples of Asia, Africa and Latin America, where the issues linked to extreme poverty, hunger, the AIDS pandemic, mass unemployment, damage to the environment and civil war are uppermost in people's minds. It is, moreover, a church in which the majority of the faithful at present predominantly speak the two Iberian languages – Castillian Spanish and Portuguese – and no longer French or Italian.

Nonetheless, the presence of the churches of Latin America, Asia and Africa in the decision-making structures of Catholicism is extremely weak, and the predominant vision of the world continues to be European and to a lesser extent North American.

The overall number of Catholics increased approximately fourfold in the course of the 20th century, growing at a rate slightly faster than the world population (3.7 times), which from 1.6 billion in 1900 rose to 6 billion by the end of the century. However, the increase was 5.5 times in North America, a little over 8 times in Australasia and in Latin America, but almost 10 times in Asia and 63 times in Africa, while it was only 1.5 times in Europe. This uneven rate of growth explains the shift of the numerical predominance of Catholics from Europe to the

Americas and, increasingly, to Asia, and above all Africa. Catholicism has definitely left its European cradle and in the third millennium it will be a church that is increasingly Latin American and African, to a lesser degree Asian, and only after that North American and European. Without a doubt the star of the third millennium will be Africa, which will entail a quite profound cultural and historical reconfiguration of Catholic tradition.

Modernity

Generally, it can be said that in the West modernity begins at the end of the Latin Middle Ages and the awakening of the Renaissance. There are those, however, who prefer to trace the roots of modernity back to the founding of the universities in the flourishing European cities of the 13th century and the intellectual adventure arising from the encounter of medieval Christian thinking with the philosophical corpus of Aristotle and Greek-Islamic science, with its resulting synthesis, which found its most complete expression in the *Summa Theologica* of St Thomas Aquinas. [15]

Modernity in its many manifestations

Modernity takes on many forms, but its central concern is always the human individual and the independence of reason, freed from the tutelage of religion. Descartes' *Cogito ergo sum* ("I think, therefore I am") in his *Discourse on Method* shows with crystal clarity this break with earlier medieval thought and the transcendence under which it functioned. Aristotelian "science" experienced a slow but progressive decline with the introduction of the experimental method and the firm establishment of the principles that, after Copernicus, Galileo and Newton, came to govern the sciences of astronomy, physics, mathematics and chemistry, and later of biology and genetics, initiating the vast modern development of science and technology, and the controversies between science and faith.

The Protestant Reformation marked the emergence of a fresh religious sensibility concentrating more on the individual and free will than on the church and its magisterium. In the Catholic world, the Society of Jesus (the Jesuits) marked a break with the earlier monastic tradition and even with the medieval mendicant orders, which maintained the choral and thus communal observance of the divine office. The Jesuits, following Gutenberg's technical advance of printing books with movable type, were able to live separately from the community as they undertook their missionary task, while individually maintaining their private recitation of the Breviary. They were still linked with their companions by the invisible thread of their reciting the offices at the same hour of the day.

The secularization of political power, which received its theoretical expression in Machiavelli's *Prince* (separating as far as possible morality from politics), from its beginning in the Italian city-states, resulted in the modern nation-states, forged in the crucible of the English revolution of Cromwell, in the declaration of the rights of the citizen in the constitution of the United States, in the ideas of "liberty, equality and fraternity" in the French revolution of 1789 and in the Italian *rissorgimento* and unification in 1860.

It is also possible to speak of another face of modernity, which is not bourgeois but proletarian and socialist, in the proposals for the state coming from the utopian socialists, in the revolutions of 1848, the Paris commune of 1870 and, ultimately, in the Russian revolution of 1917. The Marxist analysis of capitalism led later to criticism of all colonialism and neo-colonialism, which in practice were a denial of the equality of all peoples, races and cultures, and denied to colonized countries and peoples the right to independence and self-determination. In the field of economics, modernity merged with the commercial revolution and later with the industrial, technical and scientific revolutions, thus giving rise to a multiplicity of interpretations, highlighting sometimes one of its aspects and sometimes another.

Among its classical interpreters, Auguste Comte (1798–1857) gives pride of place to the advances in science and technology. For him, modernity represents progress from an initial theological age, dominated by a religious interpretation of the world, through a second metaphysical age, where the lead is taken by rational philosophical interpretation, but without experimental investigation into reality, to a third age, which he called "positive", characterized by science and scientific principles. Comte sees modernity as the establishment of science and technology as the main motors of human progress.

Another interpreter, Alexis de Tocqueville (1805–59) cast his gaze on the world of politics. Born into an aristocratic family, as a young French deputy only just emerging from the whirlwind of revolution he was sent at the age of 26 to the United States to study their prison system (1831–32) in order to gain ideas for reforming the French system. Faced with the collapse of monarchist France, which was bringing his own social class down with it, and before the impact of the emerging American democracy, de Tocqueville views the advent of modernity as a political revolution, involving an end to absolutes, the abolition of the monarchy, the aristocracy and the power of the clergy, and the rise of other social strata, based on the principle of citizenship and universal human rights. For him, modernity finds its expression in the democratization of society.

Karl Marx (1818–83), for his part, interprets modernity by seeking its roots in the field of economics, in the passage from commercial to industrial capitalism achieved by the bourgeois revolutions and their attendant increasing social division and conflict, as the number of factory workers increased. In the factories and in society the industrial revolution resulted in the creation of two opposing social classes: the bourgeoisie, who possessed the ownership of the means of production, and the proletariat, who had nothing to call their own and were compelled to sell their labour. The bourgeoisie remained under the influence of the liberal ideas of the Enlightenment and the working class was sustained by its vision of social equality, which would be achieved by the abolition of the private ownership of the means of production and the consequent disappearance of social class.

Max Weber (1864–1920) regards modernity, in the cultural and religious sphere, as *Entzäuberung*, the disenchantment of the world, or secularization. In the economic and social realm, bureaucratic rationalization, also adopted by the state, would be the key to understanding modernity. The Calvinist Protestant work ethic, with its understanding of vocation *(Beruf)* and frugality, which postpones consumption, was to be the initial basis for modern capitalist wealth accumulation.

In the field of philosophy, the trajectory linking Descartes with Kant and Hegel with Marx shows the establishment of a philosophy increasingly removed from the presuppositions underlying the dialogue between Christian belief and Greek philosophy, which had achieved a balanced synthesis in the 13th century.

The Catholic tradition of intransigence in the face of modernity

What has all this to do with Vatican II? Over a long period of time the main impact of the Council was that it represented the beginning of a dialogue with modernity, which the church had been systematically resisting for four centuries.

At the beginning, important sectors of the church had gladly welcomed the cultural movement of the Renaissance. Figures such as Erasmus of Rotterdam, Thomas More and many others within Catholicism broke with medieval scholasticism and creatively and freely revisited classical antiquity. Artists of the calibre of Pinturicchio, Raphael and Michelangelo flocked to the papal court in Rome, considerably influenced by the Renaissance winds from Florence, the home city of Leo X, son of Lorenzo the Magnificent of the powerful Medici family, which also provided other popes during that period.

Among historians there is today a growing consensus that there were in many parts of Europe significant but dispersed and isolated reform movements within Catholicism at the end of the 15th and beginning of the 16th centuries. They met, however, with little acceptance in Rome. According to Martina, the results of these spontaneous movements "were still slight and far from being a serious and profound renewal, all the more so because resistance to religious renewal came above all from the Roman curia, where pontiffs and their functionaries were really unaware of the seriousness of the danger and were living complacent lives in idleness and worldliness". [16]

The failure of the reforms proposed by the fifth Lateran council (1512–17) convened unwillingly by Julius II (1503–13) and unenthusiastically concluded by Leo X (1513–21), and the subsequent break with Luther in Germany (1517), forced changes on Rome, which was frightened by the direction being taken by the new trends: free will, freedom of investigation in the sciences and arts, a critical spirit and also the demand for the church to be more evangelical *in capite et in membris*, in its head and members. Within the ranks of the church, Savonarola, Giordano Bruno and Galileo Galilei were only some of the victims of the desire to put a stop to the movement that had already escaped elsewhere from pontifical control. Even the dilatory convening of the council of Trent (1545–63), which was long overdue, and its fitful progress were unable to suppress it.

The council of Trent, which was intended to re-establish a bridge with the Protestant reformers and provide a response to the call for reforms within the church, became better known as the departure point for the Catholic Counter-Reformation, thus placing itself in opposition not only to the Protestant Reformation but also to modernity, then in its early stages.

The church was to find itself in a position further opposed to the 18th-century Enlightenment and the French revolution, which represented a break with its centuries-long alliance with the state and, in particular, the monarchy, which had until then been regarded as by divine right. With Gregory XVI, pope from 1831 to 1846, and Pius IX, who succeeded him from 1846 to 1878, these intransigent positions found expression in documents that were increasingly hardline: the encyclical *Mirari Vos* (1832) against indifferentism and rationalism; *Quanta Cura* (1864) against naturalism, socialism and the doctrine of separation of civil power from religion; and, finally, a tirade against modern errors, spelt out and condemned in *Syllabus Errorum* (1864). This intransigent position was softened, but not abandoned, under Leo XIII (1878–1903), who in a letter to the archbishop of Baltimore (1899) condemned the close relationship between Catholicism and democracy in the United States. This hard position made a strong comeback in the encyclical *Pascendi* (1907), in which Pius X condemned modernism, and in *Humani Generis* by Pius XII (1950), against dangerous trends in modern philosophy, particularly evolution and relativism, and against the so-called "new theology" and new methods of biblical exegesis. This stream of thought was to surface during the Council in the *Coetus Internationalis Patrum*, a minority group led by the French archbishop Marcel Lefebvre, and supported by two Brazilian bishops, who had played a leading role in his organization and campaigns: the archbishop of Diamantina, Minas Gerais, Geraldo de Proença Sigaud, the secretary of the group, and the bishop of Campos, Rio de Janeiro, Antônio de Castro Mayer, who was one of its most high-profile spokesmen.

This intransigent position condemned modernity wholesale and was incapable of seeing any redeeming positive aspect in its long history from the Renaissance onwards. It is against this background that we can understand what a veritable earthquake Vatican II was, since the intransigent current, with the exception of brief interludes of timid openness under Leo XIII and Benedict XV, had held unassailable sway in Rome.

The Council and the modern world

John XXIII surprised the world when, on 25 January 1959, he announced the calling of an ecumenical council, together with a synod for the diocesan church of Rome and the reform of the code of canon law. [17] Many Roman theologians were of the opinion that further councils could be dispensed with, after Vatican I had concentrated so much power in the hands of the pope and defined his magisterium to be infallible in *ex cathedra* pronouncements.

The new element introduced by John XXIII was the specific proposal to initiate dialogue with other Christian churches and to undertake the internal renewal of the church. There was no wish to make any fresh condemnations, which marked a departure from the position that had been dominant since the council of Trent. By declaring that ecumenism was an aim of the Council, though not clearly defining the consequent steps, John XXIII was in a certain way marking the end of the Counter-Reformation, which had been based more on condemnation of the Protestant world than on dialogue with it, whether in its Lutheran version, its Reformed version, or its many subsequent versions.

Roger Garaudy, a French intellectual outside the church and a member of the central committee of the French communist party, captured this change of approach initiated by John XXIII very well in the title of his book on this new departure for the church: *From Anathema to Dialogue*. [18] John XXIII, and subsequently the Council, took on this new approach to modernity, leaving behind the period of condemnation and entering into a period of listening and dialogue.

The most telling metaphor for understanding the attitude of Vatican II to modernity is the document on the Pastoral Constitution on the Church in the Modern World, which was given the attractive title *Gaudium et Spes* (Joy and Hope). The force of this metaphor lies in the shift represented by this pastoral constitution: from an attitude of opposition to the world and a clear separation between the spheres of world and church, the profane and the sacred, to one of encounter and dialogue. [19] Flight from the world is replaced by incarnation in the world. In an image common at the time and which became the title of a book by that powerful prefect of the Congregation of the Holy Office, Cardinal Ottaviani, the church had been seen as a "bulwark" against the modern world, protecting itself from contamination by it and thus maintaining its sacred language, Latin (which was different from profane languages), its dress and its sacred institutions over against the institutions of the world. [20] Flight from the world was the best description of its project for a society that was perfect and thus a distinctive hallowed alternative to other societies in the world.

Gaudium et Spes, by placing the church in the world of today, was a statement that the church was relocating into the world, with the idea that it was within the world that dialogue had to be conducted, overcoming conflict in a common quest so as better to serve humankind with its hopes and its sufferings.

We shall now examine briefly some of the conciliar documents with a view to ascertaining how these issues were translated into practice in the Council and how this open door to modernity operated within the Council.

The liturgy and the vernacular

The first question to be discussed in the Council, in October 1962, was the question of the liturgy. Paradoxically, it would seem to be the issue furthest removed from the concerns of the world and modernity, but only apparently, for it deals with two key issues in the modern world.

The first is that the liturgy comes to be regarded, not with the celebrant, the priest, the one presiding over the celebration, but with the assembly of the faithful as the starting point. The central focus is on the gathered congregation, within which there will be various actors, the principal one being the congregation itself. In this we thus see, as it were, a democratization of the liturgy, where all – and not only the clergy and ordained ministers – can speak or have a role to perform. This also entails a break with the exclusion of women. In the liturgy up to that time they had been forbidden to enter the sanctuary, to speak, to touch the chalice or administer communion. Their role is still very limited, but this represents the breaking of a mould and a departure from the previous model.

The other break, perhaps the most obvious for people to see, was, in the area of the Latin Church, the end of the exclusive use of Latin in the liturgy and in ecclesiastical study. Latin had been regarded – wrongly, it must be acknowledged – as the one and only language in the Catholic Church. Wrongly, because there were other languages used in the liturgy of the Eastern Catholic churches. Greek still continued as the liturgical language in the Constantinopolitan rite; Armenian in the Armenian ritual tradition; Syriac in the Antiochene rite; and the Slav languages in the churches of Ukraine and the other Slav regions united with Rome. It is easily forgotten that within the Catholic Church, alongside the Latin tradition, there are many other churches with their own languages and rites in five major traditions: the Alexandrine, the Antiochene, the Armenian, the Chaldean, and the Constantinopolitan, or Byzantine. The Latin Catholic branch, the largest, is easily mistakenly seen as the whole of the Catholic Church.

In a memorable speech during the first session of the Council, Maximus IV Saigh, the Antiochene patriarch of the Melkites, put his finger on this erroneous view. As noted earlier, he caused a sensation by breaking the rules of the Council and speaking in French and not Latin. This act was a way of calling attention to the incongruity of imposing on the whole Council the burden of speaking in the language of one, but not all, of the churches of the Catholic communion. He continued by saying that the Melkites were fully Catholic, but not Latin, nor Roman, in their language, theology, liturgy and pastoral practice; and that all their tradition in terms of theology, liturgy and spirituality owed nothing to the church of Rome. His speech doubtlessly speeded up the growth in awareness in the Council of the legitimate linguistic, cultural, theological, pastoral and liturgical diversity within the church.

It should be noted that many of the Eastern Catholic churches are to be found in Brazil: the Melkite Church, the Maronite Church, the Ukrainian Church and the Armenian Church. For the other faithful of Eastern rites there is also an Ordinary located in Rio de Janeiro, providing pastoral care for those who do not have an Ordinary of their own rite.

In the Constitution on the Sacred Liturgy, *Sacrosanctum Concilium* (4 December 1963), the Council finally approved the use of languages other than Latin in the liturgy of the Latin Church. This change from Latin to vernacular languages in worship has certainly been the most obvious result of the Council in the daily experience of Catholics. The liturgy has splintered into hundreds of different languages, thus making possible what St Augustine said of himself: as a pastor he preferred to speak in a non-literary, even ungrammatical way, so as to be understood by the people, rather than giving the appearance of being highly educated, presenting himself as highly educated (which he was), and not being understood by his hearers.

The motivation behind this change was pastoral. It was recognized that the world had changed, that Latin was no longer the vernacular language spoken by the people and that it had become the language of only a limited clerical section of the church. At other times in the history of the church, this same pastoral concern has produced changes of direction at the cultural level. Witnessing the collapse of the Roman empire and with it the end of the classical world and its institutions thanks to the so-called barbarian peoples, St Jerome, at the request of Pope Damasus (366–384), withdrew to Palestine and from 382 undertook the monumental task of making a fresh translation of the Bible from the Hebrew and Greek manuscripts, the Syriac versions and the so-called Old Latin versions. This new translation was to make the biblical heritage accessible in popular everyday language, which was becoming increasingly removed from the pure classical elegance of the Old Latin versions. From this Herculean labour of St Jerome we have inherited the translation of the Bible known as the Vulgate since, as its name indicates, it was intended for the vulgus, the ordinary people. Today, we could say that Jerome has bequeathed us, in the strict sense of the word, a popular version of the Bible.

Analogously, the change in liturgical language from Latin to hundreds of modern vernacular languages has represented a break with the ancient and then medieval form of the Western liturgy, standardized in the post-Tridentine reform and in the revised edition of the Roman Missal issued by St Pius V (1566–72).

The position of Vatican II, which reaffirmed the use of Latin in the liturgy while opening up the possibility of the use of the vernacular, indicated acceptance of modernity in the area of language. In today's world, there is no longer a koine, a lingua franca, as was popular Greek, which spread throughout the Mediterranean with the conquests of Alexander the Great; or ancient Latin, which the expansion of the frontiers of the Roman empire took to the four corners of the European,

North African and Middle Eastern world; or even medieval Latin, which dominated the whole of the Latin West because of the cultural supremacy of the Catholic Church. At the time of the Council the scene was one of total linguistic diversity, whereas today English is taking on the role of a modern koine, since it is the language of the new North American empire. In practice, this dominance brings with it a sombre element, since to fight for one's own language is to fight for one's own identity and one's own vision of the future. The church has thus performed a great service by restoring to all peoples the possibility of celebrating the liturgy in their own language.

The church, the people of God

In the Dogmatic Constitution on the Church, *Lumen Gentium*, two aspects stand out, of which the first gave rise to a key debate on the proper definition of the church. Should it begin with the hierarchy, as was done classically after Trent and above all after Vatican I, which dealt with the role and attributes of the Roman pontiff and the bishops in its structure? Or should it make an about turn and begin with the people of God? In a draft distributed to the bishops, chapter 1 was an introduction, chapter 2 dealt with the hierarchy, and chapter 3 with the people of God. There then followed a battle in the Council over reversing the order of the chapters so as to define the church in the first instance as the people of God. By thus defining it, the people (*laos* in Greek) were being defined as central to the church. This presupposed a radical equality between all its members and indicated that it was baptism and not ordination that was the sacrament basic to the structure of relationships within the church. That was a reversal of all previous theology, whereby lay people could only exercise an apostolate in the church if they had become members of Catholic Action and received permission from the hierarchy. The activity of lay people had not been regarded as properly theirs, based on their vocation given in baptism, but as merely derivative and dependent on the hierarchy's permission. This theology of hierarchical permission, in which Catholic Action itself had been conceived as a participation in the apostolate of the hierarchy and as a sort of bridge between church and world, was now abandoned, and the basis of the apostolate of all Christians became their baptism.

This definition of the church as "the people of God" not only had the result of giving it a radically democratic structure, but also had another important result as a by-product. For "the people of God" is central to Luther's theological thinking. Some even accused the

Catholic Church of having become Lutheran by including in its definition this concept of the people of God. But it would be correct to say
that it had become more biblical and less legalistic in its language, thus
creating a very important opportunity for dialogue with the churches
arising from the Protestant Reformation.

The second aspect to be considered is that defining the church as the
people of God enabled other forms of organization to arise within it that
would have been unimaginable but for this change of theory. A good
example are the present diocesan synods. Previously, the bishop
decided everything, practically on his own. Some still today continue
to take decisions in that way, but increasingly another direction is being
taken. The pastoral work done jointly by priests, religious, deacons and
above all by lay people has been taken so seriously that it is no longer
possible for it to remain solely in the hands of the bishop, or even in the
hands of priests and religious. It is a responsibility shared by all the baptized, men and women. Diocesan synods, which are gatherings of the
people of God, are an expression of this common shared responsibility
in the policies and tasks of the church, as are also the diocesan pastoral
councils and the parish or community councils. The ecclesial base communities were not contemplated in the Council text, but they were
immediately included and recommended in the integrated pastoral plan
of the national Brazilian bishops conference, approved in November
1965, during the Council's fourth session before it closed. They are a
more radical form of participation, with their members having much
more independence and administrative responsibility, and with no internal distinction between different forms of ministry. There has thus been
created within the Catholic Church a definite space where women can
take on a greater number of responsibilities and ministries, including
local leadership in church life. The Medellín conference aptly speaks
of the extent of these changes in its description of the ecclesial base
communities in its document on its integrated pastoral policy:

> Thus the Christian base community is the foremost and basic church
> nucleus, which at its own level should take responsibility for the richness
> and dissemination of the faith, and also for the worship which is its expres-
> sion. It is, therefore, the basic building block in the structure of the church,
> a centre for evangelization and at the present time its prime agent for human
> advancement and development.[21]

Ecumenism between *Lumen Gentium* and *Dominus Iesus*

It is worthwhile to examine a further point in *Lumen Gentium* that
is crucial for ecumenical dialogue. When it deals with the one and only

church of Jesus Christ, at once visible and invisible, which is confessed in the Nicene-Constantinopolitan Creed as one, holy, catholic and apostolic, the Council proceeds:

> This church, constituted and organized as a society in the present world, subsists in *[subsistit in]* the Catholic Church, which is governed by the successor of Peter and by the bishops in communion with him. Nevertheless, many elements of sanctification and of truth are found outside its visible confines (LG 8).

The position of the Council is that it admits that there are elements of sanctification and truth, such as the sacraments, the word of God, and holiness, to be found in other Christian churches outside the Catholic Church. It further carefully avoids wording that would imply a total identity between the church of Christ and the Catholic Church. Thus the wording "Ecclesia Christi est Ecclesia Catholica" was replaced by a different formulation stating that "Ecclesia Christi subsistit in Ecclesia Catholica". The change of the verb "is" *(est)* to the verb "subsists in" *(subsistit in)* was the result of long debate and lengthy negotiations with a view to a wider vision of the boundaries of the church of Christ, which does not stop at the visible contours of the Catholic Church but extends beyond them and is present in the other Christian churches.

However, Cardinal Ratzinger (now Pope Benedict XVI) in the declaration *Dominus Iesus* of 6 August 2000, issued by the Congregation for the Doctrine of the Faith, proposed an interpretation of the Council's text which undermines the intention of the Council fathers by saying that *subsistit in* should be interpreted as having the same sense as *est*, thus affirming complete identity between the church of Christ and the Catholic Church.[22] This interpretation has been severely criticized, not only by the churches involved in the ecumenical journey and by the theological community, but also by leading personalities such as the highly regarded theologian Walter Kasper, bishop of Rotenburg, Germany, who has been elevated to the cardinalate and to the high responsibility of directing the Pontifical Council for Promoting Christian Unity. Leonardo Boff, whose thesis on the ecclesiology of Vatican II had Ratzinger himself, then professor of theology at Munich, as one of its examiners, and was recommended by him for publication, wrote a detailed appreciation of this key passage in *Lumen Gentium*.[23]

Kasper returned to the issue in his report on the present situation and future prospects for the ecumenical movement presented to the plenary session of the Pontifical Council in November 2001. The thrust of his argument is extremely important for the future course of the ecumenical movement, while at the same time reaffirming the foundations laid by Vatican II, especially on this point of the ecclesial elements present in the other Christian churches, which is the touchstone for Catholic credibility and seriousness in ecumenical dialogue.

Catholic principles on ecumenism

Concerning the conciliar Decree on Ecumenism *Unitatis Redintegratio*, a brief note is sufficient as a reminder that initially there had been three drafts on ecumenism: one prepared by the theological commission presided over by Cardinal Alfredo Ottaviani and included as chapter 11 in the draft *De Ecclesia*; a second, prepared by the commission of the Eastern churches on ecumenical relations with the ancient Eastern churches and the Orthodox churches; and a third, prepared by the secretariat of the Pontifical Council for Promoting Christian Unity, presided over by Cardinal Augustin Bea and dealing with ecumenical relations with the churches originating in the Reformation. The Council fathers requested that they be combined in a single draft to be presented by the secretariat. An initial point in the debate concerned the wording of the proposed title for chapter 1, which was "Principles of Catholic Ecumenism". That wording was rejected on the grounds that there was no such thing as "Catholic ecumenism", since the ecumenical movement was a single whole and had come into being outside the ambit of Catholicism. What there could be was a statement of "Catholic Principles on Ecumenism"; in other words, a statement of Catholic guidelines for entry into and participation in the ecumenical journey.

Ecumenism is important in that it places dialogue and cooperation – rather than competition, let alone open war – at the centre of inter-church relations.

Religious freedom and modernity

The most crucial document for dialogue with modernity, apart from *Gaudium et Spes*, is the Declaration on Religious Freedom, *Dignitatis Humanae*.

The traditional position in countries with a Catholic majority was to affirm that in the field of religion truth had all rights and error had none. In practice, this meant that, since Catholicism was the one true religion, it alone should be supported and protected by the state. A model for church-state relations was thus presupposed, based on union between them, with the corollary that Catholicism was declared to be the official religion of the state. Other religions or churches could be at most tolerated, for the sake of public order, but never supported or encouraged or placed on an equal footing with the Catholic religion. That whole edifice was brought down by the Declaration on Religious Freedom, which formally established the right of individuals and communities to social and civil freedom in the field of religion:

> The Vatican Council declares that the human person has a right to religious freedom. Freedom of this kind means that all men should be immune from coercion on the part of individuals, social groups and every human power, so that, within due limits, nobody is forced to act against his convictions nor is anyone to be restrained from acting in accordance with his convictions in religious matters in private or in public, alone or in associations with others. The Council further declares that the right to religious freedom is based on the very dignity of the human person as known through the revealed word of God and by reason itself. This right of the human person to religious freedom must be given such recognition in the constitutional order of society as will make it a civil right. (DH 2)

In one of its most controversial points, the Council declared that this right holds good even for those who do not comply with the obligation to seek the truth, since it is a right inherent in the individual's conscience that may in no way be infringed:

> Therefore the right to religious freedom has its foundation not in the subjective attitude of the individual but in his very nature. For this reason the right to this immunity continues to exist even in those who do not live up to their obligation of seeking the truth and adhering to it. The exercise of this right cannot be interfered with as long as the just requirements of public order are observed. (DH 2)

The most vigorous support for the draft on religious freedom came from the United States. The United States is a religiously pluralist country and has never had a system in which the state supports a particular church or religion in general. Catholicism had been regarded with a degree of distrust, since it was feared that, if it became the majority religion, it would be tempted to curtail the rights of other religious groups. These feelings surfaced strongly during the election campaign of John F. Kennedy, the first Catholic to be US president. It was essential for the American bishops to allay those fears once and for all. On the other hand, the difficult situation of Catholicism in the mission field, notably in Muslim countries, could not be confronted without, similarly, the rights of persons of other religions being scrupulously safeguarded in traditionally Catholic-majority countries, such as Spain, Portugal and Italy, where Catholicism was the state religion or enjoyed extensive privileges.

The interesting aspect of the debate and the Council's Declaration was that discussion was not limited to practical issues, but also explored their doctrinal basis in an attempt to respond to a deeper understanding of human persons and their inviolable conscience, and to one of the core principles of modernity, that of the strict civil equality of all citizens, irrespective of class, colour, race or political or religious belief. The Declaration considers the rights of the individual as well as those of religious communities:

> The freedom or immunity from coercion in religious matters which is the right of individuals must also be accorded to men when they act in community. Religious communities are a requirement of the nature of man and of religion itself… Religious communities also have the right not to be hindered by legislation or administrative action on the part of the civil authority in the selection, training, appointment and transfer of their own ministers, in communicating with religious authorities and communities in other parts of the world, in erecting buildings for religious purposes, and in the acquisition and use of the property they need. (DH 4)

The provisions of the above paragraph were aimed directly at the difficult religious situation (as much for Catholics as for Orthodox and Protestants) in the socialist countries of Eastern Europe and the former Soviet Union, but also in China, North Korea, North Vietnam and Cuba. Despite the détente initiated under John XXIII, which had succeeded in bringing to the Council a considerable number of bishops, some of them released from prison, such as Joseph Beran, the archbishop of Prague, or directly from labour camps, such as Josyf Slipy of Ukraine, and the initial steps taken by Paul VI in his Ostpolitik with a view to re-establishing the Catholic hierarchy in those countries, the situation remained legally precarious and subject to swings in national policies or to international fluctuations in the cold war.

In the eyes of secular public opinion the Declaration on Religious Freedom was the passport for the entry of the Catholic Church into modernity, in its totally clear statement that the human conscience is inviolable and cannot be invaded by either church or state; and that people's religious choice should be free from all and every coercion or external constraint, and that not even God violates this sanctuary of the individual's conscience.

Modernity thus entails a whole range of freedoms, but above all the profound freedom, which is freedom of conscience and to choose one's religion. It is to be regretted that this core document for understanding the intention of the Council for the contemporary world is so little studied and so little commented on in our country and that there is as yet no authoritative commentary on it available in our language.

Gaudium et Spes : a dialogue, but with what sort of modernity?

Finally, we come to *Gaudium et Spes*, the subject matter of which was not on the Council's agenda. It initially appeared as draft 17 in the reordering of the Council material after the first session. It then became draft 13, and was finally approved as the Pastoral Constitution on the Church in the Modern World, *Gaudium et Spes*.

Great hopes surrounded it, but it also caused great disappointment. What were those hopes? There was an important fringe group in the Council that included Dom Helder Camara. The group represented the church of the poor, and bishops from the third world, for whom the Council's agenda was a European agenda, largely a church agenda for a church turned in on itself. This agenda did not include the most painful and distressing issues, such as hunger, poverty, war, colonialism, underdevelopment, exploitation and lack of opportunities for the great majority of humankind. In the eyes of this fairly large group, the Council would either take on board these issues, or it would pass by on the other side, deaf to the cries of two-thirds of the human race, in particular the poor of the earth. Great hopes were raised when the battle was won for a draft dealing with the problems of today's world. However, this major issue of the poor found its way onto the agenda only with difficulty, in a low key, which caused Helder Camara at the end of the third session to write that preparations should begin for the holding of Vatican III, which would be a Council where the voices of the third world would be heard and heeded. Paul VI, for his part, sensitive to these criticisms, promised that after the Council an encyclical would address the growing gulf between North and South. In the course of the fourth Council session, he also charged Fr Lebret (a French Dominican and author of the book *Suicide and Survival of the West*) and Helder Camara with the task of preparing the initial draft of what was later to be the encyclical on the Development of Peoples, *Populorum Progressio*.

This leads us directly to a question: What were the limits of the Council in its approach to modernity? Many European theologians in the progressive stream have made a clear, relevant criticism of the Council, particularly of the way in which it deals with the issues in the chapter on the family in *Gaudium et Spes*. Along with undeniable advances, such as the abandonment of the traditional teaching on the purposes of marriage (the first being procreation, the second mutual support of husband and wife and the avoidance of fornication), which was replaced in all clarity by "the intimate partnership of life and the love which constitutes the married state" (GS 48) and by responsible fatherhood and motherhood, other issues were only dealt with in a half-baked way or were withdrawn from consideration by the Council, such as artificial means of birth control.

These criticisms did not, however, touch on a more fundamental problem and did not confront the ambiguous nature of Western modernity. It is ambiguous in its dominant centre – Europe and the United States – since the "progress" that has been made, in particular by industrialization, has been historically achieved at the price of ruthless exploitation of the working class and an equally harsh treatment of a work-force of women and children in mines and textile mills. It is equally ambiguous as regards the countries of the South because, while the process was presented as bringing "enlightenment and material and spiritual progress", it has in practice brought with it colonialism and enslaved Indigenous peoples in America, Africa and Asia. In suppressing the rights of peoples to independence and of individuals to freedom, we can see the other face of modernity. It represented, at the world's margins, a reinforcement of political domination, economic exploitation and the denial of rights. And it continues today, as when the president of the United States brands particular countries as "the axis of evil" and arrogates to himself the right, against all international rules and conventions, to declare wars that are, according to him, "preventive". In the North American imagination, Islam has today taken the place of Ronald Reagan's "evil empire": the USSR.

The difficulty in dealing with these two sides of modernity was clearly evident in the Council, and has had repercussions in the way in which the place of the church in today's world is envisaged.

Gustavo Gutiérrez has given a graphic illustration of the shift represented by *Gaudium et Spes*. [24] The situation before the Council could be likened to two spheres, church and world, separated from each another, the one rooted in tradition and the other driven by modernity. That situation of isolation (almost always one of opposition and conflict) led to the building of bridges, particularly by lay members of Catholic Action, who saw their sphere of action to be outside the sanctuary of the churches and more particularly in work-places, educational institutions and the economic, political, artistic and scientific fields – in short, in the world. *Gaudium et Spes* was to mark the end of that separation of the two spheres, and even of the bridge-building between them, and signified a relocation of the sphere of the church – the whole church and not just lay people – into the world. The critical interpretation coming from the third world, however, was that the world was divided and riddled with conflict. Therefore, it was not enough to take a leap into the world. You had to ask where the church should be in this divided world and on what side it should be in the midst of conflicting demands and interests. Should it be on the side of the vast oppressed majority or on the side of the powerful elites? Gutiérrez then went on to say that the great question was not "Is the church in the world?" but "In what world?", "In what part of the world?" and "What groups is it in solidarity with, and what vision of the world is it espousing?" These sorts of question are rarely asked. [25] They appear here and there in the Council, but in a low key. The main thrust lies elsewhere, and that can explain why there were great repercussions but minimal practical results from the proposal to rearrange all the Council material that was presented by Cardinal Giacomo Lercaro to the Council on 6 December 1962.

Lercaro began his speech by saying, "The mystery of Christ in the church has always been, and is pre-eminently today, the mystery of Christ in the poor, since the church, as the Holy Father John XXIII has said, is the church of all, but above all 'the church of the poor'." He pleaded that this essential aspect of the Christian mystery should appear in one way or another, explicitly and sufficiently, in the various Council drafts. He added that, if the Council intended to respond to the expectations of humankind today, it should have at the centre of its thinking the mystery of Christ in the poor and the task of evangelizing them. He concluded by saying that the poor could not be one theme among many themes of the Council, but simply its theme.

That same day Lercaro was supported by the voice of the Christian East in the person of Mgr Hakim de Nazaré, bishop of Ptolemaida, who said that the Council had raised great hopes that must not be disappointed. They had arisen mainly from the approach proposed by John XXIII in his opening speech:

> The pope has certainly opened up a new way, which is a response to the aspirations of the world, this world of which St Paul says that it is suffering the pangs of childbirth, this world that looks to the church to be there for it as the mother of all. "The church of all and more particularly the church of the poor", as the Holy Father said on 11 September and as His Eminence Cardinal Lercaro in moving words has just reminded us.
>
> It is certain that the real results of our Council will only be felt ten or fifteen years from now. What will the world, what will the church, be like then? Whether we want it or not, a Council at the end of the 20th century must be the Council of the 21st century, when the world population will have doubled, reaching six billion, and when hunger will also have increased twofold. What will the evangelization of the world involve then?

Dom Antônio Fragoso, bishop of Crateús and one of the young Brazilian bishops attending the Council, who was a member of the group "church of the poor", in a statement to the author, thirty years on, has made this comment about the group that met in the Belgian college to discuss the stance of the Council on the poor:

> We were 36 bishops, one patriarch, Maximos IV, some cardinals, among them [Giacomo] Lercaro, and some archbishops and bishops. Of the bishops I remember Mgr [Charles-Marie] Himmer, of Tournai [in Belgium], myself, and others whom I do not remember. The group began during the first session. We had as secretaries Paul Gauthier and Marie-Thérèse Lescase. The subject for discussion was the church and the poor, beginning with Jesus identifying with the poor. I remember the main argument: when we affirm the identity between Jesus and the consecrated bread, "This is my body", we worship [it] and draw from that consequences for our spirituality, liturgy and everything else. But when we affirm the identity between Jesus and those who do not have bread or shelter, we do not draw out the consequences for our spirituality, liturgy and pastoral work. I remember that, at our final session, we went to celebrate our final eucharist in one of the catacombs. We signed a commitment that we would be there for the poor and give priority attention to the poor (not to have money in the bank, nor to build up assets), and that act of commitment was signed by 500 bishops.

Dom Fragoso, however, also made a hard discovery: "[The Council] enabled me to discover (an interpretation I made later) that the poor were not on the hearts of the bishops nor their concern. That is why the Council did not devote more attention to the subject. The Council enabled me to leave behind my pessimism about nature, and gave me happiness, but I did not see it becoming reconciled with the poor."

Although one month before opening the Council John XXIII had said that the great issue was the church of the poor and that the crucial question was what the church would be doing about the poor, who were in the ascendancy, and with poverty in the world, that was not, in fact, the central concern of the Council. The proposal presented to the Council on 4 December 1962 by Cardinal Leo Joseph Suenens of Malines-Brussels to structure all the Council material around two poles, *ecclesia ad intra* and *ecclesia ad extra*, was what attracted the majority consensus:

> That the Council be the Council "de ecclesia", and consist of two parts: "de ecclesia ad intra" and "de ecclesia ad extra".
> "De ecclesia ad intra". We should in the first place examine what the church is in itself, as the mystery of the living Christ in his mystical body: what is

in truth the nature of the church. We thus ask the church: what do you say of yourself?...

"De ecclesia ad extra". Under this heading we deal with the church in its dialogue with the world. The world is looking to the church to provide solutions to relevant questions that the world is presenting to it.

Among such questions, the Cardinal mentioned the sacredness of life and the inviolability of the human person, social justice, evangelization of the poor, international peace and war.

The dream of Dom Helder Camara of a third Vatican council in which the most urgent perspectives of the forgotten face of modernity should be really confronted was in part realized in the second general conference of Latin American bishops at Medellín, Colombia, in 1968. There, some of the issues on which no progress had been made in the Council were taken up and dealt with. In the field of ecclesiology, for instance, the Medellín document devoted to it was given the title "The Poverty of the Church".

In this regard, and taking into account the situation in Brazil and in Latin America as a whole, one of the useful – and at times essential – ways of interpreting Vatican II is to re-examine it by taking Medellín and its way of approaching various issues as the starting point. As an example of these different approaches it would be useful to examine the ways in which the Council and Medellín deal with the issues of peace, war and violence, issues that are again high on the agenda of our world.

The Cuban missile crisis of October 1962 began the week following the opening of the Council. John XXIII was greatly shaken by the realization that the world had arrived at the brink of a nuclear war, in which the whole human race could have been wiped out, without there having been channels of direct communication between the main world leaders. Two months before his death, the pope bequeathed a wise and illuminating legacy in the form of the encyclical *Pacem in Terris* (Peace on Earth).

Medellín: peace versus institutionalized violence

During the Council the theme of peace was addressed and developed in the second part of *Gaudium et Spes*, and for this greatly differing demands came together. The background was of course the traditional teaching of the church on the "just war", with its threefold function of condemning war as evil, limiting the damage it causes, and making the way in which it is conducted as humane as possible. This doctrine had been considerably whittled away as a result of the slaughter of the two world wars. Could war still be considered a "just" recourse in order to settle conflicts between nations and peoples?

Pius XII had taken on board the growing doubts in public opinion and among moral theologians and had become a spokesperson for the advances in ethical thinking on this issue, clearly setting out contemporary teaching. "Pius XII condemned all wars except those undertaken in self-defence. Previous traditional definitions of the just war had allowed a variety of legitimate reasons for taking up arms. But, influenced by his own experiences, Pius XII insisted that the sole legitimate moral reason for war was self-defence."[26]

John XXIII contributed to the subject with *Pacem in Terris* in April 1963:

> Men nowadays are becoming more and more convinced that any disputes which may arise between nations must be resolved by negotiation and agreement, and not by recourse to arms.
> We acknowledge that this conviction owes its origin chiefly to the terrifying destructive force of modern weapons. It arises from fear of the ghastly and catastrophic consequences of their use. Thus, in this age which boasts of its atomic power, it no longer makes sense to maintain that war is a fit instrument with which to repair the violation of justice.

What is new in John XXIII is a departure from the traditional position, and even from that of Pius XII, in that it shows an advance towards a more radical perspective for peace: even in cases of the violation of justice, war could not be regarded as an appropriate instrument to right it.

In the course of debate on *Gaudium et Spes* during the fourth session of the Council, there was a clash (at times sharp) between three positions: that of the more radical pacifists, who were following the line of John XXIII; that of the supporters of the traditional doctrine of the just war, supported by those who believed the possession of nuclear weapons was an effective deterrent for maintaining peace; and, finally, those who shifted the debate to the threat to peace presented by the gulf of inequality between social classes and countries, and the poverty, hunger and underdevelopment that was the cruel burden shouldered by two-thirds of humankind. A compromise between the two first positions was reached in the document, while the third position was downgraded and only managed to appear in a few places, such as in the condemnation of the arms race: "Therefore, we declare once again: the arms race is one of the greatest curses on the human race and the harm it inflicts on the poor is more than can be endured."

Medellín devoted its first two documents in a very clear way to issues that had not been given a space of their own in the Council:

justice and peace. Its bold stance in the specific circumstances of Latin America can be summarized in one of its pastoral proposals: "The fight against poverty is the real war in which our nations should be engaged" (Med. 2,29b). Consistent with this vision, Medellín begins its reflection on peace with the dictum from *Populorum Progressio*: "If the new name for peace is development, underdevelopment in Latin America, with its distinctive manifestations in different countries, is an unjust situation giving rise to tensions that conspire against peace" (Med. 2,1).

Medellín examines these tensions in three groups: those arising out of the clash between social classes and internal colonialism; those that result from neo-colonialism from abroad; and those that emerge between the countries of Latin America.

The first group lists the various forms of social, economic, political, cultural, racial and religious marginalization; excessive inequality between social classes; growing frustration in those sectors of society that have been constantly ignored in their countries; the various forms of oppression by dominant groups and sectors, where there is evidently a "lamentable insensitivity by the most privileged sectors in face of the misery of the marginalized sectors"; and the power unjustly used by certain dominant sectors, who quickly resort to "the use of force in order to repress with drastic measures any attempt to react" (Med. 2,2–6). These tensions were becoming much sharper, as the oppressed sectors were growing in awareness, as Paul VI recalled in a speech to the peasants in Bogotá in 1968: "But today, the problem has become more acute, because you have become more aware of your needs and your suffering, and you are no longer willing to accept that these conditions should continue without appropriate steps being taken to remedy them" (Med. 2,7).

The second group of tensions was to do with economics and politics. Economically, neo-colonialism was seen in the growing imbalance in international trade relations, with countries producing raw materials increasingly at a disadvantage vis-à-vis industrialized countries, capital flight, the brain drain, tax evasion, and profits and dividends going abroad; progressive indebtedness; powerful international monopolies; and international monetary imperialism, resulting in nothing less than economic dictatorship (Med. 2,8–9). Politically, there was condemnation of the constant pressure exerted by imperialism "of whatever ideological shade" on Latin American countries, even going as far as direct intervention. In practice, such interventions were almost always made by the United States (Med. 2,10).

The third group listed the tensions between Latin American countries resulting from extreme nationalism or the arms race, which was condemned without qualification, using the words of *Populorum Progressio*: "When so many people are hungry, when so many families suffer from destitution, when so many remain steeped in ignorance... every exhausting armaments race becomes an intolerable scandal" (Med. 2,11–13).

The Medellín conference could not ignore the phenomenon of violence in Latin America. In its examination of violence and its causes, it introduced the concept of "structural institutionalized violence", the underlying violence that often provokes desperate resistance by the oppressed sectors of society in the form of revolutionary violence. Medellín identified among the signs of the times the growing awareness of these impoverished and oppressed sectors (Med. 2,7).

In his opening speech to the second conference, Paul VI had vehemently condemned "those systems and structures that disguise and encourage serious and oppressive inequality between classes and citizens of the same country", but also those who had chosen the path of "systematic rebellion, shedding of blood, anarchy".[27] The background to the pope's speech was the growing confrontation between the population and the military dictatorships and oligarchical political systems in Latin America, and at the same time the growing phenomenon of urban and rural guerrilla movements. In Colombia, it had attracted into its ranks a brilliant priest and social scientist, Fr Camilo Torres Restrepo, who had died in combat on 15 February 1966. His death had had enormous repercussions in Colombia and throughout the continent, and his image had become a symbol, similar to that of Che Guevara, of legitimate revolution by the poor. Camilo Torres was not an isolated case and various clergy and lay movements were sympathetic towards him.

Medellín closely links peace with the struggle for justice and the removal of inequality and poverty, which together comprise continuous war against the poor. It attempts to distinguish various existing types of violence, identifying the underlying cause of them all.

If Christians believe in the fruitfulness of peace as a means of achieving justice, they also believe that justice is an indispensable condition for peace. It can be clearly seen that Latin America is in many parts facing a situation of injustice that can be described as institutionalized violence, when, through lack of structures for agricultural and industrial enterprise, for economic activity at home and abroad and for cultural and political life, "whole populations destitute of necessities live in a state of dependence barring them from all initiative and responsibility, and all opportunity to advance culturally and share in social and political life",[28] thus violating their fundamental rights. This situation demands worldwide, bold, urgent changes and far-reaching renewal. It is not surprising, therefore, that there is coming into being in Latin America a "grave temptation to have recourse to violence". We should not try the patience of a people who for years have been enduring conditions which those who have greater awareness of human rights would find difficult to accept. (Med. 2,16)

On receiving and reading the conclusions of Medellín, Paul VI said, in an audience with Mgr Eduardo Pironio, the general secretary of CELAM (Latin American Council of Bishops), that he agreed with the stance taken by the document on institutionalized violence. He would therefore suggest that some examples be added to clarify what was being described. Following Paul VI's suggestion, an addition was made to the official document in the form of a paragraph taken from the encyclical *Populorum Progressio*, as above, giving examples of structural violence.

This novel way of thinking about war and peace in the circumstances of Latin America in no way lessened the perplexing dilemma for those engaged in pastoral work in face of the violence there. That clearly surfaces in the paragraph in which the bishops state their appreciation of the struggle for peace, even in sometimes tragic circumstances:

> When we consider the combination of circumstances in our countries and take into account Christians' desire for peace, the immense difficulties created by civil war and its logic of violence, the evil cruelty it gives rise to and the risk of attracting foreign intervention, however illegitimate, and the difficulty of building a regime of justice and freedom through violent means, it is our desire that the dynamism of the people, conscientized and organized, should be placed at the service of justice and peace. (Med. 2,19)

Conclusion

Medellín, by taking its own stance on peace, different from that of Vatican II, introduced into the debate themes that are crucial for Latin America, Africa and Asia, but which were somewhat downplayed during the Council. It added an original thought to the theme of violence, drawing attention to the structural violence of hunger, disease, unemployment and lack of education, which are a burden constantly borne by the great majority of the people in the third world. Medellín prevented uprising by the poor from being regarded as the only form of violence, for it is so often a desperate cry in the face of insensitivity, let alone repression, by regimes set up to maintain privilege and to reinforce anti-democratic structures, politically, economically and socially.

Medellín completes and enriches Vatican II. It is a sort of faithful reception of it, but it is at the same time creative, selective and very distinctive. It also sheds light on the questionable relationship between the Council and modernity, in particular modernity viewed from the point of view of the anguish and suffering, the dreams and hopes of the poor, who are excluded from its benefits and concerns.

By way of a final thought, it can be said that the Council was an essential step for this dialogue of the Catholic Church with modernity, enabling it to move forward in many areas, to give official recognition to ecumenism, interfaith dialogue and dialogue with those of no faith. Many of its results, however, came afterwards in unexpected ways, both in the liberation struggles in Latin America and the liberation theology behind them, and in the more radical demands for inculturation in Africa and in the attempts at dialogue with the great cultures and religions of Asia. These are certainly developments from seeds sown by the Council, which are only now coming to fruition and pointing to some of the new features that Catholicism will assume in the course of the 21st century.

NOTES

[1] Vatican II documents referred to here can be found in Austin Flannery ed., *Vatican Council II*, Dublin and Grand Rapids MI, Dominican Pubs and Eerdmans, 1988 and 1984:
SC = Constitution on the Sacred Liturgy, *Sacrosanctum Concilium*
LG = Dogmatic Constitution on the Church, *Lumen Gentium*
UR = Decree on Ecumenism, *Unitatis Redintegratio*
DH = Declaration on Religious Freedom, *Dignitatis Humanae*
GS = Pastoral Constitution on the Church in the Modern World, *Gaudium et Spes*
Other documents are published by the Catholic Truth Society, London:
PT = Encyclical Letter, *Pacem in Terris*, 1963
PP = Encyclical Letter, *Populorum Progressio*, 1967
EN = Apostolic Exhortation, *Evangelii Nuntiandi*, 1976
UUS = Encyclical Letter, *Ut Unum Sint*, 1995
DI = Declaration, *Dominus Iesus*, 2000
Publication has recently been completed, in five volumes and six languages (Italian, English, Portuguese, French, Spanish and German), of the most comprehensive and fully documented history of the Council itself and its initial reception, written with wide international collaboration and coordinated by the Instituto per le Scienze Religiose of Bologna, under the direction of Giuseppe Alberigo. English edition: Joseph Komonchak ed., *History of Vatican II*, Louvain and Maryknoll NY, Peeters and Orbis, 1995–2003.

² The Eastern Catholic churches following the Byzantine rite are also known as Greek Catholics of the group of Chalcedonian churches and are autocephalous: the Melkites of the patriarchates of Antioch, Alexandria and Jerusalem; the Ukrainians of the archbishopric of Lemberg (known as Lwow by the Polish, L'viv by the Ukrainians and L'vov by the Russians), united with Rome since the Union of Brest-Litovsk (1596); the Romanian Eastern Catholic Church of the metropolitan see of Alba Julia; the Bulgarian Eastern Catholic Church of the apostolic exarchate of Sophia; the Greek Catholics of Serbia, Macedonia and Croatia; the Eastern Italo-Abanians with dioceses in Albania and the south of Italy: Lungro (Calabria), Piana (Sicily) and the Nullius Abbey of Grottaferrata; the Ruthenians in the Czech Republic and Slovakia.

³ The Chaldean Catholic churches belong to Syrian Eastern Christianity and have a pre-Ephesian tradition. They have communities in Syria and Iraq, the largest group, however, being the Syrian-Malabar Church in India. They call themselves Mar Thomas Christians, claiming to be the apostolic legacy of St Thomas.

⁴ These Eastern Catholic churches, in the group of pre-Chalcedonian churches, are divided into three blocs: (1) those belonging to the Western Syrian tradition, such as the Syrian Catholic Church, the Maronite Church and the Syrian Malabar Church in India; (2) those belonging to the Coptic tradition, following the Alexandrine rite: the Coptic Catholic Church in Egypt and the Ethiopian Catholic Church; and (3) one church in the Armenian tradition: the Armenian Catholic Church. For a comprehensive overview, see *Lexicon für Theologie und Kirche*, Freiburg, Verlag Herder, 1961 (hereafter referred to as LTK), vol. 6, article on Lemberg, pp. 939–41, and LTK vol. 7, article on the Orthodox churches, pp. 1246–56.

⁵ The term "Latin", on the other hand, has other connotations in the East, as Maximos IV reminded those present at the last meeting of the preparatory central commission for the Second Vatican Council in January 1962: "If Eastern Catholics can be Catholic without becoming Latin, I ask: why then maintain in the East, in the 20th century, and in a Muslim country, a Western Latin patriarchate, which can only exist as a latinizing presence, to the detriment of the Eastern church?... The Latinization of the East, undertaken by the Latin patriarchate of Jerusalem, constitutes a lamentable contradiction of the formal statements by the popes, which promised Eastern Catholics re-establishing their unity with Rome that they would not be obliged to become Latin." This intervention and other interventions by the patriarch and other Melkite bishops during the preparations for the Council and during the Council itself have been published in *L'Église grecque melkite au Concile: Discours et notes du patriarche Maximos IV*, Beirut, Dar Al-Kalima, 1967.

⁶ See Hans Maier, "Katholizismus", in LTK, vol. 6, pp. 88–90.

⁷ The name "uniate" is given to the Eastern churches that, after the schism of 1054, re-established their communion with the see of Rome. They have always been looked upon with disapproval and criticized by Eastern Christians, and seen as a divisive element among the Eastern faithful.

⁸ Intervention by Maximos IV Saigh, Antiochene Patriarch of the Melkites, in the 28th general congregation, 27 Nov. 1962, AS I/3, pp.616-18.

⁹ Alivisatos, in the journal *Virma* ("Tribune"), Athens, 9–11 Jan. 1966; quoted in Antoine Wenger, *Vatican II – chronique de la quatrième session*, vol. 4, Paris, Centurion, 1966, p. 466.

¹⁰ In the printed order of worship there was a brief historical introduction to the rite: *Liturgia mozarabica liturgia occidentalis est et latina, efformata ac evoluta in Hispania sub dominatione wisigothorum, maxime ab eorum conversione, anno 589, usque ad initium saec. VIII. Hinc vetus hispanicus ritus melius et proprius liurgia hispanowisigothica vel, ut saepe dicitur "toletana" denominaretur quia Toletum, caput regni, centrum religiosum et sedes conciliorum, recognitione ordinum, textuum et melodiae unitati cultuali norma fuit. Non raro etiam ritus isidorianus nuncupatur. In*

Ordo Missae Ritu Mozarabico peragendae Toleti, Editorial Católica Toledana, 1963, AP 1994, p. 1716.

[11] These and other challenges to the Catholic Church at the beginning of the new millennium are listed in José Oscar Beozzo, "Documentation: The Future of Particular Churches", *Concilium*, 279, 1999-2001, pp. 124–38.

[12] Report by Philip Potter in *SEDOC* 7, Jan. 1975, p. 717.

[13] M.P. Carvalheira, Gérard Dupont et al., *"O Sínodo de 1974 – A Evangelização no Mundo de Hoje", Reflexões teológico-pastorais*, São Paulo, Loyola, 1975, pp. 6–7.

[14] Paul VI, *Evangelization in the Modern World*, London, Catholic Truth Society, 1976, sections 29–31, p. 16.

[15] See the particularly stimulating essay "Raízes da Modernidade"by Henrique Cláudio de Lima Vaz (1921–2002), published within a few days of his death in *Belo Horizonte* on 23 May 2002, São Paulo, Loyola.

[16] Giacomo Martina, *História da igreja de Lutero a nossos dias. I – O período da Reforma*, São Paulo, Loyola, 1997, p. 189.

[17] On John XXIII and the significance of his pontificate, see Peter Hebblethwaite, *John XXIII, Pope of the Council*, London, Chapman, 1984; Giuseppe e Angelina Alberigo, *Profezia nella fedeltà*, Brescia, Querigniana, 1978; Giuseppe Alberigo (a cura), *Papa Giovanni*, Bari, Laterza, 1987.

[18] Roger Garaudy, *From Anathema to Dialogue: A Marxist Challenge to the Christian Churches*, New York, Herder & Herder, 1966.

[19] Dialogue was the core proposal in the first encyclical of Paul VI, *Ecclesiam Suam*. He has been described by one of his biographers as the first modern pope. See Peter Hebblethwaite, *Paul VI, the First Modern Pope*, London and New York, Harper Collins and Paulist, 1993.

[20] His book *Il Baluardo* (The Bulwark), a collection of his articles, was also published in French, but with a different title. A. Ottaviani, *L'Église et la Cité*, Rome, Polyglotte Vaticane, 1963.

[21] Latin American Council of Bishops (CELAM), *A igreja na atual transformação da América Latina à luz do Concílio – Conclusões de Medellín*, Petrópolis, Vozes, 1969; English translation: *The Church in the Present-Day Transformation of Latin America in the Light of the Council*, Washington DC, US Catholic Council, 1970, Doc. 15, 10.

[22] Congregation for the Doctrine of the Faith, *Dominus Iesus*, London, Catholic Truth Society, 2000.

[23] Leonardo Boff, "Quem subverte o Concílio? Resposta ao Card. J Ratzinger, a propósito da Dominus Jesus" (Who is subverting the Council – A Response to Cardinal J. Ratzinger concerning *Dominus Iesus*). This study was published in book form in Austria, together with articles of a more journalistic nature previously published in the *Jornal do Brasil*, 4, 5 and 6, October 2000, with the title "Ratzinger: exterminador do futuro?" (Ratzinger – Exterminator of the Future?)

[24] I am indebted here to notes of a lecture given by him to a group of bishops in the Casa Siloé of the Vinhedo Benedictine Monastery in the 1980s.

[25] The same sorts of questions in the theological field, together with a criticism of Western modernity, are raised by Gustavo Gutiérrez in *The Power of the Poor in History*, London, SCM Press, 1983.

[26] Kenneth Himes, "The Religious Rhetoric of Just War", *Concilium*, 290, 2001-2002, pp. 43–51.

[27] Paul VI, speech at the opening of the Second Conference, Bogotá, 24 Aug. 1968, in CELAM, *Conclusões de Medellín*, Petrópolis, 1969, pp. 17–18.

[28] *Ibid.*, p. 30.

12
Reform and Reconciliation between Religion and State

Some Trends in Contemporary Islam

RADWAN AL-SAYYID

Neither modern history nor, perhaps, ancient history has ever known an age like the present, dominated as it is by such intense struggles between religion and the state. From a historical standpoint, it may be appropriate to take the assassination of Sheikh Hassan al-Banna by the Egyptian political police in 1949 as marking the outbreak of that struggle, and to regard the assassination of President Anwar Sadat at the hands of the *jihad* movement in 1981 as one of its culminating events. Between those two dates, the quarrel intensified and broadened, spreading beyond the Arab world to engulf the entirety of Islam, developing new aspects and a much more diversified discourse.

Originally, it was a straightforward fight between Islamists and political regimes, but as time went by new divisions appeared: between Islamists and the traditional religious establishment, Islamists and reformists, Islamists and secularists... – thus, the issue spilled over from the political to the cultural sphere, raising questions of Islam's ultimate authority and the underlying legitimacy of the Islamic community. For a long time now, the struggle has been far more than an internal matter affecting only the Arab and Islamic worlds, as is clear from such phenomena as the war in Afghanistan, which brought Islamists on to the international scene. They reached centre stage, so to speak, with the events of 11 September 2001, when Islam was declared to be a world problem.

Since that time, all and sundry have been talking about the war on terrorism and Islamic extremism, but many of the cultural and military aspects of that war have affected more than violent extremist movements: they have been aimed at Islam as such in some instances, and at Muslims generally in others. An example of the former is the assertion that fundamentalism leading to violence is part of the nature of Islam; an example of the latter is the assertion that Islam is not to blame for these hard-liners and terrorists. As a practical matter, the result is the same in both cases. Different views and opinions have been expressed about the phenomenon of violent fundamentalism in contemporary Arab and Islamic countries, the causes of its conflict with those countries' governments and political regimes, and the reasons why the fundamentalists have turned that conflict into a global one aimed directly at the United States and, secondarily, other Western regimes. But while there has been much diversity of views about these matters, there has been a much greater diversity of views and beliefs over the issues of relations among different Islamist movements and their approaches to other players on the domestic scene, political regimes, and the world at large.

Accordingly, it is useful to survey the range of discourse and events on the Islamic scene today, and to consider their implications in terms of attitudes towards various social forces, political regimes and the contemporary world. In two of my books I have explored some of the phenomena and aspects of contemporary Islamic discourse under the heading *Weltanschauung* (world-view), which is a technical term in philosophy meaning approximately the same as discourse, but more comprehensive and serving more adequately to express collective or party orientations rather than those of individual thinkers exclusively.

Needless to say, there is no space here for me to present all the various contending views in detail, and consequently we shall focus on the content of discourse, outlooks and events as they bear on two fundamental issues: the relationship between religion and the state, and relations with the contemporary world. While these two issues are certainly highly explosive today, they may seem less important tomorrow, and there are various other possibilities that might have been more advantageous for our present purpose. For the moment, however, those possibilities are less immediate and less relevant in terms of this study, although they will be taken into consideration when we come to examine particular aspects of some movement's views or discourse.

One further point should be made here: we must bear in mind that the men whose discourse we shall be investigating are active in the sphere of Islamic thought or Islamic action, and they regard Islam, in the most general sense, as the ultimate source of authority for society and the state, regardless of any differences among them as to what that means or what its outcome might be.

Between tradition and change

Islamic revivalists and members of Islamic political parties are more inclined than those who call for reform and renewal to avoid clashing with religious institutions concerned with education, the issuing of *fatwas* or general research. Both revivalists and reformists, however, are very different from those to whom they refer by such terms as "traditionalists", "fossils" and the like. There is nothing new about this; it goes back to the days of Muhammad Abduh, whose relations with Al-Azhar were strained. As is well known, Muhammad Abduh's pupil, Rashid Rida (who was a *salafi* sympathizer), collected his master's articles calling for the reform of Al-Azhar (previously printed in the journal *Al-manr*) into a thick volume which he published under the title *Al-manr* and *al-Azhar*. However, the traditionalists whom the reformists, *salafis* and revivalists talk about, the religious scholars of the four classical schools of law, have actually been something of an endangered species for some time.

States have intervened to bring about renewal in traditional religious institutions, adopting many of the reformists' proposals. Furthermore, there has been a long line of sheikhs (i.e. heads of Islamic religious institutions) who have taken steps to foster reform and bring about reconciliation with the modern age and its social, economic and political innovations. Indeed, sheikhs of educational institutions and *fatwa*-issuing institutions today tend to place much less emphasis on their distinctive doctrinal positions than the Islamists, whether members of political parties or reformists. This is the case not simply with members of the religious establishment who hold appointments at Al-Azhar, the Zaitouna Mosque or Al-Qarawiya College, or with research institutions, *fatwa*-issuing institutions or academies; it is also true of many graduates of Islamic universities who work in other fields unrelated to teaching or the issuing of *fatwas*. However, persons in the latter category are on much the same footing as the sheikhs of those institutions as far as our portrayal of the general situation of traditional Islamic institutions is concerned.

The watchword of the long-standing Sunni religious establishment is harmony: harmony with the modern world and its innovations, and harmony with the requirements of states and governments. In point of fact, this central issue is all that remains of the ancient tradition of the schools of law. The four schools do not advocate violent opposition; they see the existing authority as sheltering them, and their priority concerns amount to little more than working in and with society to promote the welfare of people's daily lives and rituals, and to educate young people to follow the same path in what is known as the conveyance and assumption of learning. Historically, when one of these sheikhs rose to become a mufti, he acquired, in a sense, the authority to decide legal questions on the basis of his independent judgment, within the limits of the doctrine of the school to which he belonged. He and other sheikhs constituted what had been, since the Mamluk period, a sort of council comprising muftis, judges and senior jurists of all schools that served to advise the ruler or governing authority in matters relating to both religious ritual and social life.

In Ottoman times there was a rather similar official body, consisting of the sheikhs of Islam, as they were known, and their staffs. The innovative feature of that period, however, was that the Ottomans incorporated Sufi sheikhs (those who were interested) into the religious scholarly elite, in contrast to later educational and *fatwa*-issuing institutions, which have always been based on law and learned jurists. The resources by means of which these scholars were supported came not from the state (or rather, only secondarily from the state); their main source of support was the charitable endowments known as *waqfs* and the salaried posts that they provided. This arrangement meant that the religious establishment was not far from the seat of government, yet its members were not directly employed by the government. For over half a century now, however, an overwhelming majority of practising Islamic scholars and muftis have been state employees, even as their specialized knowledge and the functions they serve have dwindled in importance everywhere except in the Gulf states.

As is well known, the early decades of the 20th century, down to the 1930s, were marked by an increasingly acrimonious dispute between the traditional religious establishment on the one hand and the reformists and the early *salafis* on the other. The problem the *salafis* had with the traditionalist sheikhs was their lack of concern with doctrinal matters, their embrace of Sufism, or at any rate their acceptance of it since the Mamluk era, and their reliance on tradition and their insistence that there was no longer any scope for innovative decisions on religious and legal issues. The reformists, for their part, wanted to see existing institutions comprehensively overhauled and their sheikhs ushered into the modern age as a means of responding to the challenges of that age and the needs arising from it. These reformists (and those known in Morocco as *salafis*) were allied at that time with contemporary efforts to renew the state, and they adopted a model of renewal and progress that owed much to current Western thinking. The traditionalist sheikhs, for their part, found it impossible to keep their distance from the state, as the role played by *waqfs* receded and became less central to their lives and their resources. At the same time, however, harmony (or the concept of necessary interests) had remained the main philosophy underlying their discourse as partners in the effort to realize the overarching Islamic ideal and the political ideal within it. Moreover, every traditionalist sheikh thoroughly abhorred civil strife, and did not regard violence as part of his general duty to advocate what was right and dissuade from what was wrong. Accordingly, while he might not support the government, he could not openly oppose it. His only alternatives were thus either to withdraw to a quiet life of teaching and writing or to seek refuge in Sufism, becoming an adherent of an authority consisting of enlightened individuals, rather than one wielding coercive power.

The task of achieving cultural and social harmony through renewal and the exercise of independent legal judgment was no easy matter, calling as it did for changes that no sheikh working in a religious institution could hope to bring about on his own. The state was taking action to modernize institutions and universities and to modernize its discourse with those who worked in them. Sheikhs whose business was teaching and issuing *fatwas* might be prepared to make their information more up to date and to accept the reformists' urging to exercise independent judgment, but they never managed to take the initiative, as the early reformists had done.

Radicalism in the air

Sheikhs of Islamic institutions devoted much effort to the question of the exercise of independent judgment in matters of law during the 1960s and 1970s, but they were shunted aside with the rise of revivalism, whose adherents also worked actively on the issue and were not hampered by the restrictions that hemmed in the traditionalists as a result of their responsibilities towards the state and the community. The question of doctrine was also a very thorny one. The traditionalist Ash'arite theology was subjected to attacks from various quarters: *salafis* old and new, who alleged that it was contaminated with idolatrous beliefs; reformists, who called it rigid and irrational; and modernists, who disapproved of its evasiveness, its middle-of-the-road position and its eclectic approach, in contrast to mu'tazilism and Shiism, both of which attracted substantial support from various quarters for various reasons.

The fact was that Islamic traditionalism, after overhauling and renewing itself, found itself compelled to fight on a number of fronts at a time when it was still fragile and was trying to maintain harmonious relations with the state and the community. Its adherents managed to defend its legal positions, publishing articles in various journals and issuing *fatwas* which did not necessarily please the state in all cases, but the problem was, on the one hand, the doctrinal aspect and, on the other hand, the fact that the setting and the community were changing. Scholastic theology held little appeal for ordinary Sunnis, and Ash'arism had provided an accommodating formula that was acceptable to various schools of thought. It had remained open to the law, to which it assigned the highest importance, partly because it was law that mattered more than anything else in people's lives, and partly because Sunni Islam has nothing comparable to what Christians call creeds. Sunnis agree on the unity of God, the prophets and the Last Day, but Ash'arism is tolerant about everything else.

Meanwhile, the *salafis* were being unbendingly rigid on many points, relying on Koran and Tradition and maintaining that debate and discussion were unlawful in matters of belief. Thus it came about in the 1950s and 1960s that traditionalist sheikhs found themselves assailed from various quarters: *salafis* charged them with being doctrinally flabby, secularists and progressives accused them of hostility to reason and logic, while the advocates of renewal and the exercise of independent judgment in matters of law alleged that they were hopelessly out of step with the demands of the modern world. Radicalism was in the air, with a rising wave of Islamist apologists on the one hand and another rising wave of secularists and progressives on the other. Traditionalists arrived at reformist positions only after a lengthy struggle, but they did arrive at them in the end, only to be told that they were hopelessly backward, reactionary, hidebound and the like. Worst and most painful of all, they were accused of working for the interests of the state against the interests of the people; they were derisively dubbed "the religious scholars who serve the power establishment".

Search for religious leadership

The 1960s were thus decisive for a number of issues, including the fate of long-established Islamic traditionalism. The national/progress-oriented model of society and the state had crystallized through the political systems in leading Arab countries, Indonesia, Pakistan, and prominent African Islamic countries, while the new Islamic model, or its discourse, had crystallized through the al-Mawdudi – al-Nadawi – Sayyid Qutb line, which stood for the pursuit of power, the application of Islamic law and the Islamic state. Traditional religious scholars were unable to summon much enthusiasm for either approach. As a result, the picture of "harmony" became nebulous: it supposedly stood for harmony between theology and Islamic law, between religion and the state, and between the state and society, but no such harmony was to be seen and nothing of it had been realized, while traditionalism itself was being subjected to scurrilous attacks by its opponents. More dangerous yet was the significance of those attacks: they implied that the members of the religious and cultural elite no longer spoke with authority as religious scholars or clerics, sometimes on the grounds that their commitment to the true faith was inadequate, and sometimes on the grounds that they were members of the ruling establishment or government.

The relaxed attitude of Ash'arite "men of religion" towards the absence of a formal Islamic creed meant that theological issues could conveniently be entrusted to them. Other faiths, however, both Abrahamic and non-Abrahamic, had "men of religion" who exercised functions and played roles that made them authoritative sources of reference (another aspect that is somewhat deficient in Sunni Islam). Not only were the sacraments in their keeping (again, there is no such function in Islam), but they were specially qualified to officiate at religious ceremonies and rituals, whereas Islam has nothing corresponding to a mass that can be celebrated only by an ordained priest. Nor does Sunni Islam have an official statement of "sources of tradition" of the kind found in Imamite Shiism. Another important function of religion is supervision of the ethical system by which the community lives, and here again, the Muslim religious establishment has no special competence in that area. Lastly, in the field of religious teaching and education, the Islamists were challenging the religious establishment for control, but the latter was still predominant.

New understanding of power and authority

After all this, what are we to say about the authority to issue *fatwas*? What is its place among the duties of the Islamic religious scholar? *Fatwas* had long been part of the ethical guidance role exercised by sheikhs and jurists, and the function of mufti had been an official post for centuries, but it was closely connected with the ultimate source of authority, or the recognition of some religious scholars as possessing such authority. As long as education and training remained largely in the hands of traditionalist religious scholars, and the authority to issue *fatwas* depended on religious knowledge and the mufti's good reputation, a religious scholar would hardly encounter any serious problems in that respect.

In reality, however, the situation was not quite so straightforward, because it was bound up with the political issue. From the 1960s to the present day, every traditionalist religious scholar has been confronted with the challenge of relations with those in power, his neutrality always suspect, constantly being put in the position of having to toady to the political establishment or being in its pocket. Far-reaching changes have occurred in the course of these past decades. Positions of power endowed with legitimacy have receded, and competitors with agendas of their own – Islamists and neo-reformists – have become steadily more prominent. This split between political establishment and people on the one hand, and between political establishment and neo-Islamists on the other, has left traditionalist Islamic scholars in a difficult position with few options and little room for choice. It is no longer feasible for them to protect themselves by siding with power in the comprehensive sense, the people, because of the split just mentioned; at the same time, they cannot think of calling for support for the established authority in the name of Islam, because the revolutionary Islamists are also speaking in the name of Islam *against* the established power and authority. Nor can they continue to assert an exclusive claim to being the source of authority or the right to issue *fatwas* or utter authoritative opinions, now that another concept of power and authority and their relations with religion has arisen. A traditionalist sheikh may debate that concept, but he cannot oppose and combat it in the name of religion.

Traditional leadership under question

Yet there is one issue left to the men of the old-fashioned institutions, one that simultaneously fulfils the demands of tradition and the new harmony while also commanding some attention from the mass of the people, and has, for the time being, enabled them to retain their new/old rule of intermediary between the political establishment and its Islamist adversaries: the role of advocates of social calm and peace, moderation and the denunciation of disorder. Traditionalist religious scholars lavished a great deal of effort on that role between the 1960s and the 1980s, but the radical atmosphere of the time meant that they achieved nothing lasting. Governments consistently wanted them to issue combative and supportive *fatwas*. The Islamists regarded them as hypocrites or unimaginative. As terrifying clashes occurred in rapid succession between the 1970s and the 1990s, there ceased to be any room for compromise, even between regimes and those who did not engage in violence, but rather sought to exert pressure by peaceful political means.

The situation of traditionalist religious scholars, or the scholarly religious establishment, was different in the Gulf states until the 1980s. Their influence grew as a result of the fact that governments in those states left some areas under their control, areas which their counterparts in other Arab states had lost. However, with the advent of the neo-*salafis*, breaking away from the religious and political institutions, the scholars of the religious establishment found themselves compelled to take a stand. For a long time they hesitated, but the acts of violence attributed to the *salafi* advocates of *jihad*, both within the Gulf states and elsewhere, ultimately forced them to speak out against the movement in the interests of governments or for the sake of preventing disorder and bloodshed. The scholars of the religious establishment thus found themselves in the same situation as their Egyptian, Syrian and Moroccan counterparts before them: doubt cast on their status as the source of authority by the hard-liners, and the hopes of governments dashed as the scholars' influence waned, despite the advantageous treatment they had received.

Consequently, the "harmony" discourse, which had always been severely strained, was on the point of disintegrating or becoming unrealizable amid the new circumstances that were growing daily more radical and were driving the scholars of the religious establishment in various mutually incompatible directions. Some of them (a hard-core remnant) insisted that their role was one of teaching and guidance and nothing more, while others became more radical in order to show impartiality and approach the populism of the Islamist party. There was also a third faction that turned to Sufism, which was also experiencing a new vitality, or to the mass appeal of the media.

At all events, the outcome was that the religious establishment ceased to be relevant in any areas apart from religious education and, to a certain extent, the issuing of *fatwas*. To be sure, these are important matters, and ordinary people found themselves in a state of uncertainty, between the long-established religious institution on the one hand and, on the other, the tools of education and information and the mobilizing institutions being developed by the Islamists, including both those who were organized into formal parties and those who were not.

Islamic awakening: opportunities and risks

If the ability to maintain harmony was the problem of the religious establishment, the problem of the new Islamic revivalism was maintaining its identity through a purifying dynamism and fashioning tools and means capable of bringing that about. The Islamic revivalist discourse had emerged, or had become organized, in the second half of the 1920s, during the unprecedented crisis of the abolition of the Caliphate in 1924. At that time, a number of factors and phenomena had combined to generate dread and fear: the fall of the Ottoman state, the occupation of the rest of the Islamic world, the abolition of the Caliphate, projects involving displacement and fragmentation, and nation-states that were neutral towards Islam or biased against it. Traditionalists and reformists alike did their utmost to confront the challenge of the abolition of the Caliphate and attempt to create an alternative source of ultimate authority. Those efforts crystallized in the holding of a series of conferences, in some cases under the auspices of the Egyptian authorities, in others under those of the Saudi authorities. Meanwhile, the Hashemites, who had been driven out of the Hijaz, continued to be concerned with the issue of the Caliphate; their leader, the Sherif Hussein, had used the title of Caliph on occasion before 1924.

However, the conferences led to nothing, as the Arab regimes fell out over the question of which of them should succeed the Ottomans as the holder of (religious) authority, while the British and French were opposed to any renewal of the Caliphate. The feeling of frustration and futility grew as elements that were angry with the feebleness of the traditionalists and the Westernization of the reformists went their own way by founding associations, organizations and mechanisms to assert their identity. These included the Muslim Youth movement, the Muslim Brotherhood, the Ansar al-Sunna, the Shar'ia Association, the Islamic Youth Union in Syria, the Youth of Muhammad in Iraq, the Jama'at al-Islami party in India, and the Khilafat movement in India and subsequently in Indonesia.

What began as a kind of secession born of protest soon evolved into a general movement that came to be known as the Islamic Awakening. At first, these various associations and movements were doctrinal and educational in nature, with no clearcut political concerns. Thanks to their attention to social and cultural issues with which people were directly involved, they won a substantial measure of popular backing, and this was reinforced by their ability to use religious symbolism to attract people, win their support, and enlist their participation in ritual, educational and sporting activities. By this means they gave young people hope, confidence, and an organizational framework such as Muslims had traditionally known only in the form of state institutions or Sufi orders.

It is clear from Hassan al-Banna's letters and from his addresses and remarks at conferences and meetings between 1934 and 1945, and from the writings of Abu'l-A'la al-Mawdudi, the leader of the Jama'at al-Islami party in Pakistan between 1941 and 1950, that the leaders of those movements had no coherent discourse in the early stages, except on two issues: combating Westernization and the cultural and political presence of the West in the Islamic world, and providing Muslims with an education that was far removed from the recent waves of evangelization, dissolution and factionalism. It might have been possible for those two movements and others like them to retreat to or be converted into charitable or Sufi institutions, had it not been for the powerful purifying identity discourse that dominated them and the mass following that they had attracted, and above all the crucial moment of trial to which each of them was subjected: the Jam'at al-Islami party's moment of trial came with the establishment of the Islamic state of Pakistan in 1947, while that of the Muslim Brotherhood was the assassination of its founder and leader, Hassan al-Banna, in 1949. It might have been supposed that the Jam'at al-Islami party would hasten to support the concept of an Islamic Pakistan, in view of its repeated allegations about the distinctiveness and purity of Islam. But it stood in confusion at the division which the founding of the separate state had left in the ranks of Muslims themselves. Approximately one third of the subcontinent's Muslims had remained under Indian sovereignty; moreover, the secular elite that had created Pakistan wanted a nation-state in which Islam would play a unifying nationalist role. Al-Mawdudi was opposed to the concept of two authorities, and consequently he was impelled to embrace a theory that religion should be incorporated into the state, or that the state should be based on religion, which he subsequently termed *hakimiya* (approximately, "sovereignty"), to denote that doctrinal distinctiveness which, according to him, was the only justification for Pakistan's separation from India.

At the time when legal experts in the new state were engrossed in their ultimately unsuccessful attempt to produce an Islamic constitution for the new state, al-Mawdudi wrote the first Islamic constitution, which defined the Islamic political regime as a "theodemocracy" (i.e. a divinely ordained *hakimiya* at the level of the ultimate source of authority, managed by the people at the level of public issues having to do with day-to-day human life). Until al-Mawdudi's death in 1979, his Jama'at al-Islami party continued to be the leading Islamic opposition party in the country. Al-Mawdudi was imprisoned on a number of occasions, and the party, unable to win significant numbers of seats in successive parliaments, made its peace with Zia ul-Haq's military rule and went back to wrangling with other governments, and has continued to do so to this day.

Hakimiya vision in the context of the cold war

The assassination of Hassan al-Banna in Egypt occurred after the monarchy had lost patience with a movement that refused to behave like a charitable or religious association, but at the same time did not want to be dealt with like a political party. Sometimes it intervened in public affairs, while at other times it refrained from doing so, as it saw fit. Al-Banna's assassination led to the politicization of the movement and a shift in its discourse. According to al-Banna, Islam was both religion and the earthly world, both Koran and sword. Abd al-Qadir 'Awda wrote about Islam and the law and about Islam and politics. Sayyid Qutb wrote about the social situation in Islam, and then, after discovering the writings of al-Mawdudi and al-Nadawi, he proceeded to refine the theory of *hakimiya*. In his view, that theory was not a means of confronting despotism and tyranny, as al-Mawdudi had conceived of it, but rather a means of confronting a state of affairs comparable to the pre-Islamic condition of ignorance. This became an issue on which the Islamist movement has been divided from the mid-1960s to the present day. All factions advocated an Islamic state that applied the Shari'a, but they differed in their views of what to do about the existing situation. Those who saw it as analogous to pre-Islamic ignorance tended to regard state and society as consisting of infidels, or to regard the state in those terms while sparing society. The main school of thought, which crystallized in the early 1980s, called for partnership in governance in the name of Islam, but using mechanisms that were recognized in the contemporary world. The adherents of this position have continued to develop their writings, initiatives and experimental projects in a number of Arab and Islamic states.

Our main concern here is to consider the positions of the neo-Islamists on the same matters that were discussed above in the case of the traditional religious scholars: their *Weltanschauung*, their position with respect to modern civilization, international relations, and relations between religion and the state. As regards the first of these, revivalist writings during and after the second world war tended to focus on the evils of the West and Western culture; the revivalists sought to build an independent Islamic identity modelled after the "virtuous ancestors" *(al-salaf al-salih)*, but the problems and mechanisms associated with that approach are modern and controversial.

Then came the cold war between the two great powers, with the Pakistani regime allied with the United States. Accordingly, the writings of the Islamist movement, including its Eastern adherents, continued to attack Western culture. In the 1960s, however, a shift occurred in the stance of the Arab revivalists, who began to direct their fire against Marxism and apostasy as a result of the way the Arab countries were aligning themselves in the cold war, and because of the emergence of the Arab progressive camp, with its tilt towards the Soviet Union, in contrast to the pro-American Islamic alliance. As the Islamists in Egypt and Syria were in a position of conflict with the regimes in those countries, they joined the other camp, while at the same time their denunciation of capitalism and Marxism alike continued unabated.

The *hakimiya* vision led to the maturing of an independent discourse or integral third type of alternative regime, one that would constitute an Islamic solution (Yusuf al-Qardawi), characterized by an independent view of a state founded upon religion, with a distinctive legal system (application of the Shari'a) and a distinctive economic system (banks that did not charge interest, an Islamic economy).

Cross-fertilization between fundamentalism and neo-salafism

In the atmosphere of violent conflict between Islamists and regimes in the 1960s and 1970s, first in the Arab Levant, then in North Africa, and finally spreading to the rest of the Islamic world in the 1980s, a third phenomenon arose alongside the concepts of *hakimiya* and integral Islamic regime: this was a cross-fertilization between fundamentalism and neo-salafism. Islamic revivalist movements were populist movements that ordinarily avoided discussion of the details of dogma, with their potential for sectarian fragmentation. But as doctrinal conflict increased in intensity, fundamentalists and *salafis* found a middle ground: the former adopted the *salafi* discourse, while the latter became politicized, both in the Arab countries and among Indian Muslims. The dogmatism of the integral Islamic regime concept meant a breach with the world system (i.e. both the capitalist and Marxist components of Western culture). As far as that went, there was not a great deal of difference between the non-violent mainstream and the violent splinter groups. Virtually all the literature condemning the West, Western culture, Western hegemony and Western materialism was written by members of the mainstream or majority position.

As regards the other issue, the relationship between religion and the state, the concept of the integral Islamic regime, with a political system based on religion, meant the rejection of all existing political regimes. This is not to say that Islam had been devoid of political concerns either in the classical era or in the age of Islamic reformism. In the classical era, the Commander of the Faithful (i.e. the Caliph) was, according to al-Mawardi, the successor to Muhammad, the Apostle of God (God's blessing and peace be upon him), and as such, responsible both for safe-guarding religion and managing worldly affairs. However, this implied two institutions, one to direct the polity and be in charge of public matters, and the other to be in charge of religious matters, and this involved some sort of separation between political life and the Shari'a, although not between religion and the state as such, inasmuch as the ultimate source of authority for the system as a whole was Islam. It is that separation that explains Islamic jurists' attacks upon any form of "politics" that overstepped the bounds of the Shari'a in responding to the needs of the state or the public interest. This led to the fashioning of what was known as 'Shari'a politics': a middle-way solution or reconciliation between politics and the Shari'a.

In the period of Islamic reformism, from the Ottoman tanzimat to the innovations of the school founded by Muhammad Abduh, the religious scholars intervened in political matters and public affairs. However, they were calling for a renewal of the state; they did not claim to possess an independent system. The politicized Islamic reformists, for their part, who called for an integral regime based on *hakimiya* and application of the Shari'a, were effectively advocating a system in which political and religious affairs would be merged into a single institution. The main task or function of the Islamic state, according to the reformists, was to apply the Shari'a. It followed that an Arab regime in its doctrinaire, nationalist, socialist phase must necessarily be in conflict with reformism, which regarded the Shari'a as the ultimate source of divine authority (although it was not), and must also be in conflict with it in its continuing, present-day phase, when the issue has come to be seen as being over power and the question of who will govern. Doubtless this conflict had many causes, including the legacy of the cold war, the United States assault on the Middle East, the way the regimes were barred from participation, and the alternation of power. The most important reason, however, was the dogmatic nature of the concept of the state in the Islamist view, and the clash between discourse and practice.

Forms of relationships between religion and the state in the Arab world

The past five decades have known four forms of relationship between religion and the state in the Arab world. When we speak of relationship we mean the relationship between the political system and the traditional religious institution or institutions. Our aim is to eluci-date contemporary attempts by the neo-Islamists to create other institutions, conceived of as potential alternatives to non-Islamic regimes and traditional institutions alike.

The first of these forms has been a relationship of antipathy and aversion. States that practise this form of relationship are few in number (no more than two or three). During the 1960s, 1970s and 1980s, matters reached the point where the media were carrying open propaganda directed against religion and religious scholars. In the past two decades the aim of these states has been to put such pressure on the religious establishment as partly to annihilate it. Severe restrictions have been placed on movements dedicated to religious education, gatherings in mosques outside ritual times of prayer have been curtailed, and there have been harsh campaigns against neo-Islamist movements, membership of which has been made an offence liable to prosecution.

The second form of that relationship is the union of religion and state, which is the case in Iran and the Sudan. In Iran the religious establishment came to power at the head of a vast popular movement. The traditional religious institution was still powerful and coherent enough to have been able to oppose the shah's regime, and ultimately overthrow and destroy it. What happened in the Sudan was the reverse: it was neo-Islamic revivalists, advocates of an alternative integral system, who came to power there, under the leadership of Hassan al-Turabi, in alliance with military officers, but it appears the latter shared the revivalist outlook.

The third form of the relationship between religion and state is benevolent or hostile neutrality: a situation in which traditional religious institutions are allowed to survive, their favour is solicited, and support is made available to them at times, while at the same time they are not allowed to intervene directly in public affairs, or at any rate are not welcomed. The political institutions of approximately half the Arab states have relations of this kind with their religious establishments.

The fourth and most prominent form of relationship between religion and state in the Arab world is subordination, in the sense that the religious establishment is placed in a subservient position by the political institution. This form is found in some of the leading Arab states, such as Egypt, Saudi Arabia and Morocco. Typically, the religious establishment retains its structure and its ritual and social functions, while being firmly controlled by the state organization and obliged to meet its requirements and serve its needs. The political apparatus has been able to achieve this position of dominance because of the historical strength of the concept of the state, the nurturing relations that had been maintained for centuries, the attacks of the neo-Islamists against both state and sheikhs, and the fact that the state has lavished money on the religious establishment after having despoiled it of the basis of its independence by confiscating or ruining the charitable endowments known as *waqfs*. Another factor has been the weakening of the traditional religious establishment as a result of its conflict with the fundamentalists over the issue of the ultimate source of authority. At the same time, the state very much needs the traditional religious establishment to issue *fatwas* and provide religious education, and to work against the fundamentalists.

It is noteworthy that of these four forms of relationship, the one that gives rise to fewest problems has been the relationship of neutrality, or positive neutrality, to phrase it more correctly. The other three – hostility, union and subordination – have resulted in serious problems that have not been resolved. Nearly all the states that have adopted an attitude of hostility and coldness towards the religious establishment and those that have placed it in a subservient position have experienced serious religious agitation, with effects that continue to this day. And even where the new Islam has succeeded in coming to power, its success has not meant fewer or less challenging problems; on the contrary, Islam in the guise of a political party has aroused the susceptibilities of similar Islamist movements, as well as their conservative and reformist counterparts, to say nothing of other social forces.

We may note at this point that states that have adopted the line of hostility and coldness and states that have placed the religious establishment in a position of subservience have not stood idly by: they have offered what they regard as concessions to the neo-Islamic forces, such as including provisions in the country's constitution stating that the official state religion is Islam, or that the religion of the head of state must be Islam, or that the Islamic Shari'a is the country's sole, fundamental or main source of law.

This approach has availed them nothing, for various reasons – some having to do with the state itself, others having to do with the political and social context, and still others having to do with the religious institutions concerned and the neo-Islamists. At the very time when the nationalist, progressive Arab states were offering these concessions, they were coming to regard the Islamist problem as a security problem, and proceeded to subject its adherents to the most extreme forms of coercion and intimidation, prosecuting them and throwing them into prison. They then sought to pressure the religious establishment into helping them meet the requirements of modernization and combat fundamentalism, thereby destroying or seriously weakening it. Moreover, the traditionalist religious scholars had little knowledge of the age in which they were living, and they were unable to look closely and critically at their heritage, or to differentiate between neo-Islamists and the existing political establishment with the same degree of objectivity and lucidity.

One of the most important causes of the unrelenting struggle that has pitted religion against the state in the cultural sphere in recent decades is that both sides have changed radically, while each of them continues to treat the other and call it to account as though it were only the other that had changed, having itself held unswervingly to its unchanging religious (or, as the case may be, national) principles. The nation-state is no longer the state of the community and the people, having abandoned for some decades both traditional and contemporary mechanisms for consulting the general public and enlisting its participation in any meaningful way. This is true both of progressives, who tend to think of themselves as representing the people, and of conservatives, who like to claim that they are guided by the traditions, customs and values of the clan, family and household and the rule of first among equals. In my 2004 study on Arab political reform I looked at the concepts of legitimacy and law in contemporary Arab states and concluded that the dominant pattern was one of appropriation, in which the state takes over and fragments society, then seeks to consolidate it in its supposed ethnic, regional and denominational origins in an endeavour to compel its obedience by subjecting it to two forms of violence, material and symbolic.

The members of the traditional religious establishment, for their part, are no longer able to perform their two traditional functions other than performing rituals, namely ensuring harmony between religion and new contexts, and mediating between the state and the various social groups. The first of those functions would require them to possess both a sound knowledge of the fundamental characteristics of religion and its doctrinal and legal heritage, and also a sound knowledge of the fundamental characteristics of the present age and its various contexts. The second function would require recognition by the state and the people of the status of the religious establishment as the ultimate source of authority, so that it could wield its learning and knowledge effectively, command respect and act independently. In most cases, the members of the traditional religious establishment, who are employed by the various institutions, do not meet these conditions. They are challenged on all fronts by the fundamentalist revivalists who are an irritant to the state and despise the religious establishment. They also have an aversion to the masses of the people, the contemporary world and its teachings, and the state as currently constituted, considering as they do that they possess the key to a full-fledged divinely ordained alternative to it.

Reconciliation between the state and the old and new religious elites would thus require a change in the state's understanding of itself, its functions and its relations with the people. As regards religious groups in particular, this would mean abandoning take-over in favour of partnership, and abandoning a security-based approach in favour of a political approach. The fundamentalists, for their part, are exclusivist, even if they are not violent, as they usually are. In recent years there has been an intensive debate over priorities: political reform or religious reform? The Americans concentrated on religious reform after the events of 11 September 2001, but once the Europeans had joined them in their Greater Middle East project, they reverted to emphasizing political reform and strengthening civil society.

Lessons to be followed

In my own view, the state experiment has been a failure in the sphere with which we are here concerned. It has been the cause of the most serious and most acute problems, including the rise of Islamic fundamentalism. Accordingly, I consider that it is more urgent to pursue political reform, especially in view of the fact that the mechanisms of political reform, and its beginnings and ends, are well known. There have been many successful contemporary experiments which we can examine and from which we can benefit. Religious reform, as such, has two components. One of these has to do with rereading the texts and heritage; this will call for elites that are deeply steeped in culture and training, and will involve a long-term effort. The other component has to do with public action (i.e. the relationship between state and society) and this will call for a different *Weltanschauung* and a different view of the role of religion in the world and in the lives of people here. Many people have already embarked seriously on that task, and its first fruits are already appearing. We shall return to this matter in due course.

Over the past two decades a number of groups of Islamic and Muslim thinkers have appeared. An overwhelming majority of these thinkers emerged from the Muslim Brotherhood movement (either the original Egyptian organization or one of its offshoots in other parts of the Arab world) or were close to the Pakistani Jama'at al-Islami movement. However, they became completely independent in the 1980s and 1990s and proceeded to review the arguments made by the hardline and moderate Islamists in an effort to comprehend and transcend them. They claimed at the outset that they wanted to "guide the Awakening", and their concern in that connection was how to confront the issues of violence and charges of unbelief. As time went on they directed their efforts to the challenges of renewal, openness and reconciliation between state and people, and between state and Islamists. With respect to renewal and openness, they held to such considerations as identity and distinctiveness. They proceeded to publish statements and Islamic proclamations about human rights, women's issues, the welfare of the family, the rights of children and environmental issues.

Their underlying purpose in all this was to show that Muslims had something to say to the world on these various issues, which are of widespread interest today, in contrast to the Islamists, who were not concerned with them, being absorbed in their struggles with political regimes and the world at large. At the same time, these thinkers were saying to Muslims generally that through enlightened reconciliation, open-mindedness and persuasion, they would be able to participate meaningfully and effectively in change for the benefit of all, with no need for violence or the threat of violence. Today's world, they argued, is characterized by interdependence, and while there can be no doubt about the injustice and double standards of the global system, violence is unproductive and self-defeating; indeed, it makes matters worse. In any case, Islam, according to the Koran, teaches mutual knowledge and recognition among people of different religions, different colours, different interests, different customs and different temperaments.

With respect to the theory of the state, these thinkers reverted to a position of advocating citizenship of the political system in Islam. They regarded a binding advisory assembly as the basis of the Islamic political system and held that it was close to democracy. They were unable to reach agreement on the place of the Shari'a in the system. The Islamists and fundamentalists, for their part, placed great emphasis on the Shari'a, assigning to it the place that had been held by "the community" as the ultimate source of authority among the early Muslims. They thus held unanimously that the Shari'a was the ultimate source of authority and guide to the management of public affairs.

They regarded the antagonism between religion and the state in the Arab and Muslim worlds as a disaster for religion and state alike. As evidence, they pointed to the severe erosion of legitimacy that was affecting governments, and the terrible toll of victims that had been taken by violence on both sides at home, and the catastrophes that had befallen and continue to befall Muslims as a result of world indignation at indiscriminate suicide bombings.

They identified a number of causes for the anarchy prevailing in the Arab and Muslim worlds, including in particular the failure of political regimes, the decline of the guiding and directing roles played by Islamic sources of authority, the fact that traditional institutions were not respected either by governments or by ordinary people, and the fact that neither governments nor their opponents hesitate to resort to violence.

The discourse of identity and revival that the neo-Islamists have maintained for the past six decades was a discourse of crisis, and it continues today. However, this must not cause us to overlook the fact that no religious source of ultimate authority is currently available, nor any structuring framework for one. Most of us attached little importance to the abolition of the Caliphate, despite the fact that it had wielded political power for centuries; yet in the consciousness of Muslims, it had been just such a structuring framework. There are other nations and states for which the state itself has occupied the place formerly held by traditional sources of authority in the management of public life, and the people have been enlisted as participants in the process; where this is the case, revivalist groups have not arisen, or if they have, they have remained weak.

A successful state is one that is able to associate its people as equal partners in the management of public life. In Malaysia, for example, the fundamentalists won no more than 7 percent of the votes cast in recent elections, while in Indonesia the people elected a retired general because of his honesty and unblemished reputation. When the Indonesian authorities arrested the fundamentalist leader Abu Bakr Bashir, no more than 200 Indonesians demonstrated in protest, out of the country's total population of 200 million! The traditional truce between religion (jurists) and state (Caliphate and Sultanate) rested on a division of powers: the religious establishment was in charge of education, the issuing of *fatwas*, judicial matters, the inspection of markets, and charitable endowments *(waqfs)*, while the wielders of the sword (i.e. the temporal authorities) were in charge of all secular matters. That arrangement collapsed with the fall of the Sultanate and Caliphate and the rise of the nation-state, which does not rely on religion as its ultimate source of authority and does not share any of its material or symbolic power. Then the Islamic tradition crumbled under the hammer blows of the neo-fundamentalists on the one hand and exclusivist governments on the other. There was no way to achieve any kind of harmonious arrangement or neutrality between fundamentalists and governments because of the insistence of the latter on having control of all aspects of public life, while at the same time failing to perform the usual functions of successful modern states: maintaining the existence of the nation and improving people's lives through participation. The fundamentalists wanted no part of any *rapprochement* in any case, believing as they did that they possessed a complete alternative, and holding a bleak view of the world and our community's situation in it. Because governments were incapable of fulfilling their functions or acknowledging that change and alternation of power were necessary, the Islamists set out to work against them, and against the world as a whole. The relative popularity that the fundamentalist discourse has acquired suffers from the weakness that that discourse grows and gains strength when a political regime is unable to persuade the people that it is maintaining their security, dignity and sovereignty in their own country.

There is another matter as well, related to the international system. Because of the extremely serious Arab and Islamic issues in Palestine, Iraq, Kashmir, Chechnya and elsewhere, which are not being resolved or even noticed, many young people are coming together to resist injustice, in an effort to contribute to the liberation of those lands. No one can deny the determination of Hamas and Islamic Jihad in resisting Israel. Consequently, in my view, beyond sound, successful states there are global contexts upon which states with good governance must of necessity have an impact, acting as our representatives and upholding our interests, instead of the matter being left to *salafis* who advocate *jihad*, or to hired surrogates. The Lebanese constitution of 1989–90 refers in its preamble to "the principle of harmony between religion and the state". This is a vitally important goal attainable only by free democratic states having new and enlightened Islamic sources of ultimate authority.

The discourse of Islamic revivalism has passed its peak, after having dominated the agenda of thought and practice for approximately four decades. There is no hope of a renewal of tradition; rather, hope lies in the work of those who are calling old assumptions into question and advocating a new renaissance and reform between religion and the state, and between Islam and the world.

Some years ago a French scholar, Gilles Kepel, published a book entitled *Jihad* in which he discussed Islamist hardliners' understanding of relations with the world. Three months later, however, he published another book, this one entitled *Fitna: Guerre au cœur de l'Islam*, with reference to the fact that the real struggle in this important arena is taking place within the Islamic world and Muslim communities. To God is the power before and after.

13
Secularization:
The European Experience

GRACE DAVIE

Some reference to secularization has already been made in the first part of this book, which deals with the theoretical tools available to us in our attempts to understand the place of religion in the modern world. This chapter will deal primarily with the realities of secularization rather than the theoretical approaches associated with this term. It must, however, start with the complexities embedded within the concept of secularization itself in order to set out the kind of data that we need to include. This will be our first task. The second will be to identify those parts of the world where the process of secularization is most marked and the different forms that this has taken. The final paragraphs will underline once again the limitations of the term and the need to think very carefully about its applicability outside the context from which it emerged in the first place.

Secularization: a multidimensional concept

One of the clearest definitions of secularization can be found in the work of Jose Casanova. It is worth quoting this in full, as it sets out with great clarity the different dimensions that are contained within this concept and the problems that emerge if these are confused with each other:

> A central thesis and main theoretical premise of this work has been that what usually passes for a single theory of secularization is actually made up of three very different, uneven and unintegrated propositions: secularization as differentiation of the secular spheres from religious institutions and norms, secularization as decline of religious beliefs and practices, and secularization as marginalization of religion to a privatized sphere. If the premise is correct, it should follow from the analytical distinction that the fruitless secularization debate can end only when sociologists of religion

begin to examine and test the validity of each of the three propositions independently of each other.[1]

Casanova is entirely correct: a great deal of fruitless debate has been generated by conflating these propositions rather than thinking of them separately. It becomes increasingly clear, for example, that those parts of the Western world which have endorsed the principle of institutional separation or differentiation most fully are not those where there has been a decline in religious beliefs and practices or where religion has necessarily been excluded from public life. The reverse is more likely to be the case.

It is at this point that the contrast between Europe and the United States is at its most marked. The separation of church and state not only exists in practice in American life, but it is also endorsed by law and (most important of all) embedded in cultural awareness. The first amendment and its implications for modern living are part and parcel of American self-understanding. It is simply not the case, however, that there is a corresponding decline in religious activity or that religion as such is marginalized from the public sphere. It is true that there is considerable discussion about exactly how many Americans do attend places of worship on a regular basis;[2] this is an important area of enquiry, provoking among other things interesting methodological questions. But whatever the outcome of these continuing exchanges, no one disputes the fact that political life in the United States is heavily influenced by religious people and religious lobbies. Whether or not this is a good thing is a separate and much-debated issue, but it is not evidence of secularization.

Almost the reverse is true in Europe. Here, as in America, there has been a partial separation of powers. All Europeans, for example, look primarily to the state rather than to religious institutions to provide education, health care and welfare for the population as a whole, though the churches continue to play important (and sometimes increasing) responsibilities in all these spheres.[3] The separation of church and state in Europe has, however, taken a very different path from that found in the United States – unsurprisingly, given the very different histories of the old and new world.[4] And even where a legal or constitutional separation has taken place in Europe (sometimes harmoniously and sometimes rather less so), the residues of the old system remain, most noticeably in attitudes towards the churches. This is the principal reason why the historic churches in Europe are still regarded as public utilities rather than free-standing or voluntary organizations. Europeans expect their churches to be there when they need them, mostly at the time of a death; whether or not they choose to attend them on a regular basis is an entirely different issue.

It is in Western Europe, moreover, that the decline of religious activity has been most marked and where the most obvious indices of secularization can be found.[5] Paradoxically (or perhaps not) it is the part of the Western world where the process of institutional differentiation has been most retarded.

The decline in institutional religion

Some facts and figures have been set out in chapter 2; more detailed information about the European case can be found in *Religion in Modern Europe: A Memory Mutates.*[6] The statistics speak for themselves. There has been a substantial reduction in institutional religion in most parts of the continent and over a wide range of indicators – a shift that began, broadly speaking, with the onset of industrialization and urbanization. Here is evidence of secularization. Even in Europe, however, the process is far from uniform; it takes place differently in different parts of the continent and with different social, political and cultural implications.[7] There is first of all a marked discrepancy between the Protestant north where the indicators of religious activity are particularly low, and the Catholic south where (with the exception of France) they remain relatively high. Whether or not the Catholic south will imitate the Protestant north a generation or so later remains a very open question. It is the Protestant north moreover which has, by and large, retained the notion of a state church – an institution which exists alongside a moderately secularized population but with little animosity. In Catholic cultures, the opposition between church and state has been noticeably more marked, and most of all in France.

Bearing such complexities in mind, we need to think further about the patterns of religious life in modern Europe. Two concepts are helpful in this respect. First, the notion of "believing without belonging".[8] Europeans no longer attend their churches with any regularity, nor do they subscribe to the historic formularies of the Christian tradition (indeed, many Europeans no longer know what these are). The majority of Europeans retain, however, a passive attachment to their churches, while being free to experiment with new forms of religious life (both practice and belief). Religion becomes therefore increasingly individualized, heterogeneous and open to change. Exactly the same point can be put in a different way: Europeans who detach themselves from the churches do not necessarily turn into secular rationalists. Convinced unbelievers certainly exist – more so in Europe than in other parts of the world – but they remain a minority, clustered in certain milieux and over-represented in the "chattering classes" (notably in the media).

It is at this point that the second concept becomes important – that of "vicarious religion".[9] By "vicarious" is meant the notion of religion performed by an active minority but on behalf of a much larger number, who (implicitly at least) not only understand, but also quite clearly approve of what the minority are doing. The most obvious examples of this process can be found in the Nordic countries (Sweden, Norway, Denmark, Finland and Iceland), but it penetrates throughout Europe. Nordic populations, more than most, remain members of their Lutheran churches; they use them extensively for the occasional offices and regard membership as part of national just as much as religious identity. More pertinently for the churches themselves, Nordic people continue to pay appreciable amounts of tax to their churches – resulting, among other things, in large numbers of religious professionals (not least musicians) and beautifully maintained buildings in even the tiniest village. The cultural aspects of religion are well cared for.

This does not mean that Nordic populations attend their churches with any frequency, nor do they necessarily believe in the tenets of Lutheranism. Indeed, they appear on every comparative scale to be among the least believing and least practising (most secularized) populations in the world. So how should we understand their continuing membership of and support for their churches? This question is not only central to the understanding of religion in Europe, but also poses a significant methodological challenge. How is it possible to get beneath the surface of the Nordic (or indeed any other) society in order to investigate the deep but largely hidden reflexes of a population?

An iceberg may provide a helpful analogy. It is easy enough both to measure and to take note of the part that emerges from the water. Large numbers of studies have done precisely that and have concluded that the visible tip of the religious iceberg in Europe is getting smaller and less significant almost by the day. But this is to ignore the vast mass under the water which is invisible for most of the time, but without which the visible part would not be there at all. How, though, can the investigator penetrate beneath the surface in order to understand what is going on? A further discussion of the methodological issues lies beyond the scope of this chapter. The point to retain is that even in the most secularized part of the Western world (i.e. Western Europe), the detachment of the population from their churches is partial rather than complete.

New habits are forming, however, in Europe as in other parts of the world, and such habits are part of the process of secularization. A good example can be found in the changing motivations for religious activity.

More precisely, the understanding of religion as a form of obligation or duty is giving way to an increasing emphasis on "consumption" or choosing. What until moderately recently was simply imposed by the historic churches (with all the negative connotations of this word), or inherited (a rather more positive spin), becomes instead a matter of personal choice. I go to church or to another religious organization because I want to, maybe for a short period or maybe for longer, to fulfil a particular rather than a general need in my life and where I will continue my attachment so long as it provides what I want, but I have no *obligation* either to attend in the first place or to continue if I do not want to.

As such this pattern is entirely compatible with vicariousness: the churches need to be there in order that an individual may attend them if they so choose. The chemistry, however, gradually changes, a shift which is discernible in both practice and belief of Europeans, not to mention the connections between them. There is, for example, a clearly observable change in the patterns of confirmation in the Church of England. The first point to make is that the overall numbers of confirmations have dropped dramatically in the post-war period, evidence once again of institutional decline. In England, though not yet in the Nordic countries, confirmation is no longer a teenage rite of passage, but a relatively rare event undertaken as a matter of personal choice by people of all ages. Indeed, there is a very marked rise in the proportion of adult confirmations among the candidates overall – up to 40 percent by the mid 1990s (by no means enough, however, to offset the fall among teenagers).

Confirmation becomes, therefore, a very significant event for those individuals who choose this option, an attitude that is bound to affect the rite itself – which now includes the space for a public declaration of faith. It becomes in fact an opportunity to make public what has often been an entirely private activity. It is increasingly common, moreover, to baptize an adult candidate immediately before the confirmation, a gesture which is evidence in itself of the fall in infant baptism some twenty to thirty years earlier. Taken together, these events indicate a marked change in the nature of membership in the historic churches which become, in some senses, much more like their non-established counterparts. Voluntarism is beginning to establish itself de facto, regardless of the constitutional position of the churches.

What secularization means in Europe, therefore, is a marked shift in the traditional patterns of religious life and, rather more slowly, the erosion of the Christian culture that both supports and depends on the mainstream churches. What it does not mean is the end of religious sensibilities, which in turn bring about the search for new meanings. Those religious institutions (in any denomination) which are able to respond to this seeking are those that are likely to do relatively well. Those that depend on habit or obligation are those that are collapsing very fast – the sanctions that enforced such habits have long since disappeared.

A note on the English-speaking dominions

Before moving to the final part of this chapter, it is important to include a few remarks about the English-speaking dominions: Canada, Australia and New Zealand. All three are unquestionably modern societies whose patterns of religious life are best thought of as being half-way between the European and American cases. The indices of activity are higher that those of Europe, but not as high as those in the United States. They are also subtly different from each other. It seems to be the case, however, that all three of the dominions are becoming more like Europe than America from a religious point of view, but are at the same time subject to new influences. In Australia, for instance, recent immigrations have come from Asia rather than from Europe, leading to distinctive innovations in religion as in so much else. The loosening of the old disciplines is similar to the European case; what emerges to replace these may be very different indeed.

It is worth underlining a final point with respect to the dominions. These are territorially very large – both Canada and Australia cover huge land masses. However, their populations are small. Less than 20 million relatively secular (in the sense described above) Australians live alongside 240 million Indonesians. In terms of global religiosity, the latter (the largest Muslim nation in the world) will have the greater significance.

The limitations of the concept

Carefully used, the concept of secularization (in the sense of institutional decline) describes well the state of affairs that exists in modern Europe and in the English-speaking dominions, as the power of the mainstream churches diminishes, together with their capacity to influence the habits and thought patterns of modern citizens. One reason for this was the tendency for these churches to cling too long to secular power and to inhibit the gradual separation of powers which are part of the modern state. Institutional differentiation (an entirely healthy aspiration) was restricted, bringing with it, in the long term, a decline in religious activity.

This, however, is a distinctively European process; it is not the inevitable consequence of modernization, a point already raised in part one of this book but worth repeating here. Secularization, as described here, is the outcome of modernization in the European case, and in those parts of the world most directly influenced by European institutions and European culture. It is not a universal process.[10] Modernization takes different forms in different parts of the world; hence, the combination in the United States of developed indices of modernization alongside high levels of religious activity, and in the developing world, outcomes that are different again. In short, the reasons for the relatively secular nature of Europe lie primarily in Europeanness, not in the process of modernization *per se*. Hence, among other things, the need to be cautious not only in extrapolating from the European case, but also in using indiscriminately the concepts and tools that have emerged as an integral part of the European experience. And if this is the case within the modern West, even greater care will be necessary as the debate moves further afield – to the Southern hemisphere with its rapidly growing Christian churches and to the parts of the globe dominated by the other world faiths.

Those responsible for the ecumenical movement need to bear both the practical and the conceptual points in mind as they come to terms with the nature of religion in the modern world. Leaving the secularization paradigm behind will, however, require considerable effort, especially on the part of Europeans; it is deeply embedded in popular as well as in social scientific ways of thinking. It has been formative in much of the thinking that lies behind the ecumenical movement.

NOTES

[1]   J. Casanova, *Public Religions in the Modern World*, Chicago, Univ. of Chicago Press, 1994, p. 211. This in turn builds on K. Dobbelaere, "Secularization: A Multi-dimensional Concept", *Current Sociology*, 29, 2, 1981, recently reprinted in K. Dobbelaere, *Secularization: An Analysis at Three Levels*, Brussels, PIE–Peter Lang, 2002.

[2]   K. Hadaway, P. Marler and M. Chaves, "What the Polls Don't Show: A Closer Look at Church Attendance", *American Sociological Review*, 58, 6, 1993, pp. 741–52. K. Hadaway, P. Marler and M. Chaves, "A Symposium on Church Attendance", *American Sociological Review*, 63, 1, 1998, pp. 111–45.

[3]   An interesting comparative project concerning the place of the churches in the welfare systems of contemporary Europe is in process. It is based in the University of Uppsala, Sweden.

[4]   S. Warner, "Work in Progress towards a New Paradigm for the Sociological Study of Religion in the United States", *American Journal of Sociology*, 98, 5, 1993, pp. 1044–93. S. Warner, "A Paradigm Is not a Theory: Reply to Lechner", *American Journal of Sociology*, 103, 1, 1997, pp.192–98.

[5]   The religious indicators in Central and Eastern Europe remain both varied and volatile. It is too soon yet to say whether these will settle down and follow the pattern

in Western Europe or whether a distinctively different post-communist model will eventually emerge.

6 Grace Davie, Oxford, Oxford UP, 2000.

7 D. Martin, *A General Theory of Secularization*, Oxford, Blackwell, 1978; and Davie, *Religion in Modern Europe*.

8 G. Davie, *Religion in Britain since 1945: Believing without Belonging*, Oxford, Blackwell, 1994.

9 Davie, *Religion in Modern Europe*.

10 S. Eisenstadt, "Multiple Modernities", in *Daedalus*, 129, 1, 2000, pp.1-30. G. Davie, *Europe: The Exceptional Case. Parameters of Faith in the Modern World*, London, Darton, Longman & Todd, 2002.

14
Emerging New Religious Awareness and Its Challenges to the Ecumenical Movement

S. WESLEY ARIARAJAH

Following the lead of Gustave Mensching, the Japanese Buddhist, scholar Masao Abe classifies religions into three types. This classification is open to debate because religions can be classified in many ways depending on the principles of classification used. Grouping religions into these three models, however, helps us in our understanding of how contemporary developments are affecting religions. It also helps us to discern the impact religions are having on one another, resulting in a new religious awareness in our day. [1]

Abe calls the first kind of religions nature religions. Often, these religions are too easily characterized as those in which nature is worshipped. Some historians of religion call them primal religions – having to do with early humans' fear of the unknown – the implication being that with the advancement of science and technology humans would be "cured" of the fear of nature. A chronological development is often imposed on the history of religions with the suggestion that these religions would come to an end with "advances" in human civilization.

Unfortunately, the analysis falls far short of entering the true spirit of these religions, which are very much alive and present in our own day among the native or the first peoples of the Americas, in most parts of Africa, among Aboriginal and Maori peoples of Australasia and among most of the tribal peoples of Asia and the Pacific. In reality what is at the heart of the nature religions is the conviction that nature, humans and the divine are in a continuum. The unwillingness on the part of these religions to separate the humans and the gods from nature has for centuries enabled them to respect and preserve nature, to live in harmony with it, and to see the presence of the divine in it. They consider every stage of human life as part of the natural cycles of life and death. Individual human beings come and go, but nature, the gods and human communities remain.

It is not surprising, therefore, that the native elders of the Americas were rather confused when the newcomers to the continent wanted to buy land from them. "How can you sell what you do not own?" was the question. "We do not own the land; the land owns us." For them, the concept of putting up fences to claim ownership of pieces of land was quite a mystery, especially since no one could take it with them when they "go". In these traditions no polarization is made between life and death. Rather, births and deaths are the poles marking the entry and exit points. Life continues.

According to Abe, the other two groups of religions differ from nature religions in introducing speculative thinking that separates humans from nature, and the divine from nature and humans. The introduction of the concept of transcendence in the forms of God, Brahman, Ultimate Reality, Tao, etc., over nature and humans, and the elevation of humans over the natural world, marks them off from the nature religions.

These religions can again be grouped into two. In the first type, ethnic religions, religious identity is very much linked to a race, *ethnic* group or specific geographical location. In the ancient world the religious traditions of Egypt, Persia, Greece, Rome, etc., while introducing transcendence, remained ethnic in character. With the separation of gods from nature arose the need for more complex rituals, myths, sacrifices and priesthoods to mediate the relationship between the gods on the one hand and nature and humans on the other. Now sacrifices had to be offered to gods to increase the fertility of the land and to entice rich harvest. Humans had to find ways and means to earn acts of forgiveness and favours from the divine. As long as these expressions remained ethnic, much of these practices found expression also in community regulations, feasts and festivals, contributing to the evolution of a culture that represented the religion and race of a people. Today, religious traditions like Confucianism, Taoism, Shintoism, Judaism and much of Hinduism, Sikhism and Jainism show some of the basic characteristics of the ethnic religious expression.

Religions in the third group, while sharing much with ethnic religions, differ from them in claiming to be *world* religions that runs across many ethnic, racial and national boundaries. Christianity, Islam and Buddhism, for example, had their origins as ethnic religions, but they have become complex realities by their claim to be universal religions.

Five main features are typical to religious traditions that claim to be world religions. First, they normally have founders who become the centre of the community's focus and attention. Second, they claim validity and relevance for their messages among peoples and cultures that lie well beyond the immediate cultures in which they were born. Third, while the sense of community still plays a key role, the primary emphasis shifts to the individual as the focus of the liberating or saving messages of the founders. Fourth, individuals that are not born into the community are encouraged to join these religious traditions, and thus they develop a strong missionary dimension to their expression. They end up drawing their respective religious communities from a vast variety of cultures, nations and locations. Fifth, whereas religion, culture, life and politics are seen to belong together in ethnic religions, world religions, in view of the complexities brought in by the plurality of cultures, either seek to transplant and enforce a dominant specific culture across national boundaries or, in some instances, introduce a radical separation between religion on the one hand and socio-political and cultural realities on the other.

In considering changes to religious life, one needs to be aware that all these forms of religious expression are prevalent in our day. We begin this discussion by making distinctions between these religions because in seeking to understand the rise of a new religious awareness in our day we need to see both how these religions are affected by the contemporary culture, and how they begin to affect one another as they seek to cope with the challenges posed by modernity and post-modernity.

Realities affecting religious life today

It is significant that over the past centuries all these traditions have come under pressure, and what we see today is the culmination of some of the pressures that have been mounting on them. Four of the factors deserve special consideration.

Colonization

Perhaps no other force has done more to destabilize nature religions than colonization. The colonization of the Americas, Africa, Australia-New Zealand, the Pacific and parts of Asia brought into these regions dimensions of religious self-understandings that were alien to nature religions. The imposition of the new forms of religion was accompanied by forceful introduction of teachings and cultural practices that challenged the bases of both the nature and ethnic religions. The unbridled confidence in science and technology and the denigration of the nature-based religious life as inferior, and the ethnic religions as insular, did much to undermine the concept of the nature-human-gods continuum and the internal coherence of religious communities. With new perspectives came the loss of respect for the earth and the unconscionable exploitation of the earth and its resources. Part of the new religious awareness today has to do with the attempt to recover and reown this religious dimension that brings peoples closer to nature. To this we would return.

Migration

The second important factor that has affected the neat separation of different groups of religious expressions is the large-scale migration of human communities, either by choice or due to external factors that make them refugees and asylum-seekers. Much of prehistoric and early migrations of peoples were in large communities where wars, famine, natural disasters, etc. made it imperative for whole communities to move to different locations. In so doing, the communities that moved carried with them their ethnic, religious and cultural identities. They were in sufficient numbers to be able to transplant their religio-cultural life into the new location. The impact of the new location on them was gradual. The external influences were gradually assimilated into the mainstream of religious and cultural life.

But a qualitative difference can be seen in migrations over the past century. Smaller groups of people migrate from one country to another for social, economic or political reasons, of course, carrying with them the religious cultural ethos peculiar to their communities. But their numbers are not large enough, and they often have to scatter within the new community in search of jobs and livelihood. Thus, when groups from nature religions move into a cultural ethos dominated by the world religions, it becomes difficult for them to maintain their religious life. This is aggravated by the fact that much small-scale migration is to urban areas where the immediate contact with nature that had surrounded them in the community back home no longer exists. The most obvious example of this is witnessed in the religious life of African migrants into Western Europe and North America. While the first generation of migrants attempts desperately to hold on to traditional values and practices, they find that they are at the losing end with the second and third generations.

Migrations also affect ethnic religions. Migrant Hindu communities are beginning to pay a heavy price for moving away from the geographic location that nurtured and fostered Hindu expressions of religious life. Hinduism is in fact defined as all the religious expressions that have taken place in the Indian landmass. Indianness and Hinduness are inseparable, as is it argued today by the Hindu nationalist movement in India under the banner of *Hinduthva* (Hinduness). Here again, the migrant communities build temples and observe festivals and rituals in the new locations, but a conversation with these communities would show deep anxieties about the future.

Globalization

The third factor, globalization, already discussed at length in this book, also plays a significant role in the rise of new awareness among religious communities. Globalization in all its forms militates against the nature and ethnic religions. These religions have no power to stop the impact of globalization on their communities. Whatever be the positive aspects of globalization, it affects religious communities in five different ways. First, it facilitates even greater movement of peoples into new situations. Second, it disrupts the organized socio-economic life that has been the basis on which communities have been built. Third, with the power of the mass media, it promotes a global culture and seeks to introduce cultural elements, values, priorities and ways of life that militate against the values that are particular to specific communities. Fourth, it erodes the traditional authority structures that have enabled the communities to function together. Fifth, through a gradual process, it homogenizes the human community, especially in economic terms. In other words, it militates against qualitative pluralism that encourages all forms of diversity, including religious diversity. In reality, the economic–cultural dimensions of globalization function like a world religion seeking to establish itself as an alternative to other forms of religious life.

Plurality

Colonization, migration and globalization have together introduced into all communities a plurality that is qualitatively and quantitatively different from that traditionally experienced by communities. As a result, some of the religious communities that have been in comparative isolation (e.g. Christian communities in Norway and Sweden) have to deal with new forms of religious and cultural plurality brought in by the arrival of Muslims, Buddhists, Hindus, etc. Hindu and Buddhist communities that have migrated into the Western hemisphere, even though they have come from the pluralistic Asian continent, have to deal with the reality of a new kind of pluralism in which they are no longer the dominant community. Islamic communities, where religion seeks to organize life in all its dimensions and is best practised in a homogeneous community, struggle to find a way to be Islamic in cultures that are influenced by other visions of society.

There are of course many other factors that affect religion. The examples above are sufficient to help us embark on a discussion of how a new religious consciousness has emerged.

The mutual interaction of religious streams

The impact of the factors discussed above has been different on the three different types of religious expression. At the same time, there is also an unprecedented level of interaction, mutual knowledge and actual meetings between these different streams of religious expression. These meetings have also affected each of them in different ways. The impact of other religions and the secular culture on nature religions has challenged the cultural ethos, values and ways of life that preserved them through the centuries. However, the impact has not been only one way. Their insights into the relationship between nature, human beings and the divine have begun to influence world religions deeply. This can be traced in the developments that we see in our day.

A spirituality closer to the earth

One of the dimensions of the new religious awareness has to do with a new search for a religious life that fosters a closer relationship between humanity and nature. Three distinct issues have contributed to the emergence of this new awareness.

First, the growing anxiety over the deepening ecological crisis. While there is disagreement on the causes of this crisis, many are convinced that it primarily has to do with the separation that the Semitic religious traditions have introduced between nature and humans, and nature and the divine. The scientific world-view that looks upon the universe as an object to be studied, understood and manipulated arose primarily in cultures influenced by the Semitic religions. Behind this modernist perception was also the understanding of the universe as a static reality that follows dependable permanent laws and principles. Contemporary science (especially advances in quantum physics) has deeply shaken the foundations of this understanding of the universe. Randomness and unpredictability of the universe have become matters of special interest. We realize today that even as life emerged, it can also cease to exist. Therefore, there is greater awareness today of the preciousness of life, the fragility of the earth, and the credible threat to life as we know it. Greater knowledge of the importance of bio-diversity for the continuation and evolution of life on the planet has taken the ecological debate beyond responsible use of natural resources to the protection and preservation of animal and plant species from extinction.

Some would still insist that the ecological issue is a scientific problem requiring scientific answers. However, Leonardo Boff, in his *Ecology and Liberation* argues that it is the very basis of this scientific view that stands discredited today:

> From the 1920s a new cosmology emerged with the theory of relativity of Einstein, the quantum physics of Bohr, the indeterminacy principle of Heisenberg, the findings in theoretical physics of Prigogine and Stengers, and the contributions of depth psychology (Freud and Jung), transpersonal psychology (Maslow, P. Weil), bio-genetics, cybernetics and deep ecology.

He holds that there is now "a transition from a materialistic world (linked to production of material goods) to a post-materialistic and spiritual world (interested in the integration of the everyday with the mystical dimension of things)".

This development, in his view, is nothing less than a proposal for a new cosmology, a move from a materialistic world to a post-materialistic and spiritual world. This new cosmology "proposes a vision of a unified but not hierarchical world, one that is organic, holistic, feminine/masculine, and spiritual. Living beings... are not juxtaposed or disunited. Everything is profoundly inter-related. Everything that exists is a complex bundle of energy in perpetual inter-relativity. Matter itself represents one of the possible manifestations of energy."[2]

Thus, the ecological issue is seen as a spiritual question having to do with our vision of the world, needing spiritual responses. In other words, the new religious awareness calls for a new spirituality in our understanding of our relationship to nature.

The second factor that has influenced the revolution of thinking on humanity's relation to nature is the rise of the eco-feminist movement. Strong parallels have been drawn between the patriarchal attitudes to and exploitation of the earth and of women. A new accent on the importance of the body over against preoccupation with the mind, and the affirmation of the sanctity of the life-cycle within the feminist movement, have brought the feminist and the ecological movements closer together.

Anne Primavesi, writing on ecology, feminism and Christianity, argues the patriarchal approach both to the earth and to women has been based on a concept of "power-over". Power-over, she says, shapes every institution of our society and is linked to domination and control. Extending this to the concept of the divine, she says: "For Christians, it has been consciousness modelled on the image of God who stands 'over' the world, above it and beyond it: a God outside nature whose will must be obeyed under the pain of death; a God not involved in the messy business of being human." Identifying this approach as the one that sanctions violence against the natural world, she argues: "Ecology has different models of power: power-from-within and power-with. It reunites the spirit and body, humanity and nature, God and world, in the name of immanent value."[3]

This has also resulted in attempts to recover and reinstate some of the early religious traditions that were centred on the "mother earth" and on nature in general. There is in the United States for example a close link between native women thinkers and those active in the construction of a feminist theology that is close to the earth. This attempt to recover traditions buried by patriarchal views is also undertaken by women in Asia, Africa and Latin America.

Aruna Gnanadason from India sees in the Hindu concept of Shakti some of the basic elements of "a new feminist paradigm – an eco-centred feminist spirituality". In this world-view, *Shakti*, the feminist principle that is the life energy of the universe, is the source and substance of all things, pervading everything. The manifestation of this primordial energy is called *Prakriti* (nature):

> Nature, both animate and inanimate, is thus the expression of *Shakti*, the feminine creative principle of the cosmos; in conjunction with the masculine principle *(Purusha)*, *Prakriti* creates the world. *Prakriti* is worshipped as *Aditi*, the primordial vastness, the inexhaustible, the source of abundance. She is worshipped as *Adi Shakti*, the primordial power. All the forms of nature and life in nature are the forms, the children of the Mother nature who is nature itself born of the creative play of her thought.[4]

The third factor has to do with a change in emphasis in our understanding of God. Over the past century there has been a quiet shift that places greater emphasis on God's immanence. Even though the Semitic religions, in theory, have emphasized both the transcendence and the immanence of God, transcendence played the major role in the actual understanding of humanity's relation to God. The impact of ethnic religions like Hinduism, Buddhism and Taoism has had the effect of creating a greater interest in immanence, for example, within Christianity. Much contemporary theology is deeply influenced by existentialist thinking, and there is greater interest today in theological schools that pay greater attention to elements in the metaphysics that underlie process thinking. In this stream of thinking the immanence of the divine is seen not only in relation to humans but also to the universe. The Upanishadic concept of the Brahman as the one who pervades the universe and the Vaishnava view of seeing the universe as the body of the divine find echoes in contemporary eco-theologies. This is a remarkable shift from the fear of pantheism and monism that drove Christian theologians away from the fundamentals of Hindu thought.

All these developments have contributed to a new awareness of the need for a spirituality that links humans to the earth and to the divine in a new paradigm.

Search for a new religious identity

The new religious awareness is also accompanied by a search for a new religious identity that will free people from the rigid boxes of streamlined religious traditions into which they are born.

Greater population movements, the communications explosion and interaction between the different religious streams have begun radically to weaken the hold of institutionalized religions on people's lives and spirituality. Since the world religions are based on revelations or on the teaching of the founders, they have had difficulty adjusting to the spiritual demands that arise from their adherents' exposure to the nature and ethnic religions. Further, because of their universal outreach they also needed to have more well defined doctrines and policies that preserved their identity as a religious community, while drawing adherents from all cultures. This rigid system, maintained by doctrines and clearly defined structures of authority, which served these religions well in past centuries, has itself become the primary problem in our day. There are of course new theological articulations and adaptations to meet the situation, but they appear to be too little, too late.

Wilfred Cantwell Smith, who has specialized in documenting and reflecting on this reality, says,

> However incipiently, the boundaries segregating off religious communities radically and finally from each other are beginning, just a little, to weaken or to dissolve, so that being a Hindu and being a Buddhist, or being a Christian and not being a Christian, are not so stark alternatives as once they seemed.

Smith himself takes this reality as an indication of a new religious awareness and argues that the gradual convergence between religious traditions has reached the point where we need to speak of "a common religious history of humankind" where specific religious traditions have to be seen as none other than "strands" within that common history.[5]

Even those who consider Smith, as always, to be a little ahead of his times would not deny the experiential and phenomenological reality that many religious people today have learned the art of sitting lightly on their own traditions. In some cases it only finds expression in the dissatisfaction and alienation from one's own tradition. In other cases, commitment to one's own tradition is flavoured by a lively interest and engagement in other forms of spiritual disciplines. Thus, for example, the same person that goes regularly to the United Methodist Church each Sunday would also attend on Wednesdays the Buddhist Vipasana meditation to learn to "centre down" and concentrate on Reality. Devout Jews practise Zen to have the experience of "emptiness" that releases the strains of daily life. In still other cases, people have become "multifaith" or "interfaith" in their religious orientation and are open to many religious insights and disciplines. In other words, part of the new religious awareness is the inadequacy of all labels that mark religious traditions as distinct realities from one another. There is a search for a new, broader and more freeing religious identity.

As seen in earlier parts of this book, the search for identity is a more complex reality with a great variety of manifestations, including trends towards fundamentalism, extremism and so on. For the purposes of this chapter, however, we need to note the spiritual revolution that is in progress, where many are looking for a richer and fuller meaning of what it means to be religious.

The quest for an adequate theology of religions

Even though Smith's call for a "world theology" has not yet received the attention it deserves, one dimension of the new religious awareness is the intense search for a new theology of religions that would make greater theological sense of religious plurality and diversity. Within the Christian tradition, for instance, there has been intense debate on how Christians might come to terms with the reality that they live among peoples who also "believe" but use a different symbol system to do so. The continuing debate on the theology of religions has sometimes been systematized into the threefold "exclusivist", "inclusivist" and "pluralistic" positions. Such a systematization, however, misses out the many nuances of the positions being taken, all of which, with the exception of the extreme forms of exclusivism, aim at a more generous understanding of other religious traditions.

The Roman Catholic theology after Vatican II, for example, has produced a long line of veterans in this field, such as Karl Rahner, Raimundo Panikkar, Hans Küng, Jacques Dupuis, Paul Knitter, Julius Lipner, Gavin D'Costa and a host of others who are attempting to further the openings that are provided in the documents of Vatican II to expound a theology of religions that is more adequate for our day.

It must be noted that these discussions in the theology of religions do not arise from purely intellectual curiosity, but from the need to find an adequate theology that responds to the new religious awareness on the ground. The faithful within the Roman Catholic tradition are in fact searching for handles to take account of the religious reality of their neighbours. The church's relevance in this context depends on its capacity to provide new answers.

The same is true of the Protestant tradition. Here the people engaged in the exploration are too numerous to name. Persons like John Hick and John Cobb have faced the problem in a radical way. Hick has come up with a position that validates all religions as legitimate paths to the Real, and Cobb, approaching the issue from his process perspective, sees the encounter of religions as "occasions" that would bring about their mutual transformation and evolution. While everyone seems to agree that we do not have a theology that can meet the new situation, no one seems to be satisfied with the answers that are being proposed.

The creation of the Sub-unit on Dialogue within the World Council of Churches was also a response to this new awareness. Its validity is confirmed by the way in which interfaith ministries, dialogues and organizations have flourished during the past few decades.

Asian theologians like P.D. Devanandan, Stanley Samartha, M.M. Thomas, Aloysius Pieris, Anthony Fernando, C.S. Song, Kosuke Koyama, Sachi Yagi and others argue the encounter between religious traditions needs to go much deeper than dialogue for mutual understanding and relationships. Each of them has proposed positions that aim at profound interaction that would mutually transform the meaning of being religious in our day.

Aloysius Pieris, for example, speaks about the Semitic and Asian approaches to Reality as two distinct "idioms" or "poles"; each in itself does not provide a holistic approach. Characterizing the Semitic religions as "agapaic" (love-oriented) and the Asian ones as "gnostic" (wisdom-oriented), he argues that a fuller understanding of Reality can emerge only as a result of holding these poles together. Thus, he challenges the Semitic traditions to have "a baptism by immersion" in Asian spirituality as the way of entering the holistic understanding of being truly religious in our day. The Christian emphasis on love and the Buddhist call for wisdom are not alien to one another; they belong together.[6] Similar voices in Africa call for a new assessment of Christian relations to African Traditional Religions and spirituality. African Christian theologians are beginning to point out the spiritual dimensions of religious life that have been lost due to the antagonism Christianity has had as a world religion to the nature religions of Africa.

The discussions above show that the new religious awareness related to the encounter of religions is to be traced not only to the experiential dimension, but also to a new theological awareness. In fact, Kenneth Cragg argues that we dare not do theology any longer in isolation, but with "attentiveness" to the fact that there are others who also believe and pray. He calls this "doing theology in cross-reference".[7]

Open religious quest

Ursula King argues religious plurality, the dialogue encounter of religions, greater knowledge and participation in other religious experiences have led today to the emergence of "an open religious quest" in search of a genuine spiritual freedom. Quoting the former Burmese UN general secretary U Thant, she argues all humans have to satisfy four fundamental needs: physical, mental, moral and spiritual. What we see in the new religious awareness is a longing to satisfy the spiritual needs through an open religious quest.[8]

The new religious awareness thus has to do with the struggle for greater freedom in the spiritual sphere so that there can be more open experimentations, crossings over and adaptations. The limits imposed by the world religions for the preservation of the distinctiveness of specific traditions have been challenged and often breached. It has become heretical to speak about heresy. The fears of syncretism and relativism that plagued the WCC Nairobi assembly debate on dialogue, for example, are hardly raised today. What is more visible is the freedom people demand to search for an authentic spiritual life and to look for it wherever it may be found. There is a demand to see all spiritual traditions as the common heritage of humankind.

This open quest for spirituality has had many manifestations. The search for spiritual experiences that employ the body, mind and spirit has led to the emergence of a great variety of religious beliefs, practices and observances that are rather loosely referred to as New-Age spirituality. The hope of finding new meaning to existence and its destiny has resulted in the rise of gurus, cult leaders, spiritual communities and goddess traditions that attract many, especially in the Western hemisphere. The quest for the immediacy of the spiritual experience and the longing for community has led worldwide to the emergence of charismatic renewal movements. Many who had moved away from religion as an outmoded and oppressive reality are beginning to look for new forms of spirituality to ground them in Reality, without having to accept institutionalized forms of religion.

Wars and conflicts (also in the name of religions), widening economic disparities and growing poverty, the breakdown of the sense of community, the inability of individuals and communities to have a say in their social–political life, the ambiguities of political systems, and the overall sense of the "loss of meaning of life" have all contributed to the search for meaning, and a spirituality that would sustain people in their predicament. The new religious awareness is thus a search that has led to some creative movements as well as to new forms of religious exploitation. It is not a call for the reformation of religions. Nor is it a call to return to the fundamentals. Rather, it is a call for relevance and a challenge to religions to provide meaning in the midst of all the ambiguities that beset contemporary life. This has made enormous demands on religious traditions, none of which appear able to make an adequate response.

Challenges to the ecumenical movement

These can be summarized as five clusters of issues:

1. *The nature and scope of the ecumenical movement.* As early as 1980, Wilfred Cantwell Smith complained that the word "ecumenical", which should in reality mean the search for the unity of all humankind, had unfortunately "been appropriated lately to designate a rather internal development within the ongoing church".[9] The use of "new ecumenism", "mega ecumenism", "wider ecumenism", etc. to point to the need for the religious traditions to grow closer together has not had much welcome. There is a fear that this concept will eventually undermine the Christian search for unity. Be that as it may, the ecumenical movement can no longer be satisfied with the unity of the church to the exclusion of the search for wider unity. The relationship between the two movements needs to be understood and related. In fact, there were attempts in the past to deal with this question in the Faith and Order studies on the "Unity of the Church and Unity of Humankind". The contemporary religious awareness has gone far beyond the parameters of that study. A new attempt to understand the issues has become urgent.[10]

2. The new religious awareness raises questions for the basis on which discussions on mission and dialogue are carried out within the ecumenical movement. Some of the old questions about syncretism, relativism and universalism no longer apply to the interfaith discussions of our day. There needs to be a new framework for our theological discussion on the reality of other religious traditions and our relationship to them. The discussions on "Christian missions" also need to find a new framework that takes fuller account of the new religious awareness and the dramatic challenges posed by the new socio-economic and political realities. The ecumenical move-

ment is also best placed to facilitate a rethinking of Christian theology with attentiveness to the fact that others also have a contribution to make to the subjects of our theological explorations.

3. While the issues of globalization, migration and plurality have attracted the attention of the ecumenical movement, and much has been said and done about them, there has not been a concerted effort to understand their impact on religious life and the challenges they bring to the understanding and practice of religion.

4. The search for an authentic spirituality is the foundation of the new religious awareness. Again, the ecumenical movement has made several explorations in the past on spirituality, but for the most part they have been concerned with different forms, dimensions and expressions of Christian spirituality. Here, too, a new frame of reference is needed for a fresh discussion on an authentic spiritual life.

5. Many of the issues that affect human life are experienced by people across the religious barriers. Therefore, the ecumenical movement needs to pioneer the Christian willingness to explore all issues that confront humankind, not in isolation, but in partnership with others. The Lund principle in relation to interchurch relations – that we should do separately only those things that our conscience does not permit us to do together with others – should be broadened to include our relationships and life with people of other religious traditions. The new religious awareness today provides us with a challenge for such a radical departure. Therein may also lie the key to the renewal of the ecumenical movement.

NOTES

[1] Masao Abe, "The End of World Religions", *World Faiths Insight*, New Series, Jan. 1984, pp. 8–21.

[2] Leonardo Boff, *Ecology and Liberation: A New Paradigm*, Maryknoll NY, Orbis, 1995, pp. 63–64.

[3] Anne Primavesi, *From Apocalypse to Genesis: Ecology, Feminism and Christianity*, Minneapolis, Fortress, 1991, pp. 219–20.

[4] Aruna Gnanadason, "Towards a Feminist Eco-Theology for India", in Rosemary Radford Ruether ed., *Women Healing the Earth: Third World Women on Ecology, Feminism, and Religion*, Maryknoll NY, Orbis, 1996, pp. 75–6.

[5] Wilfred Cantwell Smith, *Towards a World Theology*, London, Macmillan, 1981. See esp. his chapters on "A History of Religions in the Singular" and "Religious Life as Participation in a Process".

[6] See Aloysius Pieris, "Western Christianity and Asian Buddhism: A Theological Reading of Historical Encounters", *Dialogue*, New Series 7, no. 2, 1980, p. 66.

7   Kenneth Cragg, *The Christ and the Faiths: Theology in Cross-Reference*, London, SPCK, 1986, p. 145.

8   Ursula King, "The Freedom of the Spirit: Spirituality and the New Religions", *World Faiths Insight*, New Series 8, Jan. 1984, pp. 25–28.

9   Wilfred Cantwell Smith, "The Christian in a Religiously Plural World", in John Hick and Brian Hebblethwaite eds, *Christianity and Other Religions*, Glasgow, Collins, 1980, p. 87.

10 For a full discussion of this issues see S. Wesley Ariarajah, "Wider Ecumenism: A Threat or a Promise?" *The Ecumenical Review*, vol. 50, no. 3, July 1998, pp. 321–29.

15

The Individualization
of Religious Experience

ANDRÉ DROOGERS

From the point of view of the churches, individualization is often experienced as threatening. They believe that they lose influence not only on their members, but also generally, as an institution in public life. It is therefore worthwhile, when considering the current state of religion in the world, to draw special attention to the process of individualization of religion. An analysis of its characteristics and causes might be helpful in making the challenges to the ecumenical movement more explicit.

The problem

Today, at least in some parts of the world (mainly at both ends of the North Atlantic axis), people seem to have developed a way of living with a minimum of institutional help. What is more, their society (and paradoxically even some of its institutions, including the churches) promotes this independent attitude. The ideology of freedom is followed to its ultimate consequences. Emancipation as freedom from institutional dominance has become a positive value.

Yet a puzzle presents itself. Societies survive partly through their institutions, from the family to the municipality, from political parties to trade unions, from schools to universities. Institutions depend on the willingness of people to accept the role these institutions play in society. People are supposed to support them by identifying with them and feeling responsible for them, perhaps being a paying member and taking part in the activities that maintain it. Once people are encouraged to behave as "authentic" individuals this support seems to fall away and the institutions enter the danger zone, and perhaps society with them.

Christian institutions do not escape this development. Thus, when people begin to stay away from church or become more selective in their participation, or even leave the church, that church faces a problem. Nowadays, in some parts of the West, people have discovered that they are able to believe without belonging.[1] They may do so as a rule, for years in a row, or for the greater part of the year.

Secularization is now viewed as primarily an institutional process. Its relative nature has also become clear, as it is more the exception than the rule, in the sense that it happens particularly in West European countries. There, the churches are no longer a significant factor in the way society is organized, and they have also lost their control over the way individuals manage their lives. Accordingly, the individualization of the religious experience may seem the concern mainly of Western churches, especially in Europe. Yet, in view of the connection of individualization with Western culture and its influence on the rest of the world, the individualization process may make itself felt elsewhere as well.

Anyway, successful secularization – or "dechurching" – does not mean the disappearance of religion or religiosity. The process of individual independence may even be understood as having facilitated a retrieval of religiosity after the religious institutions lost their influence. When the relationship with the sacred was no longer a monopoly of the church or the clergy, individual religiosity represented a refuge. It could even be argued that because of its negative consequences it was precisely the trend towards individualization that created a need for such new forms of religiosity as evangelicalism and New Age.[2] The increasing individualization of religious experience may therefore also be viewed in a more positive vein, for whereas religion does not survive at the level of institutions, it succeeds (perhaps better than before) at the individual level.

Of course, the situation is much more nuanced than this suggests and also for that reason not as dramatic as one might think. In a way the new is not so new: individuality always was important and represented a stronghold for religion. It was a starting point for mysticism and other forms of religious innovation, as exemplified by the Reformation. Besides, the erosion of the churches is not total, not even in Western Europe. Thus, even atheists may view the churches as legitimate public spokespersons. And as Casanova[3] has eloquently shown, privatization need not entail loss of public influence. The fact that the individual becomes more decisive for faith praxis does not necessarily mean that public influence is lost. From theologies of liberation to various forms of fundamentalism, religion has been a public factor during the last few decades. Even in secularized Europe the churches continue to influence political processes, as is clear from the Polish and East German examples. Finally, the situation also is more complex because churches have adapted themselves – voluntarily or imperceptibly or under protest – to the new individual autonomy. In contrast to the past, such churches no longer seek to direct or limit their members in their participation in society, for example by censoring information or prescribing electoral choices.

In this complex situation between deinstitutionalizing religion and increasing individual religiosity the church's leadership will inevitably have to reconsider its policies, especially if people start thinking that they no longer need the church institution in order to have an effective world-view. The process of institutional erosion represents a policy problem for church leaders. Paradoxically, by emphasizing individual conversion, personal faith and freedom of choice, churches seem to have admitted a Trojan horse, thus creating the conditions for their own demise. What is more, individualism finds some of its roots in Christianity.

The societal context

In a way it all started with modernization, summarily defined as the application of scientific and technological findings in society. Taking a variety of forms in different countries, this process greatly influenced the manner in which societies were organized. Industrialization, as the most obvious application of scientific innovation, demanded a quite different distribution of roles. It also obliged people to migrate to centres that geographically speaking were useful to the new industries. Labour had to follow the factories. Urbanization was reinforced. People therefore left their small-scale social surroundings of the village type, and had to move into a more anonymous environment. Even though urban neighbourhoods were sometimes organized as villages within the city, social control was not as strong as in the rural areas.

The more complex society that emerged demanded a differentiation of domains within society. Even though these domains are technically interdependent (e.g. banking, production, distribution, consumption) or may contaminate each other in unexpected ways (e.g. politics and sports), they act as autonomous ways of organizing activities. In comparison to the so-called multiplexity of roles in the village, where people depended on each other for more than one role – for kinship, economic, political, religious and leisure purposes – functional relationships that serve only one purpose at a time are typical of modernized society. People perform a single role as a function of the demands of the sector in which that role is played, with work as the dominant role. Alienation has become the term to describe their position. It became "not done" in conversation to mix roles that previously were easily combined. In the course of the day, a person participates in different domains of society that are only connected by their contribution to the maintenance of society. That person may even have difficulty in managing and reconciling the various roles he or she has to play in the course of the day. There may be conflicts between these roles because of different interests and pressures, as when athletes have to boycott championships for political reasons. It has consequently become more difficult for individuals to identify themselves with the partial role they have to play in often very complicated processes, also because power usually resides elsewhere. The answer to the question "Who am I?" has become more delicate. It has become more difficult to feel at home.

The sources for the definition of identity have changed accordingly. The small-scale village society had its own ways and institutions for the prescription and imposition of role models (e.g. for the sexes, age categories, the poor and the wealthy). In industrial society the social control for such an imposition of roles has to come from other sources. One of them is industry itself. It often seeks to bind the workers to the corporate identity of the firm. Moreover, industrial production is by definition mass production and requires enormous investments. All the goods that are produced have to be sold. The change in scale of production leads to a widening globalizing market. Publicity has the role of creating a worldwide market for products. Services are also for sale on a large scale. For example, leisure became industrialized, people buying the services of the mass media and the tourist industry. So lifestyles that are invented by advertising agencies have become a source of identity. The new liberty is certainly not total and has undertones of dependency. The liberty of the consumer is limited to the choice between brands: Coke or Pepsi? Or, for that matter, Republican or Democrat? Another kind of dependency was created, less visible than that of the village, but as effective.

The liberty that came with modernization had several other consequences. In terms of morals, the "natural" rules that prevailed before were no longer so compelling. That something was tradition or that it had been done for ages was no longer an argument. To say that something is modern became a recommendation, for example in advertising. Or, in reaction to the changes, it became a word with which to criticize loose attitudes. The abandoning of traditions not only created liberty but also insecurity.[4] Liberty was experienced because new experiments were possible and new ideologies were formed for the new society that was emerging. But the search for new meanings also brought feelings of insecurity and uncertainty. The often contradictory demands of the different domains of society contributed to these feelings. Inevitably, individuals, as the centres of their own world, were increasingly thrown back upon themselves, becoming the direct criterion for making sense of life and the world. Accordingly, identity became an important notion and a therapeutic one as well. Plural identity for some time had a pathological connotation, as if one were not able to integrate the different roles one had to play. People develop means to maintain an illusion of a certain consistency in the way their different roles are played, as a compensation for a world that is too diverse and too detraditionalized to provide the necessary integrative support.[5]

Consequences for religion

In discussing what these changes mean for religion, we have to ask what exactly should be considered religious. The question presents itself because the natural position of traditional mainstream religion was undermined, especially institutionally speaking. The consequence was that alternatives presented themselves. Especially in approaches that emphasize the function religion has had from time immemorial, these alternatives caught the attention because they seemed to serve the same goals. In terms of content or form there was not necessarily a similarity, but in the net result there was. All sets of ideas and practices that directed society and individuals in the way they organized themselves fell into this category of alternatives and were consequently labelled religious. Ideology, art and sport came to be viewed as religious in nature. In connection with the secularization thesis, announcing the end of religion – in the substantial sense, as a relationship with God, gods and/or spirits – this functional view was confusing, since the alternatives were supposed to represent new forms of religion, thus seemingly denying the secularization thesis. In the end the secularization thesis was reduced to an indication of the end of institutional religion and secularization was considered a typical West European case, not to be generalized to the rest of the world.[6] A reference to alternatives proved not to be the only way to show the continuing presence of religion and religiosity. Non-institutional religiosity is another symptom of how people continue to look for meaning in their lives and the world they live in. And at that point individualization was drawn into the discussion.

As suggested above, individualization was not only a threat to institutional religion, but also at the same time represented a new possibility to practise religion. It could even be said to have been a cause of a growing religiosity. This seems contradictory, since the same phenomenon, individualization, is presented as both a cause of the end of religion and of its recovery. Yet it can be shown that the process of individualization produced these contradictory results.

The eroding effect of individualization was alluded to in the previous section. Modernization, as a societal translation of science, introduced a world-view that was in competition with the prevailing religious interpretation of life and reality. Over and against an appeal to the sacred, science underlined the exclusive validity of the rational and of the empirically verifiable. In addition, the new liberty put an end to the social control exercised by the institution (e.g. directly through clerics, or indirectly within families or even the state). The domain-wise organization of modern society made religion one of various domains, not as a factor that is as omnipresent as it was before. The institution "religion" or "church", sent to its own corner, also gradually lost its influence in society. It was no longer a necessary sector for the functioning of society. Core values were no longer provided by the churches.

As already suggested, the Christian faith and church have contributed to the individualization of the religious experience. Both as a consequence of its own message and through adaptation of that message to the signs of the times, the emphasis in belief's praxis has been on individual choices, on a personal relationship with God and Jesus, on confirmation and vocation as a personal calling – in sum, on the individual or even the soul as the basic unit of church life. Also, when it spread to other cultures, Christianity brought with it the act of conversion as the central experience, often severing the social links of the convert. Though in some sectors of Christianity communal experience was cherished, as in monastic life, even there individual vocation and vows were important. In mutual reinforcement of the Western culture, and exported through such church channels as education, the church generated individualization and as an institution thus dug its own grave.

People acted accordingly, separating their religious role from the others they performed, for example by ignoring the church's moral prescriptions. In terms of time and space the religious could be reduced to an activity on Sunday morning in a building called a church. In churches it became normal to reconsider the relevance of faith, a question that was superfluous when that relevance was uncontested. Religion became less important for the construction of people's identity and would no longer appear among the spontaneous answers to the question "Who am I?" People went shopping on an open and very inconsistent value market.

How then could individualization contribute to the recovery of religiosity and even become its cause? Several reasons could be mentioned.[7] The rationality of the modern world-view may be good at answering how-questions, but it remains silent when why-questions are raised. Professionals are trained for the functionality of their domain only. A doctor may very well be able to explain how cancer destroys the body, but the patient's question is "Why my body?" Unfortunately, that question belongs to another domain that is not available there and then. Formerly, the doctor and the pastor would meet at the patient's bedside. Now the instrumentality of the modern medical world ignores the ultimate questions that human beings raise: "Why am I here? Why will I die? And why do I have to suffer?" A pastor would have versions of answers to these questions, but is no longer a regular guest.

Besides, the new liberty has its disadvantages. True enough, the freedom of choice between alternatives for thinking and behaviour is a victory over traditional powers that imposed their views. But it can also create a sense of insecurity, for example about the criteria for choosing the right modus. The fragmented and complex structure of society in autonomous sectors and roles prevents the use of a single recipe. Each sector and each role makes its own demands. Where previously the long arm of the religious institution stretched into all sectors of public and private life and provided answers to all questions, the old answers are nowadays no longer acceptable and even ridiculed.

"I think, therefore I am" makes people self-conscious, but also uncertain. The gift of reflection often does more to worsen the situation than to resolve it, because sound thinking needs clear criteria and principles – and these the individual often seeks in vain, both within and without. Help from the outside is rare because in the name of freedom of expression society frowns on efforts to provide people with criteria, their propagators readily being called sectarian. With the so-called end of ideology the market for world-view criteria has not really improved. In this vacuum therapists of all kinds are the new and well-paid professionals.

The answer to the invitation "know yourself" is difficult to find. The multiplicity of the modern self militates against a clear answer. Basically, the self escapes reduction to some essence. Philosophers have raised the question whether the independently acting subject really exists. This would drive the individual into the arms of society again, but here coercion is waiting, though clothed in the freedom of the digital choices of the Coke/Pepsi type. The uniformity of fashions lies hidden behind the consumer's seeming freedom of choice. Just as money can be spent only once, the number of basic choices is limited – job and partner being the most important. Of course, there is a tendency to change both job and partner, but within a certain period of time the opportunities are limited. Besides, to find the right job the individual is driven on the move, obliging the self to adapt to ever new contexts with different demands. This reverse side of the coin of liberty represents insecurity, unrest and feelings of guilt.[8] The stronger the illusion that life can be constructed at will, the more profound the impact of the failure to realize this ideal. Modern society is cruel in attributing the leading role to the individual, while at the same time frustrating its freedom by leaving it at the mercy of a differentiated, inherently contradictory and at times coercive world. Even when society proclaims the freedom of the individual, this freedom is a social construct and a new commandment.

The picture drawn so far is perhaps even grimmer. The modernized world, despite its basis in science and technology, has not been able to solve the fundamental problems of poverty, violence and environment. The free individual runs the risk of hunger, violent death and pollution. This contributes to the feeling of insecurity, even when this individual has enough to eat, lives in peace, and far away from dirty industries. At least one author contributes to this pessimism by suggesting that we are now subjected to a second (type of) modernity, summarized as "risk society", urban Europe being the prototype.[9] The first modernity is characterized by people with a given identity; it is centred on industrialization, cherishes reflection, it has rule-providing institutions and provides a certain degree of optimism and linearity. The second modernity is represented by people with shifting identities; it is typical of a society that gives primacy to information, and the reflective individual is substituted by the *homo optionis*, who is an improvising rule finder on his or her own, creating as a *bricoleur* his or her own relative order (autonomy), but constantly driven by reflexes to the input of signals from the information society. This risk society is a token of the failure of the Enlightenment, and its inhabitants are sorcerer's apprentices who let themselves constantly be surprised by the unintended consequences of their deeds. One example is street violence as a way of resolving conflicts, or even without a cause; another, floods as a consequence of deforestation and global warming. Of course, this description of the second modernity is a caricature, but with recognizable traits.

Institutionalized religion runs the risk of being busy finding the answers to the challenges of the first modernity, still enjoying its corresponding institutional rule-providing role, whereas by now the questions are changing to those of the second modernity. In the meantime the *bricoleurs* of the second modernity try to survive by experimenting with new and – at least in the eyes of those who identify themselves with the first modernity – often odd combinations of reflexes, seeking the ultimate bodily feel-good experience, even though the ultimate sensation, on approaching it, behaves like the horizon. Under the label of "spirituality" he or she turns all these efforts towards the construction of the self, seeking to reconcile multiplicity and consistency, trying to be a successful individual in a society that is fond of authentic personalities. Wholeness is a central notion, as it is an effort to maintain unity in an otherwise fragmented and contradictory (yet global) world. It may take a therapeutic form. It is produced individually outside institutional control and is therefore extremely diverse. The difficulty in defining a new religious movement as New Age is partly because of its many ingredients (from UFOs to anthroposophy) and its many individual combinations. [10]

Interestingly, the old repertoire is used as well. Familiar forms from the old religiosity continue to be used as long as people can fill them with their own emotions: burning a candle, but also ritually attending an annual performance of Bach's passion according to St Matthew. Madonna's use of religious symbols is an example of how in pop music the iconology can be traditional. Mysticism and convents have been rediscovered, as has Gregorian chant, to serve as old carriers of a new experiment in meaning-making.

This religiosity is more immanent than transcendental, more inner-directed than outward-directed. The sacred over and above the people, typical of mainstream religion, has been substituted by a sacred that is to be discovered deep down within. This view of the sacred is acceptable to the critics of traditional religion because it does not enter into conflict with the scientific world-view. The gradual substitution of the word "religion" by "spirituality" is a token of the new emphasis on the individual's person and body experiencing the extraordinary from within. [11] Religion is outdated, spirituality is correct.

For its propagation and distribution, if that is what its authors are after, the new spirituality seems to depend in part on market mechanisms. Where institutional religion is no longer considered a producer of relevant meaning, world-views are now available through the channels of the information society and are arranged according to the market model. Antenna masts have come to join church spires. Mass media are prominent among the providers, from Oprah, through the electronic church, to the televised death and burial of Princess Diana. In contrast to traditional religiosity, the new religiosity is hardly transmitted through socialization. In the name of freedom, parents refrain from educating their children in a particular world-view, preparing them – if at all – for the *bricolage* that suits the participants in the second modernity. Their offspring have to find their own way.

Because of its individual character much of what happens in this field goes unnoticed and cannot be put into familiar categories, not even in social science research. Because tendencies to uniformity and to diversity go together, it is difficult to grasp what is happening. Quantitative methods that presuppose some quantifiable categorical regularity are not directly applicable. Qualitative methods have a better chance to meet the methodological challenge, but should be adapted to fit the new situation.

Consequences for the churches

One reaction to this confusing inchoate construction of a new religiosity is to withdraw to the security of the old-time religion. Fundamentalism owes part of its success, both in Christendom and Islam, to the answers it provides to modernity and even stronger to the second modernity. One may ask oneself, however, whether the return to the old forms reproduces the same meanings of old. Some reformulation of meaning is always going on, even when people confess to stick to the traditions of the fathers (more rarely the mothers). It might therefore be worthwhile considering the possibility that it is especially the familiar form that attracts people to the old-time religion, perhaps with the accompanying feeling, but not necessarily the doctrine. The evangelical emphasis on emotions points in this direction, as does the rejection of "religion" in so-called new paradigm churches (e.g. Vineyard). It may be that the political dimension is important in justifying the appeal to traditional religion, such as fundamentalism in Islam, but also in the position of the US "silent majority".

These developments have not left Christian religiosity untouched. Thus, evangelicals occupy an interesting position. Though not all evangelicals are fundamentalists, some of the anti-modernist characteristics of fundamentalism are often present. Moreover, there is a strong focus on the transcendental God and on Jesus, in a theistic spirituality. But at the same time some aspects of the type of spirituality that was just described for the second modernity can be there as well, such as the emphasis on bodily experience (most obviously in healings) and the reaction against cerebral traditional religious practice. Clearly, the *bricoleur's* repertoire is more limited in the evangelical case, in terms of what is done and not done, but mass media codes have for example been adopted. The construction of the self takes the form of conversion and uses the dramatic metaphor of being born again. In the case of the so-called "Toronto Blessing", popular in Pentecostal churches in the second half of the 1990s, reflexes seem to be addressed when people are triggered to bodily reactions such as falling backwards, having fits of laughter, or being literally drunk in the Spirit. The overall impression is that these forms attend to individuals' needs for religious experience, and thus continue the traditional focus on the believer and his or her soul as the basic unit.

The trend just described has consequences for established forms of Christianity. The individualization of religious experience is felt within the traditional churches. Members do not escape that influence. In churches with a strong popular religiosity, such as the Catholic church, there was already a strong praxis for the individualization of religious experience, parallel to the official version. Members were accustomed to use their freedom of expression, even though this could take standardized forms and was often brought under the control of the church leadership, as in the case of saints and pilgrimage. The new expressions may match the traditional popular religiosity. Examples are the smooth transition from popular Catholicism to Pentecostal churches, as is evident in many Latin American countries, and a similar migration from traditional African religion, often via or within mainstream churches, to some form of Pentecostalism.

Elsewhere, other developments may occur. One aspect is the gradual minimization of the contents of faith as a consequence of the continuing process of reformulating what it is all about, in view of the demands of (late) modern culture. Whereas from the pulpits the certainty of faith is pastorally administered, in discussion groups doubt is explicitly discussed and as it were set aside, institutionalized. In some cases, starting with John Robinson's *Honest to God* but becoming an established best-selling category for publishers and bookshops, theologians popularize critical views from their discipline. Their readers construct their selves through reflection on theological issues such as the concept of God – especially if sought deep down inside – or the person of Jesus, or perhaps just by having such theological books on the shelf.

Within the mainstream churches an aspect of modernity and individualization is present through emancipation movements such as those surrounding gender (feminist movements), local culture (rehabilitation of the pre-Christian tradition, as in African and Asian theology), or class (as in theologies of liberation and church base communities). In all these cases the believer's individual identity is an issue, and thereby the (re)construction of the self receives much attention. The ingredients for such a (re)construction are varied, but can come partly from the new religiosity. Examples are the influence of the goddess movement in feminist circles and the role of shamanism in Korean theology. Emancipation movements have often remained marginal to the churches and eventually their participants have in various cases decided to drop out, addressing themselves to other sources for identity construction.

Another symptom is the declared strategy of some local churches to be an "open" parish, accepting that people differ in their views on church and faith, thereby introducing the whole spectrum of possible views, from rather orthodox to ultra-liberal. The identity of the community then is that it has no clear identity. Other churches avoid experiments with their identity, especially in view of the financial risk they would run if members decide to leave.

One other symptom is that, just as there is a great deal of believing without belonging, there may be church members who are belonging without much believing. An example is the type of parish that primarily serves social functions for people who – for reasons of class, education or age – enjoy each other's company. The programme of such a parish may include fully secular activities. And of course an important part of the category of members who belong without believing can be found in the state churches. In such cases the absent majority keeps the church alive financially (if only as burial insurance) and accepts its public role.

Challenges to the ecumenical movement

The ecumenical movement calls itself a movement, but it depends on the institutionalized churches. Of course, the movement has become institutionalized itself in the course of time, but its more flexible organizational form as a movement could be an advantage when facing the challenge of modernity, especially in its second manifestation. One may of course choose to ignore the challenge. The WCC may remain as a service institute for that part of Christianity that succeeds in surviving in the West or North as an institution, or is not (yet) confronted with the demands of either the first or second modernity, as is mainly the case in the South and the East. It may even develop initiatives to help institutionalized churches survive. It then would represent one case of the type of religion that Woodhead and Heelas [12] describe as "religions of difference": the difference between the three composing religious elements of God, the human and the natural, as distinguished from "spiritualities of life", stressing holism and the fundamental unity between the divine, the self and the natural, and from "religions of humanity" that seek a balance between the three composing elements. The new religiosity is in large part an example of the second type of religion and would therefore not fit within the (restrictive) definition of ecumenical. In this option, the World Council of Churches would invest in a critical but hardly empathic position. It would bring the Council into the company of more fundamentalist views on modernity, especially in their reaction to institutional erosion, threatening the position of orthodox believers.

A different strategy would be to address the consequences of modernity and corresponding individualization, especially because they affect the position of the Council. If institutions are indeed losing their authority, and if member churches undergo the consequences of this development, this will certainly be reflected *mutatis mutandis* in the position of the WCC, and not only financially. In comparison with the first decades of its existence, the WCC certainly has already lost influence in the public debate, just as several national councils of churches are confronted with difficulties in addressing public issues. Of course, the tendencies are not linear. For example, there is a tendency that runs counter to privatization, when churches influence national transformations, [13] or when churches discover the role that they can play in civil society. But in other cases public manifestations have become rare or are no longer heard.

The WCC could opt for a policy that takes the religiosity of the second modernity seriously, especially as the laity in member churches are influenced by it. Consequently, the Council could adopt a wider view on ecumenicity, and its task as a service institute and as a movement should be partly reorganized. Starting from the influence of that religiosity in member churches, it could develop a department or a study programme on spirituality that focuses on forms of non-institutionalized religion. The presence of the churches in a modernized world suggests that the new religiosity is within the churches' field of interest, even more so if they themselves are changed by it. Churches are participants in this process and should speak up. One example is of course the movement in some of the mainstream churches in the direction of an evangelical view on faith. What is happening in Pentecostal churches would especially deserve attention, also because of the rapid growth of these churches. It seems that these churches, though critical of much of what the second modernity stands for, nevertheless offer something that is akin to it and that succeeds in attracting people. [14] Another quite different example is the expressive search for a Christian form of New Age, or for a spirituality that combines parallel ideas in Christianity and other religions such as mysticism.

Bodily experience is certainly not absent from member churches, especially in those from the South. If the new religiosity is a reaction to the first modernity, it implicitly also sets itself off from traditional Western forms of Christianity. The fact that an inculturation – natural or artificial – has occurred in the Southern churches suggests that often the corporeal side of faith experience has been developed. As I once heard a theologian from the South say, "For Protestants in the West it is a discovery that you can believe with your body." The popularity of sacred dance is a sign that the discovery has also been made in Western churches. In other words, exchange within the ecumenical movement can help churches that are confronted with the demands of the new religiosity.

A problem that would present itself once the WCC showed an interest in including the new religiosity in its perspective is that it should have access to the means of communication that normally carry expressions of that religiosity. This demands a change in perspective, away from the channels provided by the member institutions and much more to the media. It is certainly the case that the WCC has accumulated some experience with the media, but if it wishes to be present at the source of the new religiosity (or at least at the production of the primary material for that religiosity) it will have to adopt other policies with regard to the so-called culture industry. An example of how a world religion has gained such access is provided by Buddhism. In the last ten years or so several films have been made with Buddhist themes. The Dalai Lama has certainly contributed to this popularity. In passing, it may be noted that Buddhism represents, at least in certain forms (interestingly, not the Tibetan of the Dalai Lama), a non-theistic religion that is sufficiently open to have deeply influenced the new religiosity.

In summary, the individualization of religious experience challenges the ecumenical movement to critically follow what is developing in terms of new religiosity. A department or a study programme on spirituality is no luxury. The new religiosity should not be ignored, nor embraced automatically. Its basis in the information society and its role as a market commodity are reasons to follow closely what is happening, let alone the question of what can be said from the point of view of a cultural theology. Such a theology should base its analysis in an indepth study of the new religiosity, starting with members of the member churches. This theology has to face the vicious circle of having to form an opinion on the same cultural context of which it is in a way a product. In particular, the contribution that churches themselves have made to the popularity of the individualization of religious experience should be critically explored. The social dimension of the Christian faith should be reconsidered and rehabilitated. The difficulty of the task should not be a reason to ignore it.

NOTES

1   Grace Davie, *Religion in Britain since 1945: Believing without Belonging*, Oxford, Blackwell, 1994.

2   Anton van Harskamp, *Het nieuw-religieuze verlangen*, Kampen, Kok, 2000.

3   José Casanova, *Public Religions in the Modern World*, Chicago, Univ. of Chicago Press, 1994.

4   Harskamp, *Het nieuw-religieuze verlangen*.

5   Katherine P. Ewing, "The Illusion of Wholeness: Culture, Self, and the Experience of Inconsistency", *Ethos*, 18, 3, 1990, pp. 251–78.

6   Grace Davie, *Religion in Modern Europe: A Memory Mutates*, Oxford, Oxford UP, 2000.

7   Harskamp, *Het nieuw-religieuze verlangen*.

8   *Ibid.*

9   Ulrich Beck, *Risk Society: Towards a New Modernity*, Newbury Park CA, Sage, 1992; and *World Risk Society*, Cambridge MA, Polity, 1999. Ulrich Beck and Elisabeth Beck-Gernsheim, *Individualization: Institutionalized Individualism and Its Social and Political Consequences*, London, Sage, 2002.

10 Wouter Jacobus Hanegraaff, *New Age Religion and Western Culture: Esotericism in the Mirror of Secular Thought*, Leiden, Brill, 1996.

11 Paul Heelas, "The Spiritual Revolution: From 'Religion' to 'Spirituality'", in *Religions in the Modern World*, L. Woodhead ed., London, Routledge, 2002, pp. 357–77.

12 Linda Woodhead and Paul Heelas, *Religion in Modern Times*, Oxford, Blackwell, 2000.

13 Casanova, *Public Religions in the Modern World*.

14 André Droogers, "Globalization and Pentecostal Success", in *Between Babel and Pentecost: Transnational Pentecostalism in Africa and Latin America*, A. Corten and R. Marshall-Fratani eds, London, Hurst, 2001, pp. 41-61. Peter Versteeg, "Draw Me Close: An Ethnography of Experience in a Dutch Charismatic Church", Sl: sn, 2001.

16
Syncretism

ANDRÉ DROOGERS

In church circles and in theological parlance syncretism is often considered a dirty word. When in some way the purity of the Christian conviction is endangered, especially when strange non-Christian elements appear to have been adopted in Christian discourse and practice, the accusation of syncretism is readily made. A well-known example is the discussion begun by the presentation – or should one say performance – by the South Korean theologian Chung Hyung Kyung at the 1991 assembly of the World Council of Churches in Canberra. Her proposal for a Christian shamanism, though welcomed by some as creative theology and an interesting example of inculturation, was strongly criticized by others as utterly condemnable syncretism. But where does inculturation end and syncretism begin?

There are also those who appear to use the word in a different way: sometimes neutral, as a descriptive term for the mixing of elements from different religious sources; sometimes positively, as a recommended or unavoidable way of dealing with faith, especially when the Christian message is brought to other cultures. [1]

What is wisdom? Is syncretism wrong "by definition"? And how should it be defined in the first place? Does not a great deal depend on what we call syncretism and what not? Moreover, who decides what should be condemned or commended? Is there a safe criterion for purity and impurity?

This chapter tries to probe a bit further into the debate, not necessarily with the intention of providing final answers to such questions, but at least to make an inventory of the options that present themselves and to consider them in their connectedness, as together forming a landscape of positions. It may then also be possible to formulate some recommendations.

The history of the term

Syncretism is a term with a history of almost two millennia.[2] Plutarch (46–125) used the term in his *Moralia*. Originally, the word was a pun, on the one hand referring to the Greek *syngkrasis* ("mixing together"), and on the other hand referring to the inhabitants of Crete, who were known to quarrel among themselves, but when there was a common enemy all fights were forgotten and unity was restored. The connotation therefore is not just of mixing, but also – even stronger – mixing conflicting elements as a strategy of defence.

In the context of Plutarch's *Moralia* – which provided ethical advice – syncretism was valued positively. This positive meaning was maintained much later by Erasmus of Rotterdam (1496–1536), who used the term as a recommendable union of seemingly disparate opinions in philosophy and theology. He saw it as an attitude to be applied in debates, with the purpose of understanding one's opponent as accurately as possible and to find a common cause.

It was only in the 17th century that the negative connotation we now know so well came into use. At that time polemics revolved around the proposals of George Calixtus (1586–1656), an early ecumenical who defended the union of theological opposites. In the debate known as the syncretistic controversy, the term syncretism was for the first time used in a pejorative sense, as a mixing of ideas that should not be brought together.

In the 19th century, when the study of religion and religions really began, the term gradually came to be used for descriptive purposes. Yet, in the beginning, especially when Christianity was the religion most studied, the term syncretistic was still applied in a negative sense, referring to sect-like groups.[3] What was interesting in this period was that the study of the history of Christianity showed that the religion had syncretistic elements at its very origins, syncretism referring objectively and descriptively to the mixing of elements from different religious sources.

At the same time, there took place the expansion of Christianity in the wake of Western colonialism, or sometimes even preceding it. Just as the new study of religion and religions had done, this brought a change of meaning to the term syncretism, because till then it was used within Christian theology for the diversity of opinions within it, all exclusively Christian. Now that missionaries were confronted with other cultures and their influence on new converts, the term gained a new dimension and came to be used also for the mixing of Christian and non-Christian elements. The descriptive use of the term in comparative religion had paved the way for the application of the term outside Christianity. Thus the cornerstone for the current negative meaning was laid. Van der Leeuw, one of the founding fathers of comparative religion, maintained that missionary work without syncretism was an impossibility. [4]

A quite different contribution to the discussion came from Hendrik Kraemer, who at one stage of his life (1948–55) was the director of the Ecumenical Institute of the WCC at Bossey, but was also renowned as a scholar of comparative religion. Using the opposition between monistic and prophetic religions, contrasting Hinduism and Buddhism on the one hand, and the Abrahamic religions on the other (Judaism, Christianity and Islam), he suggested that the first were naturalistic and auto-soteriological in nature, whereas the other religions depended on revelation and salvation by divine initiative. In his view the roots of syncretism were monistic, even though he recognized that in the prophetic religions popular religiosity might contain syncretistic elements because of intercultural contact. [5] The theological distinction with which Kraemer worked was not acceptable to scholars in comparative religion and history of religions, who wanted to avoid theological bias and be as objective as possible.

When students of religion began to publish works in which religions were compared, more insight was gained into the role of mixing in the origin of world religions. Christianity obviously had roots in Judaism, just as Islam used elements of the two older religions. Buddhism used ideas from what much later came to be called Hinduism. So, interestingly, even religions that now would oppose syncretism cannot deny there is some syncretistic influence in their origins.

As syncretism came to be studied in more detail, various research questions were addressed. Thus, one may ask whether religions in syncretistic contact maintain relations of equality, influencing each other, or whether one is dominant, thus forcing syncretism upon the other. A related distinction is that between conscious, purposeful syncretism, which seeks to combine elements as well as possible (as in some forms of New Age), and unconscious, almost natural syncretism, as in popular religion. There was also the question of to what degree mixing took place: at one extreme, elements could coexist in symbiosis and minimal syncretism; at the other, elements could merge into a new consistent synthesis that made the original components unidentifiable. Another point of discussion was whether only religious elements were mixed, or whether also more general, cultural elements were involved (e.g. African polygamy among church members). A question that was also raised is whether syncretism is the *result* of the mixing, as when one says that some religions belong to a type called syncretism (e.g. the Afro-Brazilian religions), or whether syncretism is the *mixing* itself, as a process.

The large number of options in deciding what syncretism is, the seemingly general presence of the phenomenon and its vague boundaries led some scholars to propose abandoning the term completely (e.g. Baird[6]). If borrowing and blending occur in all religions and are part and parcel of religion itself, what is then the specific value of the term? Besides, its negative theological connotation was found to make the concept less useful and too corrupted for objective descriptive use. The term could still be used, but only as a theological, negatively tainted term, not for objective use in the scholarly study of religions. Another argument is that nobody actually defines themselves as syncretistic. Less contaminated terms are available, such as creolization and hybridization, even though these terms are not specifically religious.

Scholarly vocabulary does not follow such suggestions rapidly. What makes the term viable is that in the globalizing world mixing is rampant. More and more believers of different religions come into contact and influence each other. The individualization of the religious experience (see ch. 15) will stimulate syncretistic practice. Besides, poverty and affliction appear to be on the increase, and religions are used indiscriminately by the afflicted as long as their problem stands a chance of being solved. Furthermore, as long as the so-called world religions are used as basic, autonomous and separate units in the field of religion, some term is needed to describe the mixing of elements from them. The long and eventful history of the term shows that redefinition is not unthinkable. One such effort could focus on the power dimension of syncretism.

Syncretistic practice

Whereas students of comparative religion and the history of religions have a longer tradition in the study of syncretism,[7] anthropologists of religion have only recently entered the field, the American anthropologist Melville Herskovits being a forerunner.[8] They added a new dimension to the discussion. Their contribution has been to place syncretism as a religious phenomenon in a cultural context, paying attention especially to its contextualized nature, as it is connected with non-religious or pre-Christian aspects of culture.

In particular, the political aspects of syncretism have received attention, meaning power relations and power mechanisms in their widest sense. This has shed new light on the term and has contributed to its rehabilitation. In the approach founded by Max Weber, power can be defined as the capacity to influence other people's behaviour, even against their will. In this sense all human relations usually have a power dimension. In the case of syncretism, as is evident from the negative use of the term, power is involved in the sense that religious leadership usually seeks to keep believers free from the influence of other religions. The term is used as an instrument to maintain the desired purity of the religion, a policy that corresponds interestingly to the way scholars in comparative religion and the history of religions treat the world religions as separate units. Kraemer's views on syncretism are an example of how the theological interests of one religion could even be combined with an authoritative approach from comparative religion. From the point of view of the religion's leadership, the purist position with regard to syncretism can be theologically legitimated, just as the authority of the leadership to pronounce on matters such as syncretism and impose its policies can be justified by an appeal to theological notions. Stewart and Shaw[9] introduced the term anti-syncretism to emphasize this political aspect of syncretism. It may be noted in passing that leadership is usually predominantly male, whereas syncretism occurs within popular religiosity, as practised primarily by women. Thus, the power relations of gender are an integral part of the power mechanisms that accompany syncretism.

If we take a closer look at this political aspect we might ask who has access to the formulation or "production" of correct religion. The distinction between clerics and laity suggests a division of labour with distinct roles. In many cases these distinctions follow gender lines. Often, this way of distributing power is surrounded by theological notions. Thus, vocation is a category that is used to defend such a role distribution. In the Christian context, the equality of all believers before God – whether clerical or lay – and more particularly the availability of the Holy Spirit and its gifts to all members of the flock, represent a counterpoint to such a hierarchical view. It is clear from the variety of church models that emphases differ and that the preference for horizontal or vertical vectors can differ substantially, sometimes paralleling secular models of institutional organization. In other words, in some cases the power of the leadership is more outspoken than in others, discipline is an issue, and close control is maintained on what faith the faithful carry as their spiritual resource. A more liberal theology, recognizing historical critical notions and viewing the Bible as a text that must be viewed in the context of the time and region in which it came into existence, may contribute to a flexible attitude towards differences in exegesis or theology. The question of purity is then not given priority on the church's agenda. On the other side, a stricter way of reading the Bible, that some would call fundamentalist, will be surrounded by censure of deviant views, and the leadership will use their position to protect the purity of what they consider the heart of the matter. In other words, the more exclusive the theological view, the stricter the church's organization and discipline, also with regard to syncretism. Thus, in various ways, power is present in the *internal* organization of the church, and the outcome with regard to anti-syncretism will differ accordingly. Precisely because of this political aspect, syncretism is more a problem for the leadership than it is for lay members.

Power may also play a role in the *external* relationships of the church and this may influence the position with regard to anti-syncretism. When a form of dualism is defended with regard to the church and the world – the latter being considered sinful and Satan's domain – a close watch will be kept on boundary maintenance. In cases where Christianity is a relative newcomer in a culture, such as in large parts of the so-called third world, certain elements from the pre-Christian local culture may be condemned – an attitude that may have roots in earlier missionary practice. The contents of faith are subjected to constant supervision. At the other end of the spectrum, one may think of churches that have been rooted in the local culture for centuries, as is the case with European churches. There may be elements in the pre-Christian local culture that are taken for granted, or that have even become part of the church's calendar, as when the incarnation of God in Jesus is celebrated on the day that in the northern hemisphere is the shortest day of the year, following local pre-Christian lore of old, as in midwinter rituals. In such cases nobody objects to syncretism, though technically it is present. In terms of power, influences from the cultural context may lead to strict rejection or leniency – or even simple ignorance when things are taken for granted.

Somewhat more can be said, using notions from cultural anthropology. The attitude towards the cultural environment is of course a typical anthropological issue. The integration – or in theological terms, the incarnation – of the Christian message in the local culture is a particular aspect of culture contact. The whole issue of enculturation cannot be considered without going back to the cultural context of the first Christian communities, and thus to the cultural context of the founding of Christianity. The anthropological interest is in how a religion that began as a localized phenomenon first took on a West European form and then took root universally. The theological issue is how normative the original forms must be in view of their localized nature. If inculturation of the Christian message in the local (e.g. third world) context, whether purposeful or spontaneous, raises the issue of symbolism, what is then the value of the localized symbolism that prevailed when it all started? If syncretism is considered a real danger, why does another local translation of the original message carry authority, even though it was the first translation ever? Was there no syncretism involved in Christianity's early start? Why should bread and wine become universal symbols? To take a perhaps more obvious example, should women still cover their heads and remain silent in church services, as Paul ordained? The view on the normative value of the oldest Christian practice is ultimately decisive for attitudes towards syncretism. Ironically, even in those original forms some degree of syncretistic influence is present, a circumstance that may lead to some hesitation when using the word syncretism. This line of argument could be extended to the normative authority of Western expressions of Christianity, the ecclesiastical calendar being the obvious example. But, again, much depends on the theological view taken, and thereby the authority given to the biblical text.

However, theologians might accept anthropological advice, especially when the matter concerns the understanding of cultures that are subject to missionary influence or where Christian churches have been established. Too often, Western moral presuppositions have determined ways of looking at a foreign culture. Though Western Christianity is the result of a process of inculturation, and can be viewed with relative feelings (as the Christmas example has shown), it was often reified to represent the form of Christianity. The view on the local culture was thereby rather selective, emphasizing obvious aspects, usually of a moral nature, and simply ignoring elements that may be less obvious but much more in opposition to the Christian belief, even more so in its more fundamentalist versions. During the last few decades Christian churches in the third world (especially their theologians) have worked hard to develop localized and contextualized theologies. In so doing, they have encountered similar problems, dealing with the essence of Christianity as well as that of the local culture. The question of syncretism sometimes comes up in this debate.

It may be clear by now that it is not only in internal and external relationships that attitudes towards syncretism are formed. In fact, both the internal and the external dimension of a church's organization depend on the view of the relationship with God; in short, on the theology that has been adopted. This theological dimension influences the attitude taken towards internal organization and external relationships, and many of the choices that can be made between alternatives. The inverse is also possible: that the theology is influenced, willy-nilly, by the way power is distributed in the internal and external dimensions. Special interests may directly mark theologizing, as several authoritarian regimes have made clear in the course of church history, just as various leaders and theologians have had to defend themselves before secular authorities. Similarly, the cultural context may influence theology as well, as when Roman juridical categories determine views on salvation, or Greek vocabulary influences New Testament thinking. Views on the power of God have sometimes been modelled on secular examples, even in the biblical text, when God is called father or king. Generally speaking, the demands of social institutions such as churches may determine the outcome of theological debates, especially in the social need for a common basis that reinforces control over the boundaries of the institution. Thus, the theological dimension also has characteristics that refer to power. In the case of syncretism, a strong emphasis on the overwhelming revelatory power of God, primarily in the sacred inspiration of the biblical text, but also in the person of Jesus, seems to underline an exclusive view on God that prevents syncretism with notions taken from other gods, be they German, African or Papuan. However, when there is some room left for human beings to influence divine behaviour or define what God is like on the basis of their experience of God, the faithful may find ways to share in divine power, and they may use it to solve their problems. In the latter case, the practical attitude may create conditions for syncretism, even more so if the pre-Christian religiosity was aimed at practical problem-solving.

In short, syncretistic practice depends on the views that are adopted with regard to power. Such views may have to do with the internal as well as external relationships of the Christian community, but they may also refer to the theological dimension. When considering the conditions in which syncretism, as the mixture of elements from different religious sources, may occur, the total constellation of these three dimensions must be taken into account. A central concern is the question of which believers have access to the production of what is considered correct religion, and especially what is done with lay ideas present in popular religiosity.

Within this framework, syncretism can be compared to and distinguished from fundamentalism, which in a number of aspects is its opposite. It seems that the conditions under which fundamentalism emerges are more or less the inverse of those that were just described as giving rise to syncretism. The internal dimension is then usually organized along hierarchical lines that help to control the purity of the religion. The external dimension is marked by opposition with the world, which is considered unfaithful and thereby sinful. And in the theological dimension revelation is emphasized as the only source of sacred knowledge. Where syncretism celebrates plurality, fundamentalism thrives on singularity. They meet when fundamentalist leaders condemn syncretism among their followers.

Conclusion: the challenge

Is syncretism wrong "by definition"? How should it be defined? Does not a great deal depend on what we call syncretism and what not? Moreover, who decides on what is to be condemned or commended? Is there a safe criterion regarding purity and impurity?

The answer to such questions given here is that one should be aware of the type of definition used: normative in the negative or positive sense, or objective in the descriptive sense, or analytical with special reference to the power aspect, opposing anti-syncretism to syncretism. Accordingly, syncretism may be a term to be used in a theological debate on the purity of religion, or it may serve descriptive purposes in the study of religion and religiosity, or it may create some analytic awareness of how power mechanisms work within a church. The theological debate may be studied with the latter, more political type of definition. Instead of reacting as if to a threat to purity – and consequently to leadership – an awareness of the different options may invite us first of all to study the situation and discover what is really going on. The model of the internal, external and theological dimensions proposed here may be helpful in doing so. The constellation of these three dimensions will help us gain some awareness of the role of power in debates on syncretism. If this type of awareness had been available in the famous Canberra case, the debate would have been more fruitful.

This type of recommendation does not touch on theological decisions that depend on more general options in exegesis and revelation. In that sense the debate on syncretism occurs within the same parameters as that on inculturation. Yet some awareness of the power mechanisms that influence the discussion on such a phenomenon as syncretism can be salutary, especially if it leads to some form of self-examination among the religious powers that be and on their vocation in this era of ever more complex religiosity. Besides, a thorough rethinking in cultural terms of the experience and normative value of the first Christian communities is urgent.

NOTES

[1] Wolfhart Pannenberg, *Basic Questions in Theology*, London, SCM, 1970, pp. 85-88, esp. n. 37; see also M.M. Thomas, "The Absoluteness of Jesus Christ and Christ-centred Syncretism", in *The Ecumenical Review*, 37, 1985, pp. 387–97.

[2] André Droogers, "Syncretism: The Problem of Definition, the Definition of the Problem", 1989. Kurt Rudolph, "Synkretismus – vom Theologischen Scheltwort zum religionswissenschaftlichen Begriff", in *Humanitas religiosa. Festschrift H. Biezais*, Stockholm, Almqvist & Wiksell, 1979, pp. 193–212. Charles Stewart and Rosalind Shaw eds, *Syncretism/Anti-Syncretism: The Politics of Religious Synthesis*, London, Routledge, 1994.

3 Rudolph, "Synkretismus", pp. 196,197.

[4] G. van der Leeuw, *Phänomenologie der Religion*, Tübingen, Mohr, 1956, pp. 649ff.

[5] Hendrik Kraemer, *De wortelen van het syncretisme*, 's-Gravenhage, Boekencentrum, 1937; *The Christian Message in the Non-Christian World*, London, Edinburgh House, 1938; *Religion and the Christian Faith*, London, Lutterworth, 1956; "Synkretismus II: Im Wirkungsbereich der Mission", *Die Religion in Geschichte und Gegenwart: Handwörterbuch für Theologie und Religionswissenschaft*, vol. 6, Tübingen, Mohr, 1962, pp. 567–68.

[6] R.D. Baird, *Category Formation and the History of Religion*, The Hague, Mouton, 1971.

[7] U. Berner, "Heuristisches Modell der Synkretismus-Forschung (Stand August 1977)", in Gernot Wiessner ed., *Synkretismusforschung, Theorie und Praxis*, Wiesbaden, Harrassowitz, 1978, pp. 11–26; "Das 'Synkretismus-Modell' als Instrument einer historischen Religionsphänomenologie", in *ibid.*, pp. 27–37. C. Colpe, "Synkretismus, Renaissance, Säkularisation und Neubildung von Religionen in der Gegenwart", in Jes Peter Asmussen et al. eds, *Handbuch der Religionsgeschichte*, Göttingen, Vandenhoeck & Ruprecht, 1975, pp. 441–523; "Die Vereinbarkeit historischer und struktureller Bestimmungen des Synkretismus", in Albert Dietrich ed., *Synkretismus im Syrisch-Persischen Kulturgebiet: Bericht über ein Symposium in Reinhausen bei Göttingen in der Zeit von 4. bis 8. Oktober 1971*, Göttingen, Vandenhoeck & Ruprecht, 1975, pp. 17–30; "Syncretism and Secularisation: Complementary and Antithetical Trends in New Religious Movements", *Numen*, 17, 1977, pp. 158–76; "Synkretismus", *Der kleine Pauly*, vol. 5, 1979, pp. 1648–52. Gort et al. eds, *Dialogue and Syncretism: An Interdisciplinary Approach*, Grand Rapids MI and Amsterdam, Eerdmans and Rodopi, 1989, pp. 7–25. Michael Pye, "Syncretism and Ambiguity", *Numen*, 18, 1971, pp. 83–93. Rudolph, "Synkretismus".

[8] Droogers, "Syncretism", in *International Encyclopedia of the Social and Behavioural Sciences*, London, Elsevier, 2001. Sidney M. Greenfield and André Droogers eds, *Reinventing Religions: Syncretism and Transformation in Africa and the Americas*, Lanham MD, Rowman & Littlefield, 1999. Stewart and Shaw, *Syncretism/Anti-Syncretism*.

[9] Stewart and Shaw, *Syncretism/Anti-Syncretism*.

17
Pentecostalism

ANDRÉ DROOGERS

Pentecostalism appears to be the most thriving sector of Christianity. Why is it so successful? In this chapter I look for a reply to that question. I am aware of the answer that a Pentecostal believer would give: "The Spirit is moving, brother!" Yet, from a social science point of view, the current global situation appears to create promising opportunities for the Spirit. In combination, both the internal characteristics of Pentecostal praxis and the external conditions under which Pentecostals operate reinforce each other and thus, as I will argue, create an optimal situation for the expansion of this type of Christianity.

The term "Pentecostalism" applies first of all to the churches that consider themselves Pentecostal because of the emphasis they place on the believer's access to the work and gifts – charismata – of the Holy Spirit. These charismata, such as speaking in tongues, prophecy, healing and exorcism, are part of Pentecostal praxis. The churches differ greatly in size, style and organization. Pentecostalism need not be limited to these churches. Because of their emphasis on the presence of the Holy Spirit, the so-called charismatic movements in Protestant churches as well as in the Roman Catholic Church could be included in Pentecostalism. These movements operate from within the mainstream churches in order to "renew" them, without the intention of founding a separate church. Besides churches and movements there are individual ministries that stand within the Pentecostal tradition, usually centred on an evangelist whose activities as a religious entrepreneur are financed by gifts from private persons. Sometimes these ministries have a few staff members and a tiny office, sometimes they are huge organizations. It is not so easy to draw a clear line between Pentecostalism and other phenomena like Evangelical churches or Christian fundamentalism, since there may be considerable overlap. Yet it is clear that not all Pentecostals consider themselves Evangelicals or fundamentalists, and vice versa.

Though it is difficult to give a general explanation for the growth of a phenomenon that is so diverse, the external and internal aspects mentioned below offer an answer to the question why Pentecostals are so successful that in the third world alone they amount to over 150 million believers.

Diversity

In defining what Pentecostalism represents, its huge diversity frustrates efforts to attach a clear label. The minimal description would be that Pentecostalism is that form of Christianity in which the Holy Spirit occupies a central place. In view of the diversity of forms, it seems difficult to say more. There are historical reasons for such a variety of forms. Churches and movements receive their identity from the period in which they were started and from the way they then developed. The first Pentecostal churches were founded at the beginning of the 20th century. A second period of strong expansion occurred in the 1950s. The charismatic movements arose in the 1960s, introducing the Pentecostal praxis into the established mainstream churches. From the 1960s as well, churches and movements have been established that have been labelled as neo-Pentecostal. Authors differ in their way of characterizing neo-Pentecostalism, but one of the points that are often mentioned is the emphasis on prosperity as God's blessing and as a promise to the faithful, sometimes accompanied by a fierce anti-communism. Another point (less theological) is the use of PR and mass media, especially in the so-called electronic church. Some of these churches seek political influence through the command of their members' votes at elections.

In view of these successive periods of expansion, diversity is predictable. Besides, in the course of time, churches and movements may change, for example because of institutionalization, or through conflicts and fission, or by a revival, or simply through the transmission of faith from one generation to the other. A church's growth and success demand a stricter and more complex organization, usually introducing hierarchical structures that are not easily combined with the basic democracy in the believers' access to the gifts of the Spirit. As a consequence women, for example, lose the central position they sometimes had in the first years of a church's life because of their use of the Spirit's gifts, men then occupying the positions of power. So in terms of gender there is also diversity. Changes may also come from the gradual movement of believers, in the course of their lives, through different churches, in search of the perfect environment for their situation.

Such diversity means that stereotypical descriptions should be avoided. One stereotype is the generalization that Pentecostals will obey any kind of government and even support dictatorial regimes. There have been examples of such churches, but there also have been churches that opposed dictatorship. Another stereotype is the assertion that Pentecostals are focused on the after-life and promise heavenly well-being, doing nothing to improve current conditions. Here, too, examples can be given of Pentecostal churches and organizations that run extensive projects to improve the living conditions of the poor. Similarly, there are stereotypical views on church services as chaotic and enthusiastic through the impact of the Spirit, whereas most services are well structured and disciplined, just as there are third-generation churches where the expressions of the Spirit have become formalized or even rare.

One popular view is that Pentecostal churches are churches of the poor, yet there are churches that draw their members primarily from the middle and upper classes. Pentecostals are said to be anti-ecumenical and to work autonomously or even in isolation, yet there are forms of cooperation between churches, such as in evangelization campaigns. The presence of Pentecostal churches among the members of the WCC should also be mentioned in this respect, as should the participation of Pentecostal churches in ecumenical theological training institutions. Finally, there is the idea that Pentecostals are an export product of the USA. For some time American Pentecostal missions and ministries started new churches outside the US, but once Pentecostalism was established, local initiatives became prominent and gradually a counter-export movement took place, bringing "Southern" churches to the "North".

Non-specific factors of growth

Some growth factors are typical of Pentecostal Christianity and have to do with the exclusive characteristics of these churches and movements. Other factors are part of the environment in which they operate and are less specific, also because other expanding religions would be privileged by the same conditions. I will first discuss these non-specific factors, returning to the specific Pentecostal factors in the next section. A satisfactory explanation for the growth of Pentecostalism can only come from a combination of these external and internal factors. A unilateral emphasis on the external factors would result in explanations that might help us to understand the expansion of other religions as well, and would therefore be too general, producing only a partial analysis.

Similarly, an exclusive focus on the characteristics that are typical of Pentecostalism itself would ignore the influence of societal factors. In terms of academic disciplines, only in combination will social science and theology be able to produce the beginnings of an answer to the question with which this chapter started.

Basically, modernization is in some way or another at the bottom of the conditions under which Pentecostalism grows. Modernization could be described as the application of science and technology in society – as the societal consequence of Enlightenment. We are not always aware of what the scientific and industrial revolutions have done to society, first in the North Atlantic axis, then gradually, because of the system's need for expansion, in the rest of the world. Much has been changed and is being changed. The labels used for these changes are subject to terminological fashions, and some now would prefer to speak of globalization instead of modernization. The process remains more or less the same.

Modernization manifests itself in several ways. Industrialization and mass production and distribution were the most manifest expressions. They led in turn to labour migration, as in urbanization, but also as a consequence of colonial practice, as in slavery. There was more cultural and religious contact and exchange, especially when means of transport and mass communication began to work globally. Traditional boundaries were perforated. More contact also meant more conflict. Forms of social control that were effective in the traditional rural situation no longer functioned in the city. The extended family became less important, the nuclear family more important. Individualism became a central value. Social mobility and class formation were parallel developments. Education, as the preparation of young members of society for their participation in the modernization process, contributed to these changes. As the Western liberal capitalist system expanded, large parts of the world came under its impact, as a source of raw material, as a provider of cheap labour or as a new market. In Western Europe modernization led to the loss of influence of religious institutions, whereas in the rest of the world these remained influential and religions served to soften the affliction that the modernization process brought with it.

In this context Pentecostal expansion took place, corresponding to some of the felt-needs of the citizens of the modernized world. To illustrate this, let us consider some of the manifestations of the modernization process.

First, urbanization caused people to leave rural areas and migrate to the city. This brought them into a new situation that represented modernization in its most concentrated form. They had to get accustomed to it. Often, positive expectations of life in the city were not fulfilled. To survive became hard work. Networks of relatives that could be relied on in the rural context were precarious or absent, though the definition of kin was stretched to accommodate the growing need for help. Morally, as well, migrants had to adapt and often had to find their own way for lack of a clear urban value system. The Pentecostal church was one of the places that offered compensation to the newcomer in the city. The absent kin were substituted by the brothers and sisters in the Lord, the family of God. The church was very explicit with regard to what was acceptable and what not in the urban setting, and thus was a source of values and morals. Reliability was one of these values, and together with the network of church members this helped people to escape unemployment and find work. The respect for authority, as understood from a (rather literal) reading of Paul's Letter to the Romans, was supposed to make them loyal employees who would even refrain from labour unrest – an employer's dream. Through the local church network the homeless found a place to live. The church was not just a Sunday-morning phenomenon, but demanded participation through the week, and thereby made itself very much present in the lives of its members. Its network and its values were constantly maintained and reproduced. It was the new instance of social control.

Moreover, the affliction that newcomers suffered in the city found a remedy in the healing services of the church. In as far as people's misery was a consequence of what the church considered immoral life (alcoholism and prostitution, but also the lottery, all abundantly present in the city), conversion was a way of reorganizing one's life and making a fresh start. Conversion as an individual decision matched individualism as a modern value. Social mobility was part of the new perspective, because of a sober life and the wish to use one's talents for the honour of God. Out of unaccustomed migrants Pentecostal praxis made useful citizens.

Of course, this type of explanation of Pentecostal growth does not represent the ultimate answer to the question why Pentecostals are doing well. For example, it does not apply to all Pentecostals. Successful urbanites of the middle and upper classes may also convert to Pentecostalism because its value system would fit their aspirations and mentality (this would invert Weber's reasoning on Calvinism). Furthermore, there is Pentecostal expansion in areas where such urban conditions are absent, as in small rural towns. Besides, even though it makes some of the typical Pentecostal characteristics visible and integrates them into its reasoning, this mechanism does not make clear why people chose the Pentecostal church and not some other form of a new urban religion that helped them adapt to modern urban life. So there must be more.

A second aspect that is related to modernization is the fact that life became plural. This was especially visible where society had been organized in a homogeneous way, secular and religious powers maintaining a pact of cooperation that was not without its crises, but nevertheless lent continuity to society. Democratization, as a companion process to modernization, was the political translation of this pluralism. Where Protestantism had broken the monopoly of the Catholic church, religious pluralism was the result, except where a Protestant church assumed the role of state church. Pentecostalism may be viewed as a strong player in the trend towards religious pluralism, especially because at least in origin – more than the mainstream churches – it was a religion of the laity. It therefore also was in most cases a non-elite religion and thereby did not identify with a dominant group. The free access to the gifts of the spirits also worked towards pluralism because it stimulated a horizontal relationship between church members and honoured individual exploration of beliefs and experiences, though always accompanied by church discipline as well as conflict.

Yet, here again, the explanation is by itself not sufficient. Pentecostalism was not the only religious factor to contribute to modern pluralism. Besides, there almost always remains a tension between the pluralism that Pentecostals helped to bring about and the exclusiveness that is typical of certain forms of Pentecostalism. In this exclusiveness and particularly in authoritative leadership some traits of the traditional rural feudal society appear to be continued. The pastor has been compared to the rural landowner. In this sense Pentecostalism appears in an anti-modern role. More explanation is needed.

A third aspect of modernization that may play a role is the rise of class society. The presupposition is that Pentecostal churches recruit from the lower classes and that Pentecostalism is a lay movement. Pentecostal growth is then attributed to the emergence of class society. In its crudest form the Marxist claim that religion is the opium of the people is at the basis of such reasoning. But there are more sophisticated versions, in part inspired by Gramsci, thereby leaving more room for what in the jargon would be the superstructural dimension.

Basically, the idea is that what happens in economic life is compensated for by a similar but inverted process in religious life. Those who have been dispossessed in economic terms and do not enjoy access to the economic means of production, gain control over the religious means of production and become the owners of a religious product that – under current market conditions – sells well. If the gifts of the Spirit are for everyone, this religious capital is democratized. The economically poor become – religiously speaking – rich and blessed. Pentecostal churches are characterized by the multiplicity of tasks that members fulfil and through which they construct their identity. During the day they may be anonymous workers, whereas in church they have the guarantee of being somebody. No clergy serve as owners of the religious means of production. The language is that of the poor classes, not that of a theological well-educated elite. Especially when prosperity is viewed as God's promise to the faithful, the religious rich live from the hope that they will also become economically rich. They then have come full circle and have succeeded – through the Pentecostal church – to find their place in class society.

However, the other side of the coin is that small religious entrepreneurs are enabled to start their own religious businesses, and some of them have made it to CEO of a mega-church. This degree of institutionalization and hierarchy reduces free access, even when doctrine continues to defend that very idea. In addition, the presupposition of this type of explanation is that Pentecostalism is the poor person's religion. It does not serve to explain expansion among middle- and upper-class people. Especially in urban Africa, Pentecostal churches are often populated by educated middle-class members. And again, there are other religions that operate among poor people. In itself this third type of explanation is not sufficient.

In its most recent form, modernization theory deals with the tension between global developments and local experiences of the global world. Globalization – and sometimes glocalization – is the buzzword. The emphasis on the local suggests that globalization is not a matter of a uniform world culture, but of the translation of the global to local proportions. It strangely combines change in scale (as in the formation of the European Union) and reinforced local identities in reaction to that process.

More than anything else, globalization is a cognitive process, and not a political or even economic homogeneity. Mass media maintain the collective global knowledge. For an expanding religion such as Pentecostalism, the global perspective offers new opportunities. The claim (now twenty centuries old) that the message is meant for the whole world can nowadays be taken literally. The corporeal manifestation of the Spirit is an experience that can be felt universally, especially where similar extra-sensorial experiences were part of pre-Christian tradition. To converts, participation in the global Pentecostal expansion may be a way of feeling integrated into this change of scale, even when belonging to a small local community. It may serve as an entry to global facilities, such as when East European Pentecostals offer and follow courses in English. Simultaneously, means of mass communication are being used that reach millions across national borders. On a market that sells very diverse and complex identities, often linked with fashion and commodities, Pentecostalism represents a clear spiritual identity, in its neo-Pentecostal form even combined with access to the prosperity of the commodities. Entrepreneurial tactics are similar to those of secular global entrepreneurs. Conversion stories present role models to potential converts. The above-mentioned diversity of forms of Pentecostalism serves at the local level to attend to a diversity of audiences and preferences. In fact, from the very beginning, the Pentecostal message has shown itself to be flexible, despite the reputation of rigidity and dogmatism.

This way of explaining Pentecostal expansion is valid, but it has its limits. The global framework may play a role in the local community, but it need not be the case. Much depends on the selection of meanings that individual members make from the views that are on offer. If the world is experienced as fundamentally sinful, they could just as well have closed themselves off from it, globalization or not. A global awareness of belonging to the Pentecostal shadow world need not be present everywhere and at all times. The change in scale is not an inevitable and inescapable mechanism; it can be ignored to a large degree. The view from globalization, though valid, is as partial as the other perspectives.

One last type of explanation that refers to external conditions can be mentioned. It has to do with the suggestion that in situations of underdevelopment and poverty, modernization stimulates religious revival and innovation. Modernization does not lead to secularization, but to sacralization. Though modernization seems identical with progress, to many people suffering is abundant, especially in the third world, but also in the urban margins of so-called developed countries. The wealth of the few is paid for by the poverty of the many. Because Pentecostalism applies the gifts of the Spirit to the instant resolution of problems (especially through healing), the link with suffering and problem-solving is only natural. The Pentecostal church is one of the addresses where healing and health appear to be available. When modernization has not produced an adequate medical infrastructure, despite the illusion of progress, such help is more than welcome.

However, there are other such addresses as well. Moreover, Pentecostalism is more than a source of help, as it also brings a way of life and a world-view that are integral to the help it provides. It is a religion that makes itself part of the assistance.

In sum, the explanations that start from these four processes appear to contain some grain of truth and are applicable to some forms of Pentecostalism, but not to all. Besides, they are applicable to certain non-Pentecostal forms of religion as well and therefore do not explain why people opt for Pentecostalism instead of another religion with similar facilities. All explanations start from a process that is supposed to be typical of society in a certain context, and all attribute a role to religion in that process. Usually, religion's role is viewed as functional in maintaining some form of order or equilibrium in society, such as when changes occur as a consequence of modernization. Whether it is a matter of urbanization or pluralism or class society or suffering, in all these cases religion (in this case Pentecostalism) grows because it is useful for society and offers some form of compensation. In that light it is understandable that the explanations apply to other religions and cannot be specific enough to interpret the growth of *Pentecostal* expansion. They might be called reductionist in that religion and religious growth (or decline) are explained by reducing them to non-religious circumstances – here, modernization and all it brought with it. We therefore have to turn to more specific Pentecostal characteristics.

Specific factors of growth

The focus on the gifts of the Holy Spirit is the primary characteristic of Pentecostalism. Thus, a more specific explanation has to start from this point. If Pentecostalism proves to be attractive to so many people, it is only natural that they are impressed by this aspect. Of course, the impression that the Pentecostal praxis makes cannot be isolated from the external context of the convert or the believer, but it is a significant datum that can remain invisible if one begins analysis of Pentecostal growth via general social theory. Similar social conditions provoke a variety of religious reactions. As a consequence these reactions cannot be explained from the social conditions alone. Besides personal idiosyncrasies, a religion's typical profile influences people's decision to adhere to a religious group.

Why then is the emphasis on the Holy Spirit so significant? An important consequence of receiving the gifts of the Holy Spirit – being "baptized in the Holy Spirit" – is the rehabilitation of the person. Conversion is a social process, but also an individual decision regarding one's identity. It is a way (sometimes a dramatic way) of deciding to belong to a particular group of people. In the Pentecostal case the gifts of the Spirit often play a role, as a proof of the relevance of this type of Christian faith, but also as a form of empowerment of the person and their peers. These gifts also obtain their relevance from their application in controlling and organizing life. Especially in a situation that makes people vulnerable, such a form of empowerment is experienced as valuable. This need not be restricted to people who are marginal in society. All people, poor and rich, face problems when confronted with disease and death. Rich people cannot fully buy their health.

Another consequence of (on principle) equal access to the gifts of the Spirit is that the church group tends to be organized horizontally: there is no *a priori* class of religious specialists who through some form of legitimization – a vocation, a vision, a theological education – establish religious authority. This makes for a very special kind of church organization. Of course, it should be added immediately that this picture is the ideal and that vertical structures become visible as soon as a church grows and requires institutionalization. In practice the Spirit's gifts are not as equally distributed as scripture would suggest. Differences in personality influence the way power – the capacity to influence other people's behaviour – is distributed. Here charisma, in the non-theological sense, may come in. Churches may even formally adopt a vertical model for their organization. Thus, there are Pentecostal churches led by bishops. Yet, even then, a certain informality and personal ambience may exist.

Furthermore, Pentecostal praxis is marked by the importance of the conversion experience as such. This is not a Pentecostal monopoly, but its focus on the Spirit certainly is. If the gifts of the Spirit are central to the church and believers, the moment of getting acquainted with them is important. Conversion therefore often coincides with the first time that a person speaks in tongues or prophesies or is able to heal or be healed. Conversion then serves as a ritual of transition, as an initiation. Its dramatic nature not only comes from the forceful experience of the Spirit's gifts, but also from the rupture with a past that is considered sinful. Giving witness of this "rebirth" is a way of almost re-enacting it and experiencing it anew. The repeated story of one's conversion is also a way of reproducing the values that have been embraced there and then. The claim that accompanies the conversion experience is total because it regards the whole person and everything in their life. Again, practice may be different and deviant, but this is what gives Pentecostals their identity.

The drastic claim is also visible in the dualistic world-view. What happens at the personal level, but also in society, is brought under the label of the struggle between God and the devil. The coming of the Spirit and the use of the Spirit's gifts are important weapons in this all-out war. The world is by definition evil and sinful because people have not converted. They must be viewed as the other and the opposite, but also as the potential new member, waiting to be converted. In the fight against the devil it is therefore important to gain new souls for God.

There is one other dimension to this dualism. Because of their negative attitude towards the world, Pentecostals are often treated as "strange" Christians, even by members of mainstream churches. They might feel marginalized, but their dualist view helps them to retain a certain pride. They are sure to be on the right track and thereby are able to bear whatever scorn they may be subjected to. That in the end God will win the war against the devil and against sin justifies such a certainty. This in turn is a strong motivation to convince non-Pentecostals of the importance of Pentecostal belief.

Finally the Pentecostal identity is characterized by a particular way of combining seemingly paradoxical ideas and practices. With regard to the attraction that Pentecostalism exerts on potential converts, this would mean that disparate interests can be met, despite their contradictory nature. Some of these paradoxes have been mentioned in passing. One example is the focus on the after-life and heaven, or on the second coming of Christ, whereas at the same time current problem-solving through the Spirit's gifts receives much attention. In some cases social work or development projects are part of a church's activities. The promise of the final victory does not prevent Pentecostals from waging the war against Satan.

Another example is freedom of expression, best summarized by the image of collective prayer spoken aloud during a church service, easily combined with a rather strict and disciplined way of directing the service on the part of the pastor or leader. The same strictness can also be found in terms of beliefs and morality. A third case in point is the coexistence of a fundamental equality between believers based on common access to the charismata, with hierarchical forms of church organization, especially in second- and third-generation churches. With regard to the world, a similar paradoxical position can be found. On the one hand, the world is rejected as sinful and as Satan's domain, yet it also is the field for recruitment of new members and the battlefield for the war against evil. Pentecostals are successful modern citizens, yet show anti-modern traits, especially in terms of morals. Finally, the double relationship regarding tradition must be mentioned. On the one hand, a critical position is taken towards certain aspects of tradition (e.g. popular Catholicism or African traditional religion), but on the other hand some form of continuity with tradition may be visible, such as in the problem-solving nature of religiosity, or – as was shown above – in the authoritarian form of leadership.

These and other paradoxes produce a situation in which people may find room for their own preferences, despite the apparent strictness of church discipline. In the current global situation of affliction, the help that is offered here and now in combination with a preview of a happy end of times certainly is an attractive message. At the same time, the contradictions may nourish conflicts as soon as people opt for one extreme within the options represented by these paradoxes. The tension between equality and hierarchy, for example, has served as the basis of fission.

Conclusion

In searching for an answer to the causes of Pentecostal expansion, we have a series of partial answers that may serve as a checklist of possible factors that are active in specific cases, from the living-room community at somebody's home, to the mass meeting of the star evangelist. It is difficult to establish the relative importance of each of these factors. Moreover, the diversity of Pentecostal phenomena frustrates efforts to generalize. It is the specific correlation of elements in a local situation that offers an appealing identity. The appeal may come from the answer to a migrant's needs, or the demands of growing pluralism, or the needs of a particular class (both poor and well-off), or from the combination of global and local elements, or as a welcome problem-solver. It may come from the clear identity, the sympathetic democratization of roles and tasks, from the dramatic force of conversion ritual, from the dualist world-view, or from the ambiguity of paradoxical combinations of extremes. Each person will make his or her own selection from these and other meanings that Pentecostalism presents.

Recommendations

What challenges does Pentecostalism pose to the ecumenical movement?

A first lesson from the Pentecostal experience may be that growth results from a complex constellation of factors that happen to reinforce each other. In any case, a message is by itself not sufficient to guarantee success. The sometimes unpredictable chemistry of different elements may lead to surprising results at the local and personal level, both positive and negative. The role of the Holy Spirit in moving people to enthusiasm and empowerment is crucial. A social-science view must complement a theological appreciation.

A second lesson may be that the Pentecostal expansion shows how, in an often natural and less often artificial way, the relevance of a global message for the local situation of modernity can be implemented, appealing to what persons experience universally, in their bodies, as a consequence of global trends.

In the third place it can be observed that a theological elite is not only privileged by its education but also hampered when its members no longer speak the language of popular religiosity.

Fourth, Pentecostals are not by definition anti-ecumenical. Dialogue with Pentecostals can be fruitful to the ecumenical movement, just as it may bring Pentecostals to new insights. Ecumenicals may feel challenged in describing what the Holy Spirit represents to them. They may also reconsider the importance of the body to the experience of faith. Furthermore, methods of spreading the gospel may be reconsidered in the light of Pentecostal experience. The appreciation of dominant cultural values is a common concern in the context of modernization. Pentecostals may re-evaluate the gender role distribution in their churches.

Fifth, the Pentecostal experience must not only be admired but also evaluated critically. It may be that its expansion on the wings of modernization has made it less critical of the system distributed by the processes derived from modernization. When prosperity is given a central place or entrepreneurial models are copied, the parallel with the economic system seems too obvious and uncritical.

18
Religious Fundamentalism

HEINRICH SCHÄFER

Fundamentalism, today, is one of the most important ways in which religion makes itself present in everyday life, in culture and in politics. Be it the Christian Right in the USA, or the Free Presbyterian Church in Ulster, the Jewish Gush Emunim or Kach, Islamic Hamas, Muslim Brethren or Islamic Jihad, the Catholic Opus Dei, Buddhist Sri Lankan monks, the Indian Baratiya Janata Party or Rashtriya Svayamsevak Sangh – the list of today's movements and organizations deemed fundamentalist is long. However, there are huge differences between such movements and it is not clear what fundamentalist trait they share.

The very term "fundamentalism" is problematic. First, its use can be very polemical. To be a fundamentalist means to be outside the limits of modern common sense. Taking this into account, some religious believers of the Christian Right proudly call themselves fundamentalists, while others (e.g. Muslim or Jewish traditionalists) are not happy with this label, although they are in no way identified with Western modernity. What is the difference between traditionalism and fundamentalism? Are fundamentalists integrists? Is fundamentalism, in the end, only a Christian praxis, confined to conservative Christians? Is it a specific form of biblical literalism? Or is it a broader category of social and political habitus, so that it is even possible to think of a Western technocratic fundamentalism?

In this chapter, we will not come to define fundamentalism. Rather, we will try to focus on some family resemblances of fundamentalist praxis. These might help us to distinguish between what might be called fundamentalism and other, similar religious practices. We will examine some basic traits, using the example of Christian fundamentalism. We will do this for two reasons. First, this book is written from a Christian perspective; thus, we should begin with the log in our own eye rather than with the speck in our neighbour's. Second, it was American Christianity that first brought forth the phenomenon labelled fundamentalism.

We can permit ourselves one general statement at the outset: in the contemporary framework of globalization and modernization, fundamentalism can be seen as a "thoroughly modern phenomenon".[1] It arose as a modern answer to the core of modernity itself: reflexivity.

Modernity, reflexivity and fundamentalism

According to Shmuel Eisenstadt, the

> reflexivity that developed in the modern programme not only focused on the possibility of different interpretations of core transcendental visions and basic ontological conceptions prevalent in a particular society or civilization; it came to question the very givenness of such visions and the institutional patterns related to them. It gave rise to an awareness of the possibility of multiple visions that could, in fact, be contested.[2]

After the birth of modern subjectivity during the Renaissance and with Descartes and (in the religious sense) Luther, individuals became aware of themselves as able to decide and to be responsible for themselves. Religious wars, the subsequent learning of tolerance, and the secularization of political legitimation under the will of the people in the French revolution changed politics into a realm of decisions that had to be taken reflexively. Even the holy scriptures and human existence itself were seen as historical and in constant change, relative to other possibilities. Modernity spells itself out through feelings of autonomy, through the possibility to construct a variety of social identities and to consciously form social and political life by democratic procedures. It brings about new symbols such as freedom, solidarity, justice and identity. The task of granting legitimacy to given forms of life is transferred from transcendental agents and values to those who live in society. The awareness that individuals, their beliefs and their values are relative over against others led to pluralist tolerance, and an awareness of risk invaded the modern self-conception. So it became necessary for all social actors – individuals, institutions and even the democratic political system – continually to observe and correct themselves. Reflexivity thus became a crucial practice for modern identity construction as well as social and political life. Reflexivity is the central operator of political democracy, liberty, human rights and solidarity.

A second, equally important trait of modernity is instrumental reason, as well as technological and imperial political development. Economic and political action became emancipated from clerical and aristocratic rule. The logic of economic maximization unfolds an enormous power over social and political relations and private life. What

was once ruled by kings and bishops is now developing freely according to the laws of the market. Colonial wars, exploitation and domination of large parts of the world corroborated in politics the universalistic pretensions of instrumental reason. The modern West came to be
known to other cultures as a universal warlord that ruthlessly exploited
their property and dictated its conditions on social and political life. A
reaction against "the West" goes primarily against *this* face of modernity.[3] The question is, what logic does this reaction follow?

Modernity can thus be distinguished by two types of reason. On the
one hand, it is *reflexive*; on the other, it is *instrumental*.[4] Reflexive
modernity tends to lead to democratic political practice, tolerance of
plurality, human rights, open political discourse, etc. Instrumental
modernity goes with technological development, colonial domination,
cultural unification, expansion by war and the overall dominance of
instrumental (economic) reason.

Both these characteristics of modernity acted upon religion. Reflexivity went hand in hand with the growing awareness of the "nasty gap"
(Lessing's *der garstige Graben*) between the present and the time of the
Bible. Historical research, hermeneutical thinking and an awareness of
historicity changed the habitus of many Christians, but questioned age-
old authorities. At the same time, instrumental reason emancipated
more and more from traditional norms and values, and equally began to
threaten religious authorities and believers. Social differentiation and
secularization did not extinguish religion, but with a new distinction
between the public and the private spheres, religion became a matter of
private choice. In Western nations, religious authority lost its power
over society.

As religion withdrew, freedom increased and technical management
of the future became more and more mandatory. Risk became
omnipresent. This means the future is consciously seen to be dependent upon present human action. "The concept of risk becomes fundamental to the way both lay actors and technical specialists organize the
social world."[5] This, in turn, questions feelings of deep-rooted trust in
the world's future. It is hard to believe that "He's got the whole world
in his hands". Trust has to be gained as "ontological security" in individual socialization according to lucky circumstances, a caring
mother's hand and individual faith.[6] Or it has to be restored in universalist ways by the claim to absolute truth for certain modes of organizing the social world.

This function has been fulfilled by the secular myths of modernity.[7]
The narratives of holy scripture were replaced by the great tale of technical and social evolution, of revolution and eternal betterment. The old

prophecy of final fulfilment was given secular shape. History could now be seen as a teleological process culminating in whatever reign of perfection. Secular prophecies took the place of religious ones. However, when the limits of growth became visible towards the end of the 20th century, the quasi-religious timeframe of modern identity – the expectation of eternal fulfilment – turned into apocalyptic nightmares.

Fundamentalism seems to be a religious and political reaction to this overall situation. In fact, a closer look will show that it is the other face of modernity. It is anti-modern only in relation to reflexive modernity. It subverts the basic civilizational paradigm shift at the brink of modernity: reflexivity as consciously relative, procedural legitimation and organization of political and social life. Where modernity puts reflexivity, tolerance and pluralism in place, fundamentalism installs absolute "truths" as orientations for social organization.

Fundamentalism is a religious strategy to gain (or regain) perspectives for action in what is perceived as a crisis. This strategy identifies its supporters with the Absolute (God, scripture, the Qur'an, the Spirit, etc.), makes an exclusive claim to truth and validity, aims as far as possible to bring whatever differs from it wholly under its dominion, and goes along (up to a certain point) with strategies of defensive affirmation of cultural identity.

How fundamentalism works

The theological roots of fundamentalism in the USA are in the 19th century: in the premillenialist movement and in "Princeton theology" with its Reformed background. For outright fundamentalism, however, it is Princeton theology that is determinative.[8] Premillenialism had its roots in white lower classes, while academic Princeton theology – and likewise the fundamentalism of the early 20th century – was a matter of the religious Establishment and the middle classes.

Fundamentalism was born in the 19th century amid social and economic crises in the USA. It is important to notice that the theologies generally attributed to fundamentalism have different emphases in different social classes. Common to all of them, however, are two characteristics. They operate so as to allow believers to dissociate themselves from the crisis they are experiencing. And they associate, on the level of religious content, specific and appropriate theological themes that contrast with the specific form of crisis according to the social status of their adherents.

Establishing absoluteness and absolutizing one's own position of power

Fundamentalism is widely perceived as an ideology that grants its adherents the belief that they possess the absolute truth. However, we should note the difference between naive religious certainty and conscious absolutism.

The white lower and lower-middle classes of the Northern states of the USA found the second half of the 19th century to be a radical change from everything that had previously existed. The civil war, industrialization, urbanization and immigration drowned the "promised land" in the rising tide of modernity. The Bible, taken as it stood, became a rock amid the flood. It offered itself to naive biblicism as the old truth that remained as valid as ever. The main emphasis for believers lay in the fact that the Bible and "old-time religion" offered certainty, so that they were not swallowed up by the wave of social change. However, such certainty is not part of a universalistic strategy of social domination. To the contrary, this naive biblicism combines with a strong expectation of the imminent return of Christ within a premillennialist framework: the church will be raptured out of the world instead of being the main actor in the "restoration of the kingdom". This religious option allows the defence of social identity, but it does not tend to project its own logic upon society.

The evangelical theological elites and educated upper middle class were much more concerned with the influences of cultural modernity on theology, philosophy, the "moral foundations" of society and, in the end, political power. They were threatened by the Enlightenment rationalist critique, naturalist denial of God's guiding hand on world issues, historicist interpretation of the scriptures and, finally, Darwin's equation of man, the "crown of creation", with the fool of creation, the ape. It was time to defend the truth of the scriptures and, with it, their own legitimacy for claiming to have the correct definition of society's rules. These intellectuals were firmly grounded in Baconian empiricism and Scottish "common-sense" philosophy. So they developed their own brand of rationalism in order to defend their position against modernity. Thus, such fundamentalists were not anti-scientific or even anti-intellectual; they simply judged "the standards of the later scientific revolution by the standards of the first – the evolution of Bacon and Newton.[9] In other words, they countered reflexive, hermeneutical thinking with an instrumental concept of reason.

Theological truth thus was an object of correct scientific procedure, source and knowledge. The Bible became a book of natural and supernatural facts. Alexander A. Hodge, one of the most important theologians in Princeton, could state that "all the affirmations of scripture of all kinds whether of spiritual doctrine or duty, or of physical or historical fact, or of psychological or philosophical principle, are without any error". [10] All these facts, the natural and the supernatural, are accessible without distortion to reason; and reason works empirically and instrumentally. Thus, conceptual realism assumes that the supernatural truths are depicted in the Bible and that behind any concept of the Bible there is a supernatural reality. And, finally, every such thing is subject to the scientific knowledge of the theologian. In more pointed terms, fundamentalist epistemology and ontology relativize the absolute and identify it with the contents of the fundamentalist's own understanding. This means that human beings claim their own cognition to be capable of the absolute. And as biblical knowledge is pertinent for any science, knowledge or social and political order, fundamentalists claim an absolute and universalistic authority over the definition of truth and practice in society.

Time and the mental dispositions to understand it were important issues for 19th-century fundamentalism in the USA. Modern sciences and biblical research are based upon the notion of the historicity of existence, symbolized in the theory of evolution. This raised a twofold problem for fundamentalist theologians. First, evolutionist thought was going to inherit and secularize the great biblical narrative of final perfection. This would deprive the church of important symbolic capital. Second, the teleological trait of history as such could not be denied without losing the great narrative itself. The doctrine of dispensationalism took up the challenge and offered a solution. Those theologians conceive of history – in accordance with evolutionism – as a teleological process towards fulfilment, but the process is not linear: it is subdivided into smaller circles (dispensations). Human agency (autonomy) brings every circle to a fatal end, and God's mercy establishes a new opportunity, another circle. This goes on until the final judgment and restoration of the kingdom of God. Thus, the teleological sense of history is being saved, but human agency – the most important element of modern evolutionary thought – is only valid if it works according to fundamentalist precepts.

This brief look at early US fundamentalism allows us to make four observations. First, the basic cognitive strategy is to construct a sense of absoluteness and exclusivity of one's own truth claims. Second, there is a difference between the offensive strategy of upper-middle-class intellectuals and the defensive retreat to old time religion in the lower classes. Both are triggered by perceived social and cultural crisis, but the defensive strategy affirms the identity and (physical) integrity of people in a weak position, while the offensive strategy acts as a social power strategy in order to impose particular criteria and rules upon society as a whole.

Third, it is quite clear that the social position of adherents is crucial for the movement's performance in religious terms. Actors without real possibilities to influence major developments will concentrate on the construction of social spaces for survival with dignity. They confine themselves to their "enclave".[11] Actors with access to political, economic, cultural and social means will use these resources to influence society. They use their enclave as a base for authoritarian power strategies. Thus, the social effect of the claim to absolute knowledge is different. From a weak position it allows the affirmation of the space for retreat. From a strong position it is a rationale for social domination and oppression of different practices and points of view. The former creates a world for its adherents; the latter seeks to conquer the world on its own behalf.

Fourth, the dispensationalist schema for understanding time offers an applied strategy for risk management. As modern thought understood historical time as an evolutionary process with human agency, risk became visible (though not to the extent it is today). The fundamentalist proposal manages this situation by means of its own model that facilitates successful social and political action under the conditions of fundamentalist rule.

Different contents, one strategy

These different basic strategies can combine with very different religious and political contents, furthered by discourse and practice. Thus, it is not necessarily so that fundamentalism depends upon the use of scriptures. It can pivot around virtually any emblematic practice with enough symbolic power to mobilize people.

Our observations showed that classical US fundamentalism aimed at countering cultural change into reflexive modernity by imposing an older, instrumental form of reason. Scripture was in this context not only a general security and point of reference for fundamentalist identity. Scripture, in its realist understanding, was itself the central contents of the message: there is no change to eternal truth; truth and reason coincide in the plain text. Dispensationalism answered the challenge of evolutionism. According to this doctrine, there is no progress in history by human agency. Thus, fundamentalists counter the theory of evolution and the notion of the historicity and relativity of human existence with their own (unhistoric) theory of history. Scriptures and dispensations, in this sense, are not the "essence" of fundamentalism. They are simply religious themes of their time and place. The important thing is that they are operators that make the logic of fundamentalism work in an applied way.

Thus, it is not surprising that a century later the neo-Pentecostal movement in the USA operates the same logic with different contents. [12] From an upper-middle-class and upper-class perspective, the question is how to foster political change towards the betterment of the economic and political position (prosperity and power) of neo-Pentecostals within a strongly competitive industrial and post-industrial society. The stance of the movement is generally in favour of technological development, with a notable tendency against reflexive modernity. Neo-Pentecostals normally are strong supporters of technological, financial and cultural globalization in Western patterns and look with a very sceptical attitude at cultural and political pluralism. For example, they identify non-Western (non-Christian) cultures with demonic spirits and forces. Neo-Pentecostals construct their own absolute standpoint not so much on the Bible as on ecstatic experiences with the Holy Spirit that confer a direct "knowledge of the supernatural" and the "empirical reality of God". Scripture loses importance to *rhema*, the direct inspirational discourse. Ecstatic experiences can even reveal truths contrary to the Bible. The identification of the believers with the Holy Spirit comes to be the standpoint from which they can wage "spiritual warfare" against everything and everybody they believe to be demonic. Exorcism turns out to be the major pattern of religious, social and political strategies. Here, the conquest of the world takes place by the expulsion of the other. Neo-Pentecostalism has no problem with historical progress. Its members want to have a big share of it. So empowerment for action by the Holy Spirit and God's blessing by prosperity are the central operators for this particular fundamentalism.

In spite of considerable differences in content between classical fundamentalism and neo-Pentecostalism, the operational logic is the same: both create an absolute standpoint over against social challenges and present a rationale for a universalistic pretension of power. In both actors this operation excludes any notion of historical relativity and self-critical reflexivity. This means the same result for both, only under different historical circumstances and therefore with different contents.

Logic of power

As we have seen, the most important ingredient of fundamentalism is a certain cognitive operation that aims against reflexivity and historical relativity. This logic can operate with different contents, objects or practices. Generally, it takes four steps. First, religious specialists establish a cognitive connection between the demands of a specific population in a situation of change and/or crisis and some agent of the divine. Second, they construct a stable collective relationship to the main religious object (e.g. a rational relationship to a book, an ecstatic relationship to a spirit, a juridical relationship to an ecclesiastical authority, etc.). Third, the religious actors identify with the object and ascribe to themselves the (supposed) absoluteness of the religious object. This means that they reappropriate their social claims in a new way: as religiously legitimate and with other means of pursuing them. Fourth, the actors claim – according to the absoluteness of the religious object with which they identify – absolute and universal validity for their own social and religious claims.

Thus, fundamentalism turns out to be a specific social strategy to extend power over other people, groups and society. The fact that this logic can generally go along with any set of contents and practices means that fundamentalism is very adaptable. It can work with a great variety of traditions, moulding some of their elements into an ideology with universal validity claims. It is not itself traditionalism, even if it builds on traditions. Christian fundamentalists, for example, do not have a particularly good knowledge of Christian tradition.[13] Instead, they condense some traditional terms into symbolic triggers that mobilize people into the logic of the fundamentalist power play.

However, it is important to notice that not every claim for the absoluteness of one's own position necessarily develops into a universalist politics of power. It might remain as a means of defending the last place for the survival of a group. Only where power is already accumulated and combined with opportunities for mobilization can defensive attitudes be mobilized into universalist fundamentalism and its strivings for power.

Different fundamentalisms

If we consider the distinction between the operation of the practical logic of fundamentalism and its exchangeable contents, it is possible to identify fundamentalistic logic in different cultural and religious settings without risking an inflational use of the term.

Today, it is common to talk about different fundamentalisms, according to different religious and cultural backgrounds: Christian, Jewish, Islamic, Sikh, Hindu, Buddhist, etc. This is a response to the fact that fundamentalism is not so much a matter of content, as it depends on the logic of producing the habitus of absoluteness and transforming it into an offensive strategy of domination.

Modernity expanded from Europe to other places in the world together with military, economic and political domination. The face of modernity abroad was thus primarily one of belligerent and technological instrumental modernity. The reflexive, self-correcting contents and procedures of modern identity were not so easy to perceive from outside Europe. To some extent, the dominant classes in some countries (e.g. India) took into account the benefits of secular government and democratic procedures for economic development. But this does not entail a thorough democratization of society (neither was it the overall effect in the West). Strong differences and contradictions between classes in society may remain (e.g. the caste system in India). If this happens, domination will be identified with a "Western" orientation of the political or social upper class in general; in India, this would be the secularized Brahman caste; in Iran, it was the Shah; and in Egypt, it was Nasser's brand of socialism. For most of the population, rationalist political strategies (e.g. leftist people's movements) are not the habitual way of opposing "Western" domination within their own societies. Instead, such options are thought to be another trick of the West. But religious and ethnic traditions have deep roots in the daily life of poor populations. Thus, religion and ethnicity become important for mobilizing opposition to economic exclusion, social domination and political rule. The first accusation against the ruling classes is that they are non-Hindu, non-Islamic or non-Christian, and so forth.

However, simple reference to traditional religious and ethnic values is not necessarily fundamentalist. In many cultures religious teachings govern the whole of human life (politics, economics, partnership and personal behaviour) without modern Western distinctions between public and private, secular and religious. Such patterns of social life are not simply models of political and economic organization. They are profoundly rooted in the habitus of any person who has grown up with them. Thus, they deeply influence any social practice, from the most personal to the most public. The traditional orientation in religious and ethnic forms of life is premodern or non-modern. It is not in itself anti-modern because it existed long before modern political and economic organization spread from the West to other cultures.

It is only the confrontation of traditional cultures with Western ways of organizing political and economic life that creates the necessity of pronouncing traditional values against modern ones. And it is not social classes that are capable of moulding a new specific modernity, but the social classes that suffer harm by the modernization of the economy and politics that turn to a revitalization of traditional values. For example, they actively promote the Hindu way of life as the *Hindutva* against Muslim and Christian mission in India and against a secularized national government. Similarly, Sri Lankan Buddhists proclaim Buddhism as the national religion and the island of Sri Lanka as a sacred Buddhist realm over against a loss of importance in the process of globalization and the involvement of Christians, Hindus and Muslims in Sri Lankan society and politics. This kind of pronouncement requires a unifying effort in the articulation of religion. Neither Hinduism nor Buddhism has any orthodoxy as such, for both are traditionally very plural. But under the pressure of an outside challenge, the dynamics of an articulation and unification of implicit traditional religious and ethnic orientations take shape. As a consequence, activists formulate Hindu doctrines or proclaim the "Sinhala race as the chosen race for the preservation of Buddhism". [14] It is at this point that traditions can be drawn into the logic of fundamentalism analyzed above.

However, an attempt to establish one's own position as absolute does not strictly imply universal domination. In the Buddhist and Hindu cases, movements do not tend towards mission and world conquest, but claim reactively what they perceive as their territorial, economic and political rights by using religious terms in an ethnic way. In these cases religion might define ethnicity and corresponding territorial and social claims, but it does not instigate the subjugation of extra-territorial populations under religious legislation. This also seems to be the case with Jewish traditionalist groups. Only the interpretation of territorial claims against the Palestinian population and its religious legitimation can be interpreted as an expansionist policy. And in any case, Judaism does not focus on world mission. On the other hand, Christian and Islamic fundamentalisms possess strong universalistic missionary zeal. Their one basic idea is to make public law out of holy texts and extend domination worldwide.

If we compare both types of fundamentalism from a macro-sociological view of the impacts of globalization, we will find an important difference. The feeling of being culturally threatened seems to be much stronger among Muslim activists than among those of the American Christian Right. The colonial domination of Islam by Western powers is important in the history of the Muslim world and in Islamic fundamentalist thought. Thus, Islamic fundamentalism is likely to be understood as a counter-movement to Western domination. The Islamist movement developed armed militancy after the end of direct colonial domination, a general strengthening of Islamic countries and less direct repression of Islamist activists by secularist regimes. The exclusivistic politics of governing national elites and rising social injustice fuelled conflictive constellations. Nevertheless, radical Islamic activism has all the traits of an outright fundamentalism. It sets its own position as absolute without any hesitation, claims universal validity for its own religious law and way of life, and actively promotes campaigns to subdue opponents, regardless of such modern inventions as international law and the sovereignty of states.

The Christian Right in the USA has a different point of departure and slightly different methods. After the first decades of open counter-culture fundamentalism at the beginning of the 20th century, the movement was partially absorbed in evangelicalism. It came back in a new guise (partly neo-Pentecostal) in the 1980s. Under President Reagan it identified with the governing system and it came to be a nationalist affirmative pro-culture movement. Active militancy did not attain the degree it did in some Islamist movements, but there was strong advocacy for US military supremacy against the "reign of evil", as well as public support for US military expeditions such as the Gulf war. In addition, parts of the movement actively engaged in counter-insurgency warfare in Guatemala and the Contra-war against Nicaragua, showing the same disrespect for international law and the sovereignty of states as their Islamic counterparts. Moreover, there is notable affirmation of neo-liberal economics. Neo-Pentecostal emphasis on the so-called Prosperity Gospel stands out as an elaborate and mass-oriented apology for neo-liberal economics. This close identification with imperial politics and the satanization of non-Christian religions gives American missionary enterprises such as Youth with a Mission a strong "world conqueror" image. The programme is to evangelize the world, to give it a unitary religious and cultural outlook, and to bring everybody under the rule of scripture in its one and only true version.

As American fundamentalism turned into a pro-culture movement, the scriptures were shaped much more to cultural conditions. The idea is not so much to shape US public institutions according to a precooked Christian shari'a, as it is to legitimate existing social structures and to foster some minor changes within them. As Jerry Falwell stated, the "free enterprise system is clearly outlined in the Bible". [15]

Thus, for the time being, US fundamentalism possesses the two most important factors of fundamentalism in general: setting as absolute its own position and striving (not just in fantasy) to dominate the world. The same is true of Islamic fundamentalism. Both are utterly modern: they have developed "overarching totalitarian and all encompassing world ideologies, which emphasize a total reconstitution of the social and political order, and which espouse a strong universalistic, missionary zeal". [16] The difference is that Muslim fundamentalism acts out of a defensive setting and the identity of its protagonists is moulded by this condition. Both these fundamentalisms are modern in the sense of instrumental, technocratic modernity, in order to be effectively anti-modern in the sense of reflexive modernity and the abolition of the separation between religion and state.

The logic of fundamentalism today works under complex conditions. First, there are the dynamics of modernization in different cultures which, at the same time, create multiple modernities and maintain within each one of them a tension between Western influences and traditional ways of life. These tensions exist on social and cultural fault lines. Ethnic and religious tensions can be mobilized for opposition to "Westernization". Whether or not they develop into a fundamentalism depends on the specific degree of tension, the access to power of oppositional actors, circumstantial opportunities and the disposition within religious tradition to generate universalistic power strategies.

Democracy and power-broking: two different forms of reason

Fundamentalism turns out to be a partial answer to modernity. It generally affirms instrumental and technological modernity while it opposes reflexive modernity – both for the sake of its own power. It is *modern* in so far as it uses religious tradition as an ideology and modern technology in order to foster its practices, can get along with modern social institutions and traces universalistic perspectives. It is *anti-modern* in so far as it rejects the understanding of principles of social organization as historical and therefore relative to other times and cultures, refuses self-critical observation with checks and balances, counteracts pluralism, and refuses social differentiation and the distinction between religion and politics and promotes the integration of state and society under religious rule.

Reflexive reason is a core characteristic of modern democracy. This does not mean that it is a reality in the West; instead, it represents a challenge to Western culture, politics and economics. Nor should we claim that other cultures do not have similar systems of self-reflexive checks and balances to which Western reflexive reason may be able to link very well. But it is first and foremost to Western modernity that fundamentalism reacts, so we must focus on the Western brand of modern reflexivity. In the democratic tradition of the West, reflexive reason is based on the recognition that all human beings are relative to each other, and that no social actor possesses an absolute position and clear knowledge of the truth. Reflexive reason operates by the *processes* of regulating this relativity and not with substantial (religious or cultural) traditions. Thus, modern reflexive rationality derives legitimacy from its ability to mediate the conflicting interests of different societal actors, acknowledging the basic individual and social rights of any and every human being. This means it is social, plural and democratic, or it does not exist at all. In this sense, it represents a constant challenge to any society and policy, foremost in the West.

Fundamentalisms develop within the framework of globalization as an answer to Western modernity. On the one hand, the programme of globalism [17] means the concentration and extension of financial and other economic capital and brings about the extension of technocratic and instrumental rationality. On the other hand, cultural and political inter-relatedness brings a certain amount of reflexive reason (e.g. in democratic international institutions and processes). Economic globalism acts as the background against which reflexive traits of globalization are perceived by many non-Westerners. And Western governments and economic actors are not reflexively democratic in many of their policies.

This situation produces a downwards spiral and makes fundamentalist counter-strategies seem plausible. Many people perceive globalism as a threat to their very existence and their customary ways of life. Under this pressure, they are also likely to perceive changes in customary methods of legitimation as a threat. So even if rational legitimation with a democratic form of government might be the best way to face the threats of economic exclusion and loss of cultural self-esteem, people might prefer habitual traditional legitimation. As an addition to the problems of Western globalism, reflexive democratic modernity might appear only to deepen the problems. The actors concerned cannot conceive of procedural legitimation (by democratic processes) as an opportunity for the management of diversity and conflicting interests. This tendency is reinforced by the undemocratic and hegemonic strategies of Western countries. The consequent revival of traditional cultural values gains plausibility and at the same time offers a linkage for the logic of fundamentalisms. The more that non-Western actors perceive global players as constituting nothing but sheer domination by force instead of reflexive democracy, the more the plausibility of fundamentalist and violent counter-strategies increases.

As noted above, fundamentalism builds upon an ideological exaggeration of its own cultural traditions over against a perceived threat from outside. Fundamentalism stresses very much the importance of traditional values. But true tradition only means some accentuated elements of its own world-view. Tradition turns into ideology. So, even in modern and plural societies such as Brazil, fundamentalists can try to codify patriarchal family relationships in law, while the patriarchal orientation of Islamic fundamentalism boils down to the male rule of women's bodies. Tradition is not so much an orientation for critical self-examination as it is a rationale to legitimize the group's interests. Thus, the fact that Christian (upper-middle-class) fundamentalism sees the liberal economy as part of the divine order is no more astonishing than the fact that globally marginalized Hindus depict the divine order in conflict with the free market economy. Instead of complex processes designed to discover feasible policies, traditional texts serve to provide simplistic models that legitimize the group (class) interests of fundamentalist believers. This simply means that tradition serves as a disguise for instrumental teleology: everything serves that fosters our interest. Nothing is more harmful to such a position as reflexive reason.

Nevertheless, the revival of traditional culture is not by itself fundamentalism. It might work as the defence of a given population against overwhelming social change and the threat of extinction. The affirmation of cultural identity might make a certain culture absolute for its members, but this does not imply its belligerent imposition on outsiders. On the contrary, traditionalists like the Amish, for example, look inside to the details of their culture in order to preserve it against any modernity, be it reflexive or instrumental.

Fundamentalism, on the other hand, moulds tradition and important traits of instrumental modernity into one – with a preference for the latter. In Iran under Khomeini, for example, no one seemed to have a problem with the hybrid construction of an Islamic republic. It worked well for the double strategy of overthrowing the non-republican government of the Shah and installing Shari'a under the rule of the specially created office of the *faqih*. Fundamentalism, generally, does not reject the use of modern organization or technology if this promotes its goals. Neo-Pentecostal fundamentalists in Guatemala, for example, were the first in the religions there to use computers (in order to coordinate with the military a missionary campaign in a guerrilla stronghold). Anything goes if it serves "our" interests. It seems that today's fundamentalists endeavour within their limits to locate themselves at the spearhead of instrumental reason. They do so without the hindrance of reflexive self-criticism and recognition of the rights of others. In this sense, today's Western fundamentalism is a late affirmation of Marcuse's unidimensional man. It reacts to the challenges of Beck's Second Modernity (globally inter-related, reflexive and pluralist) with the means of the First (instrumental, unilinear and orthodox).

The social perception of time plays an even more important role in fundamentalist success than in the 19th century, when historical thinking was only in its beginnings. In today's social and technological conditions it has been transformed into an almost total awareness of risk. Living in the modern risk society means living with a clear idea of the fact that the future depends upon human agency, with all its flaws and shortcomings. Ontological trust is a scarce good under these circumstances and has to be created by favourable living conditions. But what if those conditions do not exist? Where ontological trust is fragile, fundamentalism installs metaphysical trust with its teleological concept of a history that points towards the final victory of God's people. Fundamentalist time management, once again, turns into risk management.

This is especially applicable to the crisis of (the first) modernity and the appearance of post-modern talk since the early 1970s. Up to the late 1960s, Western modernity had its "grand narratives": utopias of eternal fulfilment in the garments of revolution, technical evolution, a Third Reich of a thousand years, and so forth. These utopias directed collective orientation to ends that helped withstand the inner contradictions of modern life. But when the limits of growth became visible, these utopias gave way to apocalyptic fears. The future was no longer the utopia of a teleological historic reason; instead, it became a source of fear. In such a context fundamentalism gets straight to the point, for it does not deny the possibility or even necessity of the apocalypse. It binds its followers into a group of winners and restores an old-new story of fear and security that spans history. At the moment when the secular myths of modernity crumble, fundamentalism proposes instrumental modernity combined with a religious myth. The teleology of means and ends in instrumental rationality finds a counterpart of historic dimensions.

The price that fundamentalism imposes for this consolation is the reintegration of religion and politics. One of the most important features of Western modernity is the separation of politics and religion. Secularization means not so much the disappearance of religion as the privatization and individualization of religious belief. Especially in the French version of European modernity, this separation is strong. This might be one reason why French observers perceive fundamentalism as integrism. In this sense, religious fundamentalism always has a strong political dimension. Integration of religion and politics at a first glance seems to have very much in common with traditional cultures and religious systems. However, the fundamentalist programme overstates again a trait of traditional belief and turns it into an ideology. Religion in many cultures pervades the daily life of the people, is quite strongly identified with ethnic identity and plays a role in political decision-making. But it normally does not dictate political decisions. Religion usually plays a consultative role, with no last and definitive word in politics. In this sense, it is more than doubtful that fundamentalism guarantees something like public faith. Instead, it subdues religion to political calculus.

Those religions with the most strongly developed fundamentalist movements – Christianity, Islam and Judaism – are prophetic and messianic religions. Why should they react to reflexive modernity and democratic plurality with a proposal for religious jurisdiction over politics and society? All three of them are intimately involved in the development of Western modernity itself. And it seems to be precisely the utopian trait of modern grand narratives and their universalism which goes back to a messianic and prophetic origin. All three religions go back to one basic story: the overcoming of slavery in Egypt and scarcity in the desert with the promise of a sacred land. Overcoming the afflictions of the present with fulfilment in the future has since become common. This fulfilment has to be universal, valid for all, and it has to have the shape that religious believers have in mind – if it were not like this, what promise would it be? Such a promise cannot be relative to other promises given to other people, and it cannot be relative to the course of time, so that it might be fulfilled or not. Thus, the messianic tradition gave rise to strong expansionist activities in Christianity and in classical Islam (today, in a defensive position). And they gave rise to the great promise of instrumental, technological modernity: the overcoming of scarcity in the future. The messianic current in the three religions tends to share the consequences: universalist exclusivism and belligerent propagation of the promise. Thus, these religions share the contradictions of modernity as well. Western Christianity struggles against post-modern decomposition of the great modern stories and with them the perspective of a future fulfilment of hopes. Islam struggles against the overwhelming power of Western technology, politics and a military presence that constantly challenges the doctrine of the universal superiority of Islam. And Jewish fundamentalists struggle against an Islamic presence that obstructs the reconstruction of Zion, and against post-modern secular decay in Israeli society. All three fundamentalisms are fighting for their messianic identity. However, these religions have also developed other choices during their history.

The messianic trait of Christianity has its counterparts in the grand narratives of evolution, revolution and Western superiority. These narratives are told in the language of instrumental modernity. They are far from self-critical reflexivity and pretend to universal validity. The logic of globalism is unidimensional and oriented in unilateral domination. Yet these are characteristics that are countered, within the West itself, by reflexive, democratic rationality. Under the conditions of developed globality and multiple modernities, however, the grand narratives of the West also face a crisis. The plurality of cultures that give their own interpretation to modernity and their increasingly strong presence on the global scene relativizes the West. Believers in the secular religion of Western superiority now tend to give secular fundamentalist responses. The thesis of the "end of history" with modern capitalist society is basically fundamentalist. It reacts to the crisis of the grand narrative in almost the same way as dispensationalism. Proclaiming the end of history means to deny historical relativity and thus the necessity of reflexive self-examination and rendering account to others as a constant condition for legitimizing social and political systems. A second reaction is to set the underlying rationality of Western globalism as an absolute value over against human life and dignity and to promote it by any and every means, including violence and violation of international law. Thus, the myth of Western superiority can create a secular political fundamentalism in the core of Western modernity itself – again, by strengthening instrumental and weakening reflexive reason. In the worst case, global politics would have to count on confrontation with two fundamentalisms: a globally religious Islamic fundamentalism and a religiously global Western fundamentalism.

Religion and reflexive reason

To answer one fundamentalism with another fuels fundamentalist resentment and confirms its logic, as the situation in Palestine shows quite clearly. Democratic organization of society and possibilities for everybody to participate in the benefits of social welfare and peaceful change diminish the plausibility of fundamentalist radicalism. Islamist movements, for example, are likely to be absorbed by democratic structures that provide opportunities to participate in the shaping of social structures and which are strongly against armed militancy. This does not mean that core activists stop being fundamentalists, but it does mean the enclave culture loses its plausibility, rank and file members diminish, the strong borderline with the devil or the "system" blurs, and armed militancy loses its appeal. If perceived opportunities for action generate mobilization, political actors have to create specific opportunities that respond to the demands at the social basis of fundamentalism. If democratic participation in local and global processes brings a real chance to achieve one's goal, then fundamentalist strategies of domination and violence do not make much sense.

Any answer to religious fundamentalism that only names secular democracy and social participation is too brief, however. Religion itself should be an important component of any answer. The contrast of modernity and traditional societies shows that the secular trend to privatize religion tends to exclude religion from political and social ethics. Religion turns into a private means to satisfy personal needs. In traditional societies, religion generally is primarily a general code of understanding basic matters in the daily life of the community. It is part of the common habitus and can be made explicit by religious specialists in cases of conflicting interpretations. In modernity this basic function is lost. But the arguments of religious ethics, nevertheless, can have weight. They have weight if they target precisely the point at stake and offer from their special perspective relevant answers to relevant problems. What counts is competence.

Modern secularism produces a loss of belonging. The same is the case for any other culture affected by the rapid social change of globalization. Contradictions that arise as multiple modernities develop – uprooting by migration, social marginalization, destruction of dignity – call for new sources of identity, a new belonging. This is where religion enters in. It is far from fundamentalism.

In this context, the plurality of religious and cultural options even in very small local spaces presents a special problem. Religion could play a special role here. In its fundamentalist use, religion has the capability to produce a sense of absoluteness and to foster aggressive exclusion of the other. But religion has the opposite ability as well: to show that over against the ultimate, every human being is relative, yet still has a firm ground for hope and existence. The essential characteristic of a faith state is not the cognitive knowledge of "truths", but the emotional (and ontological) sense of security and stability. This makes it possible to perceive oneself as relative over against others in a plural world without despair or losing responsible ties to other human beings.

Fundamentalism as a modern phenomenon turns out to be a challenge to religion in that it forces religious people to become more reflexive about themselves.

Recommendations

Fundamentalism, according to the above analysis, mirrors instrumental modernity. To those who favour the concept of the rational individual and its exclusive interest in maximizing benefits, fundamentalism reveals the same instrumental logic at work, only for the benefit of others with different goals. In this sense, fundamentalism first calls for a self-critical assessment of Western modernity in order to nourish its reflexive traits.

A closer examination shows a continuum between defensive traditionalist identities and outright fundamentalism. Not every traditionalist is fundamentalist, but there can be circumstances that can forge fundamentalism out of a defensive identity affirmation. Thus, it is important to examine carefully any religious actor the ecumenical movement has to deal with, in order not to discriminate and to detect concerns with which the ecumenical movement might identify.

A careful assessment might also discover elements in an actor's praxis of which the ecumenical movement might not approve. In case of strong doubts about certain fundamentalist practices, a clear ecumenical position should be established.

Fundamentalists mobilize people who suffer assaults to their human dignity, their ability to act on their own behalf and to live in an acceptable way. Democratic participation in politics and economic life, as well as recognition of plural cultural traditions, are means of restoring dignity. Fundamentalist activists are neither democratic nor plural, so direct dialogue with them does not seem to be of much use. But members of movements might be interested in social participation. So it makes sense to foster democratic and participative opportunities and structures, addressing and including members of fundamentalist groups. More democracy and participation in society at large counteracts fundamentalism.

For inter-religious dialogue, this means that discussions about religious dogmatics and codified truths do not lead to anything in relation to fundamentalism. An alternative strategy might be to contact the religious organizations of other cultures and religions in order to address together the social, political and cultural demands at the basis of fundamentalist mobilization.

As ecumenical Christianity partly is identified with the West, Western tendencies towards an excess of instrumental reason and thus technological, political or even military fundamentalism are an important challenge to the ecumenical movement. The ecumenical movement should detect fundamentalist trends in Western culture and foster reflexive reason in general.

A theological orientation that focuses on confessionalist interests and reaffirmation of confessional positions does not seem to be a creative reaction to fundamentalism. To simply state one's own opinion against that of others does not lead us very far. Instead, while one's own position should be clear, ecumenical theology should cultivate liberal approaches to inter-religious relations that permit the joint development of inter-religious policies over against fundamentalist movements in the different religions.

NOTES

[1] For many of our observations we rely on the findings of the "fundamentalism project" by Marty and Appleby (1991, 1993, 1993, 1994, 1995). Shmuel Eisenstadt, "Fundamentalism, Phenomenology, and Comparative Dimensions", in Martin Marty and R. Scott Appleby eds, *Fundamentalisms Comprehended*, Chicago, Univ. of Chicago Press, 1995, p. 259.

[2] Shmuel Eisenstadt, "Multiple Modernities", *Daedalus*, vol. 129, 2000, p. 4.

[3] Wolfgang Geiger, "Das Gespenst des Fundamentalismus", in *Die Neue Gesellschaft. Frankfurter Hefte*, 36. Jg., 1989, no. 3, p. 245.

[4] Another way to approach fundamentalism systematically within the framework of modernity is that of Julio de Santa Ana. See "Fundamentalisms, Integralisms, Religious Conservatisms", paper presented at Bossey working group, "The present situation of religious life in the world and its challenge to the ecumenical movement", Bossey, 2001. He points out five characteristics of modernity: the autonomy of the individual, instrumental reason, historicity of truth, the "death of God", and religion as a private matter. Using these orientations he discusses fundamentalism with many interesting results.

[5] Anthony Giddens, *Modernity and Self-Identity: Self and Society in the Late Modern Age*, Stanford CA, Stanford UP, 1991, p. 3.

[6] Modernity does not erase religious faith as such, but religious institutions and their claim to publicly administer religion and morality (see Ronald Inglehart and Wayne Baker, "Modernization, Cultural Change, and the Persistence of Traditional Values", *American Sociological Review*, vol. 65, Feb. 2000, pp. 19–51). The idea that reason could question religious *faith* is wrong, since reflexive reason may foster relativity but cannot do away with personal attitudes, as hermeneutical religious science states (see Reinhold Bernhardt, *Der Absolutheitsanspruch des Christentums. Von der Aufklärung bis zur Pluralistischen Religionstheologie*, Gütersloh, Mohr, 1990). Religion is a "practical logic" (Heinrich Schäfer, *Theologie und Religion. Praxeologische Untersuchungen zu zwei zentralen Themen ökumenischer Forschung*, Habilitationsschrift, Ev.-Theol. Fakultät, Ruhr-Universität Bochum, 2001, p. 179), based in "faith states". See William James, *Die Vielfalt religiöser Erfahrung*, Frankfurt, Insel, 1997, p. 485.

[7] Thomas Meyer, *Fundamentalismus. Aufstand gegen die Moderne*, Reinbek, Rowohlt, 1989, pp. 10,62.

[8] There is discussion about the role of premillennialism in the origins of fundamentalism. Sandeen (Ernest R. Sandeen, *The Roots of Fundamentalism: British and American Millenarianism. 1800–1930*, Chicago, Univ. of Chicago Press, 1970) derives fundamentalism from millennialism. Marsden (George Marsden, "From Fundamentalism to Evangelicalism: A Historical Analysis", in David F. Wells and John D. Woodbridge eds, *The Evangelicals*, Nashville TN, Abingdon, 1975, p.126) sees important differences. So do I. For more detailed information see Heinrich Schäfer, *Protestantismus in Zentralamerika. Christliches Zeugnis im Spannungsfeld von US-amerikanischem Fundamentalismus, Unterdrückung und Wiederbelebung "indianischer" Kultur*, Frankfurt, Lang, 1992.

9 George M. Marsden, *Fundamentalism and American Culture: The Shaping of 20th Century Evangelicalism, 1870–1925*, New York, Oxford UP, 1980, p. 214.

10 A.A. Hodge and B.B. Warfield, "Inspiration", *Presbyterian Review*, 2, 1881, p. 238, quoted in Sandeen, *The Roots of Fundamentalism*, p. 126.

11 For fundamentalism as an enclave culture see Emmanuel Sivan, "The Enclave Culture", in Martin Marty and Scott Appleby eds, *Fundamentalism*, Chicago, Univ. of Chicago Press, 1995, pp.11–68; and "Kultur und Identität im Vergleich unterschiedlicher Ausprägungen des Fundamentalismus", in Aleida Assmann and Heidrun Freise eds, *Identitäten*, Frankfurt, Suhrkamp, 1999, pp. 427–55.

12 See Schafer, *Protestantismus in Zentralamerika*, pp. 67ff.

13 Nor do Muslim fundamentalists, according to Bassam Tibi (*Die Krise des modernen Islam*, Frankfurt, Suhrkamp, 1991).

14 S. Wesley Ariarajah, "Religion and Politics", paper presented at Bossey working group, "The present situation of religious life in the world and its challenge to the ecumenical movement", Bossey, 2001, p. 11.

15 Jerry Falwell, *Listen America!*, New York, Doubleday, 1980, p. 13.

16 Eisenstadt, "Fundamentalism", p. 264.

17 See Beck (*Was ist Globalisierung?*, Frankfurth, Suhrkamp, 1997, pp. 26ff.), who makes the following distinction: *globalism* is the deliberate spreading of neo-liberal practices; *globality* is the fact of non-revisable global inter-relatedness; *globalization* is the complex process of spreading different forms of inter-relations.

19

Looking Ahead

The modern ecumenical movement arose in the Christian churches from the efforts of lay persons in the European West. In the 17th century, diplomats made contacts in various ways with the intention of motivating the churches to overcome their hostility and division.[1] Particularly in the 19th century, the vision of Christian unity became the inspiration behind lay movements, above all of young people: the World Alliance of Young Men's Christian Associations, the World Young Women's Christian Association and the World Student Christian Federation are just some of the bodies noted for their efforts to reunite Christians, especially lay people in the churches. These movements began to have an impact on the life of the churches themselves. The Anglican communion produced a platform for interchurch relationships, which came to be known as the Lambeth Quadrilateral.[2] According to the Anglican bishops, the basis for conversation between separated churches was acknowledgment of (1) the holy scriptures as the source of the Christian faith; (2) the Nicene Creed as a sufficient statement of that faith; (3) administration of the sacraments of baptism and the Lord's supper by all the churches participating in dialogues promoting the rapprochement of the various Christian confessions; and (4) the existence of a ministry duly recognized between the churches. This development shows how, starting with the efforts of lay people, church leaders began to take an interest in ecumenism.

The missionary movement gave a great impetus to the cause of Christian unity at the beginning of the 20th century. The first world missionary conference took place in Edinburgh in 1910. Its participants were above all drawn from the missionary bodies that had been formed among the churches of the West. There were few representatives from the churches that were beginning to develop in Asia and Africa. Thus, the modern ecumenical movement began to take shape within the setting of Western Europe and modern culture. Today, despite its considerable growth in "peripheral" parts of the world, most of the earth's inhabitants still regard Christianity as a Western religion, propagated from Europe. Despite the fact that Christian communities originated in the Near East, and their faith had Jewish roots, the peoples of the periphery perceive Christianity to have a predominantly Western character. The ecumenical movement is not immune from this attitude. However, over the past century the Christian faith has spread throughout the so-called third world and (as has already been shown in this book) very soon the vast majority of Christians will be Latin American, African and Asian.

Thus, *the first great challenge facing ecumenism (above all in these days of globalization) consists in overcoming its Western character.* The Christian faith is a catholic faith, valid for all the peoples and all the cultures of the world. The ecumenical movement has to acknowledge that many of its constituent elements have belonged largely in a Western environment: its advocates; the vision that initially inspired it; the understanding of the Christian faith that still inspires it; the institutions that support it; the statements it has made; and the funding that has enabled it to develop. All these things are largely Western. "Largely", because significant contributions have been made by some of its leaders from the South (the Caribbean, South America, Africa, Asia and the Pacific). However, as with most expressions of the Christian faith, most churches and most of their teaching, the prevailing opinion is that they are substantially bound up with the history of Europe and, particularly as regards the ecumenical movement, bound up with the modernization pursued by the peoples of the European West.

As this book has emphasized, although the process of modernization originated in Western Europe, it has developed and is still developing along different paths in other contexts. The process of modernization in Asia, for example, is different to that in the West. Similarly in Africa and Latin America. The process of secularization experienced in Western Europe for more than a century is an exception in today's world. This does not imply that those societies that have not undergone secularization have not attempted to modernize in their own distinctive ways. There are different versions of modernization, reached by different paths.

Modernity manifests itself in very different ways, yet there is a tendency to standardize the world's cultures by following the dominant Western economic model. It is our belief that the ecumenical movement should not only reject this tendency, but also acknowledge the intrinsic importance of the cultural diversity of the world's peoples. At the beginning of the 1980s, when he was general secretary of the World

Council of Churches, Philip Potter stressed that the ecumenical task for the last two decades of the 20th century would be to establish a platform for a global dialogue of cultures on an equal footing.[3] Such a global dialogue has also to do with relations between men and women, between different churches and between majorities and minorities.

The *second challenge* facing the ecumenical movement concerns women. One of the most salient features of modernization in its various forms is the emancipation of women and the recognition of women's rights. The ecumenical movement took up the challenge presented by the feminist movement in the second half of the 20th century. However, most of the churches have not yet faced this challenge. Our study group thus believes that *a more inclusive ecumenism requires ecumenical organizations and churches to give greater attention to gender issues*. Here we would underline three points:

a) As pastors, theologians and teachers in the new millennium consider the formulation (or reformulation) of a new theology that takes into account the changing realities of our current world, we invite them to pay attention to the contributions of feminist scholars and theologians. What might a contemporary Christian theology of the church look like if it took seriously, and attempted to integrate, some of the basic assumptions of feminism and feminist theology?

b) The church as a whole, the various denominations, and the individual churches need to become more attuned to the different ways in which the message of the gospel is understood. Part of that different understanding is reflected in the experiences of women as they deliberate their relationship to the texts and structures of the faith. Can the new voices contributing to the development of various forms of feminist theology merge with and complement each other? Or does the recognition of the importance of context mean that a number of different theologies must be developed to serve the church in its various manifestations?

c) The development of various forms of feminist theology (by whatever name it is given in different contexts) clearly challenges many of the established power structures of the Christian church and its various denominations. Need the church necessarily give up those traditional structures in order for the message of Christian feminists to be both heard and heeded? What is truly at risk in taking seriously the challenges brought up by these feminists?

In another area, albeit consistent with Philip Potter's remarks above, José Míguez Bonino has been insisting for more than thirty years on the fact that ecumenism in Latin America has been pursuing its own course.[4] The World Council of Churches, which should be regarded as one of the most important expressions of the ecumenical movement, if not the major expression, has made immense efforts to make room within its own life for churches and individuals to make a contribution from their own distinctive cultures, and to lay down quotas enabling greater participation by women in its programmes and in the life of its member churches. None the less, despite those efforts, it still has a Western look about it. It seems to us that it is crucial for its future that the challenge for ecumenism to overcome its Western limitations should be faced.

The *third challenge* is linked to the second, and it too is not limited to ecumenical organizations, since it is above all aimed at church institutions that have decided to participate in the movement for Christian unity, whether or not they belong to the World Council of Churches.

As we have stated several times, the impact of the processes of modernization, including its manifestations in the form of secularization, migrations, large-scale population movements, as well as the current forces involved in globalization have radically challenged the basic assumption on which the ecumenical movement has been built. The primary vision of the movement was to call the churches to their own unity and to express their common calling to witness and service to the world. This vision was based on the assumption that the church itself was firmly rooted in expressions of faith that gave meaning and certainty to its adherents.

Today the mainline denominations and the confessional bodies that came together to participate in the ecumenical movement are in crisis. The decline of these bodies is accompanied by a diminishing confidence in the traditional doctrinal formulations and authorities, an erosion of the sense of belonging, and a search for a new spirituality in a world that has changed rapidly and continues to change. *The ecumenical movement therefore is faced with the task of enabling the churches to discover together relevant expressions and practice of the faith for our time. Our vision needs to take the present with the seriousness it deserves and work towards a future that none of the early pioneers of the movement could have anticipated. Creative imagination, unprecedented courage and a lively hope need to mark our ecumenical future. And these can come into being only by engaging the current issues with determination and by creating structures that can address these issues. What does this mean for the visions, programmes, relationships and institutional structures of the ecumenical movement of our day?*

Religious communities that dominate the ecumenical movement have, for a long time, looked upon Pentecostal, charismatic and new religious movements as marginal to the religious reality. The rise of fundamentalist and conservative religious expressions was treated as an aberration. Our research shows that these expressions of religious life, with all their weaknesses and strengths, are very much a part of the responses of the world we live in. They have become integral to religious life in our time. *Thus, a fourth challenge is for the ecumenical movement to pay greater attention to these religious expressions as part of the new religious consciousness that is emerging in today's world.*

It is very possible that these contemporary expressions of religious life may show no interest in participating in the ecumenical movement. However, that should not prevent the movement from making greater efforts than hitherto to understand these new phenomena developing within Christianity, and engaging in a more intensive dialogue with them.

As a result of population movements in various parts of the world, different cultures are living more and more closely together, resulting in unmistakable religious pluralism. This is taking place both within nations and internationally. We are witnessing new social situations produced by vast numbers of people migrating from the South to the North, from the East to the West, from Africa to Europe, and from the Caribbean and Central and South America to the USA, Canada and Europe. In some cases, these situations result in conflict and tension between followers of different faiths. The result is unprecedented in the history of humankind. The ecumenical movement cannot ignore it.

Yet religions have the potential for cooperation, not only for clashes. *Here we perceive a fifth challenge: the ecumenical movement is called to widen itself at the level of interfaith relationships.* This challenge calls for the acknowledgment of those movements that are born at the margin of the established religions, trying to renew old patterns of belief and religious practices. This implies that, on the one hand, the movement is challenged to recognize the strong faith that animates other religious communities. At this point we remember that the search for Christian unity also began to grow from marginal sectors of the main Christian confessions. We think that ecumenism may be fruitfully fermented also if it takes into account the common marginality of religious founders (e.g. Buddha, Moses, Jesus, Mohamed, etc.). The importance of the renewal strength of different religions can be appreciated if we think of some spatial metaphors such as "the desert", "the way", "mountain tops", "caves", "beaches", or "travels/pilgrimages" that prevent a sedentary, established life. In their origin, religious movements explore the symbolic potential of the marginal metaphor.

On the other hand, our research also shows that the impact of modernity and globalization is also radically changing the patterns that characterized the relationship between different faith communities. Other religious traditions stand in a new relationship to the Christian faith in this post-colonial era. Greater knowledge of other religions and participation in the lives of others has strongly challenged some Christian assumptions about themselves and others. Other religions, faced with similar challenges, are also in the process of searching for an appropriate spirituality for our times. As we have already said, there are increasing tensions between religions as they play a greater role in public life and discourse. At the same time there has been a phenomenal increase in interfaith dialogue and cooperation. The search for spirituality has crossed all religious boundaries. The call for a "new", "wider" or "interfaith" ecumenism is continually growing. What implications does this reality have for the way Christian ecumenism has been conceived and is practised? The conviction shared by all members of our research group is that the future of the ecumenical movement can no longer be envisioned without taking full account of the way in which all human communities and ways of being and believing have been thrown together and face a common future. The search for a wider unity and the discovery of a new ecumenism, more inclusive than the one that existed up till now, appear to have become integral to the Christian ecumenical movement as it looks to the future. This challenge is particularly relevant in our time, when the powers-that-be use religious symbols in order to legitimize their desire to dominate more and more the different peoples of the world.

A *sixth challenge is related to the increasing involvement of religions in power conflicts of our world.* In the view of some, the powers-that-be manipulate religious symbols, beliefs, even religious institutions. That is, the involvement of religions in power confrontations indicates that, in many cases, religions have lost their autonomy as public institutions. Others support the view that it is inherent to religious life to become involved in political life. Therefore, religions cannot be separated from other manifestations of human power; the sacred is not only "religious" but also has sociological and political dimensions. We recognize that the factual relationship between different faith communities has been heavily influenced by social and political contradictions. For example, the tensions between Islam and Christianity have to a large extent to do with the history of colonialism, political dominance of one or the other in different periods of the history of Mediterranean peoples, with the development of Christian mission itself as an instrument of political interests. Inter-religious encounters should not ignore these elements of the background of our present situations.

Different processes of modernization are quite strongly influenced by religious *habitus* (even if the main actors are sometimes not aware of this fact).[5] Thus, it is not possible to separate social thought and action from religious differences or religious encounters from the social conditions that exist within the global network of relations in which men and women participate. This means that, in most of the cases, dialogue on doctrinal matters is strongly linked with political convictions. However, it is also necessary to recognize that social and environmental issues present great opportunities for inter-religious encounter and understanding. We have seen that the concern for these issues is growing among all religions.

- It is true that these problems can give rise to fundamentalist mobilization, defensive and even violent action, as well as to exclusivist and particular attitudes.
- However, they may also provide opportunities to cosmopolitan movements in the realm of the associations that are part of civil society. These movements manifest a human concern for more justice, a better environmental situation as well as better gender relationships. They favour the development of open societies rather than the use of inclusive strategies and convincing arguments.
- In any case, these factors (that some have called "non-theological", while others insist that they should be understood as "theological") have great importance in the field of inter-religious relationships.

We do not mean that "visible unity" should exist among different religions. Diversity exists and must be respected. Nevertheless, we recognize that we are all part of the human race. Even among Christian churches the search for "visible unity" has not yet led to great results. Instead of searching for doctrinal agreements among religions, we think a fruitful approach would be to follow the so-called Lund principle, that is, to act together in everything that we are able to do together in order to find more and more things in common. This means, for example, to develop common action in the face of such issues as social marginalization, poverty, violence, terror, gender relations, environment and others that depend on specific contexts. This would be a demonstration of the religious will to break with the increasing manipulation of religions by the powers of this world.

We agree that power mechanisms tend to obliterate the origin of religions on the periphery. Power is linked with the centre and the establishment. It needs control and predictability, and therefore freezes and codifies the original message of each religion. Religious power, in itself, is ambiguous, because on the one hand a good message mobilizes and needs massive support, but on the other hand power then introduces its own inevitable mechanisms that exclude the marginal origin from collective memory and transform the movement into an institution at the centre. Religious power-wielders mobilize religious resources in order to influence other people's behaviour. However, there are always prophets, visionaries who revive the original message and who – if successful – start a new cycle from the periphery to the centre.

A seventh challenge to the ecumenical movement is put by the current development of what now we call a "network society". Manuel Castells[6] recognizes that there are some networks which could be hierarchically organized; although increasingly in our time (and above all at the level of civil society, which is the most appropriate for the life of religious institutions and ecumenical organizations) "network" implies a non-hierarchical structure. Even in a network there are areas with a "thicker", "denser fabric" and others with a faded, scattered fabric.[7] The former are strong and dominant, while the second are weak. However, "the thin" have the potential to resource people's life better than the "thick" ones. When the "thick" and "dense" prevail, the model that dominates the network is that one of "centre"–"periphery". Even if there is a clear intention to avoid the formalization of hierarchical structures, the inherent trend of this model moves towards such a kind of order. When we mentioned the first challenge that the ecumenical movement faces today, we underlined the need to cease to be "European-centred". More and more ecumenists talk about the need to reconfigure the movement, especially in the context of globalization. This challenge calls for more attention to collegial forms of organization, to give orientation to the movement. The regional ecumenical organizations, most of which are considered of secondary importance, need to be perceived as those who keep alive the ecumenical movement in the peripheral regions of the world. It is true that there are economic and geo-political conceptions that view these areas as "dependent". However, the conception of the whole inhabited world (oikoumene) in the ecumenical movement has tried to correct this understanding. Unfortunately, up to now, the movement appears to be too centred in traditional Christian lands. In the context of the network society it is time to change.

If we follow the prevailing patterns that conceive and imagine networks, we should take into consideration that religions are part of the overall social network and may be localized in stronger or weaker areas. According to their position they can be more or less identified with the advantaged or disadvantaged participants in the current hierarchy of network relationships. Nevertheless, *the challenge is to change this hierarchical order (which is inherent in the tradition of many churches in the modern ecumenical movement) and to shape organizations where power and authority is more equally shared.* The response to the challenge of network society will give the ecumenical movement a more diffuse presence rather than an institutional one. This does not mean that institution and structure should be neglected. Religions have become part of global information streams. A reconfiguration of the ecumenical movement will imply, unavoidably, a shift in its forms of communication towards more participation among its members.

Eighth, the different responses of diverse manifestations of the ecumenical movement to problems related to social justice, environment, social (ethnic, race and other forms) discrimination are not simply an application of dogmatic truisms. Rather, they have been and still are points of departure from which churches and religions can begin to search for the truth in different contexts. For Christians, the "mystery of God" is veiled behind the "masks" of human misery, of the suffering people who live on the margins of their societies. Experiences of social injustice impel people to reflect on and struggle for social justice. It was through awareness of racial injustice that Joseph H. Oldham stated that Christian mission and racism are incompatible. His book on *Christianity and the Race Problem* (1924) was the response of the most advanced ecumenical awareness of that time to the challenge of an unacceptable racial discrimination. The challenge for a more social justice grows out of the existing conditions in different contexts of the ecumenical movement. It calls not only for a response to the context, but also for introducing, as far as possible, conditions for greater justice. *This challenge for social justice is particularly relevant in a time when* la pensée unique, *with its requirement for adjustment to the market culture and uniformity of thought and behaviour that the powers-that-be try to impose on our societies, denies the right to be different and free.*

The challenge of social justice today cannot be dissociated from the common commitment of ecumenical organizations and churches to the cause of human rights. This demands, above all, that human rights be respected and promoted within ecclesiastical institutions and ecumenical associations themselves. As happened during the cold war, the primary concern with regard to human-rights violations is those committed by the religious bodies to which we belong. Then come the violations that others commit. But most important is the implementation of human rights everywhere. We are aware that there are diverse conceptions of human rights among religious families; nevertheless, we affirm that the defence and promotion of human liberties is a priority that the ecumenical movement should affirm in thought and action.

The ecumenical movement is also challenged to conserve its memory. It is important to remember that, when the cause of Christian unity began to captivate the minds and hearts of younger generations of Christians, they often became members of communities where believers of different Christian confessions and denominations came together. They became friends, trusted each other, and were courageous enough to implement actions that challenged their churches. This element is similar to what Victor Turner called *communitas*.[8]

People who were almost at the margin of their own churches, and who remained loyal to them and above all to the witness of the Christian faith found in the holy scriptures, formed communities that were ready to move forward in favour of the renewal of their churches. At the beginning of the modern ecumenical movement these communities were not "structured", institutionalized. They neither rejected nor neglected the relevance of ecclesiastical institutions, but they kept an open mind. This could be clearly perceived by the renewal of the mind and language of ecumenical communities. At a time when voices from different corners of the world criticize the ecumenical movement because it seems to be bound and controlled by an "ecumenically correct language" as well as a way of being ecumenical which has also been consecrated as "correct", it is important to remember that the modern ecumenical movement manifested its inspiration and strength through communities of people who longed for Christian unity, biblical and liturgical renewal, and theological freshness. Very often they are at the margin of ecclesiastical structures, but they set in motion a movement which, as Ernst Lange wrote, "still moves". And it is called by God to continue moving forward.

NOTES

[1]   See Ruth Rouse and Stephen Charles Neill eds, *History of the Ecumenical Movement. Vol. 1: 1517–1948*, WCC, repr. 2004, pp. 75–114.

[2]   On the Lambeth Quadrilateral see J. Draper ed., *Communion and Episcopacy*, Cuddesdon UK, Ripon College, 1988. See also J.R. Wright ed., *Quadrilateral at One Hundred*, Cincinatti OH, Forward Movement, 1988.

[3]   Philip Potter, *Life in All Its Fullness*, WCC, 1980, pp. 154–64.

[4]   José Míguez Bonino has noted on several occasions that the ecumenical movement in Latin America and the Caribbean has its own characteristics, and does not resemble the modern ecumenical movement as manifested in Europe.

[5]   On *"habitus"* see Pierre Bourdieu with J.-C. Passeron, *La reproduction: Éléments d'une théorie du système d'enseignement*, Paris, Ed. de Minuit, 1971.